Democracy and Trust

Surveys suggest an erosion of trust in government, among individuals, and between groups. Although these trends are often thought to be bad for democracy, the relationship between democracy and trust is paradoxical. Trust can develop where interests converge, but in politics interest conflict. Democracy builds on a recognition that politics does not provide a natural terrain for robust trust relations, and so includes a healthy distrust of the interests of others, especially the powerful. Democratic systems institutionalize distrust by providing many opportunities for citizens to oversee those empowered with the public trust. At the same time, trust is a generic social building block of collective action, and for this reason alone democracy cannot do without trust. At a minimum, democratic institutions depend on a trust among citizens sufficient for representation, resistance, and alternative forms of governance. Bringing together social science and political theory, this book provides a valuable exploration of these central issues.

MARK WARREN is Associate Professor of Government at Georgetown University. He is the author of *Nietzsche and Political Thought* (1988), and many articles and essays on Continental political thought, philosophy of social science and democratic theory.

Democracy and Trust

Edited by

Mark E. Warren

Georgetown University

CAMBRIDGE
UNIVERSITY PRESS

PUBLISHED BY THE PRESS SYNDICATE OF THE UNIVERSITY OF CAMBRIDGE
The Pitt Building, Trumpington Street, Cambridge, United Kingdom

CAMBRIDGE UNIVERSITY PRESS
The Edinburgh Building, Cambridge CB2 2RU, UK http://www.cup.cam.ac.uk
40 West 20th Street, New York NY 10011–4211, USA http://www.cup.org
10 Stamford Road, Oakleigh, Melbourne 3166, Australia

First published 1999

Printed in the United Kingdom at the University Press, Cambridge

Typeset in 10/12pt Plantin   [GC]

A catalogue record for this book is available from the British Library

Library of Congress cataloguing in publication data

Democracy and trust/edited by Mark E. Warren.
    p.   cm.
    Includes bibliographical references.
    ISBN 0 521 64083 0 — ISBN 0 521 64687 1 (pbk.)
    1. Democracy.   2. Trust.   I. Warren, Mark (Mark E.)
    JC423.D43984   1999
    321.8 – dc21   98–53586 CIP

ISBN 0 521 64083 0 hardback
ISBN 0 521 64687 1 paperback

Contents

Figures

Tables

Contributors

JEAN COHEN is Professor of Political Science, Columbia University

RUSSELL HARDIN is Professor of Political Science, New York University

ROM HARRÉ is Professor of Pyschology and Philosophy, Oxford University and Georgetown University

RONALD INGLEHART is Professor of Political Science, University of Michigan

JANE MANSBRIDGE is Professor of Government, Harvard University

CLAUS OFFE is Professor of Political Science, Humboldt University

ORLANDO PATTERSON is Professor of Sociology, Harvard University

JAMES C. SCOTT is Professor of Political Science and Agrarian Studies, Yale University

ERIC M. USLANER is Professor of Political Science, University of Maryland

MARK E. WARREN is Associate Professor of Government, Georgetown University

Acknowledgments

This volume had its origins in an initiative at Georgetown University to strengthen teaching and research in political theory, and particularly to strengthen its interdisciplinary dimensions. The initiative was conceived and developed by Bruce Douglass and generously funded by a grant from the Andrew Mellon Foundation. As one part of that initiative, Gerald Mara and I convened a small group of the Georgetown faculty to discuss problems of democracy that were both widely recognized and yet so unsettled that they would engage a wide range of interests and approaches. I am grateful to Sam Barnes, David Crystal, Rom Harré, Gerry Mara, Eusebio Mujal-Leon, and Diana Owen for their excellent ideas and solid instincts about what are and are not problems for democracy. We eventually converged on the problematic relationship between democracy and trust, and agreed to organize a conference on the topic, preceded by a faculty seminar. During the 1995–1996 academic year, I convened an exploratory seminar which included Tom Banchoff, Sam Barnes, Alisa Carse, David Crystal, Rom Harré, Daniel McAllister, Gerry Mara, Joshua Mitchell, Eusebio Mujal-Leon, Diana Owen, Peter Pfeiffer, Terry Pinkard, Dennis Quinn, Henry Richardson, Aviel Roshwald, Mark Tushnet, Tim Wickham-Crowley, and Diane Yeager. Without the discussions, arguments, guidance, and distinctive disciplinary contributions of these seminar participants, my understanding of the problem of democracy and trust would be much more shallow than it is. Seminar participants also provided guidance to Gerry Mara and myself as we convened a small, three-day conference at Georgetown in November, 1996 entitled "Democracy and Trust." The invited speakers provided copies of their papers in advance, which were in turn made available to the audience. The audience reciprocated by providing thoughtful and challenging interventions. This volume consists of the revised versions of these papers, some of which have evolved considerably since the conference, and in many cases in response to the excellent discussions. Jennifer Kerslake handled most of the organization of the conference, which came off without a hitch owing to her meticulous competence. Many graduate students from the

Georgetown Department of Government helped with logistics. Donna Lee Van Cott put in extra hours. Richard Schwarz, Dean of the Graduate School at Georgetown, provided encouragement and administrative support. I am especially indebted to Gerry Mara for his continued support and feedback during the process of editing the volume. Jennifer Kerslake copy-edited the initial drafts, again with extraordinary competence. Mark Mitchell compiled the index with diligence and speed. John Haslam, of the Cambridge University Press, saw the volume through from start to finish with excellent advice, good humor, flexibility, and patience.

Washington, DC   MARK E. WARREN
October, 1998

1 Introduction

Mark E. Warren

It was not self-evident until recently that there might be important questions to be asked about the relationship between democracy and trust. Considered historically, we can appreciate why: Liberalism, and then liberal democracy, emerged from the distrust of traditional political and clerical authorities. Liberal innovations were aimed at checking the discretionary powers implied in trust relations (Dunn 1988; Ely 1980). More democracy has meant more oversight of and less trust in authorities. The topic does not seem any more obvious when we consider the place of trust within political life from a more generic perspective. Politics is distinguished from other kinds of social relations by conflicts of interests and identities, so that the mere fact that a social relationship has become political throws into question the very conditions for trust. Trust involves a judgment, however implicit, to accept vulnerability to the potential ill will of others by granting them discretionary power over some good. When one trusts, one accepts some amount of risk for potential harm in exchange for the benefits of cooperation. As Annette Baier (1986: 235) puts it, "Where one depends on another's good will, one is necessarily vulnerable to the limits of that good will. One leaves others an opportunity to harm one when one trusts, and also shows one's confidence that they will not take it." So if I extend trust I am also judging – however habitually or tacitly – that my trust will not be abused. And this implies that there is no essential conflict of interest between myself and the person to whom I extend trust, or at least no conflict of interest that is not mitigated by other relationships, securities, or protections.

In *political* situations, however, the assumption of solidarity with others often is suspect, and herein lies the ambiguous, even paradoxical, nature of the topic of democracy and trust. What makes a situation political *is* that some issue or problem or pressing matter for collective action meets with conflicts of interests or identities, and that parties bring their resources to bear upon these conflicts (Warren 1999). An important democratic innovation was the recognition that in many relationships trust is misplaced or inappropriate, suppressing real conflicts of interest while

1

sustaining exploitative and paternalistic relations (Barber 1983: 93). Democratic mechanisms such as voting, freedoms of speech and association, and separations of power enable people to challenge supposed relations of trust, while limiting the discretion of the trusted, and thus the potential harm, in whatever trust relations remain.

Yet the fact that democracy requires mechanisms that help produce a decent political life in the absence of less than complete trust does not mean that democracy can do without trust. In almost trivial ways, without trust the most basic activities of everyday life would become impossible. Why should we not expect some fundamental relationships between this fact and the ways we govern ourselves? For example, as Claus Offe points out in Chapter 3 of this volume, trust can produce desirable means of social coordination when other means – in particular, state regulation through sanctioned rules and the unintentional coordinations of markets – are limited in their capacities to accomplish necessary and desirable social tasks. A society that fosters robust relations of trust is probably also a society that can afford fewer regulations and greater freedoms, deal with more contingencies, tap the energy and ingenuity of its citizens, limit the inefficiencies of rule-based means of coordination, and provide a greater sense of existential security and satisfaction. Precisely how do democratic modes of governance relate to these virtues?

While there is a significant literature on trust, with few exceptions it has not been directed at the complex relationship between democratic politics and trust – whether trust in political authorities or trust that is generated (or undermined) within society as an indirect consequence of political institutions, economic development, or cultural transformation. The essays collected in this volume aim at defining the issues involved in the complex of relationships between democracy and trust. They are interdisciplinary, and many combine theory with empirical findings. This eclectic mix is intentional, since defining the issues and questions indicated by the topic "democracy and trust" involves, at least, contributions from philosophy, political science, psychology, sociology, anthropology, and history. The topic also requires, if I may say so, some indulgence from the reader. While the authors have sought to speak to one another and to coordinate their disciplinary languages across fields, tensions remain that reflect distinctive disciplinary orientations and problems as much as they do disagreements about conceptualizing, explaining, and judging the phenomena in question.

In what follows, I provide some initial definition for the topic of democracy and trust as it is developed in this volume. The topic breaks down into a number of distinct, although closely related, problems. These include the problems of scale, complexity, and interdependency that often work to limit democratic ways of making decisions and to create functional pressures for trust, a problem I summarize in the first section. In the second section, I raise the issue of it means to trust institutions as opposed to individuals, and whether it can ever make sense, from a democratic perspective, to trust institutions. The third section introduces an important distinction between particularized and generalized trust. According to arguments made in this volume, generalized trust is conducive to desirable forms of democracy, while particularized trust – trust limited to family or to members of ethnic or religious groups, for example – is not. The fourth and fifth sections introduce "social capital" arguments: the view that trust is a key element of civil society's capacities to direct and discipline government, as well as to organize and coordinate collective actions. In the sixth section, I comment upon the important relationship between security, risk, and trust, emphasizing the close link between economic and political securities, and the capacities of people to organize collective actions through trust. The final section introduces the question of whether and how relations of trust might enter directly into democratic ways of doing politics.

Interdependency, complexity, and trust

As societies become more complex, more differentiated, and more interdependent, individuals increasingly confront a paradoxical situation. On the one hand, these developments can, and often do, generate expanded life-choices – choices resulting from greater efficiencies, pluralization, and mobility. On the other hand, increasing interdependencies extend the vulnerabilities of individuals, while increasing complexities reduce the chances that individuals can monitor the vulnerabilities to which they are subject (cf. Offe 1996: chap. 1). To be sure, individuals never could have had full confidence in the institutions and interdependencies to which they were subject, since that would have implied that they could have known the universe of their vulnerabilities. Today, however, the gap seems unbridgeable between the cognitive resources of individuals and their abilities to know and judge the contingencies that bear on their lives.

Individuals do bridge the gap, however. In most cases, they do so not by knowing their vulnerabilities but by *trusting* others, institutions, and systems with their fortunes. As Luhmann (1979), Giddens (1990), and others have emphasized, extensions of trust, especially to strangers embedded in institutions, enable coordination of actions over large domains of space and time, which in turn permits the benefits of more complex, differentiated, and diverse societies. At the same time, trust reduces complexity for individuals while providing them with a sense of security by allowing them to take for granted most of the relationships upon which they depend. These effects not only contribute to well-being in itself, but also enable individuals to expand their horizons of action. This is so in the most basic of ways. If I am unwilling to trust that the strangers I meet on the street will not mug me, I will be unable to leave my house. So the alternative to trust, particularly in complex societies, is not a transparent knowledge of risks and contingencies – which is impossible in any case – but rather generalized distrust, which offers a sense of security but at the cost of an impoverished existence.

Unhappily for democrats, the same factors that drive the increasing functional importance of trust also constrain the extent to which people can participate in the decisions that affect their lives either directly, or indirectly by using their political resources to direct and discipline their political representatives. Strongly democratic expectations that individuals ought to have a say in decisions that affect them merely amplify the paradox. In politics as elsewhere we are subject to many more vulnerabilities than we might affect through political participation owing to the disproportion between our political resources (such as time and knowledge) and the complex web of extended dependencies within which we live. For most of the decisions that affect our lives, we are inevitably in situations in which it would, perhaps, be *desirable* to trust, since trust – where it is warranted – would allow us to optimize the ways in which we allocate our scarce political resources. Warranted trust in specific institutions, representatives, and authorities would allow individuals in democracies to focus their resources on those issues that matter – in particular, those where they have good reason to distrust (Warren 1996). Thus, from a strictly functional perspective, we might think of trust and democracy as *distinct but complementary ways of making collective decisions and organizing collective actions.* When one trusts, one *forgoes* the opportunity to influence decision-making, on the assumption that there are shared or convergent interests between truster and trustee. If justified trust could in some instances relieve the burdens of *political* decision-making for both individuals and institutions, then democratic decision-making in complex societies might become more robust.

Should democrats trust political institutions?

Such functional expectations no doubt lie, in part, behind the widespread concern with research that shows precipitous declines in trust for political institutions and authorities in the United States and, to a lesser degree, in Western Europe over the last several decades (see Patterson,

Inglehart, and Uslaner, this volume). But whether this is a problem – as opposed, say, to a sign of an increasingly sophisticated citizenry – depends in part on whether or not it *ever* makes sense to place trust in political institutions or even in political representatives. If we are to assume that there is some important relationship between democracy, trust, and political institutions, we need to know what trust requires and when it is appropriate. In Chapter 2 ("Do we want trust in government?"), Russell Hardin turns a skeptical eye toward the thesis that declining trust in government is undesirable. Indeed, if we assume that people think and act sensibly, "we should not generally want trust in government for the simple reason that typical citizens cannot be in the relevant relation to government or the overwhelming majority of government officials to be able to trust them except by mistaken inference" (pp. 23–24). The issue, in Hardin's view, is whether *any* individual can ever be in a position, epistemologically speaking, to know all that is needed to warrant relations of trust with government – which is, after all, in most countries today made of up hundreds if not thousands of agencies, offices, branches, and levels, populated by people we can never know directly, and who act in ways we can never judge through direct experience.

Hardin's judgment depends in part on a specific conception of trust – namely, trust as an expression of "encapsulated interest" (cf. Hardin 1993), an account that extends rational choice axioms to relations of trust. According to these axioms, individuals seek to maximize (self-interested) preferences, while economizing on the effort of gaining the information necessary to know what course of action, in any instance, will maximize preferences. Thus, to "say that I trust you with respect to some matter means that I have reason to expect *you to act in my interest* with respect to that matter because you have good reasons to do so, *reasons that are grounded in my interest.*" . . . Your interest encapsulates my interest (p. 26). Still, from a rational choice perspective trust is paradoxical. On the one hand, relations of trust decrease the cost of information while increasing the utilities of cooperation. On the other hand, because individuals are self-interested, those who trust would seem to be choosing, irrationally, to increase their vulnerability to others. Hardin deals with the paradox by conceptualizing trust as "in a cognitive category with knowledge," so that trust and distrust make sense only when "I know or think I know relevant things about you, especially about your motivations toward me" (p. 24). In contrast to conceptions developed by Offe, Harré, and Mansbridge in this volume, Hardin attributes no moral content to trust (as opposed to trustworthiness). Rather, one should trust when it is in one's interest to do so, and one can *know* this to be so by knowing the motivations of the trusted.

On this meaning of trust, Hardin argues, it makes little sense to speak of trust in the institutions of government. We may *depend* upon government. We may find government reassuringly *predictable.* But we should not *trust* government: We simply are not in a position to trust or not because we can't know the relevant interests and circumstances. Thus, regarding the relations between people and government in large-scale, complex societies, not even democracy can generate trust, nor should we expect it to do so. On Hardin's account, if trust is a good thing, it should be sought, identified, explained, and encouraged in arenas where there is a chance that its basic cognitive conditions might exist – and this is typically not the case in distant relations between individuals and government, or even between individuals and their elected representatives. In this sense, the decline of trust in political institutions is not a problem. Indeed, it may even be a sign that citizens are becoming increasingly sophisticated about the conditions of trust, an argument suggested also by Ronald Inglehart in this volume and elsewhere (Inglehart 1997).

In contrast, Claus Offe (Chapter 3, "How can we trust our fellow citizens?") sees the "deficit of trust" in institutions as a problem for democracy, in the West as well as the postcommunist East. Without informal modes of social coordination, he argues, it is difficult if not impossible to solve the numerous collective-action problems that confront societies today. With the increasing interdependence of large-scale systems, the state has become more and more involved in solving problems that were once solved by spontaneous organizations of civil society. In many countries today, however, the state has become too weak to implement and enforce its policies and must rely increasingly on civic trust and cooperation (cf. Offe 1996). In complex societies, the issue cannot be conceived (as neoconservatives conceive it) as a problem of reestablishing trust based on face-to-face relations. Rather, the kinds of trust appropriate to major problems of social coordination are unavoidably institutional, because such problems are, as Offe puts it, between "me" and "everyone else," with no *personal* dimension to the "everyone else."

Offe seeks to locate precisely the sense in which institutions might speak to this particular deficit of trust by conceiving what it might mean to "trust institutions." He agrees with Hardin that trusting institutions is not the same thing as trusting individuals, but argues (as do Harré and Patterson in this volume) that nonetheless there is an important sense in which the idea is intelligible. "Trusting institutions" means something different from "trusting my neighbor": It means knowing the "basic idea" or good of an institution. If this idea makes sufficient sense to people, it will motivate their support for the institution and their compliance with its rules. Trusting one's neighbor, on Offe's view, involves the expectation of reciprocity. If we define trust in this way, it is as meaningless to trust an institution as it is to trust one's bicycle, as neither is capable of acting reciprocally. Like a bicycle, institutions can never be the object of genuine trust, but only the objects of empirical or theoretical knowledge and beliefs. Only persons, as social actors, are capable of following norms, including reciprocity, compliance with which is necessary for the reproduction of trust. Thus, Offe argues, "Knowing the repertoire of meaning and justification that is being generated by institutions allows 'me,' the participant observer, to determine the measure of trust I can extend to those who, although strangers, are still co-residents within an institutional regime and whose patterns of behavior 'I' have reasons expect to be shaped and informed by the evident meaning that is inherent in an institution" (p. 71). "Trusting an institution" amounts to knowing that its constitutive rules, values, and norms are shared by participants and that they regard them as binding.

In contrast to Hardin, then, who sees the absence of trust in institutions as a result of individuals' limited information, Offe's approach focuses on deficits in key "cultural and moral resources." Whether institutions can be trusted depends on whether they are structured so that they might recur discursively to their constitutive norms. Where institutions do not recur consistently to these norms, the bases for generalized trust erode. In the end, Offe suggests, only two strategies can address the deficit of trust in institutions. The first is "top-down": Trust can be increased if institutions develop an "impeccable record" in fulfilling the norms of truth-telling, promise-keeping, fairness, and solidarity. The other is "bottom-up" and is exemplified in the "civic communitarian" strategy that seeks to develop the habits and dispositions of extending trust to strangers by increasing citizen involvement in associational life.

The research Ronald Inglehart presents in Chapter 4, "Trust, well-being, and democracy," helps to clarify the role of trust in maintaining existing democracies. Drawing on data from the 1990–1991 and 1995–1997 World Values Surveys in 41 countries, Inglehart suggests that trust in specific political institutions and elites is not very important, at least to the long-term stability of existing democracies. Rather, stability derives from two other factors: subjective well-being and interpersonal trust. *Transitions* to democracy are likely to be accompanied by low levels of subjective well-being and trust. But once in place, democratic regimes require for their stability (1) a general culture of political trust sufficient to underwrite political opposition and transitions of power, and (2) diffuse mass support for existing political institutions. What best predicts this culture are high levels of interpersonal trust and subjective well-being rather than trust in political institutions and elites. Nor does Inglehart find that existing democratic institutions play an important role in causing interpersonal trust. This is not surprising, he suggests, since for most people political life is a relatively minor part of their life: Work, family, home, income, and friends are much more important. Rather, the interpersonal trust and subjective well-being that seem necessary for the stability of democratic institutions are most closely correlated with economic development and security. Other authors in this volume (Offe and Patterson) suggest that there are theoretical reasons to think that having more resources – such as economic wealth, status, and knowledge – makes it less risky to trust others, especially strangers removed in time and space. Inglehart's data indicate that those who fit a "postmaterial" profile – higher incomes and educations – also register higher levels of interpersonal trust. In addition, Inglehart finds a strong correlation between levels of interpersonal trust and the religious tradition of a country. Historically Catholic countries tend to be low on interpersonal trust as well as on levels of economic development, while historically Protestant and Confucian countries tend to be high. It is likely, Inglehart argues, that long-term cultural factors such as these make a strong and independent contribution both to economic development and to the dispositions that stabilize democracy.

While economic development and other cultural factors may contribute to the interpersonal trust and subjective well-being that stabilize democracies, these same factors may coexist with – indeed, possibly cause – declining trust in political institutions and elites. We should not, Inglehart suggests, necessarily assume that this development is bad for democracy (cf. The Pew Research Center 1997: 7). In the stable democracies, political institutions and elites are probably no less trustworthy than in the past. Rather, the decline in trust in institutions probably reflects a more general decline in respect for authority that has come with the development of post-material cultures. When people no longer worry for their survival, they do not need to cling unquestioningly to the authorities they hope will ensure their survival. Instead, as material well-being increases, trust in political institutions and elites is likely to decline as publics begin to evaluate their leaders and institutions by more demanding standards.

Generalized and particularized trust: What kinds of trust are good for democracy?

While a number of contributors to this volume suggest that democracy depends more on interpersonal trust than on trust in political institutions and elites, not all kinds of interpersonal trust are good for democracy. Eric Uslaner argues in Chapter 5, "Democracy and social capital," that trust matters for democracy in large part because trust is the key component of "social capital" – but not all forms of interpersonal trust contribute to social capital.

The term "social capital," introduced by James Coleman (1990: chap. 5), was intially coined to describe the social norms and expectations that underwrite economic activity, but which could not be accounted for from a strictly economic perspective. In particular, the term explained the capacities possessed by economically successful groups of people to extend their transactions over time and space, and more generally to control transaction costs through the "soft" regulations of norms and mutual expectations rather than through, for example, the "hard" rules of commercial law or even through the logic of instrumental reciprocity. By analogy to economic capital, groups with accummulated "social" capital can be more productive (cf. Fukuyama 1995). The term has expanded beyond its economic genesis, however, to indicate the networks, associations, and shared habits that enable individuals to act collectively.

On Uslaner's account, the kind of trust that contributes to social capital is trust that can be *generalized* to people who are strangers, as compared to trust that is *particular*, limited to one's family or group. Particularized trust tends to be attached to the kinds of group identities that are solidified against outsiders, which in turn increases factionalization and decreases chances that conflicts can be negotiated by democratic means. Generalized trust, on the other hand, helps to build large-scale, complex, interdependent social networks and institutions and for this reason is a key disposition for developing social capital. Moreover, generalized trust is connected to a number of dispositions that underwrite democratic culture, including tolerance for pluralism and criticism. Like Inglehart, however, Uslaner suggests that optimism about economic security is also closely associated with generalized trust, both as cause and effect. Perceptions of economic security reduce the perceived risks of trust, while generalized trust also enables economic development through its contributions to social capital.

For these reasons, Uslaner argues, we *should* be concerned about the fact that generalized trust in the United States has declined in the last several decades – although this is clearly a different matter than the decline of trust in government, addressed by Hardin and Inglehart: "In 1960, 58 percent of Americans believed that 'most people can be trusted.' By 1994 and 1995, a bit more than one-third (35 percent) of Americans had faith in their fellow men and women" (p. 13). Uslaner is interested in pinpointing the degree to which generalized trust has declined in the United States, and the reasons for the decline. While agreeing with Robert Putnam's (1995a, 1996) general conclusion that social capital is "disappearing" in the United States, he takes issue with Putnam's claim that television is the main cause for the erosion of social capital. Uslaner argues instead that trust has to do with the psychological dispositions of optimism and pessimism that in turn reflect perceptions of key life experiences, such as economic security. Are there life experiences other than economic security that create generalized trust? Uslaner examines the civic-republican view that participation in associational life can create trust. Although some kinds of associations create generalized trust, not all do. He finds the strongest effects in sports associations. These associations do not merely select for people who are likely to be trusting anyway; they actually transform people, creating generalized forms of trust. Perhaps there is more to the common analogy between sports and politics than meets the eye: If one can trust a competitor to play by the rules in sports, might this disposition generalize to politics? Do associations that cultivate competition within the context of clearly defined and generally accepted rules develop more general capacities for collective action in the face of difference and competition?

In Chapter 6, "Liberty against the democratic state: on the historical and contemporary sources of american distrust," Orlando Patterson rejects the view advanced by Putnam and Uslaner (cf. The Pew Research Center 1997) that the United States is experiencing an erosion of the trust that underwrites civic engagement and social capital. Instead, Patterson argues, we must place the relatively short time period measured by the surveys within a broader theoretical and historical context. American democracy incorporates several different kinds of trust and has done so in different ways at different times. Patterson distinguishes four kinds of trust: (a) affective based on face-to-face relations and incorporating direct normative sanction; (b) intermediary trust, which relies on the same mechanisms but works at a distance through intermediaries; (c) collective trust, involving situations in which persons have direct, but impersonal, contact with "familiar strangers" within their midst; and (d) delegated trust, which depends upon third-party, institutional guarantees. From the earliest days America incorporated two very different models of democracy, each depending upon different kinds of trust. In the Northern colonies, democracy evolved on the basis of direct personal trust, combined with the important generalizing element of a shared religious belief in duty to others. In the Southern colonies, however, democracy depended upon an opposition between the *demos* and the other. In this model, reminiscent of Athenian democracy, the liberties of white Americans were defined in opposition to slavery. Here, trust among citizens depended on particular boundaries of exclusion. So the trust that mediated this kind of democracy was a variant of the "collective trust" that holds together the group against the "familiar stranger," the slave. In this "primal *herrenvolk* democracy," the image of liberty defined in opposition to slavery became paramount, as did, eventually, a distrust of government, both of which helped align Southern democracy with *laissez-faire* capitalism and allowed for a marriage of convenience with a Northern "elite capitalist democracy." The combination of Southern *herrenvolk* democracy and Northern elite capitalist democracy came to define the American political landscape. But the Northern model also included the image of democracy that originated in the colonies and eventually incorporated the values of pluralism, inclusion, and participation. The kinds of trust that mediated this model – affective, intermediary, and delegated trust – differed from the trust necessary for the *herrenvolk* democracy of the South. This alternative model, Patterson argues, represents the most desirable configuration of democracy and trust.

Patterson combines his theoretical argument and historical analysis with an analysis of General Social Survey data to make two general arguments. First, the United States is not experiencing a long-term decline in the kind of trust necessary for a democracy of pluralism, inclusion, and participation. To be sure, there are ups and downs. But the broad historical measures of participation show remarkable stability rather than crisis. Nor should we be particularly nostalgic about declines in the kind of trust that enabled *herrenvolk* democracy in the past.

But Patterson does not conclude that all is well. He finds a close relationship between high socioeconomic status and generalized trust, which in turn correlates with trust in political institutions. He argues that these factors are connected through a feedback loop that advantages high socioeconomic status groups and disadvantages low socioeconomic status groups. "Political influence and attendant gains lead to a realistic perception of political effectiveness, which reinforces generalized trust, political trust, and the tendency to be more politically active. The opposite set of linkages operates with persons from lower SES groups" (p. 196). The group most disadvantaged by these linkages are African-Americans, a finding that is disturbingly predictable given the incentives to distrust built into the history of slavery, semifeudal sharecropping, segregation, and disenfranchisement. Patterson's second general argument is more optimistic. He suggests that we are witnessing the end of *herrenvolk* democracy, the form of democracy that has solidified itself by means of a rhetoric and practice of racial exclusion.

Patterson's argument concurs with a number of other arguments in this volume (see especially the chapters by Offe, Inglehart, and Uslaner) that hold that generalized trust is associated with economic security or perceptions of security as well as with other resources such as education.

All other things being equal, the wealthy and well-educated tend to have higher levels of generalized trust, while the poor and less-educated tend toward distrust. Generalized trust makes it easier for the wealthy and well-educated to combine for purposes of collective action – whether for purposes of political influence or other goals – whereas distrust tends to discourage collective action. Offe and Patterson in particular suggest a novel way of looking at the relationship between economic class and political capacities. In general, they argue, those whose lives are more insecure can less afford to trust, since for them betrayed trust is relatively more consequential. On the other hand, the rich in resources can afford to trust, and when they do trust they also benefit. Economic insecurity and educational disadvantage may, then, be not only direct causes of what might be called the "social decapitalization" of the poor, but also indirect causes through the mediating factor of trust.

Civil society's capacities for political resistance and direction

Inclusive and pluralistic democracies, then, may depend upon a discriminating trust in political institutions. But they more certainly depend upon generalized trust among individuals and groups within society. Generalized trust is a key dimension of the political capacities of civil society, which in turn reflect the capacities of individuals and groups to act for common ends as well as to represent their interests to the state. Conversely, high levels of distrust within society erode these capacities, the absence of which is one condition for detached, unresponsive, and corrupt governments as Putnam's (1993) work on Italy suggested (cf. Gambetta 1988). The importance of civil society in generating democratic resistance and direction was reinforced by the recent revolutions in Eastern Europe. Especially in those countries most likely to consolidate into constitutional democracies (Germany, Poland, the Czech Republic, Slovakia, Hungary, and the Baltic states), those leading the revolutions were able to overcome state strategies that sought to discourage political organization by cultivating distrust among individuals. Against state-induced distrust, they formed organizations such as Solidarity and Charta 77 that resisted the state, developed public spaces characterized by dialogue about issues of principle, and initiated political change through counter-hegemonic cultural transformations (Cohen and Arato 1992: chap. 1; Preuss 1995: chap. 5; Seligman 1992: 169ff.).

While there is now broad agreement that a robust civil society "makes democracy work," the conceptual contribution of the notion of "social capital" and the associated notion of generalized trust is less clear. In

Chapter 7, "Trust, voluntary association and workable democracy: the contemporary American discourse of civil society," Jean Cohen takes a critical look at the recent popularity of the notion of civil society, especially in the American context. In current usage, Cohen argues, the term has lost the progressive theoretical importance it once had, from Tocqueville in the nineteenth century to its rediscovery in the context of the democratization of Eastern Europe in the more recent past. In the current American context, the term has become equated with traditional forms of association, including traditional forms of the family. This analysis has been overlaid with a rhetoric of moral decline, so that the "social decapitalization" of America is often reduced to a problem of identifying sources of moral corruption within civil society. In this (neoconservative) view, the meaning of "democracy" is equated with the state's non-interference with the voluntary associations of civil society. On this view, social trust, a key element of voluntary associations, can only be eroded, never generalized, by the means that states have available, democratic or otherwise.

Cohen argues that this appropriation of the concept of civil society is theoretically impoverished and politically suspect. In democratic theory from Tocqueville to Habermas, the concept of civil society has served to identify key conditions of the public spheres through which individuals communicate about matters of mutual concern. The concept of civil society gained its meaning not only from its communicative role in public judgment, but also from its capacities to generate the norms that underwrite the rule of law. Finally, owing to their communicative functions, public spheres mediate among numerous associations, movements, religious organizations, and other foci of interests and ideas, thus enabling a vibrant pluralism within society.

The current rhetoric, however, has reduced these complex functions to a vague conception of "social trust," which is assumed to be generated only by traditional family structures or traditional voluntary associations – both of which are in decline. Cohen agrees that voluntary associations are central to robust democracies. But the current rhetoric discounts the central role of legal and political institutions in making possible these associations and the social capital they represent. The rhetoric also fails to specify exactly what "social capital" is. In Putnam's (1993, 1995a) studies, for example, a key weakness stems from the fact that the theory locates the genesis of social trust exclusively in face-to-face interpersonal relations among members of voluntary associations, an approach that cannot account for the generalization of norms such as those of law-abidingness and reciprocity. Sociologically speaking, the tools with which to account for the functions of civil society within large-scale, complex, differentiated societies are simply not there if one discounts, as does Putnam, the integrating effects of legal and political institutions. Not recognizing the role that legal and political institutions play in providing conditions for social trust places the entire burden for "making democracy work" onto traditional voluntary associations, including the traditional family.

Cohen argues that numerous other kinds of institutions, especially legal institutions and their associated rights, play crucial roles in protecting, fostering, and generalizing social trust. In addition, many new nontraditional forms of association are taking the place of traditional associations. Like Patterson, Cohen also questions whether traditional forms of association should be valorized. The neoconservative rhetoric of civil society tends to hold up 1950s America as an ideal. But it was also an era, Cohen reminds us (as does Patterson), in which political speech was chilled by McCarthyism, and when traditional associations were involved in segregation, in denying civil rights, and in pushing women out of the work force. For these and other reasons, we must be much more exacting in the ways we conceptualize "social capital," "social trust," and their relation to civil society.

How does trust enable nonstate forms of collective action?

Democratic theorists increasingly have come to accept a principle first associated with Tocqueville: there are inherent limits to collective actions organized by states or state-like organizations (Cohen and Rogers 1995; Habermas 1996). States get things done through the medium of laws sanctioned by power. But laws and sanctions are limited as means of organizing collective actions. The issue is analogous to Wittgenstein's account of linguistic meaning: grammatical rules underdetermine meaning owing to the multiple contributions of context and usage. Likewise, even the most explicit set of laws or administrative rules is almost always insufficient to organize a collective action. Ultimately, collective action depends upon the good will of participants, their shared understandings, their common interests, and their skilled attention to contingencies (Baier 1986: 245–253). "Trust" is a way of describing the way groups of individuals presume the good will of others with respect to shared interests as well as the divisions of knowledge necessary to make use of explicit rules for collective action. Whatever capacities the state has for collective action draw upon trust – not as deference, but as the grasp individuals have of the contingencies and shared understandings necessary for working together. Trust is required not only within the domain of the state proper, but also outside the state, especially in those many social tasks for which high-level organization is inappropriate. Yet trust cannot itself be created, at least directly, by the means the state has available. Instead, trust, like many other capacities for organization, flows from civil society. As Tocqueville (1969: 517) so famously put it, "In democratic countries knowledge of how to combine is the mother of all other forms of knowledge; on its progress depends that of all the others." Similarly, those who study the sociology of economics are increasingly drawing attention to the extent to which market relations depend upon socially embedded backgrounds of trust, without which "transaction costs" would be prohibitively high (Dasgupta 1988; Fukuyama 1995; Granovetter 1992; McAllister 1995; Michalos 1990; Sabel 1993; Zucker 1986).

In Chapter 8, Rom Harré ("Trust and its surrogates: psychological foundations of political process") seeks to identify psychological sources of trust, in part by clarifying the semantics of the word "trust." Following Wittgenstein, Harré notes that the meanings of trust are embedded in our usages. When Harré looks at our usages, he finds a complex mix of meanings that, in the end, refer back to relations between individuals. Most significantly, trust between persons and institutions is a "species of the person-to-person" relation, an account that concurs with Offe's analysis. "Our beliefs about, as well as our affective and social relations to, the personnel account for standing in a trust relation to the institution they staff" (p. 260). Institutions work well when they take into account the "thick" context of interpersonal relations, habits, and customs that determine the meanings and associated expectations of formal rules.

These clarifications allow Harré to locate a paradoxical relation between democracy and trust. On the one hand, "democracy" ideally resolves issues through discursive rather than authoritarian means. On the other hand, democracy also increases inclusiveness and, as it does so, tends to shift from "custom to code" because wider inclusiveness means fewer "thick" relations can be taken for granted. Discursive resolution of political issues requires some level of background trust, which in turn depends on shared but inexplicit understandings and practices. Inclusiveness, however, tends to draw this background into question, thus forcing participants to rely more upon explicitly codified rules and procedures and less upon trust. Individuals depend upon code when they cannot, or do not, trust. But code cannot replace trust for the same kinds of reasons that grammar cannot replace language. So we should expect inclusive and pluralistic democracies to experience tensions between political (including democratic) procedures that tend toward the explicit codes, and the uncodifiable relations that make social life possible. In the United States, Harré suggests, the tension is exacerbated by an individualistic, rights-based political culture that elevates code over custom. Code-based politics tend toward rigidity and lose the subtle possibilities, efficiencies, and flexibilities inherent in inexplicit, trust-based modes of social regulation. Harré prefers a political culture based on obligation, which, he argues, has a greater capacity to reinforce the kinds of trust that make democracy work.

Like Harré, James Scott notes that the subtle relationships between thick, multifaceted social relations and capacities for collective actions are far harder to engineer than to destroy. In Chapter 9, "Geographies of trust, geographies of hierarchy," Scott examines the generally adversarial relationship between the state (and state-like powers) and the informal, unplanned, and apparently chaotic relations of trust that develop over time among people in a community. Criticizing the state-sponsored planners of "high modernity," Scott notes that rationalized plans and rules typically disrupt thick relations of social trust and produce dysfunctional communities. This is in part because rationalized plans cannot accommodate the complexity and apparent irrationality of working social relationships. In part this is because where rationalized plans are actually implemented, they must be imposed by authoritarian means on communities that are recalcitrant just to the degree that they are functional. While the relations that make a community may be protected and enabled (often by liberal-democratic means), they cannot be planned and engineered. Insofar as the most complete visions of top-down planning have worked at all – Scott notes the examples of the Soviet collective farms – they have done so only because of an unofficial tolerance of unplanned activities, such as the cultivation of private plots or "borrowed" supplies and equipment. Similarly, Brasilia, a planned city, works only because of the unofficial tolerance of a much larger unplanned city. Scott's essay suggests democracies must evolve distinctions among spheres sufficient to keep power relations from overgrowing their bounds – not only, as some would have it, to protect the rights of individuals, but more importantly to protect and enable the creative anarchy of civil society.

The politics of trust and risk

Taken together, one might find within Chapters 8 and 9 an argument for that kind of conservatism rooted in a suspicion of reason as applied to human affairs. The conservative tradition, from Burke to Hayek, does indeed contain important insight with regard to the limits of rational planning. Yet progressive democracies also depend upon this insight. If every change must be planned and its full consequences known, then every new initiative will be unacceptably risky. In this sense, almost all of the creative and progressive possibilities of politics depend upon trust, while defensive fears of change, including a distrust of what "everyone else" might do with one's future, can impede actions that can be good for all. A progressive approach to democracy must therefore attend to the ways political institutions generate or undermine the background of trust against which political issues emerge. The reason for this is that political issues emerge when existing ways of doing things are no longer taken for granted. Owing to the future-oriented nature of politics, collective decisions inevitably involve some amount of uncertainty about future outcomes. This is why those with vested interests almost always oppose changes by seeking to undermine trust in their proponents, thus magnifying fears of malign uncertainties. An emphasis on the risks of new initiatives is usually related to a policy focus on security, whether in the domestic politics of health care (or crime, trade policy, etc.) or in foreign-policy choices between military and diplomatic/developmental strategies. When security-based political strategies are successful in focusing on uncertainties, individuals are less likely to extend the trust necessary for new collective actions, preferring known vulnerabilities to unknown (and perhaps unknowable) future risks. Absence of trust paralyzes collective action, democratic or otherwise.

Such tensions between politics and trust suggest that in political situations good forms of trust may be hard to get going. In Chapter 10, "Altruistic trust," Jane Mansbridge examines how trust is initially established, especially in view of its risky nature (a point emphasized especially by Russell Hardin). Mansbridge argues that trust may draw on common kinds of moral resources and that there is a kind of trust that is morally praiseworthy. One account of trust – what Hardin conceptualizes as "encapsulated interest" – depends entirely upon the potential truster's predictions about whether someone is trustworthy or not. Mansbridge argues that trust can be extended on other grounds as well. For purely moral or altruistic reasons, one may take on a risk beyond one's ability to predict. Thus, one may extend trust out of respect for the other, in this way treating the other as one would oneself wish to be treated. One may extend trust out of a concern for the relationship. Or one may extend trust as a way of demonstrating virtuous action to others. To extend trust in these ways is not, Mansbridge argues, simply to make mistakes about the risks one is incurring. Rather, this kind of trust is motivated by independent moral reasons, and these reasons may be quite common in everyday relations of trust.

The democratic importance of altruistic trust is that it explains how relations of trust might get going in ways that become self-reinforcing, a problem especially pressing in political contexts that lack social and cultural forms of assurance. To be sure, altruistic trust is fragile: Mansbridge speculates that it is likely to flourish only where the potential costs of defection are mitigated by relatively high levels of economic well-being (a point made by Patterson, Uslaner, and Offe as well) and where networks of moral sanction have some impact. But where these conditions exist – as, she suggests, they did in the American Midwest in the post-homesteading era – then altruistic trust may induce the development of cooperative relations.

Politics by means of deliberation and promise

If democracy at its best – politics by means of deliberation and promise – requires trust, strong democrats are presented with a particular difficulty. Trust may be especially hard to get going in political situations, if only because the issues that require dialogue are often marked by a distinctive lack of the shared understandings and practices to which, for example, Harré refers. Deliberation, we must remember, is only one way of responding to political problems; other possibilities include coercion, blackmail, reliance on habit and tradition, and exit. Of these alternatives, deliberation is perhaps the most robust in its outcomes (producing either consensus or issues clarified sufficiently for a meaningful vote), but the most fragile in its preconditions. Without some degree of trust between them, conflicting parties may prefer the alternatives to deliberation. Moreover, the problem is not only one of getting dialogue going, which is hard enough. In addition, the typical outcome of a successful deliberation is a *promise* – codified, perhaps, in law, but also depending upon the good will of the parties for the law to work, and therefore leaving each party more vulnerable than each would seem to be were it to pursue strategies of distrust, each seeking to monopolize all resources necessary to security.

Race relations in America are so troubling in part because mutual distrust is often the norm. Critical numbers of individuals thus exit from dialogue in favor of relying on resources that would seem to offer more security. Surveys suggest that African-Americans trust government institutions more than do Euro-Americans, who, for their part, are relatively more supportive of liberal protections against government intervention (Jaynes and Williams 1989: 214) and relatively more likely to trust other individuals than government (Patterson, this volume). Clearly, for many African-Americans, the relative security of laws is preferable to the perhaps suspect (and historically often malign) intentions of Euro-Americans. This pattern of response leaves those who desire more racial equality and solidarity with something of a dilemma. Even when government intervention can be organized, it often requires the willing cooperation of Euro-Americans, without which government programs can generate zero-sum dynamics and actually increase distrust between the groups. Some affirmative-action programs provide bitter examples. Although trust is not the only condition of politics by means of deliberation and promise, without trust these means are paralyzed.

Those who favor the politics of deliberation and promise will need to look closely at such paradoxical relations between politics and trust. My aim in Chapter 11 ("Democratic theory and trust") is to provide a survey of the difficulties, initially by specifying what these paradoxical relationships are. Our received models of trust, I argue, tend to miss these paradoxes, primarily because they tend to be modeled from social relations generally rather than from political relations specifically. The most important features of social relations are that they are typically based on shared interests, as well as upon shared cultures that provide information about trusted individuals or institutions. Political relations, on the other hand, are typically those in which shared interests cannot be taken for granted and parties are, at least potentially, less likely to be constrained in their actions by shared culture. When we combine these points with the fact that political conflicts usually involve the deployment, or threatened deployment, of power, we can see that politics does not provide a natural environment for trust.

Democratic theorists who seek to conceptualize how the advantages of trust might be harnessed must pay close attention to its qualities within political contexts. The extent to which these problematic qualities are conceptualized and engaged distinguishes three emerging approaches to trust in democratic theory: what I refer to as *neoconservative, rational choice*, and *deliberative* approaches. These approaches locate sources of trust, respectively, within culture, within the rational monitoring of risks by individuals, and within discursive processes. They favor the political designs of neoconservatism (withdrawal of demands from the state in favor of social and economic modes of organization), traditional liberalism (interest-based monitoring of the state), and deliberative democracy (guidance of economic and political systems by deliberative publics).

The neoconservative approach, I argue, is theoretically inadequate as well as ethically suspect. As Jean Cohen also argues (this volume), this approach sees trust as an effect only of shared moral identities, enforced by traditional voluntary associations. The approach fails, however, to conceptualize the vulnerabilities and potential power relations involved in trust, which means that it cannot distinguish trust that is ethically warranted from trust that is not. Likewise, the neoconservative approach excludes the contributions that legal and political institutions might make to nurturing and generalizing trust. In this approach, many of the problems of relating trust to politics are defined away at the outset. More promising, I suggest, are emerging rational choice approaches to trust – not, I think, because of the general adequacy of rational choice methodology in social science, but because the rational choice emphasis upon the risks and vulnerabilities in trust are especially appropriate to political contexts. In particular, rational choice approaches reveal how various legal devices, including rights, can produce trust indirectly by limiting vulnerabilities. But because rational choice approaches remain, in Mansbridge's terms, "predictive" (or, in Hardin's terms, trust is "encapsulated interest"), it is difficult to see how political interactions might, in principle, generate relations of trust. In contrast, emerging deliberative approaches to democracy focus on the generative nature of political interactions. This approach allows us to ask which kinds of political institutions – which kinds of protections and inducements – might best generate *warranted* relations of trust among individuals, groups, and between these and government. Close attention to the ways that democratic institutions manage and reduce the risks of trust may allow us to see how warranted trust and its benefits might be protected, enhanced, and generated.

REFERENCES

Baier, Annette, 1986. Trust and antitrust. *Ethics* 96, 231–260
Barber, Bernard, 1983. *The Logic and Limits of Trust*, New Brunswick, N.J.: Rutgers University Press
Cohen, Jean L. and Arato, Andrew, 1992. *Civil Society and Political Theory*, Cambridge, Mass.: MIT Press
Cohen, Joshua, and Joel Rogers, 1995. Secondary associations and democratic governance, in Eric Olin Wright (ed.) *Associations and Democracy*, New York: Routledge, 7–98.
Coleman, James S., 1990. *Foundations of Social Theory*, Cambridge, Mass.: Harvard University Press
Dasgupta, Partha, 1988. Trust as a commodity, in Diego Gambetta (ed.), *Trust: Making and Breaking Cooperative Relations*, Oxford: Basil Blackwell
Dunn, John, 1988. Trust and political agency, in Diego Gambetta (ed.), *Trust: Making and Breaking Cooperative Relations*, Oxford: Basil Blackwell
Ely, John Hart, 1980. *Democracy and Distrust: A Theory of Judicial Review*, Cambridge, Mass.: Harvard University Press
Fukuyama, Francis, 1995. *Trust: The Social Virtues and the Creation of Prosperity*, New York: Free Press
Gambetta, Diego. 1988. Mafia: The price of distrust, in Diego Gambetta (ed.), *Trust: Making and Breaking Cooperative Relations*, Oxford: Basil Blackwell
Giddens, Anthony, 1990. *The Consequences of Modernity*, Stanford: Stanford University Press

Granovetter, Mark, 1992. Problems of explanation in economic sociology, in Nitin Nohria and Robert G. Eccles (eds.), *Networks and Organizations: Structure, Form, and Action*, Boston: Harvard Business School Press

Habermas, Jürgen. 1996. *Between Facts and Norms: Contributions to a Discourse Theory of Law and Democracy*, William Rehg (trans.), Cambridge, Mass: MIT Press

Inglehart, Ronald, 1997. *Modernization and Postmodernization: Cultural, Economic, and Political Change in 43 Societies*, Princeton, NJ: Princeton University Press

Jaynes, Gerald D. and Williams, Robin M., Jr., 1989. *A Common Destiny: Blacks and American Society*, Washington, D.C.: National Academy Press

Luhmann, Niklas. 1979. Trust: A mechanism for the reduction of social complexity, in *Trust and Power: Two Works by Niklas Luhmann*, Chichester: John Wiley and Sons

McAllister, Daniel J., 1995. Affect- and cognition-based trust as foundations for interpersonal cooperation in organizations. *Academy of Management Journal* 38, 24–59

Michalos, Alex C., 1990. The impact of trust on business, international security and the quality of life. *Journal of Business Ethics* 9, 619–638

Offe, Claus. 1996. *Modernity and the State: East, West*, Cambridge, Mass.: MIT Press

Preuss, Ulrich, 1995. *Constitutional Revolution: The Link Between Constitutionalism and Progress*, Deborah Lucas Schneider (trans.), Atlantic Highlands, N.J.: Humanities Press

Putnam, Robert, 1993. *Making Democracy Work: Civic Traditions in Modern Italy*, Princeton, N.J.: Princeton University Press

  1995a. Bowling alone: America's declining social capital. *Journal of Democracy* 6, January, 65–78

Sabel, Charles F., 1993. Studied trust: Building new forms of cooperation in a volatile economy. *Human Relations* 46, 1133–1170

Seligman, Adam B., 1992. *The Idea of Civil Society*, New York: Free Press

The Pew Research Center for the People and the Press, 1997. *Trust and Citizen Engagement in Metropolitan Philadelphia: A Case Study*, Washington, D.C.: The Pew Research Center

Tocqueville, Alexis de, 1969. *Democracy in America*, George Lawrence (trans.), J. P. Mayer (ed.), Garden City, N.Y.: Doubleday

Warren, Mark E., 1996. Deliberative democracy and authority. *American Political Science Review* 90, 46–60

  1999. What is political? *Journal of Theoretical Politics* 11, 207–231

Zucker, Lynne G., 1986. Production of trust: Institutional sources of economic structure, 1840–1920. *Research in Organizational Behavior* 8, 53–111

2   Do we want trust in government?*

Russell Hardin

In the analysis of trust and government, we may focus on two quite distinct causal issues: citizen trust in other citizens as a result, in part, of governmental institutions and citizen trust in government itself. The former is a variant of the central thesis of Thomas Hobbes. We need government in order to maintain the order that enables us to invest effort in our own well-being and to deal with others in the expectation that we will not be violated. Almost no one other than anarchists disagrees with this view, although some writers have supposed that large government is disruptive of relations between citizens. The American Anti-Federalists and such anti-urban thinkers as Ibn Khaldun (Gellner 1988) therefore opposed large government or urbanization.

The second issue – that citizens might specifically trust government – is suggested in a passage by John Locke. Locke (1988: 381) wrote that society turns power over to its governors, "whom society hath set over it self, with this express or tacit Trust, That it shall be imployed for their good, and the preservation of their Property."[1] Niklas Luhmann (1979: 54) says that this "old theme of political trust, which played a large role, especially in the period after the end of the religious wars, has virtually disappeared from contemporary political theory." If it had disappeared, it has come back in force, at least in consideration of the United States and other advanced democratic societies. Now, the supposition that citizens could trust government lies behind a large contemporary literature.

That literature commonly assumes that citizens must trust government if government is to work well and that a reputed decline in citizen trust of government bodes ill for many contemporary democratic societies.

* This paper was presented to the Conference on Democracy and Trust at Georgetown University, November 7–9, 1996. Its writing has been supported by the Center for Advanced Study in the Behavioral Sciences, the Guggenheim Foundation, the National Science Foundation (grant number SBR–9022192), and New York University. It has benefited from comments by participants at the Georgetown conference and from extensive written comments by Mark Warren.
[1] For discussion, see Dunn (1984, 1988), Laslett (1988: 114–117), and Hardin (1998).

Occasionally, it includes normative claims that people should trust a particular government. By a standard dictum of ethics, one cannot have a moral duty to do what one cannot do. This is expressed in the rule "Ought implies can." Unless we mean something very different when we speak of trusting government than when we speak of trusting a person, however, citizens typically cannot trust government.

A striking thing about the contemporary vision of society that citizens should trust government (and that it is a failing of either citizens or government if they do not) is that it is starkly contrary to traditional liberalism. Among the core understandings of liberalism is that citizens should distrust and be wary of government. David Hume supposed we should design government institutions so they would serve our interests even if they were staffed by knaves. And James Madison and other federalists attempted to do just that in the US Constitution. Madison's view was essentially that the incentives to anyone with power are at least partly to abuse that power for their own interests. That is to say that government agents will have incentive not to act in the citizens' interests.

I wish to address the second of the concerns above – trust in government – rather than the first – the effect of orderly government on individual trust. And I wish even for that issue to focus on epistemological issues of what citizens can know that they must know if they are intelligently to trust government. In general, citizens cannot know enough of what they must to be able to trust government. As Luhmann (1979: 46; cf. 1988: 102) notes, "Modern differentiated social orders are much too complex for the social trust essential to ordinary living to be created solely by trust-orientations toward persons; it is all too obvious that the social order does not stand and fall by the few people one knows and trusts." Trusting institutions makes little sense for most people most of the time.

Trust and distrust are an odd pair in that they do not fully cover the range of possibilities. Between active trust and active distrust there can be simple lack of either trust or distrust. In the vernacular English usage, to say "I don't trust you" commonly means "I distrust you," as though lack of any knowledge on which to base a judgment of either trust or distrust were not a possibility. The stance of citizens toward government could, in principle, be one of trust, distrust, or lack of either. I wish to pursue the plausibility of supposing that the relevant response for citizens, both rationally and actually, is commonly the lack of either trust or distrust because we typically lack the relevant knowledge for going further than that. Moreover, I think it plausible that we should not generally want trust in government for the simple reason that typical citizens cannot be in the relevant relation to government or to the overwhelming majority of government officials to be able to trust them except by mistaken inference. It may even be true that the conditions for distrust can be met more readily than can the conditions for trust.

Trust is in a cognitive category with knowledge. To say "I trust you" means that I know or think I know relevant things about you, especially about your motivations toward me. It is such knowledge that many of us cannot sensibly claim to have with respect to most government officials or with respect to government generally (Hardin, 1998). The easy answer to the question of my title, therefore, is that, insofar as trust is not possible except by mistake, we do not want it. Because the term "trust" is used in many ways, it is useful to stipulate how it will be used here. Therefore, let us briefly spell out the notion of trust as "encapsulated interest."

Trust as encapsulated interest

Before we turn to the problem of trust in government, consider trust in another person, from which we might expect conceptually to be able to generalize to claims about trust in groups, organizations, or institutions. It is often asserted that trust is an inherently moral notion or that it means Q or P. Against any such view, it seems clear that there are no "inherently anything" notions in social discourse. The term "trust" is used in manifold ways in ordinary language as it is in both philosophy and the social sciences. There is little point in quibbling over the essential meaning of trust: It has no essential meaning. Rather, it has a variety of meanings that often conflict. Serious discussion begins with making clear what is to be at issue. Because I wish to explain behavior with respect to government, I am interested in an explanatory account of trust. And I want that account to mirror trust at the level of individuals because an account of trust in government should be consistent with a general account of trust.

Two broad conceptions of trust that I will not consider here are purely normative accounts and purely expectations accounts. First, briefly consider purely normative accounts, in which it is commonly asserted that trust is a moral notion. It is moral to trust and immoral not to trust. In general, it is compelling to argue that trustworthiness can be morally required on many moral theories (Hardin 1996a). It is not generally sensible to claim that trust is morally required by any moral theory, because it cannot be morally required that we trust those who would clearly take advantage of our trust to cheat or harm us or others. If trust is moral, it is moral only contingently. This fact makes it a misfit for anti-consequentialist moral theories. And it makes trust essentially otiose for a utilitarian consequentialist theory, which commands only actions and not attitudes. A utilitarian might be required to cooperate when cooperation would be generally beneficial. The fact that the cooperation would be beneficial is ground for trust, but the trust adds nothing to the obligation, if there is one, to cooperate.

Jane Mansbridge (chapter 10, this volume) speaks of "altruistic trust" as an apparently normative conception of trust. In her actual discussions, however, what she conceives is *acting altruistically* to cooperate with another despite having inadequate grounds for trusting that other. Many, perhaps most, of us have done that on occasion, especially with respect to children whom we are trying to teach the value of reliability in keeping agreements.

It is perhaps a matter of linguistic taste whether we call this another kind of trust or merely an instance of acting beyond trust. But I think it is not merely a matter of taste. The view of trust as cognitive, and therefore not a matter of choice, can be fitted to *various kinds of action*. My degree of trust or distrust does not alone determine my action. (As a trivial case in point, note that there are many people in the world whom I trust very much in various realms but with whom I may not ever have reason to cooperate again or at all.) That I risk cooperation when either I have no grounds to trust or I even have grounds to distrust is a matter of sometime rational choice and sometime moral, or altruistic, choice. There is no advantage in conceiving of a separate category of trust to handle each of these varied ranges of action.

Other authors speak of risking trust (Luhmann 1979: 24) or choosing trust. There is similarly no point in such usages because they add nothing to the simpler account of trust as cognitive and of actions taken in the light of one's trust. I might risk cooperating or choose to cooperate with you despite inadequate trust. It is confusing to elide this claim into saying I risk or choose trust. In this elision, my cognitive state and my action are somehow combined into a single concept.

Second, consider purely expectations accounts. If trust is nothing more than the reasonable factual expectation that another will behave in a relevant manner, then it is nothing more than, say, the trust with which we sometimes inductively assert that the sun will rise tomorrow morning because, after all, it has always risen every morning that we can remember. We may similarly inductively trust some part of the government in this very limited sense because we may simply extrapolate from behavior until this moment to predict future behavior. Of course, this means, among other things, that we can trust some government bodies and agents to continue to act corruptly against our interests, we can trust others to continue to be incompetent to do what they are appointed to do, and we can trust many agents of government to lie to us with regularity about important matters for which they are responsible. While this usage of the term "trust" is common in everyday speech, it trivializes what is of concern in general debates about whether we should trust government. If trust is merely expectations, then the claim that we should trust government is equivalent to some claim such as that we should expect government to do good. The latter would be a stupid claim much of the time. Should Martin Luther King and Ernest Hemingway have expected the FBI not to be spying on and harassing them even though they may have had evidence that it was?

Anyone who wishes to insist that either of these notions (or any other notion) of trust is *the* true meaning of the term is whistling nonsense, for which, of course, there is a grand tradition in social thought, a tradition that may be both older and more copious than any more nearly analytical tradition. No one need be deterred from contributing to that hoary tradition, which has seductive, rhetorical pleasures that are not to be denied.

My central concern is with the explanation of behavior that is grounded in a particular, coherent vision of trust. That vision is of trust as an expression of encapsulated interest (Hardin 1991). To say that I trust you with respect to some matter means that I have reason to expect *you to act in my interest* with respect to that matter because you have good reasons to do so, *reasons that are grounded in my interest*. In other words, to say that I trust you means I have reason to expect you to act, for your own reasons, *as my agent* with respect to the relevant matter. Your interest encapsulates my interest.

Trust is generally a three-part relation: A trusts B to do x (or with respect to x). There are several important considerations in this formula. Perhaps most obviously, there is the final clause, which is commonly omitted from ordinary expressions of trust. In virtually all cases of trust, the trust is limited to certain areas. I trust you to return the money for your morning cup of coffee, but I might not trust you with an unsecured loan of thousands of dollars for your down payment on a house. As Tolstoy (1949: 347) wryly notes, a Russian nobleman of his time could be trusted with gambling debts to another nobleman, but not with another nobleman's wife or with debts to his tailor. We each generally differ from Tolstoy's noblemen only with respect to the categories in which we can be trusted and distrusted.

More centrally, however, my trust of another individual typically turns on expectations grounded in the interest the relevant person has to do various things. It is trust rather than mere expectation *if* A expects B to do x *because B has a reason to do it that is grounded in A*. That reason could be an ongoing relationship – including love, friendship, or mere exchange, as in business – a relationship with A that B wants to maintain. Or it could be some other interest B has that A somehow influences. For example, A may influence B's prospects for re-election.

There is a common conception of trust that holds it to be grounded in thick, ongoing relationships (e.g. Williams 1988). In this conception, I can trust only a person with whom I associate frequently and fairly intensively, so that I am in a position to know that person's motivations toward me and to know whether my risk in giving him or her power of agency over some aspect of my life is justified. I will be justified in trusting you if you can be supposed to have a strong interest in maintaining good relations with me for future exchanges or dependencies. While the gist of this limited model of trust fits the encapsulated-interest account, it is not true that the relevant expectations can be grounded only in thick relationships. I can expect you to act well as my agent for the reason that you will suffer loss if you do not. This can happen because of the iterated nature of our interaction, as in the thick-relationship model, or because of reputational effects that will enable you to benefit from relationships other than ours, or because there is an imposed structure of incentives to get you to act well as my agent.

There is an intermediate kind of case in which all but one of the elements of the encapsulated-interest model of trust are present. Consider an example. Suppose I think environmental protection, depending on its costs, is in my interest. I may not know very much about the basic technical issues involved, so I am not competent to judge my own interest in detail. For example, I may not understand the account of ozone depletion and its significance for me or my children. But I still may think I have good reason to suppose that, say, the Sierra Club policy experts are competent to understand these matters and that the Club shares my interest in environmental protection. Suppose further that I do not contribute to the Sierra Club and therefore do not think that its stance depends on my interest either directly or indirectly. Rather, it simply does share my interest, just as some of my neighbors also do, and it and my neighbors act in ways that forward my interest merely for the reason that forwarding their own interest coincidentally forwards mine.

This coincidence of interests is a spurious causal relationship. The Club and my neighbors are not my agents, although, of course, I may be glad they are there and working in ways that forward my interest. In the vernacular, one might say both that I trust them and that I have put no trust in them. In the encapsulated-interest account, however, I do not trust them with respect to my environmental interest, nor should I distrust them. Their interest does not encapsulate mine; it merely correlates with mine. To refer to such a relationship, let us call it near-trust.

Note, however, that agencies and persons – such as the Sierra Club or my neighbors – that share our interests can be useful in certifying the trustworthiness of others. Hence, they can help to give us the grounds for trusting or distrusting these others. For example, my neighbor, whom I know to be a close associate of yours and whom I trust with respect to my interests in some matter, might advise me that I can trust you. Here, my neighbor has the role of providing the knowledge base for informing judgments of trustworthiness (see Warren chapter 11, this volume). Organizations also can perform this role for us, as they do in simple contexts of informing us of someone's credit worthiness. (I will return below to the general issue of agencies for judging trustworthiness in politics.)

Now consider this model of trust applied to trust in government. Again, A trusts B to do x (or with respect to x). For the case in which A is a citizen and B is an officeholder, office seeker, organization, or institution, the most likely reason for A's trust in B is that there is a structure of organizational or political incentives imposed on B that will get B to act well as A's agent with respect to x. Of course, it is possible that I could actually know a particular government official in ways that fit the ordinary account of individual trust in another individual, because we might have a thick or iterated relationship. This cannot be typical of anyone's trust in much of government, however, because in a large society we simply cannot have thick relationships with enough people.

Our common, and commonly justified, reaction to people who regularly tell us that very many people are their very close friends is to suppose they do not mean what we mean when we say someone is a close friend. It is not possible to have many very close friends for the simple reason that there are not enough hours in life to sustain many close relationships. Similarly, there are not enough hours to sustain enough thick relationships to be able to claim to trust many people for reasons of their dependence on our direct future relations with them. Indeed, we have created many institutions in effect to handle the problem of lack of direct relations with others that would enable us to live well.

Finally, there are two central elements in this model of trust that have been only implicit so far. First, if A is to trust B, then B must have not only the motivation to do x but also the competence. An agent who cannot act on my behalf is a poor agent. Second, if A's trust is to be fulfilled, A must have the competence to judge B. A's judgment might be delegated to relevant agencies when they exist, but in politics finding a trustworthy agency for such delegation is often difficult. Moreover, there are likely to be competing agencies attached to conflicting interests, and these agencies are apt to produce contrary, not congruent, judgments.

There are conceptions of trust other than the three-part relationship of trust as encapsulated interest. Indeed, there are other conceptions included in this volume. In addition, trust is often discussed very loosely without a clear sense of what would or would not count as an instance of trusting. Loose usage, as in several recent books on trust, allows authors to make inconsistent claims without awareness and sometimes to make very grand claims whose content is, at best, vague. Such usage then forces readers to interpret in their own ways. In part, this results from the normal, confusing richness of terms in ordinary language. Terms often have the quality of family resemblance. Any two notions of trust might have some common ground. But the set of all notions in use might have no element in common, just as the set of faces from some family might clearly resemble one another without having any particular element in common to all the faces. One might have supposed (as I do) that a notion of trust that does not include at least some sense of expectation is of no interest to us, but there are some odd claims for purely normative conceptions of trust that include no element of expectations.

Representation and bureaucracy[2]

The nature of democratic government in modern states, which are far too populous for direct democracy on most matters, is representative. Furthermore, even representative bodies cannot handle the mass of detail involved in governance, so modern government is necessarily handled by large bureaucratic organizations. Hence, our governors are often twice removed from oversight by citizens. Given the size of the constituencies of both representatives and governmental bureaus, citizens cannot be expected to know their representatives or the bureaucratic agents who govern them well enough for the model of thick relationships to characterize their trust in government.

How, then, can we make sense of trusting an institution if trust requires grounding in the interests of the institution and its agents? There are at least two ways we might unpack our trust of an institution. First, we could trust every individual in the organization, each in the relevant ways, to do what each must do if the organization is to fulfill our trust. Second, we could know that the design of the roles and their related incentives will induce role-holders to do what they must do if the organization is to fulfill our trust. Here we essentially trust the structure of incentives to get individual officeholders to act well as our agents. In this case, the individual role-holders might be broadly interchangeable, and we need know few, if any, of them.

Neither of these visions is plausible for citizen trust of modern governmental institutions. Scale factors make the first of these implausible. Virtually no one can know enough of the large number of individual

---

[2] Most of this section is borrowed from Hardin (1998).

role-holders to claim to trust them in the strong sense of seeing that they have interests in fulfilling trust placed in them. Against the second of these ways of establishing trust in government, few people can have an articulate understanding of the structures of various agencies and the roles within them or of the overall government to be confident of the incentives that role-holders have to be trustworthy. Hence, as a matter of actual practice, it is utterly implausible that trust underlies most citizens' views and expectations of government.

In actual life, we might often not trust an organization but might merely depend on its apparent predictability by induction from its past behavior. Then we have merely an expectations account of the organization's behavior. Inductive knowledge in some contexts seems very compelling. Most of us expect the sun to rise tomorrow just because that is what has always happened so far as we know. For many people, that expectation is reinforced by the belief that there are physical laws to govern the sun's rising. Their expectations are Newtonian and not merely inductive.

Expectations of human behavior are much less reliable than the merely inductive expectations about the sun's behavior. Indeed, their unreliability is the central driving force of most great literature. In a cute moment, one might say that one of the strongest expectations we must have of people in the long run is that they will defy our expectations. While there is no analogue of Newtonian physics to reinforce our expectations of human behavior, there is a consideration that is arguably far more widely understood than is Newtonian physics. We base much of our expectations of people's actions on beliefs about human psychology. Among the most compelling and generalizable of psychological traits is that people are motivated by their interests. Hence, trust – expectations grounded in encapsulated interest – may be more widely motivated than beliefs about physical relationships that are grounded in nothing more than induction.

Of a large part of the population, perhaps, we can claim no more than that they have inductive expectations about government, not that they have grounds for trust as encapsulated interest. That an agency or its role-holders are trustworthy might matter to some people, but to most there is nothing beyond expectations. Kant's neighbors may have relied on his punctuality in his morning walk to set their schedules. To trust requires more: that they rely on his having their interests at heart in deciding when to take his walk. If they could not think he did, they could not be said to trust him (Baier 1986: 234). Like Kant's neighbors, those people who have merely inductive expectations cannot be said to trust government. Inductive expectations that government will be capricious might be sufficient to ground distrust, but for most people there might be neither trust nor distrust of a reliable government or agency.

The trustworthiness of government might matter enormously to some citizens, but it might count only by default for many others. Distrust comes easily; trust requires too rich an understanding of the other's incentives for it to come easily to many people. If our understanding of government is that it must be grounded in trust to be legitimate, then no major government of modern times is legitimate. Indeed, even if all we require is the near-trust of merely correlated rather than encapsulated interests, no modern government is likely to be legitimate for more than passing moments. For example, the government of the Czech Republic in its early days or the governments of England and the United States during World War II might have been legitimate in this limited sense in the eyes of most citizens. Even during these periods, near-trust cannot have been at all complete, because citizens' interests cannot have been correlated on any but certain central matters such as prosecuting the war or establishing a non-dictatorial government.

Even in this limited sense of near-trust, the government of the United States since World War II cannot have counted as legitimate. Evidently, government need not be legitimate in this sense for it to survive and even manage a nation through major difficulties and into prosperity. It may suffice that government not be generally distrusted. If some core of the populace genuinely trusts at least parts of a government and not too much of the rest of the populace actively distrusts it, then it likely has done well by historical standards for large states.

In the end, trust still may be crucial to the success of government. Those most attentive to government also will be those most likely to know enough about governmental actions and structures to know whether the government or at least some of its agents are trustworthy. If they are also the people most likely to oppose government in response to its failings, then the possibility of trustworthiness and the epistemological possibility of trust could be important to the stability of government. The significance of their role in support of government might be ramified by the implicit support of those who act from mere expectations without articulate knowledge of the trustworthiness of government. The expectations of the latter group might be based in large part on the expectations of others, just as most of us know many of the things we know only in the sense that we gather that others think those things are true. Our crippled epistemology is little more than mimicry.

Low voter turnouts in many nations – including, notoriously, the United States – are commonly taken as evidence that government has failed to elicit support. But, *prima facie,* an equally or even more plausible conclusion may be that such turnouts are evidence that government has not engendered grievous distrust and opposition. Silence cannot unambiguously prove the case for or against government. If mimicry underpins many of our expectations of government, then the limited commitment of most people to try to change or affect government makes epistemologically good sense.

Democracy and knowledge

Pragmatists such as Charles S. Peirce and John Dewey justified democracy in part with the claim that democracy is necessary for the optimal generation of knowledge in a society. The inclusiveness of democracy would bring greater input of ideas. Dewey may have held somewhat contradictory views. He supposed that the best way to fix beliefs is with a community such as that of science, with canons of testing, experimentation, and openness. Communities of science are, however, not democratic and inclusive. Rather, they are highly meritocratic and openly exclude some people, indeed, most people. Dewey wanted to extend the purview of such communities to cover moral and political issues as well as the standard issues of the putatively objective sciences. In such an extension, one might see the requirement for inclusiveness and therefore reject the model of communities of science. Moreover, one might reject Dewey's seeming supposition that there is an underlying objectivity for our value concerns to which a community of science could direct its attention.

Against the pragmatic claim that we need democracy to generate knowledge, it seems very clear that the market in a highly advanced market economy generates vastly more knowledge than politics can and that the knowledge it generates, much of it diffused through society, enables us to accomplish things far beyond what central control of the economy could accomplish for us. The broad failure and recent demise of state-run economies in much of the world suggest that politics can be a disastrous system for generating important kinds of knowledge. Indeed, the idea that the generation and evaluation of knowledge require anything vaguely like equal inputs or even broadly representative inputs is odd. Nobel Prizes are rightly not awarded equally or representatively to all. More generally, it is arguments from knowledge that commend meritocracy of the modern kind, that is, expertise or competence (as opposed to putative merit from birth or position).

Contrary to Dewey's and Peirce's pragmatic arguments, therefore, the central problem of competence in governance inherently involves a combination of democratic choice and meritocratic decision-making. The crux of the problem is that the meritocrats have to be selected through democratic devices. This means democratic devices somehow must be good at choosing meritocrats even though they are surely not capable of directly meritocratic assessment of policies. In principle, it is not impossible that we could democratically judge competence. For example, it seems likely that democratic choice of the most competent basketball player of the 1990s would overwhelmingly confirm the views of some selection of supposed experts such as, say, National Basketball Association coaches. But it is implausible that we can democratically assess who is the smartest or most competent person in many areas of endeavor. For example, democratic choice of whose views on AIDS, secondary education, or the design of a new aircraft are best would plausibly be a travesty, especially when such choices become a regular part of politics, so that interests begin to coalesce around various positions on such matters.

Competence

We want governors to be competent, even expert, with respect to many things. We have social systems for establishing credentials for competence in many social realms in which ordinary citizens could not expect to evaluate individual competence. For example, universities certify the competence of professionals in engineering, law, medicine, and so forth. Professional organizations also evaluate and certify individuals in various realms. And large organizations such as firms, hospitals, and research laboratories evaluate competence. The striking feature of politics in purely electoral and, on occasion, even appointive offices is that there is little or no such evaluation of merit. Voters must choose candidates who essentially bundle competence, value commitments, and interests.

While no one of these always trumps, interests often seem to be the predominant factor in electoral choice. This is an almost uniquely different feature of politics. In other arenas, we do have some concern with problems of interest, as in conflict between particular experts' interests and the interests of their clientele. And we even may have some concern with problems of the conflicting values of particular experts such as, for example, the doctor who recommends against amniocentesis because she is opposed to abortion rather than because she is concerned for the interests of her patient. We have many institutional devices to manage these problems, which often may seem negligible. Moreover, we have the important institutional device of competition between experts at the level of the particular decision of the moment rather than merely for a substantial term of office commonly without much respect to particular decisions or issues.

Suppose, however, that we did not have the problem of bundling competence with other considerations in our potential officeholders. Could we expect democratic procedures to select for competence or merit? We might be able to do so for evaluating, say, candidates for Nobel Prizes if – and this is a very big if – we had reliable agencies to inform us of the competence of the candidates. While we are not completely without such resources in political choice, we do not have such reliable agencies in general. If competence were the only issue, we might expect such agencies to arise and help us make better judgments. Indeed, in many jurisdictions in which judges are elected in the United States, there are agencies, such as the Independent Voters of Illinois, that evaluate for competence and whose evaluations evidently affect voter choices.

In politics we have, oddly, competing agencies for the evaluation of competence. For example, when scientific judgments are of concern in the policy arena, we generally can expect to hear competing "experts" making claims about the scientific merits of various matters. Certified scientists still can be found to say that smoking is not causally responsible for lung cancer. The correlation is greater than virtually all that any social scientist has ever been impressed with in her own causal accounts of social matters, and it convinces the overwhelming majority of scientists of all, and especially of relevant, disciplines and may even convince most smokers. But the political arena is one in which stupid and disreputable claims often get great play and even carry the day, especially if there is money behind them.

In many such matters, energetic competition in the evaluation of the competence of politicians leads to confusion on the part of many electors. Moreover, the task of evaluation is inherently complicated by a consideration that is often much less important or not important at all in ordinary, more nearly technical matters. Part of what we must discover or come to understand is our interests, and therefore we often are forced to reach simultaneous judgment on what our interests are and on who can best deal with them. Our interests are not simply given in many policy issues. My interest when I go to a doctor with my broken finger, take my stalled car to a mechanic, or seek insurance is relatively clear and straightforward. My interest in the potential redesign of the public school system, the regulation of some industry, or such complex issues as pollution commonly, even most likely, is not. One of the most important inputs to my assessment of my interests commonly may be the claims of politicians who want my vote. My choice of a candidate for office who stands on one side or the other of such issues is doubly complex and difficult.

One way to restate this doubly complex problem is to say that in cases such as my broken finger the definition of my welfare is quite clear, so that the only issue is the means to serve that welfare. And even the means may be quite clear. In the politics of pollution, however, I first do not even know what my welfare is and typically cannot know what means would serve it. I choose both at once, so that these concerns are bundled. This problem is not unique to politics, but is distinctively central to politics. For medical care, plumbing, building, and so forth, we have long-established institutional devices for assessing means to various ends, and we have relatively clear senses of what our ends are. Moreover, there is commonly little difference in your and my ends. Politics often lacks all of these features.

Even if there were no problem in evaluating competence, in many contexts there is virtually no chance of finding competence, not least because theory and institutional devices are inadequate to handle the problems at issue. Competition in the evaluation of policies occurs even within government agencies. If the government's own supposed experts contest the issues, the implementing agents of government are in trouble. William Eskridge (1996) suggests that intra-agency problems often are compounded by the fact that regulation involves lawyers and judges, who are apt to be "morons" on scientific issues. The problems of incompetence are severe even for relatively technical problems, such as auto safety (see Mashaw and Harfst 1990), that do not involve massive social issues, such as school busing and endemic poverty (see Nelson 1977).

Trust and democracy

To trust someone with respect to some matter entails delegating that matter to them to some extent. That is why trust is at issue. Because we delegate, we empower someone to cause us harm or to fail in some task on our behalf. We do, of course, delegate many matters to government officials. But in this case, delegation is inherently necessary merely to accomplish various things, such as social order. We therefore can delegate without trusting. To some large extent, that is what we rationally should do with respect to government and its officials. This is nothing unusual. Indeed, we should rationally take most of our knowledge more or less on faith from a hodgepodge of ill- to well-qualified experts or authorities (Hardin 1996b).

When we give someone power over x, we very often implicitly and inescapably give them power over other matters. Libertarians do not want government to have power to manage the economy or to override individual freedoms, but only to maintain social order. Besides wanting government to maintain social order, liberals are willing to let government have power to manage the economy, but they do not want it to have power to override individual freedoms. Both therefore want government with limits. Yet if we empower government enough to allow it to accomplish the tasks we delegate to it, we likely empower it to go well beyond our delegations. Again, we must delegate, but it does not follow that we must or can trust.

Delegation of authority via democratic procedures is more complex than merely this account, however, in that it is accomplished by devices shot through with logical problems of the fallacy of composition. I vote for one thing, you vote for another, and yet we get the same representative. We seemingly collectively delegate power to our candidate to decide numerous issues, yet neither of us might actually want much of what the candidate does once in office. On any given issue, we might be able to escape this problem by deciding via referendum. But for the whole range of issues that concern us, the outcome of referenda would likely depend on the order in which we considered issues and the way in which we packaged them. It is almost logically excluded that I can genuinely delegate what I want to delegate if political choice is over a relatively complex range of matters, as it is in a modern polity.

Agencies for judging trustworthiness

Historically, the chief agencies for judging trustworthiness of politicians were political parties. In principle, parties could be good at judging both the competence and the commitment of potential officeholders. Hence, they could supply citizens with the knowledge they needed to determine whether candidates were trustworthy even when the citizens could not directly know the candidates well enough to make such assessments on their own. There are at least two problems with this possibility today. First, at one time we might have believed we could delegate to a party as our agency because we could have thought most issues came under a fairly coherent ideological system. That is an implausible assumption today in stable, advanced democracies. It still might make sense for the transitional period from state control of the economy to market control in some newly democratizing and marketizing states, as it still might make sense for brief periods of crisis in advanced democracies when concern with ideological issues might briefly dwarf other concerns in apparent importance. In the late twentieth-century United States, it is arguably implausible for any significant group other than fundamentalist religious voters.

Second, parties in the United States do not have much control over candidate selection. And indirectly, therefore, they also do not have much control over the selection of appointive officeholders. Strangely, then, the chief controlling agency for citizens' judgments are citizens' judgments. This raises complex issues in street-level epistemology.

If individual judgment is not good, collective judgment might never-theless be good in some choice contexts, such as those covered by the Condorcet jury theorem. According to this theorem, if the average juror is likely to have at least a slightly better than even chance of correctly assessing the truth of the innocence or guilt of an accused, then a very large jury will approach certainty of getting it right. Unfortunately, how-ever, the conditions for the jury theorem are not met in candidate selec-tion. First, the choice is not a binary one analogous to the choice between guilt and innocence. And, second, my fellow citizens cannot generally be expected to get the judgment of candidates more likely right than wrong. Therefore, an election may well come closer to getting the choice wholly wrong than wholly right.

In some matters, conventional collective knowledge is good. Often this is because there is a matter of objective rightness or wrongness that is put to test over an extended range of experiences, so that it becomes more or less perfected over time. Nevertheless, collective knowledge that is bad often may be sorely resistant to correction simply because the collectivity cannot see it put to test altogether. You may have seen correcting evid-ence, whose conclusion you report to me. But twelve other associates, who have not seen such evidence, question my good sense if I now reject the currently dominant collective view of the matter. I may have no inde-pendent judgment of the relative authority of my various associates and may naturally yield to the force of numbers. Hence, collective knowledge is apt to be relatively conservative.

The problem is even worse for politics. In politics, there is often little convincing evidence one way or the other for how good a policy will be. This is true already at the level of the best-informed experts. Consider debates a generation ago over school busing, for example, or currently over school choice. The typical citizen is in no position to judge such matters well, although sometimes the citizen can judge the immediate impact of a particular policy on her own immediate life, as many citizens did in the case of school busing.

Because candidates might be seen more or less as bundles of policy positions, they are similarly hard to assess. The so-called incumbency effect – incumbents have a strong advantage over challengers – may be in large part the result of two things related to this problem of collective knowledge. First, citizens typically may have more knowledge about the effects of an incumbent's positions than about the effects of a challenger's positions. Second, citizens typically may have far more knowledge about the competence of an incumbent than about that of a challenger.

For some policy issues, although less commonly for candidates, there are independent agencies whose judgments are relatively effective in reaching large publics. For example, the medical profession has been relatively effective in conveying the belief that smoking is causally associated with lung cancer. Even for many of the best such independent-agency judgments, however, there often are competing judgments that publics must weigh in adopting their own beliefs. Here, "adopting" is perhaps too strong a term, but it is rightly suggestive. Beliefs generally happen to people; they are not a matter of choice. I come to believe that you have lied to me because the evidence tips the scales against you. But for some hotly debated public issues, we often may simply be inclined to credit one source more than another. We accept some bit of putative knowledge on the weight of the authority of expertise after weighing the authoritative expertise rather than the bit of knowledge itself.

Nevertheless, democratic choice and the search for scientific understanding are confused already for relatively simple problems, such as the evaluation of a new treatment for AIDS. Because there are interests at stake, as in the controversy over AIDS drugs, tobacco, school busing, and virtually all policy issues, we finally cannot trust supposedly independent agencies genuinely to be independent. Moneyed interests have deliberately created agencies to pursue particular political lines rather than to seek truths. Not even a citizen who agrees with the judgments of the American Enterprise Institute or Americans for Democratic Action can seriously believe that their judgments are not tainted by, or even driven by, interests rather than by a concern for truth. It would be foolish to suppose they do not deliberately seek out expert analyses that reach the right bottom line. At some level, we might not be able even to trust ourselves to reach good judgments over issues in which we might have a personal stake. For example, a liberal might finally come to believe that welfare programs do not work partly because they cost the liberal too much. People who readily trust the judgments of many nonpolitical agencies, such as encyclopedias, heavily discount virtually every agency involved in political judgments.

Concluding remarks

Again we may ask: How can we make sense of "trusting an organization" if such trust is conceived on analogy with trusting an individual? It is commonly implausible that we could trust enough individuals in the organization, each in the relevant ways, to do what they must do if the organization is to live up to our trust. For many cases, including most governmental organizations, scale factors make this epistemologically virtually impossible. And it is implausible that most people could know the design of the roles and their related incentives to get role-holders to do what they must do if the organization is to live up to our trust. In this case, the individual role-holders might be broadly interchangeable, and we need know few if any of them, as is typically true of, say, banks, which we may confidently expect to handle our money reasonably well and honorably. But it is not plausible that many governmental organizations have such simple tasks as banks have.

Alternatively, we might not trust the organization but might depend on its apparent predictability. I may not be able to break down the organization into roles whose occupants I can judge, and I may not be able to figure out the functional relation of the various roles to the things I want or expect from the organization. But I still can possibly know enough about the history of the organization to have strong expectations of how it will respond to my query. This device formally raises David Hume's problem of induction, although at the street level this may not be an obstacle to belief. But it does eliminate concern with trust. Again, I think this is likely the most compelling claim for the relationship of citizens to government in general. It is not a relationship of trust or distrust. At best, much of the time it is a relationship of inductive expectations.

How does the account here fit the current thesis that there is declining trust by citizens both in their government and in each other? In the current discussions, there is often a focus on how to get citizens to be more trusting. This would make sense under the common thesis that trust is per se good because it enables us to enter relationships that will be beneficial.[3] But that thesis is false as a general thesis, because it is generally beneficial to trust only those who are trustworthy – not everyone, including the patently untrustworthy. If there is declining trust, the reason seems most likely to be that there is declining trustworthiness. There are at least two ways in which this might be true. First, there may be increasing exposure to or need to deal with less trustworthy people. Second, there may be declining trustworthiness of any given person or kind of person.

Consider the first of these. Data from various sources suggest that individuals trust each other less today than a few decades ago in the United States. Unfortunately, anyone trying to explain this trend or interpret its significance faces serious ambiguities in the data. It is plausible that comparing what people are saying at the different times is encumbered with an ecological fallacy. Those who trust people less today may be speaking of more people than those who trusted people more a generation ago. Why? Our lives today are typically more complicated with larger numbers of people with whom we interact. It is virtually a logical implication

---

[3] This is, unfortunately, the natural way to read Luhmann (1979).

of such a change that we cannot trust more people now as much as we trusted fewer people then.

Now consider the second way trustworthiness may be declining. The apparent changes might simply reflect the quasi-Hobbesian thesis that effective government is needed for citizens to trust each other. Perhaps government today is less effective at protecting citizens from each other than it was a generation ago. This could be true for technological, demographic, political, or other reasons. Hence, we genuinely do trust each other less because the backdrop of reliable sanctions against poor behavior is increasingly fraying.

Note, however, that neither account suggests any merit in attempting to address trust or declining trust directly. Indeed, both suggest that declining trust makes eminently good sense. It is a sound first principle of political analysis to suppose that people are behaving sensibly and to try to figure out the sense of their actions before first supposing they are behaving senselessly. People who sustained as high levels of trust after such changes as they had before the changes would be irrationally oblivious of their conditions. If levels of trust are declining, we should first take seriously accounts that make this a sensible response to the world. The second of the accounts immediately above suggests problems of governance, possibly even substantial failings of government. Some of the contemporary commentary focusing on the citizens whose trust is reputedly in decline suggests the character of Bertolt Brecht's (1976: 440) lampooning of the East German government in the 1950s. He wrote a short poem that the government, having lost faith in the people, had decided to dissolve the people and elect a new one. That, of course, misses the point of having government. Similarly, some current analyses of declining trust may miss the point of trust.

REFERENCES

Baier, Annette, 1986. Trust and antitrust. *Ethics* 96, 231–60
Brecht, Bertolt, 1976. The solution, in John Willett and Ralph Mannheim (eds.) with the cooperation of Erich Fried, *Bertolt Brecht, Poems: 1913–1956*, New York: Methuen, 440
Dunn, John, 1984. The concept of "trust" in the politics of John Locke, in Richard Rorty, J.B. Schneewind, and Quentin Skinner (eds.), *Philosophy in History: Essays on the Historiography of Philosophy*, Cambridge: Cambridge University Press, 279–301
    1988. Trust and political agency, in Diego Gambetta (ed.), *Trust: Making and Breaking Cooperative Relations*, Oxford: Basil Blackwell, 73–93
Eskridge, William, 1996. Remarks at the conference Political Consequences of Pragmatism, Washington University, St. Louis, September

Gellner, Ernst, 1988. Trust, cohesion, and the social order, in Diego Gambetta (ed.), *Trust: Making and Breaking Cooperative Relations*, Oxford: Basil Blackwell, 142–57

Hardin, Russell, 1991. Trusting persons, trusting institutions, in Richard J. Zeckhauser (ed.), *Strategy and Choice*, Cambridge, MA: MIT Press, 185–209

1996a. Trustworthiness. *Ethics* 107, 26–42

1996b. Why know. Paper presented at memorial conference in honor of James S. Coleman, Reimers Stiftung, Bad Homburg, Germany, October–November

1998. Trust in government, in Valerie Braithwaite and Margaret Levi (eds.), *Trust and Governance*, New York: Russell Sage, 9–27

Laslett, Peter, 1988. Introduction, in Peter Laslett (ed.), student edition, *Two Treatises of Government*, by John Locke, Cambridge: Cambridge University Press, 3–126

Locke, John, 1988. *Two Treatises of Government*, Peter Laslett (ed.), student edition, Cambridge: Cambridge University Press

Luhmann, Niklas, 1979. Trust: A mechanism for the reduction of social complexity, in *Trust and Power: Two Works by Niklas Luhmann*, Chichester: John Wiley and Sons

1988. Familiarity, confidence, trust: Problems and alternatives, in Diego Gambetta (ed.), *Trust: Making and Breaking Cooperative Relations*, Oxford: Basil Blackwell, 94–107

Mashaw, Jerry L. and Harfst, David L., 1990. *The Struggle for Auto Safety*, Cambridge, MA: Harvard University Press

Nelson, Richard R., 1977. *The Moon and the Ghetto*, New York: Norton

Tolstoy, Leo, 1949. *Anna Karenina*, Book I, Louise and Aylmer Maude (trans.), Oxford: Oxford University Press

Williams, Bernard, 1988. Formal structures and social reality, in Diego Gambetta (ed.), *Trust: Making and Breaking Cooperative Relations*, Oxford: Basil Blackwell, 3–13

3   How can we trust our fellow citizens?

Claus Offe

Trust is more than just another interesting, difficult, though only recently widely studied social phenomenon. The current rise in interest in this phenomenon (as reflected in recent writings by, among others, Fukuyama (1995), Seligman (1992), Gambetta (1988), Giddens (1990), Levi (1996), Misztal (1996), Putnam (1993), and Eisenstadt (1995, 1998)) as well as the closely related group of phenomena such as social capital, respect, recognition, confidence, associability, social cohesion, and civil society may have to do with a widely shared, though largely implicit, diagnosis of basic problems of public policy and the steering of social coordination, and ultimately the maintenance of social order itself. Specialists in the field of sociology of knowledge will have to reflect upon why it is that these perennial questions of social theory are widely addressed today in terms of such "soft" conceptual tools referring to informal and sub-institutional social phenomena. But there cannot be much doubt that cognitive frames and moral dispositions that prevail at the grass roots level of social life are perceived by many social theorists to be a kind of bottleneck variable upon which the viability of institutions is thought to be contingent.

What I take to be the underlying intuition that conditions the current rise in the interest in trust and related phenomena can be explicated as a skeptical three-step argument.

First, the social order of modern society is reproduced through a mix of three major media of coordination. *Money* serves to coordinate the action of market participants. Democratically constituted political *authority* backed by legitimate force constrains and enables the action of citizens through legal regulation and the enforcement of the law through the court system and executive state agencies. And *knowledge* derived from systematic observation, monitoring and research into social as well as non-social realities, as well as the storage and dissemination of this knowledge through the networks of bureaucratic and professional organizations, the mass media and educational institutions, generates a society-wide attention and awareness and cognitive skills concerning what the current and foreseeable future problems of actors are, what needs to be done, and how best to do it.

Second, the synthetic ideal resulting from these three media of coordination, call it the ideal of an *intelligently regulated market economy* is still an incomplete vision of social order, as it misses, or at any rate does not assign a proper role to, informal modes of social coordination through commitments that result from life-world-based images and beliefs that members of modern societies hold about other members of such societies, and the action that follows from such beliefs. *Trust* is a prime example of the cultural and moral resources that provide for such informal modes of social coordination. The intuition that I wish to refer to is the notion of insufficiencies of social coordination that remain even after money-driven market mechanisms, democratically legitimated law and law enforcement, and theoretically validated, systematized and formalized knowledge are combined and deployed. This is so because successful coordination depends upon cooperation, and the latter upon the presence of perceptions, dispositions, and expectations that induce agents to cooperate.

Third, these cognitive and normative dispositions share one negative quality: they defy the logic of any of the three media in that they defy strategic manipulation or provision. They can neither be bought nor ordered nor taught within the framework of formal curricula. That is to say, they are either present or absent in a given social context, but cannot easily be brought into being through strategic action. If knowledge is perceived to be lacking, we start doing research. But what do we do when trust, benevolence, or dispositions towards cooperation are perceived to be lacking? Hence the argument continues that if only the trust resources of social coordination could be better preserved and activated, both the quality of social order and the efficiency of the use of the media of power, money, and knowledge could be greatly enhanced.

To illustrate, peaceful international relations are believed to depend on the success of "trust-building measures." But are such "measures" themselves to be trusted? If not, i.e. if they are perceived as deceptive signals serving strategic interests, the result will not be trust, but cynicism. Both productivity in production and service organizations and the perceived legitimacy of governments might be enhanced by greater amounts of trust being provided. The rapid and successful transition to post-authoritarian modes of governance and the consolidation of liberal democratic regimes is seen to be greatly hindered by the absence of trust. The same applies to industrial and labor relations. In all these cases, the above three step argument applies: We would be better off if actors were to trust each other, but there is no obvious way to actually achieve this supposedly superior state of affairs. Even worse, ill-advised measures to "build" trust may well raise suspicions and backfire as a consequence.

Social trust, or the presumption of generally benign or at least non-hostile intentions on the part of partners in interaction, can be studied in several dimensions. Combining the mass/elite and horizontal/vertical dichotomies, we get four realms in which trust relations can unfold. First, trust of citizens in their fellow citizens or in sub-categories of the universe of "everyone else." Second, the trust of mass constituencies in political or other sectoral elites (such as those representing the churches, the media, the police, the court system, the military, or the medical profession). Third, the horizontal trust extending among political elites as well as other sectoral elites, such as business, labor, religious, academic, military etc. elites. And fourth, the top-down vertical dimension of trust where elites form beliefs about the behavioral dispositions of sectoral constituencies or entire mass publics. While the second variety of trust relations is most frequently studied, I'll concentrate here on horizontal trust among non-elites. Thus the question is: How can we trust our fellow citizens? Which are the favorable background conditions that induce such horizontal trust? And why is trust at all desirable, beneficial and, arguably, indispensable as a factor of social integration in modern democratic market societies?

"Trust", in a way, is the opposite of "confidence", though the two are often used interchangeably. Confidence relates to trust as facts relate to acts. Trusting someone who turns out not to have been trustworthy is my mistake; I have been imprudently willing to trust, as in the case when someone fails, out of sheer negligence, to return my car that he has borrowed at the time that was agreed upon between us. As a result, I will *regret my* imprudent assessment of the trustworthiness of the person in question and discontinue my trust relationship with him. In contrast, when my confidence in a favorable outcome is being disappointed, it must be attributed to *bad luck*, chance, or Providence, not myself.[1] In the case of disappointed confidence, the person who has used my car has been prevented from returning it in time, in spite of his sincere (and demonstrable) intentions, by the fact that he was delayed by an accident that blocked the road and thus removed the redemption of his promise from his feasible set. In that case, my psychological reaction is not regret, but (unpleasant) surprise, which provides no reason to diminish my trust in the person in question (unless, that is, I have reasons to suspect that the trustee tries to mis-represent his negligence, or failure of intentions, as

---

[1] For a somewhat different conceptual demarcation of the two phenomena – trusting the intention vs. confidence in capabilities of an actor – cf. La Porte and Metlay 1996: 342. But in essence the two demarcations converge.

causally determined by circumstances beyond his control). The analytical distinction between trust and confidence is essential because it allows us to dispose of the muddled though frequently advanced idea of "trust in institutions." Institutions are factual arrangements that provide incentives and options to actors who are involved in or live under certain institutions. As such, they are factual constraints of action, the durability and validity of which we can view with confidence. Trust, in contrast, can only be extended to actors and the ways in which they perform and enact their roles within institutions.

One of the intellectual attractions of thinking about the phenomenon of social trust is the apparent potential of this phenomenon to bridge the micro-macro-gap in social theory. Trust is the cognitive premise with which individual or collective/corporate actors enter into interaction with other actors. This cognitive premise relates to the behavioral preferences and inclinations of others in terms of their preparedness to contribute, to cooperate, and to refrain from selfish, opportunistic and hostile courses of action. These micro phenomena that result from the ongoing assessment of the likely behavior of "everyone else" are an important determinant of the macro policy options and capacities for problem solving that are available to political elites. For instance, if people think that "everyone else" is likely to succumb to moral hazards, policies that are seen to pose such hazards are unlikely to be supported and adopted in a democracy. If they are still adopted, they are likely to be subverted, as the perceived inclination of everyone else to exploit the moral hazard option provides "me" with a perfect excuse to do so myself. Thus the images and cognitive frames by which people anticipate likely reactions of other people at the micro level will constrain policies, as well as investment strategies, at the macro level. Seen from this angle, the superstructure of the political economy and the performance of its governing institutions seem to be based upon the soft underpinnings of images, perceptions, and anticipations that people form of each other.

Let me illustrate this micro-macro link by referring to a policy problem in which trust is a key strategic determinant of successful problem solving. The problem is traffic congestion with its urban and environmental externalities and inefficiencies. Gambetta (1988: 216–217) uses the following example:

"The ubiquitous problem of traffic jams in cities is often taken as a sign of the predominance of poisonous preferences for travelling by car over travelling by other means . . . [But] there are strong grounds for believing that the motives for cooperation – that is, using bicycles and public transport – are not absent. What is lacking is the belief that everybody else is going to cooperate."

At the same time, surveys he quotes indicate that a large majority of the population favors the closure of the city center to private and non-residential traffic.[2] As a result, the (in this case actually wrong) perception that people have of the non-cooperative and unreasonable behavioral inclinations of other people obstructs the chances of the policy ever being implemented. Moreover, it obstructs the chances of the people ever learning that they were wrong about their distrusting perceptions concerning the cooperative dispositions of others.

The arguments to be presented in this essay are admittedly of a tentative, experimental, and arguably even circular nature. If horizontal trust at both the elite and non-elite levels is essential for political governance and economic performance, what determines the supply of trust as a cognitive (as well as moral) resource that inspires cooperation? My tentative answer is: the qualities of the institutional and constitutional order under which "all of us" live and which engenders not just commitments pertaining to "me", but also the anticipation that others will equally be bound by these commitments. But before I enter into a discussion of that argument, let us consider the functions and favorable background conditions of the trust phenomenon more generally.

Conceptualizing trust

Trust can partly be observed and measured in negative behavioral terms. Trusting persons do *not* engage in certain types of activity. "Trust is measurable by low personal investments in information, monitoring, and sanctioning where there are, *ceteris paribus*, risks of failure to perform by the trusted with consequent high costs to the truster" (Levi 1996: 7).

---

[2] The case may be used to further illustrate the characteristic – as well as typically prohibitive – costs of actually implementing a policy so widely preferred. These involve the administrative costs of registering the cars admitted to "residential" traffic (but what about visitors' traffic?), the costs of policing the regulation, the public as well as private costs of regulating the traffic for delivery services, and the costs for providing additional public transport. Note that once the budget constraints for all these expenditures are reached, neither traffic congestion has disappeared (for that the territory to which the regulation can be applied is much too small) nor has, for the same reason, the level of air pollution been reduced. Both of these observations seem to invite the question what the policy is good for in the first place in terms of cost-effectiveness. All these costs could be saved if the trust in the civic behavior and willingness to cooperate of "everybody else" were present – although it must also be observed that this trusting belief and the behavior supporting it can well turn out to be self-limiting: The more people reciprocate my example of riding to work on a bike, the less congested the streets will be, and the more tempting it becomes for the remaining motorists to *not* reciprocate the exemplary behavior of "us" but rather to continue to use their cars. This example and its built-in dynamics suggests the need for mixing trust-based with coercion-based policy ingredients.

But, one should add, trust can also be measured in positive terms, i.e. as the preparedness to enter into relations where monitoring etc. is not feasible or prohibitively costly, or the frequency with which such relations are entered and the duration for which they are sustained by a person. For instance, someone loans some other person her car because she trusts the other person will drive carefully and return it at the agreed place and time. Conversely, lack of trust would be measured as the observed reluctance of people to enter into such relations and/or the presence of intense monitoring activities when such relations are at all entered into. Correspondingly, distrust is the perceived and behaviorally manifested assessment of great risks that result from interaction with others. Both trust and distrust can be measured in terms of its social scope (i.e., how many people are seen by an actor to be worthy of trust/distrust?) and its substantive domain of action (i.e., the kind and size of the risk an actor is prepared to enter into). For instance, I trust A and B, but not C. And I trust A with respect to a full range of activities, intentions, and judgments, while I trust B just with respect to, say, musical taste or financial advice. Trusting "too many" people in "too many" respects increases the risk of mis-allocation of trust.

Trust is the *belief* concerning the action that is to be expected from others. The belief refers to probabilities that (certain categories of) others will do certain things or refrain from doing certain things, which in either case affects the well-being of the holder of the belief, as well as possibly the well-being of others or a relevant collectivity. Trust is the belief that others, through their action or inaction, will contribute to my/ our *well-being* and refrain from inflicting damage upon me/us. The belief manifests itself in types of *actions* that signal, to direct partners of interaction as well as observing by-standers, the nature of the belief and the extent of trust involved by it. As it is in the nature of beliefs, they can be wrong. As trust is a belief concerning the impact of other actors upon my/our well-being, a mistaken belief involves not just the risk of being wrong, but the more tangible risk of suffering a damage.

Normally, the truster is aware of that risk. Therefore trust (as opposed to the deficient cases of "naive" or even "blind" trust) is a reflectively fallible *ex ante* guess based upon an assessment of others. It follows the logic: "I know it can happen, yet I believe it *won't* happen," with "it" being some undesired event caused by the trusted. This risk indicates the fact that the truster is *unable to make sure* or *know for certain* that the trusted person(s) will actually act in the way the truster expects them to act. The means by which he might be able to make this sure – coercive *power*, economic resources to be employed as *incentives*, and validated *knowledge* derived from direct observation or tested causal theories – are not at the disposal of the truster.[3]

The key problem here is that of coping with opaqueness, ignorance and social contingency. "We cannot know in advance which actions others will choose" (Sztompka 1996: 39). Trust is essentially risky because my present action is premised upon the expectation of a future favorable response that "I" can neither enforce nor "buy" nor predict with any certainty and in the absence of which I suffer a loss or damage. Hence the need to ascertain, on the basis of some second-best indicators, trustworthiness before embarking upon the risky relation of trust, be it in business, marriage, or the client relation with a professional. This operation involves costs of information, search, and monitoring.[4] For, given the risk involved, it would appear quite irrational to rely on the existing stock of trust relations and opt for the local optimum (as it happens with people who marry their primary school classmates or second degree cousins, or who rely on the family doctor even in cases where a distant specialist is called for; or in the case of Banfield's "amoral familism"). Taken to the absurd extreme, one might derive the maxim not to trust anybody before we can be nearly certain about him, at which point, however, much trust is no longer needed! In order to trust someone, you need to monitor his behavior up to a point at which you have reason to conclude that further monitoring is no longer called for, with the rule of thumb being $p > 0.5$.

There is, however, no calculus available to tell me how much investment in information gathering and monitoring yields how much information, and how much information (e.g. on the person's record of promise-keeping, bills-paying, and truth-telling) is needed before the tipping point is reached and it is seen to be safe to begin to trust. Once trust is extended to some actor, it becomes a powerful device for saving information and the cost of information. This advantage may condition an inclination for "wishful trusting," i.e. trusting too early and too easily as the costs of actual monitoring are perceived to be very high (cf. Luhmann 1973). On the other hand, and if these costs can be shifted to the agent who is competing for trust and needs to "earn" it, the tipping point from monitoring to trusting may come very late.

---

[3] This suggests that trust is a second-best solution as it plays a role only in situations where there is a manifest shortage of coercive power, purchasing power, or theoretical knowledge. But as such shortages are ubiquitous, the tendency is also ubiquitous to prudently widen the scope of cooperation by extending it by a margin beyond what can be ascertained through the use of these three "safe" media.

[4] Unless, that is, the agent is gifted with an unusual dose of the "capacity to make sound character assessments" (Levi 1996: 5).

The point at which the decision[5] is made to trust someone may be relatively early (i.e. on the basis of a short and rough assessment of trustworthiness) if the situation is such that in the case of non-cooperation "I" do not gain, but do not lose either. Trust may even be unwisely (opportunistically) overextended if the expected gains are very substantial. A more thorough assessment is called for and will probably be made if the risk of trusting involves not just no profit, but positive loss. Again, reluctance to trust will be greater if damage and loss are of a diffuse and lasting nature, and correspondingly smaller if the loss is limited in time and highly focalized.

The essential link between trusting and risk-taking raises the question why people should at all be willing to take the risk that is involved in trusting. The answer is that excessive risk avoidance and distrust cuts actors off from desired options. Trusting "too few" people in "too" narrowly defined respects is irrational because it leads the agent to opt for non-cooperation out of distrust where benefits could actually derived from a more generous belief in the trustworthiness of relevant others. But, on the other hand, excessive or "blind" trust leaves the truster vulnerable. Extending trust, in other words, is an optimization problem, although it can hardly be resolved *in terms* of an optimization problem (i.e. in analogy to weighing risk against return in an investment decision). For, for one thing, we do not have a metric to evaluate the total benefits of options obtained/foregone versus the total costs of risks avoided/accepted. Second, and more seriously, trust is a belief built upon perceptions or images of the characteristics of others. It would therefore amount to a psychologically unlikely and at any rate unstable act of self-manipulation to trust people not for what they are, but for the net benefits I expect to derive from doing so.

Hence the question emerges: If it cannot be an investment calculus, what is it that leads people to extend and allocate, or withhold and withdraw, trust, what are the criteria they employ in doing so?

---

[5] It is not clear to what extent beginning to trust is actually a "decision," rather than an unintended by-product of an ongoing interaction (Gambetta 1988: 230). But we can certainly decide *against* trusting, concluding that past signals of trustworthiness are not or no longer "good enough" to rely on. The asymmetrical relation is that there can well be compelling evidence for distrust, but not so for trust. Pursuing this idea, one might well end up with a notion of trust being the residual of non-disappointment. This idea would also elucidate the role of hypothetical distrust, or the probing attitude by which we test trustworthiness: trust is built by the repeated failure to find indications of reasons for distrust in someone's behavior. Cf. La Porte and Metlay (1996), who quote and discuss Slovic (1993) to the effect that "When it comes to winning trust, the playing field is not level. It is tilted toward distrust." But then again, "distrust may become the source of its own evidence" (Gambetta 1988: 234), at least if its intensity borders on cynicism.

Trusting and being trusted

The easiest case is building trust through continued interaction with concrete persons whom we typically know for a considerable period of time. Let us call this case "experiential" trust, or trust based upon long term experience. Here, the dynamics of trust-building can be represented on the time axis. Out of *past experience* develops a *present* orientation concerning the anticipation of *future behavior*.

But past experience is not the only basis from which actors derive their present (trusting) orientation concerning the future behavior of some other person. Even more important for this consolidation of the trust relationship is the reflexive awareness of the trustee of a history of interaction throughout which he has given *reasons* to trust him and in which the truster has accepted the risk of trusting. This poses the moral (as opposed to experiential) question concerning the continuity of the trust relationship. The trustee may continue to redeem the assumptions and expectations that the truster has come to attach to him not out of an unthinking habit or because it is "in his nature," but out of a sense of moral *obligation* to honor trust. Considering the length of time that the truster has already granted trust to the trustee, or so the latter may be envisaged to reason, it would be utterly *unfair* to betray the assumptions and beliefs of the truster. In contrast to experiential trust, we may speak of trust through obligation that applies to the trustee and that can be invoked by the truster. Trust obliges the trusted – if only because moral stigma is attached to acts of betraying or exploiting the trust of others. It is thus not just the truster's time series of accumulated past experience which generates the expectation of future behavior, but, perhaps in addition, the reliance, on the part of A, upon some *moral force* that binds B as a result of past interaction. Having trusted thus creates the conditions of trusting with good reasons and at a declining risk. "The concession of trust can generate the very behavior which might logically seem to be its precondition" (Gambetta 1988: 234). The strength of the moral obligation emerging from being trusted can make trust a self-fulfilling expectation.

But a sense of moral obligation that emerges on the part of the trustee is not the only way in which a trust relation becomes self-stabilizing. An additional mechanism is based upon rational consideration of interest of the trustee which can virtually "trap" the trustee into a behavioral pattern of complying with the expectations of the truster. For apart from moral reasons, the trustee has also strong incentives, both positive and negative, to keep the trust relationship going. As to the negative incentives, breaking trust through manifestly invalidating the beliefs of the truster involves a lasting loss of credibility. Depending on the degree of visibility[6] of the act of betrayal in question, this precludes not only the possibility of restoring the relationship with the original truster, but beyond that of building a trust relationship with any alternative agent. As to the positive incentives, being trusted is an important kind of "social capital" that can be "spent" in a variety of ways. It can also be wasted.[7] Being trusted is an important resource to the agent on the receiving side of the trust relationship. This applies way beyond the standard case of being trusted (i.e. being considered creditable) in commercial contexts. Within organizations, being trusted can be used to buffer deviation from routine – be it in the sense of experimentation and innovation, be it in the sense of partial failure and malperformance that will be, if only up to a point, more easily ignored or forgiven and less severely sanctioned if the person who commits it is being trusted.[8] In either sense, being trusted enhances the autonomy and the size of the feasible set of the agent.

There are thus two paths by which trust, once conceded, becomes self-enforcing: considerations of obligation and self-interest. But note that this twofold base of trust can also give rise to games of a less desirable outcome. That is the case when moral obligations are employed for strategic purposes. Thus a trustee may fail to develop a sense of the moral obligation that would "normally" result from being trusted while pretending to be bound by such obligation. As a result, he will be able to put himself into a position of taking unfair advantage of the truster and exploiting the trust relationship. Thus a debtor may reason: From t_1 to t_n I act in ways conducive to generating trust on the part of the creditor (the truster) in order to extract more credit which allows me to defect profitably at t_{n+1}, catching the creditor by surprise and leaving him defenseless and vulnerable. A reverse strategic use of the trust relationship is this: I act as if I believe that your (the trustee's) past behavior had given me reasons to trust you, hoping to induce you to actually honor that inauthentically invoked trust relationship. For example, a poor man may invoke the rich man's (perhaps quite fictive) reputation for generosity

---

[6] Such visibility can be manipulated, for instance, through the procedural rules of bankruptcy laws.

[7] Note the temporal asymmetry: trust-building is a very time-consuming activity, while the irreparable destruction of trust can occur in an instant. (Slovic 1993: 677)

[8] Welfare cuts and anti-inflationary incomes policies are, if only up to a point, more easily accomplished by leftist than by market-liberal parties, as these parties are trusted by their voters that they would not go "too far" and limit themselves to what is "absolutely necessary." This consideration suggests a "functionalist" explanation of why post-socialist political parties do so surprisingly well in Central East European transition societies. They can commit cruelties without being as severely punished, or without causing as much protest and unrest, as their political competitors would if they did exactly the same.

with which the latter, as an intended consequence, feels morally compelled to remain consistent.

The necessity of this reflexive loop – I am obliged by my past trust-generating behavior – is easily illustrated by the nonsensical flavor of the sentence: "I trust my bicycle." True, it has never shown any signs of malfunctioning. But my "trust" is a mere (fallible) extrapolation of past experience, or reliance upon a *regularity*, and it has nothing to do with what is the distinctive feature of trust as a sociological category: not only the experience of consistency of some observed behavior on the part of the *trusting* person, but the trusted person's *awareness of being trusted* and his/her resulting perception of the *obligation to honor trust*, which may also be mandated by an interest in the continuation of trust. Instead of an empirical regularity, we deal with a normative *rule* that obliges (rather than causes, as in empirical regularities) an agent to comply. Rules are not self-executing, as through a built-in causality. In order for rules to be kept and complied with, the actor must recognize and follow the rule as binding, rather than violating it for opportunistic reasons. Trust relationships and their robustness are as much a matter of the receiving side, the trusted, as of the providing side, the truster. Trust is a phenomenon of social reciprocity. Without a social norm (sometimes strengthened by rational interest, as in ongoing commercial transactions) being observed prescribing that trust must be honored, not betrayed by whoever is *being* trusted, trust relations would be overly risky to the truster and bound to evaporate.

This steady state of trusting and being trusted has a number of advantageous *functions* for both the truster and the trustee for which rational actors may try to achieve it, although most of these functions appear to have the status of welcome by-products. That is to say, a trust-building activity on the part of a truster that is perceived by the trusted as being motivated by instrumental considerations is unlikely to be responded to by a sense of obligation, which in turn, when and if understood by the trust-builder, will lead him to discontinue his efforts. These functions, apart from the intrinsic enjoyment of trust relations and the intimacy and passions it may give rise to, favor both the supply and the demand side of the "trust market." Suppliers of trust, the *trusters*, benefit from ("justified") trust. Trust substitutes for resources of social control and helps to economize on transaction costs. I do not need to monitor those whom I can trust, nor do I have to buy what I trust they will offer me voluntarily (such as the occasional use of a car), nor do I have to force them to do what I expect them to do or to call in third parties (such as courts) to enforce my claims. Trust opens for the truster a margin of options and activities beyond what can be directly enforced, purchased, or known for sure. Trusting begins where the reach of these media of control ends, or where we decide to stop calculating, enforcing, and monitoring – if only on the basis of an assessment based upon prior monitoring and the knowledge derived from it.

In particular, trust works as a money-saving device.[9] If an agent is trusted, and if he follows the norm of reciprocity prescribing that trust must be honored, compliance is accomplished that, in the absence of trust, would have to be either authoritatively coerced or "bought" – be it at market prices or through bribes (Elster 1989: 266). Trust is thus a highly attractive device to overcome principal-agent problems.

On the other hand, actors have also rational reasons to seek trust. It is important for them to *be trusted*. To be trusted equals to be worthy of credit. This credit can be used to cover up minor mistakes, to relieve anxiety, and to open up "a wide margin for non-conformity, innovation, originality" covered by the credit of trust (Sztompka 1996: 44, Luhmann 1973). Innovation and experimentation is encouraged by the freedom granted by trust, and such behavior may lead to the discovery of collectively beneficial opportunities that would be missed in the absence of trust. The absence of trust is rather likely to condition a type of behavior on the part of the non-trusted that is rigidly and ritualistically following orders and seeks to hide behind established rules and routines.

In spite of all these advantageous functions of the trust relationship, it implies the disadvantage of rendering the truster vulnerable. The supplier of trust can be disappointed, and the actor demanding (and having received) trust can be deprived of it, typically with the implication of never being able to regain it at any time soon. In order to minimize this risk without foregoing the beneficial effects of trust (thereby maximizing the net utility of the trust relation) actors will not only be highly selective in to whom they concede trust, but also careful in balancing trust against other resources on which they can rely should the trust relationship break down, so as to minimize the resulting overall loss. The more readily the trusted person can switch to such alternative resources – power, money, and information – the less vulnerable he is to a breakdown of trust. As a consequence, the rich, the powerful, and the well-informed can afford to trust, as they can comfortably survive the contingency of the trust being disappointed, whereas the less powerful on either the supply or demand side of trust may suffer badly from the breakdown of the trust relation.

---

[9] An illustration on how trust can be money saving can again be taken from public transport. If I trust my fellow citizens, I shall not hesitate to use public transport an night. If I do not trust them, I either have to pay the extra expenses for using a taxi or private car or I have to pay the costs of *foregone* opportunities, i.e. the costs of staying home.

This "portfolio management" perspective of the trust relationship, with trust being the most speculative of all investments, suggests that trust and the control over other social resources are also partly complementary, not just substitutes for each other. The more affluent a person is, the more easily he can trust and benefit from the trust of others, and vice versa.[10] Prosperity, transparency and control breed trust and make the risks implied affordable, while highly precarious social relations leave little space for trust. Hence Lenin's dictum: "Trust is good, control is better!," which betrays a clear understanding of the contingencies of revolutionary situation in which a single traitor can demolish the entire collective effort. In other words: The rich (or the securely in power, or the knowledgeable) "trust more," as for them the risk that is involved in all trusting is more easily bearable.

Theoretically, if I have unlimited capacity for control and enforcement, I can escape the inherent risk of a trust relationship, as I need no trust at all – except, as it were, trust in myself, my resources, and my capacity to live without trusting. Should people be inclined not to conform to my expectations and wishes, I can break their will and force them to comply. As they know this to be the case, they will not even manifest such adverse inclinations. But having to rely exclusively on coercive control rather than trust tends to become a vast misallocation of resources, and not only an inefficient (Gambetta 1988: 220–221), but ultimately also an ineffective one. No command chain, no supervision, no contract is tight enough to allow the principal to render trust entirely superfluous. Even if he minimizes the margin of trust, he is likely to pay dearly in terms of transaction costs.[11] Again, trust must be seen as a power-saving device. For the presence of trust relieves actors from anxiety, suspicion, vigilance, and watchfulness (Sztompka 1996: 43) and the costly measures to monitor every detail of the behavior of others.

A vicious cycle becomes visible here: Those lacking resources (power, wealth, information) cannot afford to trust, as misplaced trust is feared to have disastrous consequences from which actors are incapable of protecting themselves through other means. So they have to spend the severely limited resources they actually have in highly trust-saving and inefficient ways – with the consequence of perpetuating their poverty. The apparent paradox is that those who are most in need of trust-based

---

[10] A case in point is the spectacular bankruptcy of the German construction industry tycoon Schneider, whose fraudulent dealings were financed, in an incredibly negligent (i.e. irresponsibly "blindly" trusting) way, by the largest German bank, Deutsche Bank AG. After the first of the banks' ensuing losses was disclosed, worth DM 50 million, the bank's chairman tried to calm the public by describing this loss as "peanuts."

[11] This is just to paraphrase the dictum often attributed to Napoleon: "The only things you cannot do with bayonets is sit on them."

relations (because they have little else to rely upon) cannot afford the risk involved, while those who need it least enjoy it most. The seemingly perverse case of the militarism and vast military expenditures of Third World countries may be elucidated by this consideration.

Problems of building trust beyond familiarity

The main problem with trust emerging from the experience of personal interaction is the narrowness of its scope. I trust my friends, and perhaps also the friends of my friends. I may also trust long term employees or business partners, or the collective of employees of "my" company with its internal "corporate identity" (Fukuyama 1995). But in a society in which mobility and the need for cooperation with and reliance upon strangers is a prominent feature, this is not of much help. Chances are that exclusive reliance upon the old-fashioned mechanism of generating trust on the basis of personal familiarity is hopelessly insufficient, as it makes us forego, in the absence of alternative trust-generating mechanisms, many opportunities for mutually beneficial cooperation.

So far, we have discussed cases and models of trust relationships among people who are known to each other. The problem, however, is trust among strangers. Trust is known to thrive best under conditions of non-anonymity. "The conditions that make for the maintenance of trust are best met in relatively limited ranges of social activities and interaction, such as the family or kinship groups in which social interaction is regulated according to primordial and particularistic criteria." Hence the reference problem of all sociological analysis of the trust phenomenon in modern society is that of the "effective extension of the range of . . . trust beyond the narrow minimal scope of primordial units" (Eisenstadt 1995: 312–313, 366–367).

People who do not belong to primordial units need to "build" trust if they wish to enjoy the advantages to be reaped on either side of the trust relationship. Prior to the steady state of reciprocated trust, there is a period in which trust is being built by probing the evidence of trustworthiness. Trust is a thoroughly cognitive phenomenon. It depends upon knowledge and belief. Strangers do not yet have any reasons to trust nor to be trusted; they are mutually ignorant and hence encounter each other in the attitude of caution and distrust as their shared behavioral null-hypothesis. The trust that evolves is a residual – the residual that remains after an extended period of disconfirmation of reasons for distrust. "In the case of a person whose judgment is really deserving of confidence, how has it become so? Because he has kept his mind open to criticism on his opinions and conduct. Because it has been his practice to listen to all that could be said against him" (Mill 1982: 26). A trustworthy person is someone who exposes himself (and thereby enhances his autonomy) to continuous and scrupulous examination by others.

Universalized trust, i.e. trust extended to large and otherwise unspecified categories of people who are personally unknown to me, is what remains after the methodical invalidation of reasons for distrust. This, as we shall see, is the foundation of political trust in a democracy. It is the fact that multiple opportunities for testing the validity of distrust (e.g. periodic contested elections, freedom of expression, freedom of the press) are institutionalized and being used from which the trust derives that political elites enjoy (cf. Warren 1996: 259). While the intuition of conservatives is that democracy, at any rate "too much" democracy, corrodes and undermines the authority of governments, liberals rely on the productivity of institutionalized distrust. State agents, in particular members of government, can and must be trusted because they have been continuously exposed to *and* effectively withstood institutionalized distrust, such as elections, the scrutiny of the opposition within legislative bodies, and the media. In contrast to both, radicals believe that the testing procedures that supposedly generate trust out of the invalidation of distrust are themselves invalid and insufficient. According to them, it is the institutionalized system of processing distrust, as well as the agents operating these systems (e.g. the media), that cannot be trusted.

Trust in persons results from *past experience* with concrete persons. Someone has "never disappointed me," always acted competently and consistently. Here the question is: How much experience with a person over what stretch of time is sufficient for forming trust? One problem is that in order to form experientially based trust, the trusted person's behavior must be sufficiently overt and transparent, and I must be in a position to monitor it for a extended period of time. Moreover, as I argued before, the trusted person must be able to become aware that he has been trusted, and develop a sense of obligation towards the truster.

All of these are not very likely conditions to be fulfilled within the framework of a "modern" social structure and its opaqueness of most behavior of most other people for most of the time. Neither does the truster have the opportunity to know enough about others to extend trust to them nor are those actually trusted necessarily aware of who trusted them and to whom they hence owe an obligation to redeem the trust extended to them. Perhaps one could speak of a structural scarcity of opportunities to build trust, or to accumulate sufficient reasons for trust, or to reciprocate the privilege of having been trusted by a sense of obligation, in a society that is mobile, complex, differentiated, and, as a consequence, largely opaque.

Note that this opaqueness of "everyone else" (beyond the small non-anonymous subset) is of a dual nature. *Before* "they" act, "I" have no sufficient evidence to form beliefs about how they are going to act and whether there is sufficient reason to trust. But even *after* they have acted, what comes to "my" awareness is at best an aggregate effect, not the specific behavior of specific individuals that have caused it – and to whom "I" could therefore accumulate reasons to trust.

This is a particularly serious problem within the democratic regime form. In an authoritarian regime, I can watch, and perhaps even talk to, the personal holder(s) of power, and form a belief, however distorted, about the rulers' trustworthiness. Not so in a democracy: As the outcome of elections is determined by the popular sovereign, i.e. the majority of (virtually) "everyone else," and as I have no way of knowing what this quintessentially anonymous collective agent is going to do (or who has actually done what in the last elections, given the secret ballot), very high degrees of insurmountable distrust and suspicion would appear to be the normal condition within a democracy. It is in the nature of all modern political communities that the universe of fellow-citizens cannot be admitted nor excluded according to some measure of trustworthiness. The universe is "given." For one thing that "the people" cannot decide upon in a democracy is who actually belongs to the people – which is exactly the point of a democracy because this institutionalized incompetence of the citizenry protects everyone and makes the right to have rights and to participate in the political community positively inalienable. As we cannot choose our fellow citizens (nor attach some transcendent meaning to the multitude of our fellow citizens, such as all of them belonging to some "chosen people"), neither can we know or have reasons to trust the uses to which they are going to put their civic and political rights. Nor, finally, can we be certain about the aggregate outcomes of the myriad of perhaps highly idiosyncratic preferences that our fellow citizens bring to bear upon collective concerns.

At any rate, both sides of the trust relationship encounter massive problems of information gathering and the formation of reasonably reliable beliefs (cf. Hardin 1993). It is not clear how civic trust emerges among the members of mass publics within a democracy, given the condition of anonymity, diversity, and pluralism. If "emphatic understanding, acquired through love, affection, friendship, neighborliness, and the like" (Dahl 1992: 53) is held to be the essence of civic virtue, how can it conceivably come about in a mass democracy? As Dahl rightly points out, "the large scale of modern and postmodern societies poses both cognitive and affective obstacles to acquiring predispositions toward civic virtue" (Dahl 1992: 53).

Moreover, it is exactly because so much power resides with the people in a democracy that it is not obvious why individuals should extend any trust to "everyone else"; we would rather expect an attitude of methodical distrust and suspicion. To illustrate this point, let us imagine a rational citizen confronted to a situation of constitutional choice and pondering the option of overcoming an authoritarian regime. On the one hand, s/he might think, if the government's range of discretion can be limited by instituting the rule-of-law principle, and if it also can be held responsible to the electorate through universal suffrage, the introduction of both these key components of liberal democracy will effectively control the inclinations of governing powers to impose unfair burdens and limitations of freedom upon citizens, as rulers will to an extent be deprived of their powers of arbitrary and self-serving rule. On the other hand, or so the reasoning might continue, opting for a liberal democracy as the new regime form may also involve risks. True, "I" am no longer the object of autocratic rule, but instead "I" become the object of the "rule of the many" (polyarchy) and of some potential "tyranny of the majority." For opting for democracy clearly means opting for the empowerment of the vast majority of "everyone else." Hence, in case "I" opt for the liberal democratic regime form, the question emerges: Why is it that I have more to fear from the discretionary powers of autocratic (though at least conceivably benevolent) rulers than from the (potentially highly detrimental to me and "my" values) legislative will of democratically constituted representative bodies or popularly elected governments?

An answer to this question can come in one of three versions. The first answer focuses upon *elites*. According to this perspective, democracy is preferable to (or less harmful than) one of the alternative authoritarian regime forms because the democratically elected/appointed representative leaders of parties, territorial sub-units, legislatures, and governments are seen to act sufficiently responsibly so that, whatever the electoral outcomes, "my" core interests will be taken care of and protected by benevolent elites operating within the framework of constitutional legal guarantees. This trust in the elites' wisdom and fairness compensates, as it were, for my lack of trust in my fellow citizens and their political preferences. Yet this "vertical" trust rests on a rather heroic assumption. For, first, "I" do not typically have intimate and reliable knowledge (as opposed to knowledge strategically disseminated through the media and PR campaigns) about the character of elite personnel and its immunity from opportunistic temptations to sacrifice "my" interests. Second, because the quality, composition and conduct of leaders is, in a democracy, contingent upon electoral outcomes. All my trusting assumption about political elites can be perfectly true "for now," while the next election day may bring to power a selection of leaders that offer much less reason for trust.

A conceivable second way out of the problem of horizontal distrust in everyone else is to substitute confidence in the robustness and durability of institutions, specifically in the *institutional setup* of a liberal democracy, or the democratic regime form as such. Once it is put into operation, its internal structures and dynamics (bill of rights, division of powers) operate to the effect that even a highly adverse majority cannot inflict very serious damage upon me, because that would mean to interfere with my constitutionally entrenched rights, which the division and balance of powers, as it is also prescribed by the constitution, would serve to prevent anyway. This answer, as suggested by the eternity clause of the German constitution (Art. 79) is not quite compelling, as we know (among other things, from German history of the early thirties) that even perfectly democratic regime forms can be demolished as a result of pro-authoritarian mass-mobilization. Democracies have the potential for committing suicide by the "will of the people" becoming the source of the abolition of democracy itself. Such "suicidal" will of the people may emerge under a variety of circumstances: perceived lack of government effectiveness in coping with economic or military crises, the widely perceived disruptiveness and stalemate resulting from the competitive political process, or the perceived elite manipulation of the political preferences of "everyone else."

The third possible solution would overcome the problem of the absence of trust relations with my fellow citizens who are at the same time strangers by attaching some abstract and indirect bonds of trust to the *citizenry* as a whole. This encompassing extension of trust can occur by counterfactually claiming some shared commitment of (virtually) all members of the political community to the "identity" of a nation – its history, territory and culture, its laws, institutions and its constitution. Nationality and national identity would, in this case, perform a trust-conferring function bridging political divisions, anonymity, cultural diversity, and the strangeness of the vast majority of my fellow-nationals. The fates of this thin and highly generalized belief, based upon national identity, in the benevolence and hence trustworthiness of millions of fellow citizens, are uncertain in present-day Europe for at least two reasons. First, the process of European integration devalues (and is intended to devalue) the national frame of reference as the operative unit of collective self-recognition and the notion of the nation as a distinctive community of fate. Second, this imagined community of the nation and the abstract trust relations based upon it is further weakened by an ongoing process of "multicultural" and other cultural and economic fragmentations that occur (and are advocated in the name of a "politics of difference") along regional, religious, ethnic, gender, generation and other divisions.

But even within consolidated nation states, it is not easy to find reasons to trust the sovereign, i.e. the multitude of anonymous fellow citizens. Trusting them would mean to operate on the premise that these anonymous fellow citizens will by and large recognize and support the set of rules that is supposed to be binding, both in civilian and political life, to "all of us." Moreover, trusting them is equivalent to assuming that they do not tend to use these rules in the service of values and interests that are consistently inimical to my own. The basic difficulty in establishing this horizontal relationship of civic trust is that neither the *truster* has any easy way to "test," or to validate beliefs about, the trustworthiness of his fellow citizens nor *trust-seeking* citizens have any easy way to build trust by demonstrating to everyone else the rule-conforming and benign nature of their intentions and dispositions. If the problems posed by anonymity, opaqueness, and non-communication are to be overcome at all, it must be through the mediation of representative institutions, collective actors, and mass media. Note that the problem of bridging anonymity is comparatively smaller at the elite level, i.e. in the horizontal relationship between and within sectoral elites. These actors will usually have the opportunity to form and test beliefs about each other, and they have an interest in doing so as they anticipate their relations to be of a relatively lasting nature. Trust relations are also more easily built in the vertical direction between elites of associations or large manufacturers, on the one side, and their constituency or clientele, on the other. In these "vertical" cases, trustees can be observed, and they can shape observations through sending trust-inviting and trust-confirming signals.[12] In contrast, there is no equally simple and easy way to build horizontal trust, or validated opinions and expectations concerning the individually and collectively benign nature of everyone else, at the mass level. The question is how this dimension of trust, which is hypothetically so significant for the operation of a democratic political system and its governing capacity, can at all be developed.

---

[12] One technique of acquiring trust follows the potlatch-logic of conspicuously self-inflicting economic pain or sacrificing the control over power resources, such if inspections are conceded in disarmament agreements. For instance, automobile manufacturers demonstrate their scrupulous concern with product safety by expensive (and widely advertised) recall campaigns. Postcommunist governments adopt privatization schemes that are way beyond what can be deemed efficient from a purely economic point of view in order to demonstrate their determination to burn the bridges that may lead back to a command economy (Bönker and Offe 1994), thereby trying to create a favorable investment climate. Such techniques, which also include seemingly wasteful advertisement campaigns or sponsoring activities which often appear to demonstrate to the public just how well a company can cope with voluntarily self-inflicted costs, can best be thought of as the creation of *ersatz* knowledge which then serves as the basis for trust.

In modern societies, there is simply not much reason to trust those with whom we interact. Due to the mobility of people and the contingency of contractual relations, we do not know most of them for very long (so that we can trust from a record of past experience), nor do we have reasons to anticipate repeated interaction over some extended period of time (which would rationally lead us to invest in building a trust relationship by signalling and demonstrating trustworthiness).[13] This difficulty of trust-building is paid for in terms of increases in transaction costs. In the absence of trust, actors must rely on formal monitoring and enforcement. Also, low trust conditions involve opportunity costs, as potential gains from cooperation are being missed due to the prevailing (but actually untested) anticipation of non-cooperative dispositions of others.

Within a modern political community, neither civic trust that citizens extend to each other nor trust in elites can be built upon actual acquaintance, communal belonging, or symbolic codes of trustworthiness. None of the assumptions of Athenian or Renaissance city republics comes close to being fulfilled in modern societies – the assumptions of the community of active citizens being small, homogeneous, and composed of "non-anonymous individuals" (Seligman 1992: 11).

Even "vertical" trust-building, i.e. trust extended to political elites by non-elites, meets with particular obstacles in a modern democracy. For neither of the two trust-generating mechanisms discussed so far – long-term personal interaction and a sense of obligation resulting from it, shared communal background or pseudo-communal symbolism – are typically present in the relationship between mass electorates and political elites. One reason for the scarcity of trust is that opportunities for direct observation of elite actors by mass publics over extended periods of time are extremely limited, partly due to the democratic mechanism of the "coming and going" of elite personnel. The latter typically try to compensate for the structural scarcity of opportunities for trust-building by employing personality-centered dramaturgical media campaigns to earn trust, as well as to undermine the trustworthiness of political opponents. As all findings on the development of trust in political elites in Western democracies consistently demonstrate, these strategies are largely counterproductive.

---

[13] Even in repeated interaction, it is often not possible to assess competence and commitment of relevant actors. Such is the case in client interaction with professionals. Due to the vast disparity of knowledge, the client has typically no cue to assess competence – neither in an *ex ante* perspective *nor* in an *ex post* perspective, as it is beyond his competence, understanding, and scope of comparison whether or not good or bad results must be attributed to competent performance or other factors. As a consequence, I trust my dentist or tax accountant because I like the art on his office wall, or for other such wildly irrational reasons.

They generate no positive effect, as the net result of competing elites, each trying to win trust for itself and spread distrust for the opponent, may add up to zero. And these strategies may, moreover, result in a net decline of trust in elites due to the perverse effect of counter-productive intentionality: *Man merkt die Absicht und man ist verstimmt.*

It may not seem self-evident that vertical trust is in fact "a necessary condition for both civil society and democracy" (Rose 1994: 18). For as mass electorates in a democracy do have at their disposal, at least periodically, the means to sanction and control members of political elites at the ballot box, the need to develop trust in political leaders may well be questioned, following the intuition that as "we" can control and punish "them," we do not need to trust them. This proposition, however, becomes dubious if we think of the opportunities that the holders of elite positions enjoy for (a) the violation of established laws and procedures in the interest of the maintenance or increase of their *power* and (b) the use of the powers of their office for illegitimate ends of private *gain* (corruption). In spite of the efforts of the media, the opposition and the court system, these violations need not come, or only belatedly so, to the attention of the voting public. As voters thus cannot base their voting decision retrospectively on evident *outcomes* of elites' activity alone, they must also rely (prospectively) on assessments of the credibility and trustworthiness, i.e. upon ascribed *intentions* of candidates in order to form their voting decisions. And that is where "vertical" trust becomes relevant, irrespective of the various difficulties (mentioned above) that are typically encountered in elites' efforts to build trust or non-elites' efforts to ascertain trustworthiness.

What does equally seem to be a necessary condition of the stability of modern democracy is the presence of trust in the third dimension, trust *among* elites. It is safe to assume that much of political conflict resolution occurs not through arguing in public or majority voting in elections or legislative assemblies, but through bargaining behind closed doors. The latter form of conflict resolution is exceedingly trust-sensitive, for there are a number of tactics that one of the bargaining partners can turn to that will inflict serious damage on other partners. Before bargaining can start or, at any rate, continue, there must be a reasonable measure of mutual trust among participants that such tactics will *not* be resorted to by the respective other side at the bargaining table. These tactics include: breach of confidentiality through leaking bargaining positions taken by one participant to the public or to the constituency of the respective group; failure to continue bargaining from one round to the next ("politics of empty chairs"); failure to remember and honor with reciprocal concessions those concessions that the other side has made at an earlier time, which amounts to the breakdown of those inter-temporal exchange relations which are usually seen to be the unique advantage of bargaining behind closed doors; and failure to honor agreements and compromises after they have been adopted. Often none of these non-cooperative moves can be formally sanctioned in bargaining situations, which is to say that trust, often of a very personalistic kind, is what makes bargaining among representative elites at all possible.[14]

Substitutes for personal experience: categorical trust

The chain of effects that leads to the recollection of trust, the perceived obligation and interest to honor trust, and the subsequent continuation and reproduction of the trust relationship does not always need to originate with the actual long term familiarity and interaction of concrete persons. It can also originate with the symbolic representation of communities or pseudo-communities. Here, *belonging* is invoked as a non-experiential assessment rule for trustworthiness. Invoking the shared belonging to some community – be it an extended family, a religious group, a location, a college, service in a military unit, a nation, or many others – and its presumably distinctive history, identity, or spirit, may also trigger the chain effect of trusting, recollection, obligation, and reproduction of the trust relation. The logic supporting this method of allocating trust is this: As I know the tradition, culture and values of a particular group, I can generalize trust to everyone belonging to that group – particularly, but not exclusively, if the group in question happens to be a group that I myself belong to and identify with, as that increases the chance that my trusting will be reciprocated.

Attaching positive or negative trust value to entire social categories is premised upon the codes or stereotypes of trustworthiness. Group properties which appear to be particularly suitable for generating categorical trust status are those that satisfy three criteria: it should not be possible to acquire them at will, they should not be capable of being easily given up, and they should be associated with markers that are easily detected from within and from outside the group. Age is a characteristic of persons that satisfied all three of these conditions to an ideal extent. Taken together, trust-inducing group properties are those which can be *read* as

---

[14] In interviews with the leadership of various German employers' associations, I found a strong concern with generational change on the other side of the bargaining table. The concern was with whether the "new faces" would at all know and, if so, honor the code of informal rules established in past rounds of bargaining, rather than being tempted to assert their position by adopting one or more of the above non-cooperative moves. The inner life of coalition governments seems to show the same kind of vulnerabilities.

signals by the truster, but not manipulated and *sent* as signals by the trustee or trust-seeker.

Signals of categorical trustworthiness used by what I call "pseudo-communities" are the visual markers of gender, age, often ethnicity, as well as the more subtle markers of physiognomy and conformity with current esthetic ideals. But neither the markers themselves nor the meaning and trust-generating potential attached to them are entirely immune to manipulative strategies of the presentation of the self to others. Trust-*inviting* visual markers include the wearing of licensed uniforms (e.g. military, religious, professional) or chosen visual signs such as haircut, style of dress, and other such bodily signifiers of identity and belonging. They have all the advantage of being easily perceived from some distance and even in the absence of and prior to any actual communication and interaction taking place. Slightly less easily perceived are *acoustic* signals having to do with language, where not only national language, or the ability to speak other than the national language, or the use of special linguistic styles or dialects, play a role in signalling particular life styles and the implied disposition to trust and to be trusted. Finally, the oral and visual display of markers of life history, degree certificates displayed on office or shop walls being one example, serve to invite trust relations, be it trust among insiders or trust invited from the general public.[15]

The two problems associated with this mode of signalling trustworthiness and inviting and offering trust are rather obvious. First, in the case of pseudo-communities, the "post-modern" inflationary multiplication and the manipulability of at least some of these visual and linguistic codes and symbols tend to undercut their communicative function. It is actually very little that we "know" about people after seeing their age, hair style, or dress. As a consequence of this problem, we may expect an inflationary spiral to be set in motion: The increased use of trust-inviting signals is responded to by the spread of distrust in the cognitive value of these signals, which in turn is responded to by heavier doses and the accelerating innovation of such signals. Second, in the case of more authentic communities (with less easily manipulable markers of belonging, such as religious or ethno-linguistic groups), the scope of generalization of trust achieved through the use of these signals is clearly limited. Its basis is "strong loyalty to tribal, ethnic or familial groups, matched with

---

[15] The scars acquired in ritual duels by German students in the 19th and first half of the twentieth century are a particularly drastic example. Note that the trust-conferring potential of such markers vanishes if they can be acquired through purchase. For instance, military medals earned by soldiers during World War II played a significant role in the Soviet Union in conferring trust and honor to those who wore them. But after 1991, a market for these medals evolved, which undercut the valuation of these symbols.

xenophobia" (Sztompka, 1996: 45). A sum-constancy principle may be postulated here. The more trust is based upon group identity and group belonging (as a substitute for direct interaction), the more limited it is and the more likely trust is to be withheld from anybody outside of the boundaries of the group, with the result of massive discrimination and aggressive distrust directed at the outside world of those who do not clearly belong to "us." To illustrate, the intense bonds of trust that were cultivated by the youth protest culture of the sixties were purchased at the price of openly discriminatory "ageism" following the slogan: "Do not trust anybody over the age of thirty!"

As a shortcut to avoid or reduce these adverse effects of trust-building through signals and markers, *rituals* of instant trust building have become common. Purposive encounters are framed in a dramaturgy of pseudo-familiarity, including the use of first names, ample time devoted to communal eating and drinking, the dropping of names of potentially trust-conferring acquaintances, gift-giving, and the mutual sharing of views and information that reveal aspects of the persons involved which are clearly beyond the thematic focus of the interaction. Often "confidential" gossip is part of these rituals, the implication being that the speaker trusts that others won't make inappropriate use of the knowledge thus obtained. While these techniques can be very successful in lubricating the interaction within business, political and professional elites, their extension in the social and temporal dimension is obviously limited and of little political significance. It is at best a matter of building trust among sectoral elites, as are more ancient techniques, apparently well and alive in France, Britain, and the US, of the preferential recruitment of elite personnel from certain educational and military institutions.

Institutions as a substitute for trust?

A deceptively simple and easy way out of the structural scarcity of trust, in all of its dimensions, is the reliance on institutions. As we cannot trust people, we may be tempted to rely on institutions as mediators and generalizers of trust. For example, I may develop some confidence that the institutions will continue to operate according to their established rules the way I have known them to operate. Institutional rules are being relied upon, in this perspective, as self-reproductive, self-enforcing, path dependent and self-perpetuating, and nobody is expected to distort them or interfere with their expected operation. They are self-enforcing like conventions or self-correcting through a system of checks and balances. For example, once the democratic regime form is consolidated, a military coup is seen to be outside the realm of the possible. Hence no need to "trust" military leaders. Similarly, I do not need to "trust" the manufacturer of my car, as the market mechanism and the competitive pressure brought to bear by it on the manufacturer will automatically lead him, at least on average, to act as if he were to be trusted. "Business confidence" in the favorable dispositions of governments towards the interests of manufacturers may be based not upon ties of personal or categorical trust prevailing among political and economic elites, but just upon the awareness, known to be shared by all parties involved, that, within a liberal democracy, governments pursuing policies that are seen as consistently detrimental to business interests will eventually inflict damage upon themselves, both fiscally (through a declining tax base) and electorally (through increasing unemployment). Also, I do not have to trust the doctor as a person, as it is sufficient that s/he has graduated from an appropriate medical school and is licensed to practise as a doctor by the respective authorities.

In all of these cases, institutions are held to have built-in self-correcting mechanisms that rule out major deviations from the expected and known course of operation. Institutions are being counted upon because they are durable and can be taken for granted once they are put in place. Thus the impersonal operation of self-sustaining mechanisms makes personal trust relations both impossible *and dispensable*. What can be taken for granted (almost like the force of gravity) does not need to be trusted.

I wish to argue that something is profoundly wrong, naive, and reified with this "institutionalist" way out of the trust dilemma. This is so for mainly two reasons. Institutions are *incomplete* and ambiguous (at least "at the margin"), and they are *contested*.

First, institutional rules are never of a wall-to-wall nature. Rules can never provide for all contingencies and emergencies. What they leave uncovered are ever-present opportunities, as well as motives, for the opportunistic violation or subversion of institutions and their built-in self-preserving mechanisms. Both contracts and market competition are known to be *incomplete*, and the same applies to laws and constitutional regimes. More specifically, there are plenty of opportunities of *cheating* (breaking the rules) and of *subversion* (replacing the rules with alternative rules). Rules are not sacrosanct, impersonal and eternal, but authored, contingent, and incomplete, both concerning their origin and their implementation. Sometimes they need to be adjusted to changing parameters,[16]

---

[16] Occasionally, rules need to be changed – even in ways, e.g. in an emergency, that are not provided for by second-order rules (i.e. amendment procedures) concerning the change or rules. Moreover, extra-constitutional action, even if there is no demonstrable "need" for change, is never to be precluded as a possibility, and the restraint required for abstaining from the use of this option cannot be formalized. Constitutions are at best

sometimes they need to be defended against attempted violation and subversion. As a consequence, *decisions* play as much a role as *rules* – even if (and especially if) these decisions pertain only to guarding, enforcing, keeping in place, or interpreting the rules. To fly a plane on an institutional auto-pilot is no reason for concern – as long as the pilot is seen to be in his seat and trusted to perform competently. As a consequence, institutions are worthy of our confidence exactly to the extent that we have reasons to trust those who are involved in the defense, interpretation, innovation, and loyal support of institutions.

Second, institutions are not conventions, but rather the opposite, namely patterns of *precarious* and potentially contested cooperation. The potential for being challenged in the name of alternative (more equitable, more effective, more legitimate etc.) institutions is an essential feature of all institutions. Conventions, in contrast, such as the convention to drive on the right-hand side of the street, are strictly self-enforcing: nobody has an incentive to violate them, and nobody expects anyone else to have such an incentive (neglecting for the moment the *Geisterfahrer's* urge to engage in unilateral chicken games). In contrast, institutions regulate, and in potentially strongly contested ways, the distribution of values and resources (Offe 1995), most importantly liberty, or the guaranteed control of actors over spheres of action according their ends and resources. As a consequence, trust in the anonymous mechanisms of institutions is justified only by trust in the voluntary compliance of those actors to whom rules apply, as well as the trust in those actors who are mandated with the supervision and enforcement of these rules. As there is the risk of violation and breakdown, there is also the need for trust in *persons* which cannot be fully substituted for by trust in institutions.[17]

This is not the place to enter to any extensive degree into a discussion of Weber's political sociology, much of which struggles with the same problem. Weber recognizes the superiority of "authority" (*Herrschaft*) over "power" (*Macht*) as the basis of cohesion of a political community. While in the former relationship subjects as well as administrative staff

devices for semirigid self-binding and cannot be fully equated to the physical (as well as social) precautions that Ulysses took. After all, superhumanities, plebiscites, "eternity clauses," and delays (including bicameralism; these are the four major variants of constitutional self-binding) cannot definitely preclude the possibility of change, be it constitutional or non-constitutional.

[17] Given this dilemma of trust – we cannot rely on familiarity and community, but institutions are no sufficient substitute – we might be tempted to resort to the libertarian solution which proposes the minimization of the need for trust. Contracts must be unambiguously enforced, exit (including the exit from the state) must be possible, and every citizen has the right to defend himself and bear firearms in case essentially precarious and fallible trust relations break down. Once these conditions are safely in place, the need for trust is held to be obsolete or at most marginal according to libertarian thinking.

of the ruler are motivated by voluntary and un-coerced "compliance" (*Gehorsam*), in the latter relationship their opposition must be overcome by force or, in a further special case introduced later, by converging interest (*Herrschaft* qua *Interessenkonstellation*). Now, what can motivate compliance? Weber answers this question with his famous tripartite typology of legitimacy. First, compliance can be motivated by tradition. But that is not a promising mechanism in post-traditional society. Second, charismatic qualities that are attributed to the leader or the ideas he represents may motivate compliance. And third, compliance can be generated by the formal-rational correctness of the command that is to be complied with, i.e. its conformity with established rules that regulate the right to give commands.

It is not clear, however, why subjects and the personnel of the administrative apparatus should obey orders simply because they are in this sense procedurally "correct." Given that the law is not self-executing and self-enforcing (as a convention is) simply by being the formally rational law, how does it generate the compliance of those to whom it is addressed? Two kinds of answers have been suggested to this puzzle. One relies on the hidden normative content of formal correctness, i.e. the fairness and impartiality of the rules and procedures. The other is suggested by Weber's political writings of 1917 to 1919. These writings, including his proposals for the constitutional design of the Weimar Republic that were largely realized in the text of the Weimar Constitution, raise doubts whether Weber himself was unambiguously convinced that the third type of legitimation had the same compliance-generating potential that he attaches to the other two modes of legitimacy. Otherwise, he would not have had to rely on personalistic, caesaristic, presidentialist, plebiscitary, acclamationist etc. elements by which he thought the legal rational construction of effectively compliance-motivating validity beliefs (*Geltungsglaube*) must be complemented. This reintroduces an element of elitist personal decision into the framework of abstract and subjectless formalism of rules, and it is explicitly designed to preserve a residue of autonomy within the context of the "iron cage." In the last analysis, or such reading of the sociology of authority (*Herrschaftssoziologie*) as is suggested by the text of Weber's political writings, compliance of administrative apparatus and subjects alike is *not* sufficiently motivated by the rules alone; it must be co-motivated by the trust in the exceptional personal qualities and the responsible (if largely irrational) decision-making behavior of the incumbent elites that occupy the presidency, the government, and political parties, as well as the substantive values they represent.

The potential of institutionalized rules (laws) to generate generalized trust and compliance and substitute for personal trust is further cast in doubt by the fact that rules are "positive", i.e. that they have been *made* and can be *changed*, and actors can fail to change them in case such change is called for – and that the making and unmaking of laws is in the hands of *decision*-makers. Furthermore, the concrete impact that rules have, and thus the requirements that are being made upon me when I am supposed to comply, are seen to depend on the "administrative staff" of the state executive that is charged with the task of the implementation and enforcement of rules; compliance can be contingent, in addition to what the rules require and to what extent these rules conflict with my perceived interests, upon the perceived extent to which administrators make competent and fair use of their scope of discretion and how resistant they are to the temptations of opportunism. Finally (and this point broadens the Weberian model by introducing a "horizontal" or game-theoretic dimension, cf. the work of Margaret Levi (1996)), compliance will be contingent upon my assessment of the probability that everybody else is similarly motivated to comply, rather than to defect, in which case I would be in the "sucker" position. Thus, and if we keep my own level of opportunistic temptation for non-compliance constant, my disposition to follow rules stands in direct proportion to my trust in these categories of agents: law-makers, executive and administrative agents, the citizenry as a whole. More precisely, in order to be motivated to comply, I must trust that, by and large, (a) legislators do not neglect their legislative responsibilities, (b) administrators do not act opportunistically, and (c) fellow citizens do not effectively defect even in cases where they can escape formal sanctioning.

So the question remains: How can I possibly develop that kind of most inclusive and highly abstract trust in the cooperative dispositions of all those to which the law addresses itself, while not knowing from personal experience, communal or quasi-communal cues or otherwise any significant number of these agents? That is the question that needs to be answered if we want to understand trust among strangers and, as a dependent variable of trust, voluntary compliance with the law, however procedurally correctly it may have come into being. The analytical proposition that I am trying to demonstrate and defend here is that institutions, well-entrenched and time-honored though they may appear, depend for their viability upon the supportive dispositions and understanding of those involved in them. Furthermore, some institutions are more easily understood, supported, and appreciated as to their meaning than others. It is the substantive quality of institutions, their capacity to make compelling sense, that determines the extent to which they are capable of promulgating the loyalties of those whose actions they are supposed to regulate, as well as the trust on the part of agents that this support will be widely shared by other agents.

This is the point at which the quality of institutions comes in. Institutions, if appropriately designed, can enable us to trust persons whom we have never had contact with and with whom we share no relevant communal allegiance. It is not obvious how this happens, as institutions are not like persons as they cannot themselves be the object of trust. Strictly speaking, only actors can be trusted, as they are the only units capable of reciprocating trust. In contrast, institutions are, first of all, sets of rules. But more than that, they provide normative reference points and values that can be relied upon in order to justify and make sense of those rules. Institutions, in other words, are endowed with a spirit, an ethos, an implicit moral theory, an *idée directrice*, or a notion of some preferred way of conducting the life of the community. My thesis is that *it is this implied normative meaning of institutions and the moral plausibility I assume it will have for others which allows me to trust those that are involved in the same institutions* – although they are strangers and not personally known to me. From "my" point of view, it is the built-in meaning of institutions, its evidence and moral compellingness, that leads "them" to share with "me" a commitment to the norms and values represented by the institutions and thus transforms them, my anonymous fellow citizens into trustworthy and actually trusted "compatriots."

I hasten to add that not all institutions perform this function of bridging between strangers and thus of conditioning trust, but only those which "I" assume are sufficiently meaningful, plausible and compelling to "everyone else" so as to generate convergent dispositions and loyalties. Institutions which lack this quality of moral plausibility, whose meaning remains opaque to me or whose normative claims I find dubious or inconsistent with observed outcomes or unrecognizable (as in "empty rituals") will not mediate my trust in strangers. If we envisage a continuum of high vs. low trust-inducing institutions, the question is what quality institutions must have in order to score "high" on this dimension, i.e. to become "hegemonic" and to build bridges of trust between strangers.

Let me speculate further that the trust-inducing capacity of institutions depends upon their potential for a discursive self-foundation that is perceived to "make sense" – to "me" as well as, by extension and analogy, to others. Institutions are capable of discursive self-foundation if they provide reasons for their worthiness of actually being complied with and enacted. Thus "trusting institutions" means something entirely different from "trusting my neighbor": it means *knowing* and recognizing as valid the values and form of life incorporated in an institution and deriving from this recognition the assumption that this idea makes sufficient sense to a sufficient number of people to motivate their ongoing active support for the institution and the compliance with its rules. Successful institutions generate a negative feedback loop: they make sense to actors so that actors will support them and comply with what the institutionally defined order prescribes. Knowing the repertoire of meaning and justification that is being generated by institutions allows "me," the participant observer, to determine the measure of trust I can extend to those who, although strangers, are still co-residents within an institutional regime and whose patterns of behavior "I" have reasons to expect to be shaped and informed by the evident meaning that is inherent in an institution. The capacity of institutions to shape and inform behavioral dispositions is what I have called the formative function of institutions.[18]

The formative function of an institution is performed if people living in or under these institutions are both cognitively familiarized and effectively impregnated with the normative ideas embodied in the institution. Thus, the first answer to the question of how we can trust our (anonymous) fellow citizens (or what assumptions must be made before we do) is this: We trust our fellow citizens (or, for that matter, fellow human beings) due to the fact that we share a significant institutional space with a sufficiently strong meaning so as to make the overwhelming majority of "strangers" among my fellow citizens worthy of being trusted because I anticipate them to be appreciative of that meaning. At the very least, it is this meaning of institutions that lowers the risk of misallocating trust to a tolerable level.

This is the first of two mechanisms through which institutions facilitate trusting. The second mechanism through which they do so is by *lowering the risk of the truster*, thus making it easier or less worrisome for him to concede trust to anonymous others. Insurance companies, social security arrangements, and workers' protection are all examples of this second mechanism, as is the court system in general. For instance, I have better reason to trust my bank if I know that the bank participates in an inter-bank security fund (in Germany *Einlagesicherungsfonds*) which in the case of bankruptcy guarantees, at least to an extent, the security of my deposits. Trustful and cooperative labor relations are more likely to emerge if the sanctioning power of management is limited by statutory rules protecting the workers' health, safety, wages and jobs. The legal regulation of family support and the availability of family allowances makes the trust relationship leading to marriage and childbearing less risky in economic

---

[18] That institutions are not just instrumentally more or less effective, but also character-forming (or -deforming) and work as determinants of the degree of virtue (or vice) that citizens achieve is arguably one of the most time-honored axioms of political theory. "Institutions that make collective decisions in radically democratic ways will tend to generate new forms of solidarity, cooperation, and civic attachment" (Warren 1996: 241).

terms than it would be in the absence of these protective devices. In all of these cases, legal and institutional regulations make the effect of trust being disappointed relatively less harmful to the truster.[19] The stronger the status rights I enjoy, the easier and less risky it becomes to engage in trust relations (unless, that is, the status right I enjoy increases[20] my degree of risk aversion, timidity, distrust, and suspiciousness). Hence the likelihood that the remaining risk will be covered by trust, and that cooperative relations are being entered into, should increase with the scope of status rights, at least unless those perverse motivational effects intervene. This would suggest another version of the rule that the rich and secure (or knowledgeable and powerful) trust more; for they have less to lose, relative to what they already safely have, from misallocated or overextended trust. To summarize, institutions engender trust among strangers in two ways. First, they inspire compliance due to what I have called their "moral plausibility" and anticipated formative impact upon everybody else. Second, they can limit, due to the protective status rights they provide, the perceived risk of trusting strangers.

Let us return to the first of our two mechanisms, the anticipated socialization effect of institutions and the trust in strangers that results from it. The problem of building trust among strangers in this way is particularly demanding in the case of political trust. Political trust involves trusting various categories of agents whose capacity to inflict damage upon me is substantial: law-makers, administrators and the judiciary, and the citizenry in general. As I cannot possibly trust them on the basis of

[19] While, as I said before, trust is a power-saving device, the reverse is also true. State power can be seen to be a trust-saving device in the sense that it helps to reduce the risks that would have to be covered by trust in the absence of state power and its manifestation in regulatory policies. More precisely, state policies can reduce the risk involved in trust relations, thereby making them less prohibitive and more easy to enter into. It is not clear, however, whether that makes trust relations appear superfluous or, to the contrary, more attractive and ubiquitous. For instance, before the introduction of mandatory pension insurance, workers had to trust that their children or other relatives would care for them after retirement or disability to earn income. Such trust is no longer called for. Does that weaken inter-generational trust relations within families as they are no longer "needed"? Similarly, before the introduction (in Europe) of identity cards and the local registration of residents, creditors had to trust that debtors, when in trouble, would not simply escape to places where they could not be located. Such trust, or the same measure of trust, is no longer needed due to the transaction cost subsidies provided by the state. But this fact may well facilitate the spread of trust-based credit-relations, as they have become burdened with lesser risks. (cf. North 1990 and Fukuyama 1995)

[20] That can happen, as has been suspected by numerous authors since the writings of Alexis de Tocqueville, if status rights undermine the potential for trust. Welfare state institutions diminish both the need and opportunity for trust-based cooperation. As I have an enforceable right to assistance, I do not have to rely on the help of others and do not have to build the trust relationship that provides the basis on which I can expect to receive help and assistance.

	Truth	Justice
Passive	Truth-telling	Fairness
Active	Promise-keeping	Solidarity

Figure 3.1   Trust-generating values represented by institutions

personal knowledge, I need, as a substitute, knowledge of the institutions that motivate, guide and constrain these agents. The key question here is this: What is it in the quality of institutions the awareness and assessment of which allows me to derive trust in these categories of strangers? How exactly do institutions help to generalize trust?

As I have argued before, institutions mediate trust because they are seen to "stand for" and represent certain values and operate so as to provide arguments, as well as incentives, which condition loyalty and effective compliance with these values. Which values, as embodied in institutions, are trust-inducing in modern societies, and trust-destroying (up to the point of outright cynicism) in case institutions are seen to fail to live up to them?

My hypothetical (and testable) answer is that institutions can mediate political trust by committing and enforcing upon those involved in them not *any* value or valued life form, but a *specific set* of values. Inversely, their capacity for mediating trust is most critically undermined if any or all of these values are seen to be betrayed or insufficiently enforced, at any rate not embodied in the agents that act in and for an institution. I arrive at this list of values by starting with the pair of *truth* and *justice* and subdividing each of the two into a *passive* and an *active* mode. The cross-tabulation looks as follows:

(1) Institutions generalize trust to the extent they commit their members to the virtue of *truth-telling*, and to the extent they monitor and effectively detect (intentional, as in lying, or unintentional, as in erring) violations of that norm. I trust anonymous others if I encounter them within a framework of institutionalized honesty and authenticity. Truth as the key trust-engendering reference value is visible in numerous institutional patterns, ranging from the freedom of the press to formal and public court proceedings, from principles of orderly accounting to the keeping of archives and libraries, from expert committees to research organizations, from academic examens to independent product testing.

They all serve the unbiased observation, documentation, dissemination, and expression of truth about facts in the world about which either lying or ignorance might serve certain interests and violate others. As long as actors are perceived to be embedded in, educated in, and constrained by truth-enforcing institutional patterns, they are more likely to be trusted than in the absence of such embeddedness.[21] For instance, at least part of the trust that clients and potential clients extend to members of the professions derives from their being certified graduates of academic institutions and thus supposedly partake in their ethos of generating, transmitting, and applying true knowledge.

(2) Promise-keeping, and more specifically the virtue of *honoring contracts*, is just the active version of truth telling. It is truth telling not about "given" facts in the world, but actively redeeming propositions concerning my own future action, thereby *making* them true. Again, a number of institutions and institutional patterns come to mind that serve the purpose of committing agents to promise-keeping. Much of given promises can be enforced through the court system. Political promises of elites and political parties are supposedly enforced through the mechanisms of party competition and contested elections. But the guarantee of promise-keeping becomes precarious if the material resources needed to redeem legal claims cannot be generated, as in budget crises and subsequent social security cutbacks. Hence the perceived failure of policy makers to redeem their own promises or hold other actors liable for keeping promises, be it due to their lack of effort and intention, or be it due to circumstances beyond their control, will undermine the general level of trust.

(3) The generalization of trust can also be enhanced through institutions that generate practises informed by the values of *fairness*, impartiality, and neutrality. Equality before the law and equal political participation are the standard examples of fairness as abstraction, cognitive neutralization, and depersonalization.[22] In order to spread trust among strangers, the regime that these strangers are jointly subject to must be seen as

---

[21] The virtual absence of authenticity-preserving institutional patterns in state socialist societies has led some dissident intellecutuals (Havel, Konrad) to declare "living in truth" the supreme, if not only, political goal of postcommunism. It is interesting to note that the minimalist program of "living in truth" has nowhere gained a mass base, but rather remained the mark of disengaged and disenchanted intellectuals.

[22] Note the following twist here: the administrative personnel of an organization or state will be trusted to the extent that it is perceived to perform in a strictly "bureaucratic" and de-personalizing manner. The staff of an administrative agency is trustworthy if it is taken for granted that the way it deals with clients is *not* contingent upon whether officials trust the client or the client trusts them. Trust in administration, in other words, is contingent upon the perfect operative irrelevance of trust within the administration and its dealings with clients.

neutral and "color-blind", without built-in preferences, biases, and selectivities or restrictions of access. It must passively accept and recognize differences that exist between strangers as legally inconsequential.

(4) But, finally, trust can also be enhanced by an institutional regime that relates actively to, and promises to compensate for, such differences – at least to the extent these differences cannot be held to be freely chosen, but structurally imposed by unequal endowments and inescapable constraints that condition an unequal distribution of life chances. Social rights that go beyond equality "before" the law and accomplish, through redistributive intervention and selective protection, a measure of equality of life chances through and "after" the law are the underpinnings of the trust-engendering potential of *solidarity*.

Institutions generate trust among strangers (vertically as well as horizontally) if they are seen as conforming to and embodying these criteria and are believed to motivate agents accordingly, while at the same time maintaining the capacity to enforce these standards upon agents in cases where they are tempted to violate them. Conversely, impressionistic evidence suggests that the failure of any institutional complex – from government to the media, from the professions to economic institutions to the military – to live up to any or all of *these* standards is the predominant reason for denying or withdrawing generalized trust from the personnel of entire institutional sectors and ultimately "everyone else." Any evidence of institutions permitting (or failing to detect) lies, of being unable to make actors keep contracts and honor promises, of being biased and permitting unfair advantages, and of failing to compensate at least some major kinds of social inequalities appear to be the only legitimate reasons for "systemic" distrust and eventually cynicism. Such failures are taken as evidence that institutions have failed to inculcate their meaning and mission to agents and make them loyal "inhabitants" of these institutions. Persons who withdraw trust in "everyone else" do so due not to the (impossible) observation that everyone else (or, for that matter, the "political class") does in fact not deserve to be trusted, but to the perception of failure of the institutions to perform their formative and constraining role according to any or all of these four standards. The transition from the observed failure of institutional arrangements to live up to their presumed mission to the denial of trust to everyone else is made by the consideration that as institutions fail to make sense to me, I assume the same must be the case with everyone else, so that defection and unpredictability of the others' conduct must be reckoned with.

The generalization effect of institutions works in either direction. If institutional regimes are perceived to perform reasonably well according to the above four universalistic criteria, horizontal as well as vertical trust relations can flourish. As an ideal-typical result, citizens recognize and trust each other as constituent participants of a republican political community. Conversely, the observation of malfunctioning of institutional regimes can undermine the very cohesion of modern political communities and trigger regressive phenomena such as the switch from institutionally mediated to communal (e.g. ethnic and regionalist) forms of the mediation of trust.[23]

Deriving criteria for trustworthiness of strangers from the knowledge of institutions and their formative, agency-shaping and agency-enabling potential may appear to be a great alternative to trust-generation through the parochialism of "estates" or the tribalism of communities, and even more so to the trust based upon personal interaction. The advantage of this mode of generating trust is in its comparatively greater degree of generalization. This advantage, however, comes at a price. Institutions may *or may not* succeed in endowing with competence and "civilizing" their respective agents and in instilling a specific discipline, sense of mission, or "ethos" in them. Alternatively, their normative claim and mission may be perceived or suspected to function just as "ideological" pretense, i.e., as a framework of unauthentic legitimation that provides opportunities for the acquisition of power, privilege, and profit. The capacity of institutions to generate and generalize mediated trust is easily irritated by observed anomalies of their operation.

On the other hand, trust is the residue that remains after the propensity to distrust has turned out to be unfounded. "Distrust" is not the opposite of trust, but the attitude in which the cognitive assumptions are continuously tested and scrutinized which regulate the allocation of trust. This attitude and the practises flowing from it (such as investigative journalism, public hearings, or campaigns of opposition parties and movements) are essential in a democracy in order to *authenticate* the core assumptions that turn out to be capable of withstanding and disconfirming distrust. A political system in which distrust is easily articulated and listened to, and its presumed reasons easily and impartially assessed as valid or refuted, deserves to be trusted for the assurance this transparency provides to the citizens.

Re-personalizing trust relations: populism

The exceedingly demanding and roundabout process in which democratic citizens must build trust on account of what they know not about

---

[23] It must be noted here that, as a direct consequence of major incidents of manifest institutional malfunctioning, it is widely feared that two European states, Belgium and Italy, are currently (1996) seen by some observers to be on the brink of breaking apart.

the *trusted*, but about the *institutions* under which the trusted act and in which they are embedded poses significant difficulties for liberal democratic regimes. After all, who "knows" whether these institutions do actually perform according to their proclaimed rules, and whether the failure to substantiate distrust is really a sufficient reason to trust – rather than just a reason to suspect that the mechanisms of articulating and processing distrust are hopelessly inadequate? Given these precarious conditions of institutionally mediated trust, the citizen may well feel to have little reason to trust in the cognitive validity of his or her own trust.

I propose to interpret *populism* as a typical and widespread response to the cognitive emergency resulting from this doubt. Populism has to do, first of all, with a re-personalization of politics. The trust in political leaders is based not upon the track record of kept and broken promises, not on their known programmatic proposals and the constraints and possibilities afforded to them by their office, but upon their personal style, appearance, and media skills, and their reputation for moral integrity and other personality features, often referred to in terms of the Weberian concept of "charisma" (cf. Eisenstadt 1995: 313). Populism is a type of politics in which institutionally mediated credit ranks very low[24] and everything depends upon the leaders' successful pretense to charismatic personality traits and the institutionally unmediated acclaim and trust extended to him (or, as in Britain of the 1980s, her) as a quasi-familiar person. A second feature of populism is that populist mobilization does not rely on structural collectivities present within civil society (such as class, region, religion, urban vs. countryside, or ideological orientation) being invoked, but upon loyalty and support being devoted to a concrete person by a structurally often most diverse and amorphous constituency. Populist politics is an extra-institutional short-cut to political trust, and its spread and success testifies to the difficulty of mediating trust through institutions and the principles embodied in them.

Trust under postcommunist transition regimes

The characteristic weakness of the functioning of post-authoritarian new democracies is often analyzed to be the scarcity of trust and the prevalence of cynicism, the latter attitude being typically directed at both the

---

[24] Both Ronald Reagan and Margaret Thatcher have used the tactics of posing as politicians-denouncing politicians, dramaturgically exploiting the opposition between the routines of "office" vs. the creativity of genuine "leaders." Many (aspiring) populist politicians are also "anti-politicians" in that they proudly emphasize the origin of their careers being in institutional sectors other than politics, be it entertainment industries, the media, big business, the clergy, the military, or academia.

remaining (or re-emerging) elites of the old regime and not-yet-proven newcomers – that is to say, the entire political leadership personnel. As there is no widely known and firmly established set of entrenched institutional patterns capable of projecting the "meaning" and "ethos" through which trust could possibly be generalized, agents must rely on personal experience, signals substituting for such experience, and the weak forms of generalization offered by communal and quasi-communal ties and symbols.

Also, fatalism, or a cognitive frame that tends to attribute outcomes to forces that are beyond the control of ordinary humans, is characteristic of postcommunist transition societies.[25] Postcommunist Central Eastern Europe, and even more so the Russian Federation, is the ideal scene to study the failure of institutionally mediated trust-building. New institutions had very little chance so far to prove themselves in their normalizing and formative function, as well as in their capacity to guide and constrain the action of officeholders. This is particularly the case if institutional regimes consist of an incoherent patchwork of old and new rules without any evident unifying principle. The widely publicized and highly visible experience of corruption, inconsistency, fuzzily defined and hence often contested domains (e.g. between local, regional, and central governments and their respective domains and coercive or taxation powers), as well as, in many instances, the presence of leaders and administrative staff surviving in elite positions from the old regime, betray their failure to generate credible commitments to any meaningful Gestalt of principles, ideas, and functions political and economic institutions are expected to perform. This applies not only to the division of political powers (presidency vs. government vs. parliament; central state vs. federal subjects; state vs. business and interest associations) but also to property rights. Moreover, their very jurisdiction and mode of operations have often been subject to discretionary redefinition and institutional engineering that is perceived to occur "at the top" or "behind the scene",[26] in either case it being initiated by decision-making actors who stand above institutions and not formed and "internalized" by them: they are exempt from the discipline and meaning embodied in those institutions. Institutions were not given the

[25] The vast popularity of gambling in these societies, as well as of "providentialist" narratives, support this point. Cf. Sztompka (1996: 50). In my own conversations with Russian social scientists, the two ultimate forces that supposedly move – and thus must be invoked to explain – political and economic developments were "the power structures" and "the mentality of the simple people." Either of these explanatory variables is evidently seen as being beyond the reach of institutional politics (as well as, for that matter, scientific investigation) – comparable only to what the party leadership was under the old regime.

[26] cf. Nadezhda Mandelstam's epigram, quoted in Rose (1994: 21): "In Russia everything always happens at the top."

time yet to congeal into routinized patterns of legitimation and standard operating procedures to which everyone would be bound – rulers, administrators, and clients alike. (Elster et al., 1998: chap 1; Offe 1995)

The lack of trust is further indicated by the widespread reliance upon one of its functional equivalents, namely money. If schools, hospitals, and the police are seen to be insufficiently equipped to provide services fairly and competently, whoever can afford it resorts to privately purchased provision of these services, including some of the coercive state functions of enforcing contracts and titles as they are offered by hired Mafia-type organizations.

The result of the failure of encompassing institutions to mediate the generation of trust is an extreme reliance on the two other mechanisms of trust-building. Trust is being generated through *personal interaction*[27] and on the basis of *ascriptive communities*. Both of these mechanisms are clearly inferior in their reach compared to institutionally mediated trust-building. In the absence of institutionally mediated and generalized trust, there is a pervasive tendency for interaction to be of a "local", small scale and short term[28] nature. Levels of what may be called economic and political "patriotism" are extremely low, and the consideration of exit options[29] ubiquitous.

Under the conditions of post-communism, recipients of trust are likely to be an extension of friendship or collegial networks or of local and primordial communities than components of the state structure (Rose 1994: 29): clans and tribes rather than large scale and internally diverse constituted political communities with their representative agents. Placing trust in those we know, and in nobody else, may be a workable practise if what we want to avoid is disappointment; however, if we want to proceed along a path of transformation and to accomplish collective political and economic goals, we need to trust agents beyond those whom we "know" from close and extended observation. What is needed are trust-mediating institutions capable of motivating and constraining the behavior of decision-makers as well as of "everyone else."

The analyses by Rose (1994) and Sztompka (1996) each suggest one way out of the condition of extremely low trust that prevails as far as at least the civil institutions of post-communist societies are concerned. The

---

[27] "East Europeans know those whom they trust, and trust those whom they know" (Rose 1994: 29).

[28] This is illustrated not only by the extremely low rate of personal savings, but also by the priority for investments with low level of fixity of capital (trade, services, financial operations), as opposed to manufacturing and construction (Sztompka 1996: 49).

[29] This includes, in political terms, abstention from voting and non-participation in associations; and in economic terms emigration, savings in foreign currency, and a consumer preference for foreign manufactured goods.

two schools of thought can be contrasted in the following way. Rose suggests a "bottom-up" perspective. Trust, to the extent it can be generated at all, must be generated on the basis of personal knowledge and the mutual obligations that can be effectively claimed and sanctioned within the relatively small circles of families, tribes, clans, and local networks of cooperation (including, according to some authors, criminal ones). These are seen to be the only available generators of trust which are bound to remain, at least for a considerable while, of a personalistic and communal nature.

In contrast, Sztompka adopts a consistent, though arguably somewhat heroic, "republican" perspective on postcommunist trust-building. He sees the possibility to recover trust "from above" (1996: 57ff.) by eliminating arbitrariness, monocentrism, secrecy, ineptitude etc. from the operation of political institutions.

The argument between communal "bottom-up" and republican "top down" theories about how trust relationships might be extended beyond the horizon of the local, tribal, familiar and (at best) national cannot be settled here, neither concerning Central East Europe nor elsewhere, such as in the context of the emerging European Union as a new type of political community. The bottom-up perspective envisages a process of extension that involves the gradual mixing and overlapping of primordial loyalties and deals being struck among representative elites of religious, ethnic, linguistic and regional social categories (cf. Eisenstadt 1998). In contrast, the top-down perspective relies on a process in which republican universalist principles and their moral plausibility work to displace or relativize local identities and eventually create a sense of belonging, mutual obligation, and trust that is sufficiently abstract to encompass the very heterogeneous components of the political community (cf. Habermas 1998).

Enforcement problems, social capital, and the supply of trust

Applications of the problem of trust and its various partial solutions can be found not only in processes of regime transition in the East and the emergence of new supranational political communities in Western Europe. The problem is equally present on the level of public policies and their implementation. To elaborate, let me introduce two dimensions here that are meant to highlight the varying degrees of trust-dependency of public policies and their implementation. One dimension is the ease vs. costliness with which conformity of behavior with rules can be monitored and the violation of rules sanctioned. Violation of some rules (prescribing, for instance, that every car must be registered, every residential building conform to the building code, etc.) is easily detected and sanctioned, whereas others (such as legal standards pertaining to relations between members of a family, or those between professionals and clients) can be extremely difficult, or at any rate, costly, to monitor and to enforce. The more we move towards the latter extreme, the more decisive the role of "vertical" trust is likely to be – the trust, that is, that the authorities who define the rules do so in conformity with standards, values, and procedures which generate some moral obligation that "I", the citizen, actually comply with the rules in question. Such reputation of policies for their "moral reasonableness" or self-evident prudence is virtually the only way in which they can unfold some bindingness and formative or "hegemonic" force, as formal enforcement through monitoring and negative sanctions (or, for that matter, positive incentives rewarding compliance) is next to impossible to accomplish. If policies of this latter kind make a difference at all, they do so because citizens are "policing" themselves because they ("vertically") trust in the wisdom and authority of the law-makers and rely on the notion that it makes "good sense" to comply.

The other dimension has to do with the scope of (supposedly beneficial) externalities resulting from compliance. Most norms of civil and commercial law (such as corporation law, labor law, or law regulating the relationship between landlord and tenant) are relatively restricted in their incidence of benefits; these effects are limited to the holders of certain roles and positions, such as creditors, workers, tenants, etc. At the other end of the continuum, we find statutory norms and institutions with a highly diffuse incidence of benefits in which nobody "in particular" (i.e. as defined by his or her specific role or position) is going to gain, while non-compliance with such norms (such as the norms prohibiting drunk driving) implies a highly diffuse and unpredictable incidence of disutilities about which, for that reason, nobody "in particular" is likely to complain and seek remedy. Rules governing preventive medicine, the safety of traffic, the civility of relations between gender, ethnic, or religious groups, or environmental protection are instances of "collective goods" (as opposed to the protection of specific or "categorical" interests of creditors, consumers, etc.). Policies with this kind of diffuse benefits are typically subject to a logic of "contingent consent" (Levi 1996). That is to say, "my" disposition to comply with collective goods-related policies is contingent upon my "horizontal" trust that at least a relevant number of others is also going to comply, as nothing is accomplished in terms of the policy's goals and, moreover, "I" inflict damage upon myself if I remain the only one (or just a member of a small minority) to comply. If, however, I have reasons to believe (i.e. to trust) that my fellow citizens are seriously interested in promoting collective interests and public goods, this cognitive premise will eventually become self-fulfilling. Such trust in the public-regarding (or, for that matter, future-regarding) dispositions of fellow citizens is all the more called for and must be considered a decisive determinant of the successful conduct of public policy if the mode of action prescribed by the policy is not easily monitored and sanctioned, i.e. if it is located at the lower end of the first dimension.

Sometimes it is even positively dangerous to comply with a rule if there is no reason for trusting that others will do likewise. Following the rule that in foggy weather you should not exceed a maximum speed of X mph is almost as suicidal as violating that rule if you must fear to remain the only one to do so. Similarly, sorting your household garbage in order to separate recyclable substances is a messy business which remains totally meaningless as to its desired environmental effects if you do not have reasons to assume that the practise has become a mass habit. The same applies to donating to charities, paying membership dues, helping the integration of foreigners, avoiding illegal employment, providing apprenticeship training facilities, avoiding excessive air pollution and drunk driving, refraining from the use of illicit substances in cattle-breeding and food-processing, using your health insurance in cost-conscious ways, to "Buy British" or buy environmentally sound paint (even though extra costs are involved), to teach your children to stay away from dangerous drugs, and paying taxes honestly.[30] It is in the nature of an apparently growing number of public policies that they can well design and prescribe ways in which collective goods are to be produced or collective bads avoided, but that the monitoring and coercive powers of the state, as duly constrained by civil rights, are deficient, often by orders of magnitude, to implement these policies authoritatively through systematic screening and the application of positive and negative sanctions. In all of such cases, the "better selves" of citizens who are able and willing to act responsibly and reasonably are the ultimate enforcement agents, while public policy can do no more than provide guidance, moral suasion, and complementary services. But in order for those better selves of citizens to prevail and to make an impact, people must have reasons to trust that relevant numbers (often very high numbers!) of fellow citizens (or fellow consumers, or fellow competitors), are similarly disciplined, benevolent, and conscientious in their often inconspicuous modes of everyday

---

[30] Health policies aimed at containing the spread of the HIV virus are an extreme example of how the causal parameters of a political problem are virtually entirely located outside of the reach of public policies.

conduct. To be sure, the perception of effective "coercion supports and reinforces civic virtue" (Levi 1996: 26). But often must the latter substitute for the former, as monitoring cooperative behavior and sanctioning non-cooperation is not just beyond the capacity of fellow citizens, but also beyond that of the authorities. I therefore submit that we can speak of a steep increase of policies for which authoritative enforcement alone is impotent, and for the implementation of which "civic" forms of enforcement through enlightened and trusting citizens is an essential condition – of citizens who are capable of voluntary compliance and cooperation, a civic capacity that is clearly de-motivated by the distrusting perception of others being likely to take a free ride.

If this is so, two ways suggest themselves to model the relationship of state capacity and civic trust in a developmental perspective. One – the more optimistic one – is that of an inverted U-curve. That is to say, while for a long period centralized state power has gradually and cumulatively taken over functions that were previously performed through spontaneous (if incomplete and deficient) self-coordination within civil society, the process is now being reversed, as state power is manifestly too weak to perform a new generation of policies that, once again, largely depend upon civic trust and cooperation for their implementation. Hence the ubiquitous emphasis on some rather idealized concept of "civil society", as well as the equally widely shared emphasis on the need for a return from "welfare state to welfare society."

The other interpretation is less reassuring. It follows the metaphor of a "modernization trap" and questions whether this return can at all be accomplished, as the forces of spontaneous cooperation and encompassing solidarity within civil society have been effectively incapacitated by the extended experience of state-centered interventionism, and that they cannot be reactivated at the point and to the extent they are now needed, particularly as the "socio-cultural genes", so to speak, which would facilitate this return to "Tocquevillean" modes of associationalism and civic engagement are very unevenly distributed in the first place (Putnam 1993).

The key problem here is that "everyone else" is literally anonymous. The strategic actor "everyone else" cannot speak and make commitments, nor can he be spoken to, as the anonymous collectivity of all other players does not have a representation. This situation is different from politics and policies that result from bargaining and compromise in a setting of clear-cut domains and conflicts of interest, say, between partners of a coalition government, labor and employers, or doctors and patients within a system of public health insurance. Within a setting of representative interest associations, the parameters of the situation are as follows. First, both sides have diverging interests, but they also know to depend upon each other, which facilitates compromise. Second, interests are organized through representative (ideally monopolistic, or "corporatist") associations. Third, these collective actors have spokespersons and negotiators who encounter each other as persons, which allows for the opportunity of personal trust to emerge between sectoral representatives. In group negotiations participants can continually test each other's truthfulness and ability to honor promises, are aware of being tested and of being remembered for repeated rounds of negotiations, and engage in intertemporal exchanges and reciprocal concessions, thus building mutual personal trust (cf. Sartori 1975). None of these advantages applies to structurally anonymous games between "me" and "everyone else" in which the opportunity of testing trustworthiness, reciprocating trust and thus building trust is systematically lacking.

The "decline of trust" diagnosis (Putnam 1995), itself strongly contested, can be interpreted in an absolute and a relative way. In absolute terms, time series may be produced that show the decline of indicators of trust in particular agents. In relative terms, we may conceive of a growing discrepancy between trust afforded and trust "required"; even if the former remains constant or increases, the "demand" or "requirement" for trust may increase even more steeply. Two kinds of policies can be cited where this gap emerges. One is the type just mentioned: policies with low capacity for authoritative monitoring and enforcement. Here, the trust gap is *horizontal*: Successful policies depend upon cooperative dispositions that cannot be, at least not fully, enforced and coerced by state agencies. These policies can succeed only if most citizens trust that most other citizens will comply voluntarily, even if this is contrary to their short term interests.

The other has to do with high-risk policies. Here, the trust gap is *vertical*, i.e. it exists between the mass public and policy makers. These policies can well be enforced, but the widely known chances are that the balance of short term intended and long term unintended effects caused by a policy (e.g. in the fields of nuclear energy and waste disposal, information technology, regulation of chemical and biological technologies, defense technology and strategy, but also European Integration and EMU) is such that relatively small immediate gains are potentially outweighed by enormous and irreversible long term damages, and the widespread awareness and fear of such damages (cf. Slovic 1993). This is the opposite configuration from low-enforcement policies, where anticipated long term collective benefits contrast with the absence of short term individual incentives. This gap must be filled by trust – trust in the benevolent intentions and future-regardingness and responsible judgement, sufficient information and fair consideration of all relevant aspects on the part of policy-making elites.[31]

As in post-communist societies, so also in consolidated liberal democracies of the West, there are two principal strategies conceivable that can be thought of as meeting arguably (as I tried to suggest) increasing requirements of the "horizontal" trust that citizens extend to each (anonymous) other. One is the "top down" *republican* solution which operates on the demand side of the trust transaction. The solution of successfully seeking trust is that trust (in elites as well as in "everyone else") can be increased if institutions and procedures generate an impeccable record in terms of truth-telling, promise-keeping, fairness, and solidarity – and thus reasons for suspicion and cynicism are virtually nullified. Here, the formula is that good government and good laws make good citizens, i.e. citizens who are readily inclined to comply with and to cooperate in the implementation of public policies because they consider the government's authority as highly legitimate and competent. If it appears to be beyond any doubt that political institutions condition a fair and truthful conduct of government, there remains little respectable reason for non-compliance, nor is there reason to suspect that fellow citizens will fail to comply.

The other solution is a "bottom up" and, for want of a better term, "civic *communitarian*" solution of "making democracy work" (Putnam 1993; Cox 1994). It operates on the supply side of trust, making citizens less reluctant to concede trust to anonymous others. Citizens getting involved, together with strangers, in voluntary and open associative communities learn to trust each other, thereby getting habituated, as a side-effect, to the self-confirming null-hypothesis that p is in fact > 0.5 in most cases with most people. But how does this friendly attitude towards fellow citizens come about? All we know from recent debates on social capital is that it thrives where it is favored by supportive local traditions – and doesn't where it isn't. This appears to be a radical historicist answer, leaving, by implication, communities with a low perceived level of social capital with the not very helpful diagnosis that they suffer from the "wrong" kind of history and local tradition. Hence the open question with which I wish to conclude: Is it conceivable that the "social capital" of trusting and cooperative civic relations can be encouraged, acquired, and *generated* – and not just *inherited?*

---

[31] La Porte and Metlay (1996) describe, as well as prescribe, the extraordinary efforts that the US Department of Energy and its radioactive waste management operations (need to) spend on the problem of maintaining trust and restoring confidence.

REFERENCES

Bönker, Frank and Offe, Claus, 1996. The morality of restitution: reflections on some normative questions raised by the transition to a private economy, in Claus Offe (ed.) *Varieties of Transition: East European & East German Experience*, Cambridge: Polity Press, 105–130

Cox, Eva, 1994. *A Truly Civil Society*, Sidney: ABC Books

Cusack, Thomas R., 1997. On the road to Weimar? The political economy of popular satisfaction with government and regime performance in Germany, unpub. ms.

Dahl, Robert A., 1992. The problem of civic competence, *Journal of Democracy* 3, 45–59

Eisenstadt, S. N., 1995. *Power, Trust and Meaning. Essays in Sociological Theory and Analysis*, Chicago: University of Chicago Press

1998. Trust and Democracy, unpubl. ms.

Elster, Jon, 1996. *The Roundtable Talks & the Breakdown of Communism*, Chicago: Chicago University Press

1989. *Solomonic Judgements*, Cambridge: Cambridge University Press

Elster, Jon, Claus Offe, Ulrich K. Preuss, 1998. *Institutional Design in Post-Communist Societies: Rebuilding the Ship at Sea*, Cambridge: Cambridge University Press

Fukuyama, Francis, 1995. *Trust: The Social Virtues and the Creation of Prosperity*, New York: Free Press

Gambetta, Diego, 1988a. Can we trust trust? in Diego Gambetta (ed.), *Trust: Making and Breaking Cooperative Relations*, Oxford: Basil Blackwell, 213–237

Giddens, Anthony, 1990. *The Consequences of Modernity*, Stanford: Stanford University Press

Habermas, Jürgen, 1998. *The Inclusion of the Other: Studies in Political Theory*, Cambridge: MIT Press

Hardin, Russell, 1993. The street-level epistemology of trust, *Politics and Society* 21, 505–529

La Porte, Todd R. and Metlay, Daniel S., 1996. Hazards and institutional trustworthiness: Facing a deficit of trust, *Public Administration Review* 56, 341–347

Levi, Margaret, 1996. A state of trust, unpubl. ms.

Luhmann, Niklas, 1973. *Vertrauen. Ein Mechanismus der Reduktion sozialer Komplexität*, Stuttgart: Enke

Mill, John S., 1982 (1859). *On Liberty*, Harmondsworth: Penguin

Misztal, Barbara, 1996. *Trust in Modern Societies*, Cambridge: Polity Press

North, Douglas, 1990. *Institutional Change and Economic Performance*, New York: Cambridge University Press

Offe, Claus, 1995. Designing institutions for East European transitions, in Robert E. Goodin (ed.), *The Theory of Institutional Design*, Cambridge: Cambridge University Press, 199–226

1996. *Varieties of Transition*, Cambridge: Polity Press

Putnam, Robert, 1993. *Making Democracy Work: Civic Traditions in Modern Italy*, Princeton, NJ: Princeton University Press

1995a. Bowling alone: America's declining social capital. *Journal of Democracy* 6, January, 65–78

Rose, Richard, 1994. Postcommunism and the Problem of Trust, *Journal of Democracy* 5, 18–30

Sartori, Giovanni, 1975. Will democracy kill democracy? Decision-making by majorities and by committees, *Government and Opposition* 10, 131–158

Seligman, Adam B., 1992. Trust and the meaning of civil society, *International Journal of Politics, Culture and Society* 6, 5–21

Slovic, P., 1993. Perceived risk, trust, and democracy, *Risk Analysis* 13, 675–682

Sztompka, Piotr, 1996. Trust and emerging democracy, *International Sociology* 11, 37–62

Tyler, Tom R., 1990. *Why People Obey the Law*, New Haven: Yale University Press

Warren, Mark E., 1996. What should we expect from more democracy? Radically democratic responses to politics, *Political Theory* 24, 241–270

4 Trust, well-being and democracy

Ronald Inglehart

This chapter will demonstrate three points:

(1) Interpersonal trust is a relatively enduring characteristic of given societies: it reflects the entire historical heritage of a given people, including economic, political, religious, and other factors.
(2) Interpersonal trust (with other cultural factors) is conducive to stable democracy, as the political culture literature has long claimed but could not demonstrate directly.
(3) Democratic institutions do not necessarily produce interpersonal trust. A society's political institutions are only one among many factors involved in the emergence of a culture of trust or distrust.

Thus, although the United States has had democratic institutions throughout the twentieth century, interpersonal trust among the US public has declined significantly during the past four decades. Democratic institutions do not automatically produce trust. There is no institutional quick fix for the problem of creating trust and social capital.

Let us examine each of these topics, starting with the historical rootedness of interpersonal trust. Our analysis utilizes empirical measures of culture from the 1990–1991 and 1995–1997 World Values Surveys, carried out in more than 60 societies around the world and representing more than 70 percent of the world's population.[1]

---

[1] Interpersonal trust data are from the latest available World Values Survey for the given society. The data for the following 47 societies are from the 1995–1997 World Values Survey: Australia, US, China, Japan, Taiwan, South Korea, Turkey, Bangladesh, India, the Philippines, Great Britain, East Germany, West Germany, Sweden, Norway, Switzerland, Finland, Spain, Slovenia, Poland, Latvia, Estonia, Lithuania, Bulgaria, Serbia, Montenegro, Croatia, Russia, Ukraine, Belarus, Armenia, Moldova, Georgia, Azerbaijan, South Africa, Nigeria, Ghana, Argentina, Brazil, Chile, Colombia, Dominican Republic, Mexico, Puerto Rico, Uruguay, Peru, Venezuela. The data for the 14 other societies are from the 1990–1991 World Values Survey. This analysis draws on material from Inglehart (1997), chapter 6.

Trust and economic development

The people of rich societies show higher levels of interpersonal trust than the publics of poorer ones. As we will see, the World Values Survey data demonstrate this point unequivocally; the correlation is very strong. *Why* is economic development so closely linked with interpersonal trust?

Several plausible answers have been proposed. As Banfield (1958), Putnam (1993), and Fukuyama (1995) have pointed out, interpersonal trust is essential to the cooperation with strangers that is a prerequisite for large-scale economic organizations, on which modern industrial economies are based. Thus, as Putnam demonstrates, networks of collaboration and a culture of interpersonal trust developed long ago in northern Italy; their greater development in the North helps explain why that region subsequently showed much more economic development than the South.

But it seems to work both ways. Poverty can lead to distrust. As Banfield (1958) pointed out, it is safer to trust others if one has a margin of economic security. Under conditions of extreme poverty, the loss incurred from misplaced trust can be fatal. If one loans money to a neighbor and the debt is not repaid, one's family may starve to death. Under these circumstances, unless norms of reciprocity are securely reinforced by some deeply instilled religious or ethical system, interpersonal trust may be unacceptably risky.

Using game-theoretic analysis, Axelrod (1984) suggested that cooperative behavior is a rational strategy if one lives in an environment in which one can safely assume that most other players will reciprocate. But when one is faced with an exploitative player, cooperation is a losing strategy. And unless the players trust each other, they will be forced into a mutually destructive cycle of noncooperative play.

Analysis of the World Values Survey data reveals that those with relatively high levels of education and those with postmaterialist values show high levels of interpersonal trust. This reflects the fact that these groups contain the relatively secure members of a society. The postmaterialists consist of those who have experienced relatively secure conditions throughout their formative years, and the more educated have resources and skills that shield them from many of the risks of life and tend to be recruited from economically more secure families. Insofar as the members of these two groups live in a milieu in which most of the people they encounter are also reasonably secure, they can correctly assume that most of the people with whom they deal are likely to behave cooperatively. But if this is not the case, then not even the more educated or the postmaterialists can safely follow a strategy based on trust.

Table 4.1. *The impact of education and postmaterialist values on interpersonal trust: Low income societies vs. advanced industrial societies*

1. India, China and Nigeria (mean % who trust people)			
Lower education	34%	Materialist	36
Secondary education	37	Mixed	38
Tertiary education	41	Postmaterialist	39

2. Fifteen advanced industrial societies (US, Canada, Japan, Switzerland, Norway, Sweden, Denmark, Finland, West Germany, France, Austria, Netherlands, Belgium, Italy) (mean % who trust people)			
Lower education	37%	Materialist	36
Secondary education	48	Mixed	46
Tertiary education	59	Postmaterialist	59

Source: 1990–1993 World Values Survey.

An alternative interpretation would be that there is something inherent in education that makes people trust others. This does not seem to be the case. The World Values Surveys includes three low-income societies (India, China, and Nigeria), having per capita GNP below $400. As table 4.1 demonstrates, in the three low-income countries, those with more education and those with postmaterialist values are only slightly higher on interpersonal trust than those with little or no education or those with materialist values. In these societies, the postmaterialists and those with higher education constitute a very small minority. The vast majority of those in their society are people whose life experience has not conditioned them to assume that the strangers they encounter can be counted on to adhere to norms of reciprocity.

In the 15 richest societies in the 1990 World Values Survey, on the other hand, the more educated and the postmaterialists are much more likely to feel that most people can be trusted than are the less educated and the materialists. In both rich and poor societies, about the same percentage of the less educated and the materialists (roughly 35 percent) say that most people can be trusted. But within the low-income societies, the highly educated and those with postmaterialist values are only slightly higher on interpersonal trust, while among the 15 advanced industrial societies, the highly educated and the postmaterialists show much higher levels of interpersonal trust. Similarly, the postmaterialists in low-income societies rank only 3 percentage points above the materialists; in advanced

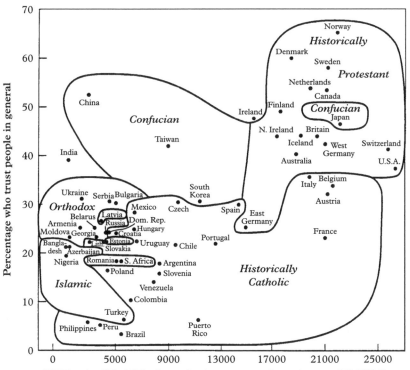

Figure 4.1   Interpersonal trust by cultural tradition and level of economic development and religious tradition. Trust by GNP/capita: r = 0.63 p < 0.000

industrial societies, they rank 23 points above them. Higher education and postmaterialist values are associated with high levels of interpersonal trust *if* one lives in a relatively secure society. But education *per se* does not seem to drive the process.

Though a society's level of economic development is closely linked with its level of interpersonal trust, it is not a process of simple economic determinism. There are plausible grounds for assuming that trust shapes economic-development rates, as well as the reverse, and empirical evidence supports the supposition that causation works in both directions.

One piece of evidence is the fact that interpersonal trust shows remarkably strong linkages with the religious tradition of the given society – and these religious traditions were established long before the industrial development of these societies. As Figure 4.1 demonstrates, interpersonal trust *is* strongly linked with economic development. Rich societies have much higher levels of trust than poor ones: the correlation across our 61 societies is 0.63. Trust levels vary immensely. Only 3 percent of the Brazilians agree that "most people can be trusted"; but at the other end of the scale, 65 percent of the Norwegian public believes that most people can be trusted. Norwegians are twenty times more likely to trust people than are Brazilians. They live in fundamentally different social climates.

The people of richer societies are indeed more trusting than those of poorer societies – but the cross-national differences also reflect the society's cultural heritage. Protestant and Confucian-influenced societies consistently show higher levels of interpersonal trust than do historically Roman Catholic or Islamic societies. Of the 18 societies in which more than 35 percent of the public believes that most people can be trusted, 13 are historically Protestant, three are Confucian-influenced, one is predominantly Hindu and only one (Ireland) is predominantly Catholic. Of the ten lowest-ranking societies in Figure 4.1, eight are historically Catholic, one is Islamic and one is historically Orthodox; *none* are historically Protestant or Confucian. Almost all historically Protestant societies show higher levels of interpersonal trust than almost all Catholic societies. Three Protestant societies rank relatively low (East Germany, Latvia, and Estonia) and all three were, until recently, dominated by communist regimes. A history of communist rule tends to reshape a society's cultural heritage: virtually all former communist societies show relatively low levels of interpersonal trust. With the sole exception of China (a Confucian society), all 21 of the ex-communist societies rank below all 13 of the non-communist Protestant societies. As Putnam (1993) has argued, rule by large, hierarchical, unresponsive, centralized bureaucracies seems to corrode interpersonal trust.

South Africa is a special case, an African society with a religiously diverse population among which the largest group is Protestant. If we were to classify her as an historically Protestant society, she would constitute an outlier. Conversely, one predominantly Catholic society (Ireland) ranks exceptionally high on interpersonal trust – but until 1922, Ireland was part of a predominantly Protestant United Kingdom of Great Britain and Ireland.

Why do Catholic societies rank lower on interpersonal trust than Protestant societies? Again, it seems to reflect the principle that horizontal, locally-controlled organizations are conducive to interpersonal trust, while remote hierarchical organizations tend to undermine it. The Roman Catholic church is the very prototype of a hierarchical, centrally controlled institution; Protestant churches were smaller, relatively decentralized and more open to local control. Though these factors may not count for much today, historically the respective churches played immensely influential roles in shaping their societies. The contrast between local control and domination by a remote hierarchy seems to have important long-term consequences for interpersonal trust.

These cross-cultural differences are not simply a reflection of the fact that richer societies tend to have higher levels of interpersonal trust than other societies. The differences in trust persist when we control for economic differences. Thus, the Catholic societies examined here have about the same average income as Confucian societies, but their average level of interpersonal trust is only *half* that of the Confucian societies – which show the same average level of trust as Protestant societies.

Relatively high levels of interpersonal trust characterize Confucian societies in general. Although we agree with most of what Fukuyama (1995) says about the importance of trust, he may be mistaken in characterizing China as a low-trust society. In both the 1990 and 1996 World Values Surveys (carried out by two different organizations) China shows about the same level of interpersonal trust as Japan (which he characterizes as a high trust society). Still another survey, carried out by Manabe (1995), finds a similar high level of interpersonal trust among the Chinese public. India is our sole example of a Hindu society, but her public manifested relatively high levels of interpersonal trust in both the 1990 and the 1995 WVS, despite her low income level. These cross-cultural differences in interpersonal trust persist in multivariate analysis that controls for GNP/capita.

As we will see below (see Figure 4.3), interpersonal trust is strongly linked with democratic institutions, as well as with economic development. One possible explanation of this configuration would be that economic development gives rise to democracy, which produces relatively high levels of interpersonal trust. But this explanation does not hold up under closer examination. A society's level of interpersonal trust seems to reflect its entire historical heritage, of which her political institutions are only one component.

In order to examine the relative impact of political, economic and cultural variables, we carried out the multivariate analysis shown in Table 4.2. We constructed dummy variables for Protestant/non-Protestant and for Confucian/non-Confucian societies and entered them in a multiple-regression analysis of interpersonal trust levels, including GNP/capita and the Freedom House ratings of levels of democracy from 1972 to 1997 as additional independent variables. As Model 1 of this analysis indicates, both the Protestant and the Confucian dummy variables show strong and statistically significant impacts on interpersonal trust levels, even when we control for GNP/capita (using the World Bank's purchasing power parity [PPP] estimates to obtain a more realistic measure of economic

Table 4.2. *The impact of economic development, level of democracy (1972–1997) and cultural heritage on interpersonal trust*

	(Model 1)	(Model 2)	(Model 3)	(Model 4)
GNP/capita, 1995 (PPP)	0.918*	0.681***	1.10****	—
($1,000s)	(0.383)	(0.189)	(0.178)	
Democ. ratings, 1972–97	0.021	—	—	—
	(0.075)			
Protestant	12.02**	12.95***	—	19.71****
	(3.70)	(3.36)		(3.02)
Confucian	14.37**	15.70**	—	18.14***
	(5.42)	(5.06)		
Adjusted R2	0.51	0.50	0.36	0.41
N	54	63	63	63

Note: Table entries are unstandardized regression coefficients with standard errors in parentheses.
*p < 0.05   **p < 0.01   ***p < 0.001   ***p < 0.0001   ****p < 0.00001

differences). Economic development also has a significant impact on trust levels. Although the Freedom House democracy ratings have a strong zero-order correlation with interpersonal trust, this linkage washes out when we control for religion and economic development. When we drop the level of democracy variable from our analysis (see Model 2), we explain almost as much variance as when we include it (50 percent vs. 51 percent). On the other hand, when we drop the dummy variable for Confucian societies, the percentage of variance explained drops from 50 to 43 percent. And when we drop *both* of the cultural variables from the analysis (Model 3), the explained variance drops even farther, to only 36 percent. On the other hand, when we drop GNP per capita from the equation (model 4), the explained variance falls to 41 percent: a society's religious tradition seems to account for even more of the cross-national variance in interpersonal trust than does its level of economic development. Nevertheless, we need to include *both* economic and religious factors in order to obtain an optimal explanatory model. Moreover, there are strong theoretical reasons to believe that democratic institutions should be conducive to democracy: if remote, hierarchical institutions erode trust, relatively horizontal, responsive ones should help develop trust. Though the analysis in Table 4.2 provides little support for this interpretation, we believe that democratic institutions probably *are* conducive to interpersonal trust – but it seems clear that they are not the whole story.

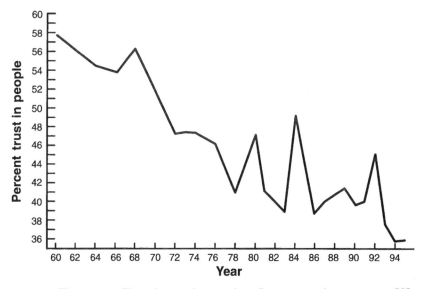

Figure 4.2   Trust in people over time: Interpersonal trust among US public, 1960–1995
Source: 1960 data from Civic Culture Survey, 1962–1994 data from National Election Surveys and General Social Surveys, 1995 data from World Values Survey

Interpersonal trust can fall as well as rise under democratic institutions. Interpersonal trust has risen in Italy since the 1950s (though it still is somewhat lower than in most democracies). But during the same period, it has fallen in the United States, as Figure 4.2 demonstrates. In 1960, 58 percent of the American public felt that most people could be trusted. A generation later in 1995, only 35 percent still held this view. The American level of interpersonal trust had fallen almost to the Italian level. The fact that trust has shown a long-term decline in one of the world's leading democracies demonstrates that life under democratic institutions does not necessarily result in rising interpersonal trust.

Both a society's cultural heritage and its level of development seem to have an important influence on interpersonal trust than its economic level. But these religious traditions overlap heavily with the developmental levels of these societies – quite possibly in a sequential fashion, as the Weberian Protestant-ethic thesis argued long ago and as more recent variations on this theme have continued to suggest. We will not attempt to unravel the complexities of this relationship here. Economic factors seem to play a major role in the emergence of interpersonal trust. But the results of this analysis suggest that a given society's religious heritage may be fully as important as its level of economic development in shaping interpersonal trust. Furthermore (as both Weber and Fukuyama have argued in different ways) a society's cultural heritage may help shape its economic growth.

These cross-national differences in interpersonal trust seem to reflect the entire historical experience of given societies, and *not* the influence of the respective churches today. For example, both the Netherlands and Germany were historically predominantly Protestant societies but (as a consequence of different birth rates and different rates of religious attrition) they have about as many practicing Catholics as Protestants today. Despite these changes in their religious makeup, both the Netherlands and Germany show relatively high trust levels today – and the Catholics and Protestants *within* these societies do not show markedly different trust levels.

We find remarkably large differences between the interpersonal-trust levels of Protestant and Catholic societies. It seems unlikely that they reflect the influence of the Catholic and Protestant churches today, for the direct influence of the church now is very slight in most of these countries. Though church attendance remains relatively high in Poland, Ireland and the United States, it has fallen drastically in most of the historically Catholic countries of Europe. It has fallen even more drastically in most historically Protestant European societies, to the point where some observers now speak of the Nordic countries as post-Christian societies: Church attendance in them has plummeted toward zero. Nevertheless, societies that were traditionally Catholic consistently show lower trust levels than those that were traditionally Protestant, even among segments of the population that have no contact with the church. Apparently, these values persist as part of the cultural heritage of given nations, not through the direct influence of religious institutions. This cultural heritage has been shaped by the economic, political, and social experience of the given people, including the fact that the Protestant societies industrialized earlier than most of the Catholic societies – which at an even earlier stage of history may, in turn, have been linked with religious differences (Weber 1958) but is certainly not a case of direct institutional determinism.

Trust and stable democracy

The hypothesis that cultural factors play an important role in sustaining democracy evoked great interest in the aftermath of World War II, but went out of fashion during the 1970s for a variety of reasons. The political-culture approach raised an important empirical question: whether given societies had political cultures that were relatively conducive to democracy. Some critics alleged this approach was "elitist" in finding that some cultures were more conducive to democracy than others: Any right-minded theory should hold that all cultures are equally conducive to democracy.

By the 1990s, though the concept of political culture was still unfashionable in American academic circles, observers in other countries from Latin America to East Asia were reaching the conclusion that cultural factors did indeed play an important role in the problems they were encountering with democratization.

Cultural factors have been omitted from most empirical analyses of democracy, partly because until now we have not had reliable measures of them from more than a handful of countries. When empirical measures of cultural factors *are* taken into account, as in Inglehart (1990) and Putnam (1993), they seem to play an important role. This chapter argues that economic development leads to cultural changes that help *stabilize* democracy.

In examining the relationship between trust and democracy, it is crucial to distinguish between three distinct aspects of democracy:

(1) Its long-term *stability*
(2) The *level* of democracy at given points in time
(3) Short-term *changes* in levels of democracy.

Relatively high levels of subjective well-being and interpersonal trust are conducive to the *stability* of democratic institutions. They are not necessarily conducive to *transitions* to democracy; quite the contrary, *low* levels of subjective well-being and interpersonal trust may play an important role in the collapse of authoritarian regimes.

It is clear that cultural variables are not the only factors involved in the emergence and survival of democratic institutions. Modernization theorists such as Lerner (1958), Deutsch (1961), and others argued that economic development brings social mobilization, giving rise to a more participant population, which helps prepare the way for democracy. We believe that they were right, but this is only part of the story. Building on the work of Almond and Verba (1963), Inglehart (1990), Diamond, Linz and Lipset (1989), and Putnam (1993), we will present evidence that economic development is conducive to democracy not only because it mobilizes mass publics, but also because it encourages supportive cultural orientations. Industrialization tends to transform a society's social structure, bringing urbanization, mass education, occupational specialization, growing organizational networks, greater income equality, and a variety of associated developments that mobilize mass participation in politics. But economic development is also conducive to *cultural* changes that help stabilize democracy. There are two particularly central factors: (1) *A culture of trust*. In authoritarian regimes, the usual way to handle the opposition is to imprison or execute its leaders. A crucial element in the rise of democracy is the emergence of the norm of the "loyal opposition": Instead of being viewed as traitors conspiring to overthrow the government, the opposition is trusted to play by the rules of the democratic game. This means that if the opposition wins an election, the ruling elite will turn power over to it, confident that they will not be executed or imprisoned for doing so and that the new elite themselves will subsequently hold elections in which they can freely compete for power.

(2) *Mass legitimacy*. Legitimacy, or diffuse mass support, can help sustain democratic institutions through difficult times. It is an asset to any regime, but it is crucial to democracies. Democratic institutions can be imposed by elites or even by foreign conquest, but whether they survive depends on whether they take root among the public – because with democratization, the public becomes a crucial political factor.

Positive outputs from a political system can generate mass support for the political incumbents. In the short term, this support is based on calculations concerning "What have you done for me lately?" But if a given regime's outputs are seen as positive over a long time, the regime may develop "diffuse support" (Easton 1953): the generalized perception that the political system is inherently good, even apart from its current outputs. This type of support can endure even through difficult times. As we will demonstrate below, a sense of subjective well-being among the public of a given society is an excellent indicator of whether or not that regime possesses legitimacy. Indeed, it is a better indicator than responses to direct questions about how strongly one supports democratic political institutions.

Three aspects of democracy

Democracy is a multidimensional phenomenon. But most empirical analyses have focused on a single aspect of democracy as the dependent variable. Thus, Inglehart (1990) analyzed the *stability* of democracy: operationally, the number of years that democratic institutions had functioned continuously in a given society. But this is just one aspect of democracy; most other analyses have focused on *levels* of democracy at a given time. And some writers have analyzed short-term *changes* in levels of democracy, such as the causes of the sudden surge of democracy that followed the collapse of socialist regimes in 1989–1991.

Careful specification of the aspect of democracy to be examined is crucial, since different causal factors are important in relation to each aspect of democratization. These factors may even reverse their polarity in connection with different aspects of democratization. Thus, though there is strong evidence that economic development is conducive to democracy, the fall of authoritarian regimes may be precipitated by economic *collapse*. The role of political culture tends to be most important in consolidating democracy and enabling it to endure through difficult times. Situation-specific factors (such as the death of a strong authoritarian leader or defeat in a war) are often the immediate cause of the transition to democracy. But once democratic institutions are in place, their long-term survival depends on whether supportive orientations develop among their citizens. The growing importance of mass preferences is inherent in the very nature of democracy: If democratic institutions do not attain enough deep-rooted mass support to weather difficult times, the citizens can simply vote democracy out of existence. They did so in Weimar Germany; they would have done so in Algeria if democracy had not been suspended; and they may do so in some of the Soviet successor states.

Long-term stability of democracy

Mass political culture is crucial to the long-term *stability* of democracy: Political culture stabilizes democracy by providing a climate of trust and an enduring base of mass support.

Democratic institutions can be implanted by a handful of elites or even imposed by foreign conquest, as they were in Germany and Austria at the end of World War I and in Germany, Japan, and elsewhere at the end of World War II. Democracy can be imposed from above or from outside, but whether a particular democracy survives through good and bad times depends on whether it has built up deep-rooted cultural attachments among the citizens. Various writers have stressed the importance of this factor. Weber emphasized the importance of legitimacy, Easton spoke of "diffuse support," and Almond and Verba discussed the "civic culture." Putnam (1993) showed how "civic orientations" contributed to the effectiveness of democracy in Italy. And in an analysis based on data from 24 societies surveyed in the 1981 World Values Survey, Inglehart (1990) demonstrated that interpersonal trust and subjective well-being are closely linked with the long-term survival of democratic institutions.

The appropriateness of using stability in measuring democracy has been debated. Lipset (1959), Muller (1988), and others measured democracy in ways that included stability along with measures of political rights and civil liberties. This practice was criticized by Jackman (1973), Bollen

(1980), and Bollen and Jackman (1985), who make a strong case for not confusing the *stability* of democracy with the *extent* of democracy – which, we emphatically agree, are two distinct things.

The present analysis does not confuse them. The *extent* or level of democracy at a given time point is a significant variable. But the *stability* of democracy is equally important. Our analysis does not use democratic stability as a proxy for *degree* of democracy; instead, it explicitly focuses on the factors that enable democratic institutions to survive over time, addressing the question "What factors enable given societies to remain above the threshold at which the top political leaders are chosen by free and competitive elections?"

In contrast with its role in sustaining democracy over the long run, political culture has a very different relationship with short-term changes to and from democracy. Indeed, the same cultural factors that stabilize and sustain democracy also tend to stabilize authoritarian regimes: Thus, though high levels of legitimacy and trust are crucial to the survival of democracy, they would not explain short-term shifts toward democracy. Instead, one would expect *low* levels of legitimacy and trust to be linked with the collapse of authoritarian regimes, possibly opening the way for a transition to democracy. The short-term consequences of cultural factors are very different from their long-term functions. Gradual cultural changes can give rise to conditions that become increasingly favorable to the rise of democratic institutions, but the immediate precipitating factor is likely to be some macro-event such as economic collapse or an intergenerational transfer of power from hard-line leaders to reformist leaders. Accordingly, the literature on transitions to democracy tends to focus on elite-level events rather than on underlying changes in culture or social structure (e.g. O'Donnell, Schmitter, and Whitehead 1986).

Cultural changes conducive to democracy

The study of political culture grew out of the tragic events that led up to World War II. In the aftermath of World War I, democratic regimes were set up in Germany, Italy, Poland, Spain, and many other formerly authoritarian societies. On paper, some of them looked like ideal democracies. But when they encountered the severe economic difficulties of the 1920s and 1930s, many democracies failed to survive. Why? Great Britain, the United States, and the Nordic countries also experienced severe economic distress during the Great Depression, but democracy survived there. In contrast, democracy gave way to fascist regimes in Germany, Italy, Japan, Spain, Hungary, and other countries, preparing the way for the greatest bloodbath in history.

The classic civic culture study (Almond and Verba 1963) addressed the question "Why did democratic institutions survive in some countries but not in others?" Manifestly, it was not just a question of constitutional engineering. The laws and constitution of the Weimar Republic were as democratic as those of any nation in the world, but they did not take root. An authoritarian outlook remained widespread throughout German society, and when distress and insecurity became severe, the Germans voted Hitler into power in free elections. Facing comparable problems, the British, Americans, and various other peoples were relatively steadfast in their support for democracy. Democracy, apparently, is not just a matter of elite-level arrangements; the basic cultural orientations of the citizens also play a crucial role in its survival. Almond and Verba set out to measure the relevant orientations empirically, to determine whether there were underlying differences in the political cultures of stable democracies, as compared with those of unstable democracies.

This question is of far more than academic interest again today, when democratic institutions recently have been installed in scores of formerly authoritarian societies from Argentina to Russia – and where their fate remains uncertain. Authoritarian forces have made a comeback in a number of the Soviet successor states, and a proto-fascist party won more votes than any other party in the 1993 Russian parliamentary elections and played a major role in the 1996 presidential elections, giving rise to the chilling question: Will Russia's fate be like that of the Weimar Republic?

The importance of societal trust

Partly, the answer depends on the development of a culture of trust, which plays a crucial role in democracy. Democratic institutions depend on trust that the opposition will accept the rules of the democratic process. You must view your political opponents as a *loyal* opposition who will not imprison or execute you if you surrender political power to them, but can be relied on to govern within the laws and to surrender power if your side wins the next election.

Banfield (1958) found that southern Italian society had much lower levels of trust than northern Italy; this hindered the cooperation between strangers that is essential to both economic development and successful democratic institutions. Almond and Verba (1963) also argued that a sense of interpersonal trust is a prerequisite for effective democracy. They found that the publics of Italy and West Germany were characterized by lower levels of interpersonal trust, readiness to participate, and other attitudes conducive to democracy than were the British and American

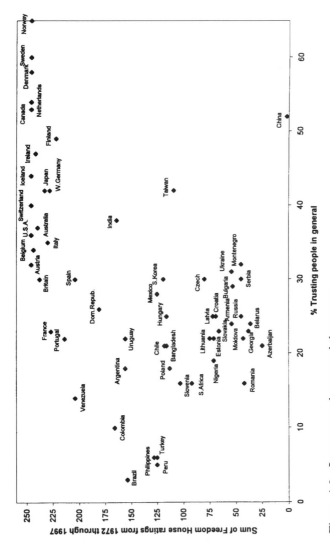

Figure 4.3   Interpersonal trust and democracy

Vertical axis is the sum of the Civil Liberties and Political Rights scores assigned to each country by Freedom House in the years from 1972 to 1997 (ratings not available for 1973, 1975 and 1977). On each of these scales, 1 is the highest possible score and 7 is the lowest possible score, producing summary scores for these countries ranging from 44 to a maximum of 288. In order to reverse polarity so that high scores indicate high levels of political rights and civil liberties, these sums were subtracted from 290, producing a new index ranging from 2 to 246. Interpersonal trust data are from latest available World Values Survey (see footnote 1). r = 0.50, significant at 0.0000 level.

publics. The relative weakness of the "civic culture" in Germany and Italy presumably contributed to the failure of democracy in those societies in the period before World War II.

Testing these ideas in a broader cross-national context, Inglehart (1990) found that interpersonal trust and related cultural orientations were strongly linked with both economic development and with stable democracy. He emphasized, however, that culture is a variable, not a constant. Though cultural characteristics tend to change slowly, they can and do change. Thus, while south Italians were still markedly less trusting than north Italians in 1990, and the Italian public still had lower levels of interpersonal trust than the publics of most democracies, levels of trust had gradually risen in Italy.

As the classic literature on political culture implied (but could not demonstrate empirically, because it was based on a handful of cases), trust is linked with the flourishing of democratic institutions. The World Values Survey data reveal a strong positive correlation between interpersonal trust and the functioning of democratic institutions throughout the world, as Figure 4.3 demonstrates. The vertical axis of this figure reflects the sum of the civil liberties and political rights scores assigned to each country by Freedom House in the years from 1972 to 1997. The countries included here range from long-established stable democracies to authoritarian states and societies in which democratic institutions have just been established – and may or may not survive.

The overall pattern in Figure 4.3 confirms theoretical expectations that have never before been tested against so broad a data base. Levels of interpersonal trust among mass publics are closely linked with a society's level of democracy during the period from 1972 to 1997. The overall correlation is 0.50, and is significant at a very high level. In most stable democracies, at least 35 percent of the public expresses the opinion that "most people can be trusted." In almost all of the nondemocratic societies or those that have only recently started to democratize, interpersonal-trust levels fall below this level.[2]

***

[2] The 1995 World Values Survey, which was carried out in China by Gallup-China, found a surprisingly high level of interpersonal trust (higher than in any other nondemocratic society). Consequently, we checked the results against other national surveys carried out in China, using the same question. An October 1993 survey of urban China carried out for Ichiro Miyake and Kazufumi Manabe by the Institute for Public Opinion Research of the People's University of China, with an N of 1,920, also shows higher levels of interpersonal trust in China than in any other nondemocratic or newly democratic society (see Manabe 1995). Moreover, the 1990 World Values Survey, which was carried out by still another organization (China Statistical Information Center), also shows a similar level of interpersonal trust. This supports the broader finding that interpersonal trust tends to be high in Confucian-influenced societies.

It seems likely that democratic institutions are conducive to interpersonal trust, as well as trust being conducive to democracy. We do not have the long time-series data base that would be needed to sort out the causal linkages between culture and institutions. But there is no reason simply to assume that institutions determine culture, rather than the other way around. We suspect that culture and social structure tend to have a mutually supportive relationship in any stable social system. The available evidence cannot conclusively determine the causal direction, but it does demonstrate that culture and political institutions tend to go together, with trust and stable democracy being closely linked as the political-culture literature has long argued.

Stable democracy and legitimacy

In recent years, formerly authoritarian regimes from East Asia to Central Europe and the former Soviet Union have held their first free elections. But it is one thing to adopt formal democracy and another thing to attain stable democracy. Immediately after World War I, a number of new democracies were established, many of which did not survive the stresses of the interwar era. The most tragic and fateful case was that of Germany.

The Weimar Republic collapsed in the face of economic difficulties because it lacked legitimacy and because an authoritarian political culture persisted. But culture is a variable, not a constant. It can change gradually, as the history of Germany after World War II demonstrates. Democracy slowly established roots among the German people after 1945 (Boynton and Loewenberg 1973; Baker, Dalton, and Hildebrandt 1981). By the 1980s, West Germany had become a stable democracy.

Weimar Germany never had a chance to develop this kind of legitimacy. Associated with defeat from its start, it soon faced the hyperinflation of the 1920s. It was unable to maintain internal order and finally collapsed under the impact of the Great Depression in the 1930s. Several decades later, the Bonn regime did develop legitimacy, but it did so gradually. Throughout the first decade of its existence, a large proportion of the German public continued to agree with the statement that "the Nazi regime was a good idea, badly carried out." As late as 1956, a plurality of the West German public still rated Hitler as one of Germany's greatest statesmen; 1967 was the first year in which an absolute majority of respondents rejected that claim (Conradt 1989: 51–52).

Democratic institutions gradually won acceptance. At first, this acceptance was based on the postwar economic miracle; by the late 1950s, the Bonn republic had achieved remarkable economic success. The 1959 *Civic Culture* survey showed that while many British and American citizens expressed pride in their political institutions, few Germans did. But the Germans *did* take pride in their economic success (Almond and Verba 1963). Mass support for the democratic regime in Bonn grew with continued economic achievement, though economic success was not the only reason for its increasing legitimacy. The institutions of the Federal Republic (unlike those of Weimar) maintained domestic order and provided for a peaceful transfer of political power from a hegemonic party to the opposition in the 1960s. By the late 1970s, the Germans were *more* apt to express satisfaction with the way their political system was functioning than were most other West European peoples, including the British. Democracy had finally taken root in German society.

Subjective well-being and legitimacy

Political-economy research deals with similar processes leading to the development of mass support, but it normally has a short-term focus. If the economic cycle has been going well, support for the incumbents increases; if the economy has done poorly, support for the incumbents declines. Support for a democratic regime has similar dynamics but is based on deeper long-term processes. Recent economic success may enhance support for the individuals in office. But if, in the long run, people feel that *life* has been good under a given regime, it gives rise to feelings of diffuse support for that regime. Thus, feelings of overall subjective well-being play a key role in the growth of legitimacy. Legitimacy is, of course, helpful to any regime, but authoritarian systems can survive through coercion. Democratic regimes *must* be legitimate in the eyes of their citizens or, like the Weimar Republic, they are likely to collapse.

In preindustrial society, chronic poverty was taken for granted as a normal part of life. But in industrial society, mass publics have come to expect their governments to provide for their well-being. Thus, in industrial society, reasonably high levels of subjective well-being have become a necessary though not sufficient condition for stable democracy: Societies with high levels of subjective well-being *can* function as democracies, though they do not necessarily become democratic unless they also have high levels of trust and other preconditions; societies with low levels of subjective well-being are likely either to have coercive governments or to collapse in the face of mass demands for radical change.

Satisfaction with one's life as a whole is one of the best available indicators of subjective well-being, and it has been surveyed regularly in the EuroBarometer studies. A society's prevailing level of subjective well-being is a reasonably stable cultural attribute – with important political consequences. If a society has a high level of subjective well-being, its

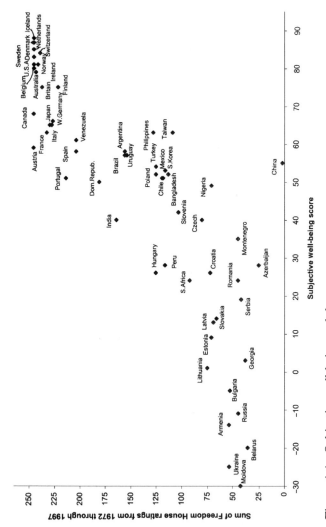

Figure 4.4 Subjective well-being and democracy

Vertical axis is the sum of the Civil Liberties and Political Rights scores assigned to each country by Freedom House in the years from 1972 to 1997 (ratings not available for 1973, 1975 and 1977). On each of these scales, 1 is the highest possible score and 7 is the lowest possible score, producing summary scores for these countries ranging from 44 to a maximum of 288. In order to reverse polarity so that high scores indicate high levels of political rights and civil liberties, these sums were subtracted from 290, producing a new index ranging from 2 to 246. Interpersonal trust data are from latest available World Values Survey (see footnote 1). r = 0.79, significant at 0.0000 level.

citizens feel that their entire way of life is fundamentally good. Their political institutions gain legitimacy by association.

Surprising as it may initially seem, satisfaction with one's *life as a whole* is far more conducive to political legitimacy than is a favorable opinion of the political system itself. Mass satisfaction with the way the *political system* is currently functioning has only a modest linkage with stable democracy, but satisfaction with one's life as a whole is a strong predictor of stable democracy (Inglehart 1990). On reflection, one can readily understand why satisfaction with one's life as a whole is a stronger predictor of stable democracy than is satisfaction with the political system. Politics is a peripheral aspect of most people's lives, and satisfaction with this specific domain can rise or fall overnight. But if one feels that one's *life as a whole* has been going well under democratic institutions, it gives rise to a relatively deep, diffuse, and enduring basis of support for those institutions. Such a regime has built up a capital of mass support that can help it weather bad times. Precisely because overall life satisfaction is deep-rooted and diffuse, it provides a more stable basis of support for a given regime than does political satisfaction.

Figure 4.4 shows the relationship between democracy and subjective well-being in more than 60 societies, using a measure of well-being based on combined responses to questions about life satisfaction and personal happiness.[3] It examines a broader range of societies than ever before, including a number of authoritarian societies and new democracies. As this figure shows, societies characterized by a relatively strong sense of subjective well-being are far likelier to be democracies than societies characterized by a low sense of well-being, confirming earlier findings (Inglehart 1990). The correlation ($r = 0.79$) is remarkably strong. Our interpretation is that, because a sense of subjective well-being is diffuse and deep-rooted, it provides a relatively stable basis of support for the regime.

When people are dissatisfied with politics, they may change the parties in office. When the people of a given society become dissatisfied with their *lives*, they may reject the regime – or even the political community, as in the case of the Soviet Union and Yugoslavia. Only rarely does mass dissatisfaction reach this level. Research on subjective well-being in many

---

[3] Subjective well-being data are from the latest available World Values Survey for the given society (see footnote 2). The subjective well-being index reflects the average between the percentage of the public in each country who (1) describe themselves as "happy" or "very happy" minus the percentage who describe themselves as "not very happy" or "unhappy"; and (2) the percentage placing themselves in the 7–10 range, minus the percentage placing themselves in the 1–4 range on a 10-point scale on which "1" indicates that the person is completely dissatisfied with his/her life as a whole, and "10" indicates that the person is completely satisfied with his/her life as a whole.

countries has virtually always found that far more people describe themselves as "happy" than as "unhappy" and that far more people describe themselves as satisfied with their lives as a whole than as dissatisfied (e.g. Andrews 1986).

The data from the 1990 World Values Survey revealed the lowest levels of subjective well-being that had ever been recorded in research on this subject up to that time. In the surveys carried out in Russia, Belarus, and Bulgaria, as many people described themselves as "unhappy" as "happy," and as many said they were "dissatisfied with their lives as a whole" as said they were "satisfied." This is an alarming finding. Normally, people tend to describe themselves as at least fairly satisfied with their lives as a whole, even in very poor societies. But in 1990, these three societies ranked far below even the poorest countries in this analysis, such as India, Nigeria, or China. Subjective well-being had fallen to unheard-of levels. It seems significant that in all three societies the system of government collapsed during the year after these surveys; in the Soviet case, the political community itself also collapsed, breaking up into successor states.

Subjective well-being levels seem to have fallen throughout the socialist world during the 1980s. Our most reliable evidence comes from Hungary, the only ex-socialist nation in which the World Values Survey was carried out in 1981 as well as 1990. Both happiness and life satisfaction fell by about 20 points from 1981 to 1990: In the former year, Hungary ranked at about where Turkey and Mexico are on Figure 4.4, but by 1990, it had fallen below the level of India. A local survey also was carried out in one region (Tambov oblast) of the Russian republic in 1981, using the World Values Survey questionnaire. Comparing these results with those from the 1990 survey of Russia as a whole suggests that subjective well-being fell even more markedly in Russia than in Hungary.

A large decline in the subjective well-being of a given public is unusual and may portend major changes in the society. The decline in subjective well-being in Hungary and Russia probably was linked with the deepening economic and political crises of the socialist world in the 1980s. In the Soviet case, it is clear that the decline of subjective well-being was not simply a mass reaction to elite-level events, for our findings of unprecedentedly low subjective well-being among the Russian people were registered before the economic and political system broke down in August 1991. The decline of subjective well-being among mass publics *preceded* the collapse of communism and the breakup of the Soviet Union.

This decline in subjective well-being among the peoples of the ex-Soviet Union continued during the 1990s. In the 1990 WVS, subjective well-being among the Russian public was at the zero point on the scale in Figure 4.4. In the 1995–1997 WVS, subjective well-being fell substantially below this level. The peoples of Russia, Armenia, Belarus, Ukraine and Moldova showed the lowest levels of subjective well-being ever recorded. We suspect that under the Weimar Republic the German public also manifested low levels of subjective well-being. It is too soon to say whether the former Soviet Union will follow the path of Weimar or that of Bonn, but it is clear that in 1995–1997 diffuse support was at alarmingly low levels. It would be rash to assume that democracy is safely installed in the former Soviet Union.

Though dependency theory itself has largely been abandoned, the heritage of its effort to discredit political culture still lingers. Recent interpretations of democratization tend to focus on elite bargaining or on economic factors outside the individual, de-emphasizing the role of mass publics. This is one-sided. It is also ironic because democracy is, by its very nature, a system in which mass preferences determine what happens. Mass political culture is certainly not the only factor; but, we argue, it plays a crucial role, particularly in consolidating democracy and enabling it to survive over the long term. It is time to reevaluate the role of political culture. We are now in a better position to do so than ever before, because the World Values Survey data enable us to examine the linkages between mass belief systems and political institutions in a global perspective.

Multivariate analyses

The following multivariate analyses are drawn from Inglehart, 1997 (Chapter 6), using data from more than 40 societies included in the 1990–1991 World Values Survey. Our central claim is that economic development is linked with democracy because it tends to bring social and cultural changes that help democracy emerge and flourish. Moreover, we believe that political culture plays its most crucial role in helping democratic institutions survive over the long run. Other types of factors account for short-term fluctuations in levels of democracy, and situation-specific events, largely at the level of elite politics, tend to determine when a transition to democracy takes place in a given society.[4]

Table 4.3 examines the impact of cultural factors on each of these three aspects of democracy, using ordinary least squares (OLS) multiple-regression analysis. We have already seen that well-being and trust are

[4] Tables 3 and 4 are reproduced from Inglehart 1997 (pages 181 and 183 respectively). A much more extensive analysis, taking many additional variables into account, appears there.

Table 4.3. *Cultural values and democracy: Multiple regression model*

Independent variable	Stability of democracy 1920–1995	Level of democracy 1990	Level of democracy 1995	Change in level 1990–1995
Culture:				
Well-being	0.74**	0.14**	0.05**	−0.09**
	(6.34)	(7.77)	(2.95)	(−4.08)
Trust	82.91**	−1.17	−0.07	1.10
	(4.00)	(−0.35)	(−0.02)	(0.28)
Intercept	−37.13	3.09	8.82	5.73
Adjusted R²	0.76	0.66	0.20	0.33
Number of Cases	41	43	43	43

Note: Entry is unstandardized OLS coefficient.
    Coefficient divided by standard error is in parentheses.
*   Variables significant at 0.05 level
** Variables significant at 0.01 level

.

closely linked with the stability of democratic institutions. Table 4.3 demonstrates that (controlling for their mutual effects) they both have powerful linkages with stable democracy, supporting Inglehart's (1990) findings from the much narrower range of countries in the 1981 World Values Survey that trust and well-being are conducive to stable democracy. The present analysis demonstrates that interpersonal trust and stable democracy are closely linked in a truly global sample. But well-being and trust have quite different relationships with each of our three dependent variables. They explain a very large proportion (76 percent) of the variance in stability of democracy and a large proportion (66 percent) of the variance in levels of democracy in 1990; but their linkage with levels of democracy in 1995 is much weaker (explaining only 20 percent of the variance).

The relatively weak linkage between culture and levels of democracy in 1995 reflects the fact that a major historical change took place from 1989 to 1995: An avalanche of new democracies emerged, partly through the collapse of communism in the former Soviet Union and Eastern Europe, but also through a major wave of democratization in other societies from South Korea to South Africa. Among the 41 independent polities in the 1990 World Values Survey, more than *one-third* began a transition to democracy during this period. Virtually all of these new democracies had much lower levels of well-being and trust than the already established democracies. This greatly weakened the relationship between political culture and democratic institutions in 1995. Whether democratic institutions survive in these new democracies may depend, in

Table 4.4. *Stability of democracy: Multiple regression model*

Independent variable	Model 1.1	Model 1.2	Model 1.3	Model 1.4
Culture:				
Well-being	0.25	—	0.36**	0.44**
	(1.90)		(3.09)	(3.03)
Trust	57.07**	—	47.51**	82.43**
	(3.08)		(2.74)	(4.02)
Social Structure:				
% Service sector	0.51	0.53	—	0.78*
	(1.59)	(1.67)		(2.00)
% Higher education	0.05	0.12	—	0.30
	(0.30)	(0.56)		(1.47)
Economic:				
GNP/capita, 1990	0.15**	0.25**	0.18**	—
($100s)	(3.91)	(6.87)	(5.23)	
Intercept	−44.40	−24.96	−24.02	−66.19
Adjusted R^2	0.86	0.80	0.86	0.81
Number of Cases	41	41	41	41

Note: Dependent variable is the number of years for which democratic institutions
functioned continuously in the given society from 1920 to 1995.
Entry is unstandardized OLS coefficient.
Coefficient divided by standard error is in parentheses.
* Variables significant at 0.05 level
** Variables significant at 0.01 level

part, on the extent to which their publics develop a sense of well-being
and interpersonal trust.

The change in the relationship between these cultural variables and
changes in the level of democracy from 1990 to 1995 is even more dramatic. Subjective well-being shows a strong *negative* linkage with this
variable: The societies that were most likely to shift toward democracy
were those in which the public showed the *lowest* levels of subjective well-
being. Thus, subjective well-being shows strong relationships with all four
dependent variables, but it reverses its role in connection with short-term
changes. While *high* levels of well-being are linked with stable democracy
and high levels of democracy, *low* levels of well-being are linked with
short-term shifts away from authoritarian institutions. This finding supports our interpretation that subjective well-being is crucial to the legitimacy of political institutions: When it is absent, neither democratic nor
authoritarian institutions are likely to endure.

Let us now undertake a more comprehensive analysis of how culture and social structure relate to stable democracy. Table 4.4 shows the results of OLS regression analyses measuring the impact of culture, social structure, and economic development on democratic stability. Model 1.1 includes all three types of independent variables, and it explains fully 86 percent of the variance in the number of years that democratic institutions have functioned consecutively in these 41 societies. When the other variables are taken into account, interpersonal trust and GNP/capita emerge as the key factors, both being significant at well above the 0.01 level. Subjective well-being also seems important, being significant at very near the 0.05 level. Neither occupational structure nor educational level shows significant effects.

When we drop the two cultural variables (in Model 1.2), the proportion of explained variance drops to 0.80 and the impact of economic development rises markedly, taking up most of the slack. But when we drop the two social-structural variables (in Model 1.3), the proportion of explained variance remains unchanged, at 0.86; the cultural and economic variables take up all of the slack, with subjective well-being and interpersonal trust both being significant at above the 0.01 level. Finally, when we drop GNP/capita from the regression (Model 1.4), the proportion of explained variance falls to 0.81; the two cultural variables take up most of the slack, though the percentage in the service sector also rises to the 0.05 level of significance.

Our model is robust, and these analyses indicate that the impact of economic development on stable democracy seems to work mainly through its tendency to bring cultural and (to a lesser degree) social changes. Dropping GNP/capita from the model reduces the explained variance by only five percentage points. Though the linkage between development and democratic stability is very strong, most of its impact seems to pass through the cultural variables (and excluding them reduces the explained variance even more than does excluding GNP/capita).

Burkhart and Lewis-Beck (1994) have argued convincingly that economic development leads to democracy, not the other way around. Building on their analysis, we conclude that the most plausible interpretation of these results is that economic development leads to stable democracy mainly (though not entirely) insofar as it brings changes in political culture and social structure.

The stability of cultural variables

Before concluding, let us take up a basic problem involved in any endeavor to measure the impact of political culture on long-term democratic stability. For a variety of reasons, empirical measures of political culture from most of the world's societies have not been available until quite recently. Consequently, any analysis of culture's impact on long-term stability will necessarily use recent measures to help explain events that took place in earlier years. Thus, the analysis in Table 4.4 uses cultural measures carried out in 1990 to explain democratic stability from 1920 to 1995. Obviously, we would prefer to have cultural measures from 1920 or earlier for this analysis, but such data are not available.

Using a 1990 measure of culture to explain the stability of democracy from 1920 to 1995 depends on the assumption that cultural variables are relatively stable. But this assumption (though fortified by countless anecdotes about the enduring characteristics of given nationalities through the ages) has never been proved empirically. As we will show, there is strong empirical evidence that the cultural characteristics dealt with here *are* relatively stable. We have already seen one piece of this evidence: the fact that, from the Almond and Verba study in 1959 to the present survey in 1990, southern Italy has been characterized by much lower levels of interpersonal trust than northern Italy – a finding that accords perfectly with Putnam's (1993) evidence that the contemporary differences in political performance that he found between northern and southern Italy can be traced to cultural differences that already existed more than a century earlier.

Though we have only fragmentary evidence about the long-term persistence of interpersonal trust, we have much more detailed evidence about another of our key variables. Overall life satisfaction has been measured in the EuroBarometer surveys carried out in the member countries of the European Union every spring and fall from 1973 to the present. As this figure demonstrates, overall life satisfaction shows an impressive degree of cross-national stability in the European Union countries from 1973 to 1995. Though a society's level of subjective well-being can change gradually over time, high or low levels are a relatively stable attribute of given societies. The correlation between a given country's level of life satisfaction at the first time point for which data are available and its level in 1995 (the latest time point for which we have data) is 0.81. For most societies, this covers a 22-year time span and represents a truly impressive level of stability. Furthermore, as detailed inspection of Figure 4.5 demonstrates, this stability maintains itself throughout the period from 1973 to 1995, not just at the two endpoints: In every year for which we have data, the Dutch and the Danes always rank near the top, while the Italians, French, and Portuguese always rank near the bottom.

To evaluate the stability of this basic cultural orientation, let us ask: How does it compare with the stability of that most frequently used of all

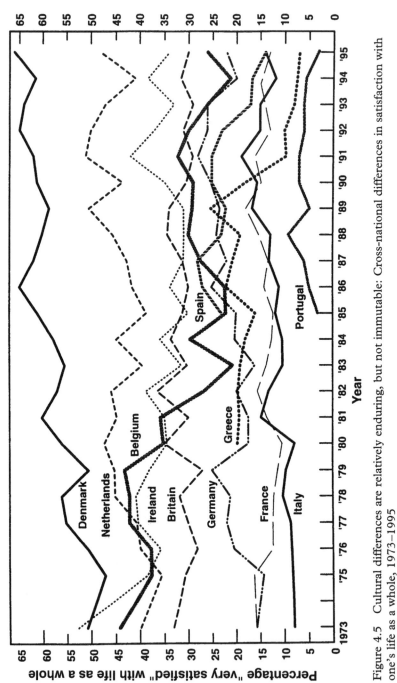

Figure 4.5 Cultural differences are relatively enduring, but not immutable: Cross-national differences in satisfaction with one's life as a whole, 1973–1995

Source: Eurobarometer surveys carried out in each respective year.

economic indicators, per capita GNP? Relative levels of wealth are generally considered very stable. This assumption is well-founded: With few exceptions, the relatively rich nations of 1900 were also the relatively rich nations of 1995, and most of the societies that were relatively poor in 1900 were still relatively poor in 1995. Accordingly, from 1970 to 1990, GNP/capita was relatively stable, showing a correlation of 0.73 among the societies in the 1990 World Values Survey. But – surprising as it may seem to those who view economic data as "hard" and cultural data as "soft" – the cultural indicator shows even *greater* stability over time than does the economic indicator!

The data from the 1981 and 1990 World Values Surveys enable us to test the stability of key cultural characteristics on a broader scale, using data from the 22 societies on five continents included in both surveys. The results are impressive. Our index of subjective well-being (based on overall life satisfaction and reported happiness) shows a correlation of 0.86 between the levels measured in 1981 and in 1990; this is even higher than the 0.81 correlation based on Figure 4.5. Moreover, interpersonal trust as measured in the 1981 survey shows an amazingly high correlation of 0.91 with interpersonal trust in 1990. By comparison, the per capita GNP of these same countries in 1980 shows a correlation of 0.88 with their per capita GNP in 1990; this is slightly higher than one of our two cultural indicators and slightly lower than the other. All of these figures are high. The available evidence indicates that relative levels of interpersonal trust and subjective well-being are attributes of given societies that are every bit as stable as their economic levels.

Figure 4.6 shows the correlations between some key cultural and social indicators and their stability over time. The first finding shown here is that subjective well-being, interpersonal trust, and postmaterialist values go together. They constitute a coherent cultural syndrome, with given societies ranking either high or low on all three of them (the mean intercorrelation being 0.60). This holds true across the 43 societies surveyed in 1990 and across the 22 societies for which we have data at both points in time. Consequently, they can be used to construct an index of pro-democratic political culture. Subjective well-being (based on the mean of the overall life satisfaction ratings and the happiness ratings of the respective publics) shows a 0.90 correlation with this index of "pro-democratic political culture" in the 1981 surveys and a 0.89 correlation with "pro-democratic political culture" in the 1990 surveys. Interpersonal trust also shows strong linkages with this underlying cultural syndrome, with correlations of 0.83 in both the 1981 and 1990 surveys. And the same is true of postmaterialist values, with linkages of 0.83 in the 1981 survey and 0.78 in the 1990 survey. These three orientations form a

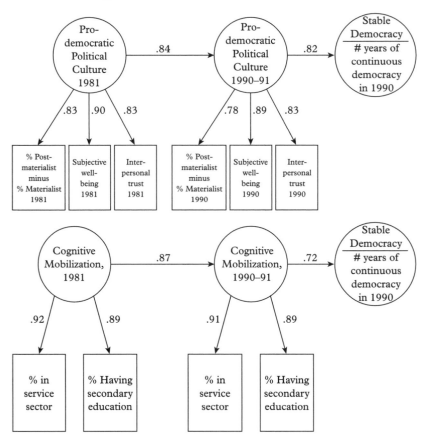

Figure 4.6   Pro-democratic political culture, cognitive mobilization and stable democracy: zero-order correlations
Source: World Bank data and 1981 and 1990–1991 World Values survey data, aggregated to national level. For political culture linkages, N = 22 (cases for which data are available for both 1981 and 1990); for cognitive mobilization linkages, N = 43.

well-integrated cultural syndrome that we refer to as "pro-democratic political culture" because it shows a remarkably strong linkage with stable democracy – even stronger than that of its components.

Let us emphasize that this is a cultural syndrome, not an individual-level worldview. At the individual level, subjective well-being is uncorrelated with postmaterialist values. Individually, postmaterialists do not have higher levels of subjective well-being than materialists, despite their higher income levels. Postmaterialism emerges when a society reaches a

threshold at which additional economic gains no longer produce significant gains in subjective well-being. Conversely, postmaterialism remains
rare until a society attains a fairly high level of subjective well-being, so
the two variables are strongly correlated at the societal level: Across the
43 societies included in the 1990–1991 surveys, r = 0.78, significant at
the 0.0000 level.

The second main finding shown in Figure 4.6 is that the "pro-
democratic political culture" syndrome manifests an impressive degree
of stability over time across these 22 societies; it shows a 0.84 continuity
coefficient from 1981 to 1990. This is almost as high as the continuity
coefficient found with the cognitive-mobilization syndrome based on the
occupational structure and educational levels of the given publics – which
are among the most stable attributes of the social structure of societies.
Key economic variables such as GNP/capita show stability coefficients
similar to these, and growth rates show much lower stability.

Cultural variables are often thought of as vague and ethereal simply
because we usually have only vague, impressionistic *measures* of them.
When measured quantitatively, basic orientations such as these display
impressive stability. This is an important finding, which supports the claim
that cultural variables have an autonomy and momentum of their own.

Conclusion

The foregoing analyses show that interpersonal trust and subjective
well-being are closely linked with stable democracy. Moreover, though
both variables are closely linked with levels of economic development, it
appears that economic development is linked with stable democracy largely
insofar as it produces changes in culture and social structure that support
democracy. When we drop GNP/capita from the regression, the cultural
and structural variables pick up almost all of the slack, explaining nearly
as much of the variance as when GNP/capita is included in the regression, and even more of the variance than is explained when the cultural
variables are dropped and GNP/capita is retained. This finding is all the
more impressive in view of the fact that one generally finds a good deal
more error in the measurement of attitudinal variables than of economic
indicators, which tends to weaken the explanatory power of the former.

Evidence from societies containing more than 70 percent of the world's
population demonstrates that political culture is closely linked with stable
democracy. But the foregoing analysis does not (and cannot) conclusively
demonstrate *why* this true.

Our interpretation is that economic development tends to bring changes
in culture and social structure that are conducive to stable democracy.

An alternative interpretation would be one of institutional determinism. It has been asserted that institutions are exogenous while culture is endogenous, which is another way of saying that institutions determine culture and never the other way around (Skocpol 1982; Jackman and Miller 1996). In the present case, this would assume that the remarkably strong link we have observed between culture and democratic institutions simply reflects the fact that democracy makes people happy and trusting.

The theoretical grounds for believing that a pro-democratic political culture is conducive to democracy are quite straightforward and were discussed at the start of this chapter. Briefly, our reasoning is (1) that if the public experiences high levels of well-being under democratic institutions, it helps legitimate them; and (2) that if the ruling elites trust the opposition, they are far more likely to put their lives in their opponents' hands by turning power over to them in free elections. The reasoning underlying the claim that democracy necessarily produces trust and subjective well-being is both theoretically vague and empirically unsubstantiated. Historical evidence indicates that democracies sometimes succeed and sometimes fail to produce well-being and trust. And survey research indicates that political life plays only a relatively minor role in shaping people's sense of subjective well-being: one's family, home, job, income, and friends all seem to have more impact on one's sense of well-being than does one's assessment of the political system (Andrews and Withey 1976; Campbell, Converse, and Rodgers 1976). To assume that democracy automatically makes people happy is to assume that the tail is wagging the dog: Political life does indeed play a role, but generally a relatively modest one. *If* democracy is accompanied by rising standards of living and an improved quality of life, then subjective well-being will increase, which tends to legitimize democratic institutions. But there is nothing inherent in democratic institutions that ensures this will happen. As we saw in Figure 4.4, more than two decades of living under democratic institutions produced no clear trend toward rising life satisfaction among the publics of the European Union countries. In some countries it rose gradually, and in others it fell. Nor did the past four decades of democracy produce any rise in interpersonal trust in the US. Similarly, the World Values Surveys show that both subjective well-being and interpersonal trust have *fallen* sharply in Russia since it adopted free elections.

A society's level of subjective well-being reflects its entire historical heritage, including economic, political, social, and religious factors. To assume that they are determined by institutions alone is simplistic.

Cultural factors play a crucial role in the long-term survival of democratic institutions. Though the transition to democracy may be initiated by elites (or even imposed by foreigners), its long-term survival is linked with relatively high levels of subjective well-being and interpersonal trust. These factors, in turn, seem to reflect both the economic development and the cultural heritage of given societies. Our findings suggest that cultural factors play a much more crucial role in democracy than the literature of the past two decades indicates. In the long run, democracy is not attained simply by making institutional changes or through clever elite-level maneuvering. Its survival also depends on what ordinary people think and feel.

REFERENCES

Almond, Gabriel and Verba, Sidney, 1963. *The Civic Culture: Political Attitudes and Democracy in Five Nations*, Princeton: Princeton University Press

Andrews, Frank M. (ed.), 1986. *Research on the Quality of Life*, Ann Arbor, Mich.: Survey Research Center, Institute for Social Research

Andrews, Frank M. and Withey, Stephen B., 1976. *Social Indicators of Well-Being in America: Americans' Perceptions of Life Quality*, New York: Plenum Press

Axelrod, Robert M., 1984. *The Evolution of Cooperation*, New York: Basic Books

Baker, Kendall L., Dalton, Russell J., and Hildebrandt, Kai, 1981. *Germany Transformed*, Cambridge, Mass.: Harvard University Press

Banfield, Edward, 1958. *The Moral Basis of a Backward Society*, New York: Free Press

Bollen, Kenneth A. and Jackman, Robert W., 1985. Political democracy and the size distribution of income, *American Sociological Review* 50, 438–457

Bollen, Kenneth A., 1980. Issues in the comparative measurement of political democracy. *American Sociological Review* 45, 370–390

Boynton, G. R. and Loewenberg, Gerhard, 1973. The development of public support for Parliament in Germany, 1951–59. *British Journal of Political Science* 3, 169–189

Burkhart, Ross E. and Lewis-Beck, Michael S., 1994. Comparative democracy: The economic development thesis. *American Political Science Review* 88, 903–910

Campbell, Angus, Converse, Philip E., and Rodgers, Willard L., 1976. *The Quality of American Life: Perceptions, Evaluations, and Satisfactions*, New York: Russell Sage Foundation

Conradt, David P., 1989. *The German Polity*, 4th ed., New York: Longman

Deutsch, Karl W., 1961. Social mobilization and political development. *American Political Science Review* 55, 493–514

Diamond, Larry, Linz, Juan J., and Lipset, Seymour Martin. (eds.), 1989. *Democracy in Developing Countries*, vol. 2, *Africa*; vol. 3, *Asia*; vol. 4, *Latin America*, Boulder, Colo: Lynne Rienner Publishers

Easton, David, 1953. *The Political System: An Inquiry into the State of Political Science*, New York: Knopf

Fukuyama, Francis, 1995. *Trust: The Social Virtues and the Creation of Prosperity*, New York: Free Press

Inglehart, Ronald, 1990. *Culture Shift in Advanced Industrial Society*, Princeton, NJ: Princeton University Press

1997. *Modernization and Postmodernization: Cultural, Economic, and Political Change in 43 Societies*, Princeton, NJ: Princeton University Press

Jackman, Robert W. and Miller, Ross A., 1996. The poverty of political culture. *American Journal of Political Science* 40, 697–716

Jackman, Robert W., 1973. On the relation of economic development to democratic performance. *American Journal of Political Science* 17, 611–621

Lerner, Daniel, 1958. *The Passing of Traditional Society: Modernizing the Middle East*, New York: Free Press

Lipset, Seymour Martin, 1959. Some social requisites of democracy: Economic development and political legitimacy. *American Political Science Review* 53, 69–105

Manabe, Kazufumi, 1995. People's attitudes toward technology and environment in China. *Kwansei Gakuin University Annual Studies*

Muller, Edward N., 1988. Democracy, economic development and income inequality. *American Sociological Review* 53, 50–68

Putnam, Robert, 1993. *Making Democracy Work: Civic Traditions in Modern Italy*, Princeton, NJ: Princeton University Press

Skocpol, Theda, 1982. Bringing the state back in. *Items* 36, 1–8; reprinted 1990, in Roy C. Macridis and Bernard E. Brown (eds.), *Comparative Politics: Notes and Readings*, 7th ed., Pacific Grove, Calif.: Brooks-Cole Publishing

Weber, Max, 1958. *The Protestant Ethic and the Spirit of Capitalism*, Talcott Parsons (trans.), New York: Scribner

5   Democracy and social capital*

Eric M. Uslaner

In August 1996, the Uslaner family took its annual sojourn to the Delaware beaches. On the way, I stopped to buy some fruit at a local stand. There was a lot of fruit and quite a few customers, but no one was minding the store. Instead, a sign directed people to put their money in a locked mailbox and take what they paid for. One of the customers seemed very impressed. He turned to others and said, "How trusting!" I bought my fruit, paid, and felt a bit warmer toward society. A week and a half later, I left a cooler to guard a parking space to load the car to go back to our rental house. When I got back with the car, the space was still there, but the cooler was gone. My wife turned to me and said, "You believe too much in what you write about. You trust people too much."

Replacing the cooler would cost about $15. The savings on the fruit, compared to buying at a neighboring stand under the watchful eye of a salesperson, was just a dollar or two. Was this a bad deal? Would I have been better off not being so trusting?

In the short run, yes. But in the long run, no. Trust in others has important payoffs. It helps to create a vibrant and virtuous community where people know their neighbors, join together in voluntary associations, give of themselves, and commit themselves to moral codes: "Virtuous citizens

* I gratefully acknowledge the support of the General Research Board of the University of Maryland-College Park, the Embassy of Canada, and the Everett McKinley Dirksen Center for the Study of Congressional Leadership. Much of the data I use were obtained from the Inter-University Consortium for Political and Social Research, which is absolved from any responsibility for the arguments in this paper. I appreciate the comments of Sue E. S. Crawford, Keith Dougherty, Morris P. Fiorina, Mark Graber, Jennifer Hochschild, Virginia Hodgkinson, Ted Jelen, Margaret Levi, Joe Oppenheimer, Anita Plotinsky, Edward Queen II, Wendy Rahn, Tara Santmire, Kay Lehman Schlozman, Mark Warren, Raymond Wolfinger, Yael Yishai, and participants in the Conference on Democracy and Trust; conversations with Robert Putnam, Karol Soltan, Jane Mansbridge, John Mueller, Russell Hardin, Ronald Inglehart, Claus Offe; and the clerical assistance of Anne Marie Clark and Yolanda Rich. Matthew Farrelly gave tremendous technical assistance. And Richard Morin and Mario Broussard of *The Washington Post* and Andrew Kohut and Margaret Petrella of the Pew Center for the People and The Press provided key data.

121

are helpful, respectful, and trustful toward one another, even when they differ on matters of substance" (Putnam 1993: 89).

Trust matters because it is part, perhaps the most essential part, of *social capital*. Putnam (1995a), following Coleman (1990: 300), argues that "social capital" refers to features of social organization, such as core values and norms (including social trust) and networks, that facilitate coordination and cooperation for mutual benefit. He argues (Putnam 1993: 169) that social capital is a "moral resource." This, I believe, is critical. I consider social capital to reflect primarily a system of values, especially social trust. Civic networks may enhance social life, but this "social connectedness" (Uslaner 1996a) is distinct from – and secondary to – moral values.

Both social capital and connectedness are important for what they produce. Communities with strong positive values (including trust in others) and ties that bind people to one another will have more powerful norms of generalized reciprocity and cooperation. Trust as a moral resource leads us to look beyond our own kind. It means that we downplay bad experiences and cooperate even when we are not sure that others will oblige (see Uslaner, in press; Whiteley 1996; Wuthnow 1997; and Mansbridge, this volume, pp. 290–307).

Trust makes for a vibrant community in several ways. Trust promotes cooperation (Putnam 1993: 171). It leads people to take active roles in their community, to behave morally, and to compromise. People who trust others aren't quite so ready to dismiss ideas they disagree with. When they can't get what they want, they are willing to listen to the other side. Communities with civic activism and moral behavior, where people give others their due, are more prosperous.

Trust in other people is in shorter supply today than it was in the 1960s, and that is something to worry about. Our society is nastier than it used to be. "In your face" and "dissing" are commonplace, sometimes even preferred, ways of dealing with others. Voices are more shrill in everyday life and in the world of policy-making. It is difficult to reach compromises when people don't respect one another's viewpoints (Uslaner 1993). Fewer people now take part in their communities and fewer trust each other. My task is to show, both theoretically and empirically, why there is a linkage between these two trends.

First, I discuss what trust is. Trust is not of one piece. We may trust those who are most like ourselves, or we may take greater risks for a more general form of trust. Only the latter is a form of social capital that you can invest and hope to reap additional income from that initial down payment. Particularlized trust (of your own kind) entails little risk, but won't make you – and the wider community – either prosperous or vibrant. Generalized trust flourishes in democracies, while particularized trust is more typical of authoritarian and totalitarian societies. Generalized trust makes people more willing to take part in their communities and to endorse moral commitments. Particularized trust makes people withdraw from civic life. There have been parallel declines in civic participation and in social trust.

And then I link the two patterns. I briefly consider arguments from critics who doubt the existence of either trend. And then I move to larger issues again: What is the relationship between trust and democracy? Why has trust declined and what, if anything, can we do about it? There is one solution that is appealing, if not immediately intuitive: People who participate in (or attend) sporting events are more trusting and join more (non-sports) voluntary associations.

The varieties of trust

Trust is a rational gamble that cooperation with others will ultimately pay off, as well as a commitment to "prosocial" behavior even if others don't always reciprocate (Bates 1988). But it is still a wager. If you bet the wrong way, you could lose a lot. You will be the "sucker" in a prisoner's dilemma game. So people rely on their experiences, updating their expectations of others' behavior from their interactions with others (Gauthier 1986: 156; Hardin 1992). If most of the people you meet are trustworthy, trusting others is reasonable. Trusters are more likely to cooperate in prisoner's dilemma games (Deutsch 1960). Fruit stands can operate on the honor system, and people will help each other without demanding, or even expecting, something in return.

If you live in a "mean world" where most people *don't* trust others, it makes sense for you not to invest too much of your social capital. It's a losing proposition and you'll be lucky if you escape with the loss of something so trivial as a cooler. In Montegrano, Sicily, Banfield (1958) found a society where people believed that ". . . any advantage that may be given to another is necessarily at the expense of one's own family. One cannot afford the luxury of charity, which is giving others more than their due, or even justice, which is giving them their due." Daily life in Montegrano is "brutal and senseless" (Banfield 1958: 109), much like Hobbes's "nasty, brutish, and short" existence. All who stand outside the immediate family are "potential enemies," battling for the meager bounty that nature has provided. People seek to protect themselves from the "threat of calamity" (Banfield 1958: 110).

Even Montegranans must trust *somebody*. Everyone – and all species – depend on others. Models from evolutionary biology suggest that reciprocity, which stems from trust, is essential for survival (first) and prosperity (second). Animals compete with each other for food and for status. Without a moral conscience, they have little incentive to share or to help each other. Yet, they do much of the time. Animals rely upon each other to share food and to warn that predators are near. But animals help out only their kin or members of their species (Hamilton 1964: 21; Trivers 1971: 48). That's all they need to do. Such reciprocity will ensure the survival of the species. People in experimental situations are also more likely to reciprocate with friends (Trivers 1971; Masters 1989: 169). Messick and Brewer (1983: 27–28, italics in original) review experiments on cooperation and find that "members of an in-group tend to perceive other in-group members in generally favorable terms, particularly as being *trustworthy, honest, and cooperative.*"

We can minimize our risks by cooperating only with our own kind or our close friends. People will burrow themselves into their own communities and trust only people they know: what Yamigishi and Yamigishi (1994) call "particularized trust." The more dependent we are on our close associates and kin, the more we think of the world in terms of "we" and "they." We won't trust "most people." Reciprocity among one's own kind ensures evolutionary "fitness," in the language of biological models. Particularized trust may suffice for animals, which do not make moral judgments as humans do. It also may work for people who rarely come into contact with people outside their immediate communities. In an interdependent world where people come into contact with strangers, trust in most people – what Yamigishi and Yamigishi (1994) call "generalized trust" – assumes a more important role. If societies are to do more than reproduce themselves, if they are to prosper, their members must interact with others. And they must make the rational gamble that others are trustworthy.

In this more expansive web, particularized trust will be inimical to social capital. We need to go beyond our kin and in-groups to trust a wide range of people, especially those whom we don't know and who are different from us. Charitable contributions exemplify this dilemma. Voluntary giving helps make a community prosperous by reducing poverty and helping the underprivileged to make a fresh start. But if we give only to our own kind, we limit what charity can do. For both ethical and practical reasons, most theological approaches to giving urge people to help strangers as well as compatriots.

For cooperation in a diverse society to emerge as the dominant strategy, a *majority* must be cooperators for the good to dominate over the nasty (Bendor and Swistak 1991). And the more widespread cooperation is, the more prosperous the community will be. Montegranans get trapped in long-term poverty because they trust only their own families. When people withdraw from – or become hostile to – the larger society, they hurt themselves as well as their perceived enemies.

The distinction between generalized and particularized trust helps solve a puzzle that has dogged those of us who believe that social capital is important. Skeptics and critics argue that social connections – and, by implication, trust – don't always serve the public good. The Ku Klux Klan, militia movements, and gangs are voluntary associations. But few would say they contribute to a virtuous society.

The Klan, militia groups, and gangs (among others) do many of the same things that "socially desirable" civic associations do. They have meetings, raise funds, and even may promote social activities. Yet they promote behavior that virtually everybody else considers repugnant. These groups are based on particularized trust: Have faith only in your own kind.; others are out to get you. Only people who trust widely can produce social capital.

Montegranans, as insular in their own way as the militias and the Klan, perpetuate their poverty when they withhold trust from strangers. Particularized trusters keep to themselves. They often develop secret rituals that only members know and in which only members may partake. They don't play in the more encompassing games of the larger society. They withdraw from them and often try to subvert them.

As the Maryland lottery television ads used to say, "You've got to play to win." It is tough to prosper when you aren't willing to take risks. If we could tell who would reciprocate and who wouldn't, we could choose when we wanted to play and when we wanted to withdraw (Frank 1988). Yet, we can't tell who is trustworthy and who is not when we walk down the street. So we often use a risk-averse strategy by trusting only our own kind. Much of our social life revolves around groups we identify with, so we minimize risk when we stick with people we know. Even if we don't know individuals, we often have more faith in people like ourselves. They share our values and may protect us from being exploited by "alien" groups (Greif 1993).

When you play this game, you might protect your species and help it to reproduce, much as animals do. But you won't prosper. Animals don't worry about affluence (or much else). If sharing with kin ensures the survival of the species, that's all to the good. Most people want more. And that means accepting risks, such as dealing with and even trusting strangers. Nations do this when they trade with other nations. Trade creates growth, but it also entails risks. Countries open their markets to countries with different economies and different cultures. Economic nationalists worry that trading can be dangerous. But when people emulate animals and stay with their own kind, they limit what they can achieve for their communities, both materially and morally. At least in market economies, generalized trust promotes economic growth and greater investment (Knack and Keefer 1996).

Similarly, trusting others means tolerating people who are different from ourselves. Particularized trusters, such as religious fundamentalists, worry that exposure to people unlike themselves might corrupt their own sense of values. So activist fundamentalists withdraw from participation in secular organizations. More liberal religous activists, who are more likely to be generalized trusters, become strongly involved in their local communities (Uslaner 1998). A tolerant society will be less rancorous and more open to compromise. It won't be so difficult for such a community to solve collective-action problems that might otherwise fester (Uslaner 1993).

Trust may make a society healthy and wealthy (if not wise). When people trust each other, they are more likely to accommodate others' preferences – and make for a more pleasant society with a better quality of life. Trust may not produce wealth directly. Yet, through tolerance, it will promote trade that in turn leads to greater prosperity.[1]

The two types of trust: measurement

I measure generalized trust by a question posed in a large number of surveys: "Do you believe that most people can be trusted or can't you be too careful in dealing with people?" While some (Smith 1996) have argued that this is not a good question, I disagree. It measures confidence in strangers, just as an indicator of generalized trust ought to do. There are no good questions on particularized trust.[2] The closest I can get with extant data may be measures of in- and out-group identifications. I constructed indices of in-group and out-group affects from feeling thermometers in the 1992 American National Election Study (Uslaner 1996). In- and out-groups are defined by demographic characteristics

---

[1] A study of civic engagement in the Philadelphia area by the Pew Center for The People and The Press (Kohut 1997) asked people a wide variety of trust questions. The overall social trust question scaled with items indicating trust in people that respondents are not particularly close to (including people who work in stores where you shop, people you meet on the street, and neighbors). The social trust measure did not scale with people that respondents are likely to be closer to (people at your church, your co-workers and boss, your family, and people you see at clubs). These results come from a factor analysis with promax (oblique) rotation. I employed 16 measures of trust, yielding a three-dimensional solution.

[2] The World Values Studies ask whether people trust their own families, immigrants, and other nationalities. But these questions don't seem to fit the bill well either theoretically (almost all people trust their own families) or empirically.

or self-identification with social or political groupings. To avoid the problem that some groups may be viewed more favorably by most people, I subtract the means from the calculated scores for each group and then compute an average for in-groups and out-groups.

Particularized trust is not of one piece. There are different reactions to demographic and political groups. Demographic groups include Asian-Americans, blacks, whites, Hispanics, Southerners, Catholics, and Jews. "Political" groups include the poor, liberals, conservatives, union members, feminists, and fundamentalists.[3] How do we interpret these measures? Suppose that whites rate white people more highly than all races do. They would have positive *in-group* scores. This could be a sign of pride. But it more likely points to tribalism and distrust of people unlike yourself. Positive scores for *out-groups* indicate greater tolerance of ideas you don't adhere to. If you are not a fundamentalist but rate adherents highly, you will have positive scores.

The in-group and out-group measures contain some surprises, perhaps reflecting the less-than-ideal measurement strategy, but also indicative of how demographic and political groups have different effects on generalized trust. There are four components of particularized trust: demographic in-groups and out-groups and political in-groups and out-groups. But only two – demographic in-groups and political out-groups – shape generalized trust. Trusters are slightly *more* likely to rate their own political groups highly (11.754) than mistrusters (11.127), a difference that is not significant (p < 0.23, r = 0.018). Trusters are more tolerant of others and are more likely to favor policies that promote civil rights for blacks, women, gays, and other minorities (Rosenberg 1956; Uslaner 1994). Yet they don't necessarily *like* other people any more than mistrusters. The mean scores for demographic out-groups are −1.631 for trusters and −1.739 for mistrusters (p < 0.43, r = 0.004).[4] Even so, we cannot rule out attitudes toward demographic out-groups as a measure of particularized trust. First, generalized and particularized trust, at least as I have measured them, are not simple substitutes for each other.[5] Second, attitudes toward out-groups play a key role in the theoretical treatment of particularized trust. Montegranans are fearful of outsiders. So even though we don't observe a strong relationship between generalized trust and this measure of particularized trust, we should not dismiss

---

[3] Putting the poor in the "political" grouping is a judgment call. One does not choose to become poor as one adopts an ideological or fundamentalist orientation. But being poor is also not an ascriptive characteristic such as race or religion. And it may not be so enduring.

[4] The t-test is one-tailed.

[5] If they were, we would expect a negative correlation between evaluations of demographic in-groups and out-groups. Instead, the correlation is strongly positive (0.522).

its role. As the theory of social capital would expect, people who have little affect for demographic out-groups withdraw from civic activity (see below).

People who see view their own demographic groups positively are not just showing pride. They are sending a message of exclusivity. Trusters rate their own demographic groups far less positively (1.864) than mis-trusters (6.899). They can put faith in others because they are less committed to their own kind – and significantly so ($p < 0.0001$, $r = -0.134$). But trusters are wary of people whom they view as suspect, especially their political opponents. Perhaps they see those on the other side of the political fence as "special interests." And they might view their adversaries as too confrontational – and, hence, not trustworthy. The differences between trusters and non-trusters for political out-groups are sharp ($p < 0.0001$, $r = -0.196$). Trusters have an average score of -5.387, compared to a positive score (0.448) for mistrusters.

Our views of generalized and particularized trust are highly stylized. The former is universally good, the latter unconditionally bad. But this view may be too simplistic. We would certainly be better off if the world had more people who are willing to invest their faith in others. Yet, few people do so unconditionally. Everybody distrusts someone and some groups (Sullivan et al. 1981).

Trust matters

Trust matters – sometimes a lot. Generalized trust in others leads people to join voluntary associations (Putnam 1995a; Brehm and Rahn 1997; Uslaner 1996b). It also makes them more likely to engage in a variety of other collective actions. Consider the range of activities that generalized trusters are more likely to engage in: voting, using the presidential campaign fund checkoff on federal income tax forms, working on community problems, giving to charity, volunteering time, and being willing to serve on a jury.

Trust in others is most important when we most need it. The effects are small for turnout, the checkoff, work on community problems, and charitable contributions. These are "consensual activities." People either (claim to) do them or don't. More than 70 percent of respondents are in the modal category for these consensual activities: 78 percent said that they give to charity, 77.6 percent don't work on a community problem, 76.6 percent said that they vote, and 71.2 percent do not contribute to the presidential campaign fund. There is far less accord on volunteering and serving on a jury: 36.5 percent say that they volunteer (cf. Wuthnow 1991: 20), while 37.1 percent are not willing to serve on a jury.

Almost 65 percent of people are in the modal category for nonconsensual activities, compared to an average of 76 percent for the consensual endeavors. The differences are not always large, but there seems to be a threshold around 70 percent. The correlation between the statistical "effect" for trust in people and the percent in the modal category for the null model is −0.92.[6] Generalized trust matters most on nonconsensual acts.

Particularized trust works to counter the effects of generalized trust. An ecumenical faith in people leads us to take part in a wide variety of collective-action measures. Particularized trust mostly leads people to withdraw from civic life. For the sorts of interactions that bring us into contact with strangers, evaluations of people who are different from ourselves matter mightily. For jury service and volunteering, the measures of particularized (demographic) trust have by far the strongest effects of any variables. On giving to charity, particularized trust ranks behind only religion and income. And people who have positive views of demographic out-groups are more likely to vote.

Attitudes toward political groups largely, though not exclusively, shape actions in the political realm. People with negative views of political out-groups are more likely to be mobilized to vote (and to volunteer). But people who have more positive attitudes toward their political opponents are more likely to use the campaign checkoff. The federal funds, after all, benefit both your own side and the opposition.

Trust also shapes moral behavior. Trusters are more likely to say that it is wrong to buy stolen goods, to claim government benefits they are not entitled to, to keep money they are not entitled to, and to fail to make a report after hitting someone's car (Uslaner in press).[7] Trust has no

[6] The "effect" refers to an estimate of the impact of an independent variable in a probit analysis (see Rosenstone and Hansen 1993). Probit permits us to estimate the probability that a person performs an action such as voting (the dependent variable). The effect tells us the impact of a particular independent variable (such as trust). It is defined as the difference in estimated probabilities from the predictor's highest and lowest values, letting other independent variables take their "natural" values. So the impact for trust is estimated by first treating all respondents as mistrusters (trust = 0) and estimating the expected probability of voting (giving to charity, etc.). Then we "pretend" that all respondents have become trusters (trust = 1) and recalculate the mean probabilities. The "effect" is the difference in the mean probabilities.

[7] These are all based on multivariate regression analyses. The pattern of trust is different in Canada and the United Kingdom. In Canada, trust has no effect on seven of the eight measures of moral behavior. Only claiming benefits has a significant impact, and then barely (p < 0.10). In the United Kingdom, trust affects buying stolen goods, joyriding, lying, and keeping money. Trust matters most in Britain for dealings among individuals rather than in one's interaction with the state. For somewhat different approaches to moral behavior, see Knack and Keefer (1996). The former uses aggregate data, the latter the World Values Study survey. Knack and Keefer envision moral values as a second measure of social capital in addition to trust that helps predict economic growth.

significant effect on approval of joyriding, lying in your own interest, cheating on taxes, and avoiding paying a fare on public transportation. On moral behavior, as on collective action, trust has stronger effects when there is less consensus on what is appropriate behavior. The correlation between the statistical effect and the level of consensus on moral behavior is −0.600. This relationship is much weaker for moral behavior than for collective action (it is statistically significant only at $p < 0.06$). The level of consensus is a moderate-to-weak predictor of what is moral behavior. In the United States (though not in Canada or the United Kingdom), what drives attitudes toward morality is the stakes involved. When the effects of doing the wrong thing are greatest, trust matters most. A measure of "big effects" correlates with the impact of trust at −0.92.[8]

Trust matters over a wide range of types of moral behavior and collective action. And there is a clear distinction between generalized and particularized trust. While the effects of social trust on collective action are not always – or even usually – large, they are consistent. No other variable affects as many types of collective action as generalized trust. When we combine multiple measures of participation into a single index, there are even more powerful effects. Beyond education and income, only frequency of prayer clearly trumps trust in other people when we predict public participation in civic and social activities (Uslaner 1996).

Trust plays a key role in creating a vibrant community. So do other measures of social capital: values such as religious ideals and social egalitarianism and ties to one's community – being married, knowing and talking to neighbors, living in the same community for many years, and being a union member. When people trust each other, they are more likely to take an active role in their community. Active and virtuous people overcome collective action problems more readily.

Opting out

When people don't trust each other, they often take potshots at each other. But they may tire of the fray and simply withdraw from active participation. Americans have always been joiners. When Alexis de Tocqueville visited the new nation in the early nineteenth century, he was struck by the vitality of civic life (1945: 109): "As soon as several of the inhabitants of the United States have taken up an opinion or a feeling

---

[8] The measure of "big effects" classifies buying stolen goods, claiming benefits, keeping money, and hitting a car at 1; lying at 0.5; and the other measures at 0. The correlation here is not with probit effects, since the estimates in Uslaner (in press) are regression coefficients. The correlations for the regression coefficients for Britain and Canada are −0.34 and 0.19, respectively.

which they wish to promote in the world, they look out for mutual assistance; and as soon as they have found one another out, they combine. From that moment they are no longer isolated men, but a power seen from afar, whose actions are seen from afar and whose language is listened to." But Americans are no longer so committed to their communities. By a variety of measures, they are withdrawing from civic life.

As Putnam (1995a) and others have noted, civic participation has fallen in a wide range of activities from the 1960s onward. Fewer people vote, write to public officials, work for political parties, attend church or synagogue, belong to labor unions, belong to parent-teachers associations, volunteer their time (Hayge 1991; Brudney 1990), belong to fraternal organizations such as the Lions, Elks, Jaycees, Shriners, or Masons, or simply belong to voluntary organizations.

Why have people withdrawn from social life? Americans have lost faith in each other. Trust in other people is a key factor in many forms of participation. When people trust only their own kind, they withdraw from civic life. I turn next to an analysis of different types of trust and how trust in most people has declined over time. This is the key to why we see a decline in some forms of participation and a stagnation in other forms, even when we expect an *increase*. And then I consider why levels of trust have fallen and what we might do about it.

Where has trust gone?

Americans join fewer groups than they used to, though the drop has not been quite as sharp as we initially thought (Helliwell and Putnam 1996). The trends in social trust track the decline in membership in voluntary associations particularly well (Putnam 1995a, 1995b). Here we have a striking confirmation of a core prediction of the social capital approach. As trust in others falls, so does participation in civic activities. Figure 5.1 documents the decline in trust in other people from the first time the question was asked in a national survey in the United States (1960) to the most recent data point (1995).[9] In 1960, 58 percent of Americans believed that "most people can be trusted." By 1994 and 1995, a bit more than one-third (35 percent) of Americans had faith in their fellow men and women.

---

[9] The sources of the data points are 1960, Civic Culture Study (Almond and Verba 1963); 1964, 1966, 1968, 1974, 1992, American National Election Studies; 1979, Temple University Institute for Survey Research; 1981, World Values Study; 1995, Washington Post/Kaiser Family Foundation/Harvard University survey; and all other years, the General Social Survey. The 1964, 1966, and 1968 ANES surveys exclude the black oversamples. The figures omit people who did not respond.

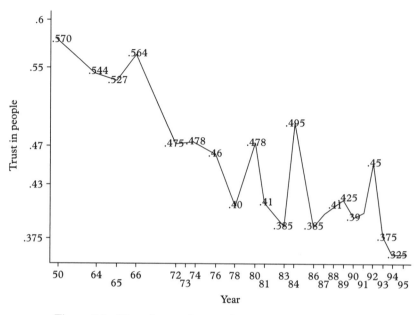

Figure 5.1   Trust in people over time

This decrease in trust produced a double whammy. First, people who trust others are more likely to participate in civic life, so fewer trusters means fewer participants. Second, social capital must be contextual. Individuals aren't lone rangers. The "Lake Wobegon effect" holds that friendly communities encourage participation. Evolutionary models of collective action games posit a threshold effect for contextual effects (Bendor and Swistak 1991). A disease, the spread of a rumor, or social trust must reach a certain critical level before it becomes contagious. When there is a lot of social capital to go around, its effects will be powerful. Even a Scrooge will feel the need to behave better in a world populated by Bob Cratchitts. Contextual trust matters most when it is plentiful. When individual-level social capital declines, there is less contextual trust to go around, and its impact will be smaller (Uslaner 1996).[10]

I estimate models of turnout for 1964 and 1992 from the American National Election Studies to test the impacts of individual-level and con-textual trusts in two eras. In 1964, trust was relatively high. It hovered around the 50 percent mark that Bendor and Swistak (1991) argue is essential to sustain cooperation in collective-action games. By 1992, trust

---

[10] Contextual trust is the mean value of trust for a region. In the ANES data, there are not sufficient cases to derive contextual measures for each state.

had fallen to less than 40 percent, hardly enough to change the Scrooges into Cratchitts.

Social capital proved more important at the individual level and less at the contextual level in 1992 than in 1964. In the more trusting era, all sorts of people voted and participated in other ways, such as joining voluntary organizations. So it didn't matter quite so much whether you were a truster or not in 1964. Individual-level trust did not have a significant impact on turnout.[11] By 1992, trust mattered; it was a significant predictor of turnout ($p < 0.05$). In an era with less social capital, trusters were more likely to participate than mistrusters When fewer people have faith in each other, trust becomes a more valuable resource in creating a civic community.

Contextual trust shows just the opposite pattern. In the more trusting environment of the 1960s, the goodwill of the Lake Wobegon effect went further than it did in the 1990s, when there was less trust in others to go around. In 1964, contextual trust in people boosted turnout by 18 percent. Its significance level was second only to interest in the campaign. By 1992, the significance level was less than half its 1964 rate, and the effect dropped by almost two-thirds. Now people living in the most trusting region were only 6 percent more likely to vote than those in the least trusting section. By the 1990s, social capital was not abundant enough to become contagious.

This same logic is likely to apply to other types of participation that depend more on social capital. Joining voluntary associations follows a similar path: Individual trust matters more when there is less social capital, while contextual trust counts more when people have greater faith in each other.[12] As we have both argued, then, the aggregate trends in trust in other people do more than track declining participation. They explain participation at the individual level as well.

A slippery slope or a seesaw?

Wait a minute. Are we explaining something that didn't happen? Are we making too much of Sherlock Holmes' dog that didn't bark. Perhaps there was no dog. Some observers look at the evidence differently. They argue that there has been no overall decline in many types of public participation, especially membership in voluntary associations. If Tocqueville came back to the contemporary United States, he would see a civic vitality that rivaled that of the early nineteenth century (Greeley 1996; Lemann

---

[11] Trust even had the wrong sign in 1964!
[12] I reported these results in an earlier version of "Faith, Hope, and Charity."

1996; Schudson 1996). Others see a more modest decline in interpersonal trust (Smith 1996). So we might be explaining something that didn't happen by something that barely happened.

First, trust. Smith (1996) notes that the General Social Survey question on trust was sometimes asked after questions about life satisfaction and sometimes asked after queries on crime, ideology, and divorce. The first series always yielded more trusters than the second, sometimes by a lot. In 1989, when the sample was split in two, the first group was almost 14 points more trusting than the second. Most other comparisons yield smaller differences, but the gaps are consistent and average about 8 percent.

Is the decline in trust ephemeral? Have Americans really lost social capital? Or have we all been duped by question-order effects? No. And Smith makes no such claim. Perhaps the fall is smaller than we believed, but it is still real. In *each* question ordering, we see a decline. For the first series, trust fell from 46.8 percent in 1973 to 36.6 percent in 1994. For the second, the decay was less precipitous. We started lower – at 39.7 percent in 1975 – and ended lower at 32.0 percent in 1994. Whatever the question ordering, there was a noticeable and significant decline in trust over time. Moreover, by the end of the time series, the question-order effect seemed to be wearing off. By 1993 (when the difference is 6.1 percent) and 1994 (when the difference is 4.6 percent), we see a convergence in responses regardless of the context.

Now to the dog. It may not bite, but it does bark. First, there is incontrovertible evidence that many types of participation have fallen sharply, as we have already noted. Second, even if membership in voluntary organizations has not plummeted (cf. Helliwell and Putnam 1996), it should have increased sharply. The single best predictor of both social trust and virtually every type of participation is education. As Brody (1978) has argued, there is a puzzle of participation in America: Turnout has declined, but it should have increased because Americans are better educated today than at any point in our history. The story is the same for membership in voluntary organizations.

We see an overall decline in membership in voluntary associations in the General Social Survey data of approximately 3 percent. This is hardly worth the *cri de coeur* of the social-capital movement. But if education has been increasing, membership in voluntary associations should have *increased*. We can estimate the direct and indirect effects of the increases in education on membership in voluntary associations in the two decades since the first General Social Survey in 1972. The direct effect focuses on how increases in education, especially college education, should have led more people to join voluntary associations. The indirect effect examines how education gains should have produced greater interpersonal trust, which in turn shapes membership in voluntary organizations.[13] The increase in education alone from 1972 to 1994 should have produced an average of 0.227 more memberships. The indirect effect – what we would expect if trust had risen with education levels – is an additional 0.065 membership. So the total effect is 0.293 memberships. This may not seem very large absolutely. But relatively it is quite powerful. From 1972 to 1994, the average American belonged to 1.849 organizations. The projected increase is 15.8 percent of the base. If we add these 0.293 memberships to the 1994 average of 1.862, we get 2.155 memberships. So in an era of rising education, voluntary organizations should have had 12.1 percent more members in 1994 than in 1972. The real 3 percent decline and the 12 percent increase that should have happened (the dog that didn't bark) point to a total decline of 15 percent, as Putnam (1995b) originally estimated without controls for education.

Civic action in a "mean world"

Trust, the core component of social capital, plays an important role in all sorts of civic activism and moral behavior. Civic participation – whether voting, membership in voluntary associations, giving to charity, or volunteering time – has fallen (either absolutely or relative to education) in the past two and a half decades. So has interpersonal trust (as well as other measures of social capital; see Putnam 1995a). We can link at least a moderate portion of Americans' withdrawal from civic life to our loss of social capital.[14]

But why have civic participation and trust ebbed? There is a host of contending forces, and we have provided strong evidence to eliminate most of the contenders. Putnam (1995a) exonerates a range of potential culprits for the decline in civic engagement. More women have joined the work force, placing a time crunch on participation, but both male and female participation fell before so many women began working. Increased mobility might account for weaker social bonds, but residential stability and homeownership have *risen* modestly since 1965, and they surely are higher now than during the 1950s, when civic engagement and social connectedness by our measures was definitely higher. Additional changes have transformed the American family since the 1960s: fewer marriages, more divorces, fewer children, and so on. Each of these changes

[13] These calculations use estimates from a probit equation predicting trust and the second stage of a simultaneous equation regression estimation for membership in voluntary associations. Both are reported in Uslaner (1998b).

[14] Even when the individual-level effects of trust are modest, contextual trust often has more powerful effects (Uslaner 1996, 1998b).

might account for some of the slackening of civic engagement, since married parents are generally more socially involved than other people. Another prominent alternative is that we are just too pressed for time in the 1990s (Schor 1991). Both Putnam (1995a) and Uslaner (1996a) show that time pressures don't keep Americans at home. Many of these potential explanations may play a role in shaping trust, but none is the likely root of the problem.

Putnam sees television as the culprit in the decline for both participation and trust. I argue below that we don't trust others as much anymore because we have lost confidence that the future will be better than the past. These are more than two alternative theses. They represent distinct arguments on how social capital works. For Putnam, the causal logic goes like this: People who watch a lot of television have less time to get involved in their communities. They also get a distorted view of the world. Television thus eats up time we would ordinarily spend in our communities; it also makes us less trusting of our fellow citizens and thus less likely to take an active role in working with them. My thesis is that trust reflects a worldview that is shaped in part by experience and in part by deeper values.

Putnam's argument for television goes like this. The single biggest change in the way Americans use their time since the 1960s has been the increase of television viewing (Robinson and Converse 1972). Simultaneously, we have withdrawn from many other forms of social activity. The connection is clear: People who watch a lot of television have neither the time nor the zeal to do much else. We sit home in front of our television sets instead of participating in our communities. And what we see on TV makes us shallow (Meyrowitz 1985).

TV viewing is the great exception to what we might call the participatory syndrome: One type of leisure activity leads to others. People who go camping visit art museums and tend their gardens. Attending sports events or playing sports, making art, going to auto races, camping, gardening, dancing, attending concerts, performing music, hunting and fishing, seeing movies, and using videocassette recorders all go together, in addition to camping and seeing art.[15] But watching television is distinctive. Viewing TV either has no significant relationship to other activities or actually discourages participation.

Television dramas bring us violence and bad guys. The news highlights crime, war, disease, and other plagues. A viewer might reasonably

---

[15] The list comes from the 1993 General Social Survey. There are some negligible relationships and a few negative ones: People who visit art museums are less likely to go to auto races. Hunters and fishermen don't dance as much or go to concerts. But most of the relationships are fairly strong.

think that the real world is cruel as well. Your local community might not be like Bosnia, but it is not Mr. Rogers' neighborhood either. Seventy percent of prime-time programs in 1978 contained violence; more than 90 percent of children's weekend morning programs did as well (Gerbner et al. 1980: 13). If you watch a lot of television, you are likely to believe that the "television world" *is* the real world.

There are clear trends in television viewing and trust in people, and they overlap strikingly. Television became a key part of American life in the 1950s. People born in the 1940s grew up with television, the first generation to become glued to the box. They and succeeding generations watched large amounts of television, particularly as children. They also became much less likely to read newspapers. Far more than pre-television generations, they got a distorted vision of the world, the "mean world." The generations raised on television – and especially the people who watch the most television and read newspapers least often – became the new misanthropes. They are less trusting and join fewer voluntary organizations (Putnam 1995b).

But the TV account does not stand up to a more elaborate statistical analysis. Allowing reciprocal effects among the variables and bringing in what I consider the key reason why trust has declined (optimism for the future), I find no effects for viewing either on trust or on membership in voluntary associations. And these results do not reflect poor measurement of viewing habits. Virtually no type of programming demobilizes people. Some types of programming – news and public broadcasting – led people to become *more* engaged.

The one show with consistent effects that persist despite controls is "Dr. Quinn, Medicine Woman." "Dr. Quinn" isn't a shoot-'em-up drama that makes people think that the real world must also be "mean." It is a heart-wrenching drama about a woman doctor in the "old West" that airs during television's "family hour" when violence is prohibited by federal regulation. The program appeals to people who attend services regularly and born-again Christians, although these variables (and others) don't wipe out the effects of the show. Perhaps people who stay home on Saturday nights to watch the show are less likely to get out and about through group memberships. If "Saturday night is the loneliest night of the week" for regular viewers, this might solve the puzzle (Uslaner 1996b).[16]

Even if television isn't the answer, it may be part of the question. Television viewers are dropouts from civic life. They opt out because they want to be alone. Heavy viewers say that they are frequently bored, don't

---

[16] The estimation procedures are two-stage and three-stage least squares.

see things going their way, and don't want friends around when they are relaxing. If they had extra free time, they wouldn't spend it helping others or improving their intellects. They probably would devote it to more television. If we took away their television sets, they still would be bored and pessimistic.

Trust and optimism

A waning optimism for the future, not television, is the reason for the decline in trust (Uslaner 1998b). Optimism is a world view, not just a summation of life experiences. Optimists believe that other people will be helpful, are tolerant of people from different backgrounds, and value both diversity and independent thinking; they have confidence in their own capacity to shape the world (Rosenberg 1956; Lane 1959: 163–66). Optimists are not worried that others will exploit them. If they take a chance and lose, their upbeat world view leads them to try again. Setbacks are temporary; the next encounter will be more cooperative (Seligman 1991: 4–5). So it makes sense to trust others (Rosenberg 1956). Optimism and pessimism are not primarily reflections of how well you fare now. They reflect your expectations for the long run, especially for whether life will be better for the next generation. The American dream stresses that tomorrow will be better than today. Optimists believe in it; pessimists don't. And our fundamental optimism and pessimism is set early in our lives. It reflects our values at least as much as our experiences.[17]

Experience matters for trust. How well things are going for you shapes your world view (cf. Hardin 1992). But so do values and family structure (cf. Brehm and Rahn 1997). Trust depends to a large degree on altruism (Mansbridge, chapter 10, this volume; Wuthnow 1997), and this calls forth moral sentiments that may be only weakly related to immediate experience (Uslaner in press).

Optimism leads to generalized trust, which promotes civic activism, which creates a prosperous community, leading to increasing optimism. Pessimistic people trust only their own kind. They withdraw from participation in the larger society, and they never get the benefits of risk-taking. They don't prosper, and their pessimism becomes ever deeper-seated. Optimism stands at the beginning and end of the causal chain. For Putnam, it is only the end product.

---

[17] Coleman's original discussion of social capital cites Glen Loury's usage. Loury formulated social capital as "the set of resources that inhere in family relations and in community social organizations and that are useful for the cognitive or social development of a child" (Coleman 1990: 300).

Optimism and trust are strongly related, but they are not the same thing. It makes little sense to trust others if you are a pessimist (though there are always some people who fit this category). But you *may* be an optimistic distruster, believing that tomorrow might be better than today for *you* because you control your own fate. Though you may not trust others to engage in cooperative behavior, you still may be an optimist. And, across several surveys, there is evidence that (1) there are considerable numbers of optimistic distrusters (but relatively few pessimistic trusters); and (2) optimistic distrusters believe, as do optimistic trusters, that they control their own fate.[18] If the two concepts were simply measuring the same underlying concept, we shouldn't see distrusters who believe that they are masters of their own future (which they expect to be bright).

While optimism and trust are not the same thing, a positive world view lays the foundation for interpersonal trust. When people believe that things are getting better and that they can control their environment, they are likely to adopt cooperative values. When the future looks bright, you can afford to take the gamble that others will be trustworthy. If you are wrong, you will lose a bit, but you can afford it. When things look bleak, you will be more skeptical of others' motivations. There is no guarantee that the future will be better than the past, and each stranger is a competitor for scarce resources. Unconditional trust is foolhardy. Even conditional trust is risky.

So people who have less have a greater incentive to look out for themselves rather than contribute to collective goods – except when things look bright for the future and taking a risk does not seem like such a long shot. But when things look bleak, as in periods of increasing income inequality that have marked contemporary America, trust makes less sense for the downtrodden. First, their proportionate risk is far greater than mine. Second, when the rich get richer and the poor don't get richer, the less well-off may well feel exploited – and not quite so charitable (or trusting) to those who benefit at their expense. During the Great Depression, when most people were suffering, giving others the benefit of the doubt

[18] I found support for this perspective in three surveys: the 1972 American National Election Study, the 1978 Quality of Life Survey, and a 1971 Survey Research Center Pilot Study of Economic Incentives, Values, and Subjective Well-Being in Baltimore and Detroit. In each survey, I created a combined measure of optimism and trust by cross-tabulating interpersonal trust with a dichotomous measure of expectations for the longer-term future (at least five years in the future). For each survey, pessimistic trusters were by far the smallest category among the fourfold classification. Optimistic distrusters strongly resembled optimistic trusters in their overall level of efficacy and belief that they could control their own destiny, while pessimistic trusters had less of a sense of mastery of their own fate. If trust and optimism were the same concept, I should not find this distinction.

was too risky for many. So stores hung out the sign "In God we trust, all others pay cash."

There has been a sharp overall decline in confidence for the future. But for most of our history the belief that tomorrow would be better than today has been paramount. In public opinion polls from the late 1930s to the 1960s, Americans expressed optimism that life would get better. We believed that our children would have a better life than we did. This creed is essential to American culture; it was the promise that guided immigrants to come to a land where streets were paved with gold. By the late 1970s, we had turned sour. Not even during Ronald Reagan's tenure did a majority believe that the next generation would fare better (Uslaner 1993: 76). By 1995, only 10 percent of Americans were "very confident" that life for their children would be better than it has been for them, while 54 percent were "not confident at all" (Kaiser Family Foundation 1996: 22).

Trust and optimism for the future reinforce each other, though the path from optimism to trust is stronger than the other way around. I use four measures of optimism and find that they are powerful determinants of social capital: A person who says that it is still all right to bring a child into the world, who says that the average person is faring better than in the past, who has faith that officials are listening, and who has a lot of confidence in science is 45 percent more likely to be trusting than a pessimist with the opposite attitudes. No other variable comes close to the combined effects of four types of optimism. In contrast, someone who watches 10 hours of television a day is only 4 percent less likely to be a truster than someone who never watches television. Television doesn't produce a "mean world" effect: Someone who watches 10 hours a day is only 4 percent more likely to be a pessimist than a person who doesn't see TV at all.

Social capital and democracy

Some years ago the noted novelist E. M. Forster (1965: 70) gave "Two Cheers for Democracy": "one because it admits variety and two because it permits criticism. Two cheers are quite enough: there is no occasion to give three. Only Love the Beloved Republic deserves that." Perhaps there is a reason for the third cheer. Democratic societies are trusting societies.

The benefits of trust and other forms of social capital are not unconditional. They depend upon a society's environment. We hear much about how developing nations accumulate social capital through rotating credit associations and the like. But credit associations are small-scale attempts to build up trust in a world that could use a good shot in the arm of more social capital. In the grander scheme of things, local efforts to build social capital pale by comparison to the larger political environment. Whatever the current crisis in industrialized societies, including the United States, democracies still outshine autocracies and other despotisms on the social capital ledger. Democracies are more trusting[19] – and trusting countries have a larger share of their citizens joining voluntary associations (Putnam 1995a; Inglehart, chapter 4, this volume).

Only in democracies is trust a rational gamble. When the heavy hand of the state looms over society, it makes little sense to put too much faith in most other people (Levi 1996). A totalitarian state will demand that its citizens conform to rigid rules and will turn one person against another in that quest. Your neighbor may be an agent of the state, so you won't invest heavily in social trust. Even less repressive autocracies have little desire to foster alternative centers of power that we might find in civil societies. In totalitarian societies, it makes little sense to trust anyone but your family and your closest friends. In authoritarian societies, you might trust a somewhat larger circle. But only in democracies – and not even in all of them – will you give your trust to strangers.

Trust works because, like Forster's democracy, it promotes variety and admits criticism. It makes us more comfortable with strangers and more willing to put our trust where we might otherwise not tread. Democracies are breeding grounds for generalized trust and social networks.

Why? Levi (1996) and Muller and Seligson (1994) argue that living in a democracy makes you more trusting. And that seems right. But Inglehart (1988) maintains that a trusting political culture is more conducive to democracy. And that seems right, too. We know that trusting people are more tolerant and acceptant of minority cultures (Uslaner 1994).

The relationship between democracy and social capital appears to be symbiotic. This seems like a chicken-and-egg problem that defies causal ordering.[20] But Inglehart (chapter 4, this volume) presents data (and an argument) that help us sort things out: Democracies can't produce trust, but autocracies will destroy it. So the causal logic seems to look like this: Democracy doesn't depend on trust. In fact, democracy, as Mueller

---

[19] Using aggregated data from the 1990 World Values Studies, supplemented by Latin American data from Muller and Seligson (1994), there is a 0.586 correlation between social trust and the measure of democracy (in 1978) in Ted Robert Gurr's POLITY III data set. I am grateful to Ronald Inglehart for the aggregate World Values Studies scores and to Ted Robert Gurr for the democracy measure.

[20] Muller and Seligson (1994) show that the number of years of continuous democracy from 1900 to 1986 has a more powerful effect on an index of civic culture (including trust) from 1981 to 1986 than the culture index has on the democracy index. But our analysis of the Gurr data set (see note 1) shows no significant effects for trust on change in democracy or for change in democracy on trust. The problem is that we have no measurement of trust (especially for many nations) before the 1980s.

(1996:117–18, italics in original) argues, doesn't seem to depend on much of anything: ". . . democracy is at base a fairly simple thing – even a rather natural one. If people feel something is wrong, they will complain about it. . . . People do not need to be encouraged or coaxed; nor do they first need to be imbued with the democratic spirit or achieve broad literacy or a high degree of development. They will just *do* it."

Constitutional engineers may come in with their democracy machines and change legal structures overnight. They may proclaim their task done and remark how easy it is to produce electoral systems with many (sometimes too many) political parties and a free press. Yet we are still left with cultures of distrust.[21] This logic would produce precisely the pattern that Inglehart observes: Both high and low levels of trust can coexist with democratic governments, but authoritarian states need to destroy civil society to maintain control. The mean level of trust in 1990 among societies that were democratic in 1978 is 0.402. The standard deviation is 0.128. For non-democratic societies, the mean is 0.281 and the standard deviation is 0.097 (see note 19 for the data sources). Democratic societies are all over the lot: In some, barely a quarter of people trusted each other, and in others 60 percent had faith in their fellow citizens.[22] In non-democracies, the range is much narrower: Between 17 and 39 percent of the public are trusters. Yet, you don't need a legacy of trust to become a democracy. By the mid-1990s, virtually every country in this database had become a democracy.[23] Brazil, where less than 10 percent of the people trust each other, and Norway and Sweden, with more than 60 percent trusters, look alike when we tote up the legal ledger.

Can democracy create trust? Inglehart's data, though very limited in time (most new democracies are simply too new), offer little hope that courts of law and a free press are sufficient to (as Israeli hawks say in a different, less trusting, context) "create facts on the ground." Under the best of circumstances, good law enforcement can create compliance. It can't produce trust – certainly not trust based on altruism (Mansbridge, chapter 10, this volume). Most people obey the law because they believe the legal system is fair, not because they fear punishment (Tyler 1990).

---

[21] Mueller's discussion stems from the experience of the former Communist states in Eastern and Central Europe. Yet Inglehart (chapter 4, this volume) shows that these countries have among the least trusting populations. Ironically, Mueller's solution to the problem of civil society is not structural, but the adoption of the norms of honesty that undergird vibrant capitalist states (Mueller 1996: 133). Without a deeply rooted sense of trust, it is difficult to see how these norms will take root in nations with patterns of pessimism fostered by authoritarianism.

[22] This eliminates extremes, taking out the top and bottom 10 percent of cases. I also exclude China, which has a high level of trust, from these calculations.

[23] This is not surprising, since it is easier to conduct survey research in democracies.

Courts can save us from rascals only if there are few rascals. Law-abiding citizens, not rogue outlaws, create constitutions that work. The "honor among thieves" is very limited. And it is easy to see why. Rational agents have no reason to trust institutions. They have every reason to base whatever faith they have on the people who run the structures (Offe, chapter 3, this volume).

Democracy is no guarantee of either trust or a vibrant community. Democracies that are badly divided by ethnic, religious, or racial clashes may be only marginally more trusting than autocracies that are similarly split. Generalized trust can be the engine of a society only where most people are willing to express at least a modicum of faith in strangers. And people are most likely to trust others (and not just their own kind) when they are doing well and expect to do better. If even small losses are very costly, trusting others may be too big a risk (Offe, chapter 3, this volume). A poor person would feel the loss of a cooler far more than I did. Patterson (chapter 6, this volume) shows that people who are less well-off and who have been treated badly by American society (especially blacks) are far less trusting than others.[24] And societies that fare well economically are more trusting (Inglehart, chapter 4, this volume). Prosperity makes people optimistic and optimism breeds trust. Yet, we don't always need prosperity to produce optimism or trust. Things can be *getting better* and people can have a sense that they *can make things better*. This is what optimism is all about, and it can occur even if prosperity seems just around the corner.

In one sense, democracy is all about optimism: the belief that people can make a difference and change the direction of the country when things go awry. In the United States, trust in others increases in presidential election years, perhaps because people look to these contests as opportunities for civic renewal (Rahn, Brehm, and Carlson 1997). Yet, the relationship between democracy and trust is not a simple equation where democracy leads to feelings of optimism and control and then to trust. Democracy can produce a sense of optimism only if people believe that they have a real chance to effect change. In some democracies, there is little opportunity for alternation of parties in power and in others people may not believe that it makes a great deal of difference whether one side or the other wins.

To have a democracy does not mean that you have a well-functioning government. Societies that are badly polarized by class or ethnic divisions

---

[24] In multivariate analysis, the impact of family income on trust is moderate, tempered by education and confidence in the future. But income is one of the strongest determinants of faith in the future, so it has both direct and strong indirect effects on trust (Uslaner 1996a.)

may have democratic constitutions, but they won't work well as democracies. Putnam (1993) got it right when he said that trust *makes democracy work* in northern Italy. It doesn't simply *make democracy*. Generalized trust, for those who can afford the risk, undergirds the attitudes that produce cooperation and prosperity. Particularized trust often seems to be the most rational strategy for those who see the risks of putting too much faith in strangers. But it is ultimately a self-defeating strategy, as Montegranans and Bosnians find out, though one that is tough to extract yourself from. A new constitution, even with all the trappings of democracy, can't turn a low-trusting society into a wealthy one.[25]

Even if democracies don't necessarily produce trusting societies, authoritarian states destroy faith in others. Citizens may or may not exercise much control in democracies, but they have little reason to believe they can control their world at all in *any* authoritarian system. Dictatorships often demand that people inform on each other and even family relationships are not always secure. So you can't take an authoritarian regime, have a small elite succeed in toppling it, and then expect it to work well as a new democracy with a strong foundation of interpersonal trust. There will still be the soft underbelly of pessimism – and, as we see in many new democracies, relatively little respect for the new legal codes guaranteeing civil liberties and other desirable things.

We can create new constitutional formats, but it is not so easy to develop trusting societies. We know little about engineering optimism and that means we don't know much about developing trust and civic engagement over the long haul. But maybe we can take some small steps.

Can we restore social capital?

While I disagree with some of the recent literature on what drives trust and in particular on the causal ordering leading to trust, I agree with Putnam and others that social capital has declined, that participation in civic life also has fallen, that both trends are disturbing, and that they are strongly connected to each other.

What, then, is to be done? Get people involved. So says Putnam (1995a), who argues that participation in civic life can build the trust that leads to further participation. Involved in what? You can't tell people

---

[25] The causal ordering isn't clear, but there are two interesting cross-national correlations using the Gurr democracy measure (see note 2) and the aggregate World Values Study measure of trust. For 42 nations, the correlation between GNP per capita and trust is considerably higher (0.771) than the correlation between GNP per capita and democracy (0.586, cf. note 1).

that they ought to feel shame for not fulfilling their civic duties. That's why they opted out in the first place.

But the right strategy can build a sense of control, which leads to a sense of optimism for the future and replaces particularized trust with general trust in others. This scheme involves a bit of deception. Don't tell people that they need to get their social capital act together. Instead, get them involved in something that seems to have little to do with molding better citizens. Get them to do something they like that has a common purpose that will unite people, rather than set them at each other's throats.

This is the strategy that Muzafer Sherif and his colleagues employed in social experiments (Sherif et al. 1961). They induced deep hostility (particularized trust) among two groups of summer campers. And then they sought to put Humpty Dumpty together again. It wasn't easy. Sherif and his colleagues found the solution through what they call "superordinate tasks." The two groups of campers had to come together to get themselves out of a collective fix. The camp made them ride in same truck on a field trip. When the truck broke down, the two groups were compelled to cooperate to help get it moving. They also found themselves "forced" to cooperate to remove boulders that were blocking the camp's water supply.

The campers did not see these "superordinate tasks" as exercises in building social capital. Instead, they were exigencies of the moment – that just happened to build trust among formerly warring groups. Social capital emerged as a by-product of digging oneself out of a ditch. Rescuing the truck built common interests and a sense of control and ultimately fostered generalized trust among all the campers.

We don't have many opportunities to dig ourselves out of ditches in everyday life. And when we do, there are plenty of opportunities for people low in social capital to opt out. So how do we build trust? Perhaps, as Putnam wryly suggested, by bowling in leagues. People who play sports or who attend sporting events are more trusting. They are also, both directly and indirectly (through increased trust), more likely to join voluntary associations.[26]

Professor Harold Hill sought four decades ago to stem the decline in morals in River City, Iowa, by starting a boys band. He should have started a Little League. No other leisure activity (see the list cited above in the discussion of television) creates interpersonal trust or membership in voluntary organizations in multivariate models. This makes sense. My causal logic goes from values and optimism to trust to membership in

---

[26] These findings stem from a simultaneous equation analysis by Uslaner from the 1987 General Social Survey.

voluntary organizations – and not the other way around (in contrast to Putnam 1993, 1995a; and Brehm and Rahn 1997). As Levi (1996) argues, it is arguable whether choral societies or other voluntary associations should produce more social capital (trust). If you put a bunch of misanthropes in a room and have them sing, they will still be Scrooges (and they may sound sour notes). The linkage between voluntary associations and trust is likely the other way around: Trusting people show up in choral societies (and other organizations), and there is substantial evidence for this (Uslaner 1998b). Contra Frost, good neighbors make good fences. A fence (or any other institution) cannot build trust (Offe, this volume).

Yet, sports are different. Sports build social capital because they build self-confidence and teach respect for rules. Student athletes – at least at Ivy League institutions – have wider social networks that permit them to "work toward common goals" (Cantor and Prentice 1996: 5). And sports, like another major determinant of trust (education), impart values. People of all backgrounds meet on the playing fields, helping to build the tolerance that is essential for generalized trust.[27] Egalitarian attitudes help create – and may be necessary for – sustained social trust (Putnam 1993: 174; Uslaner 1996). Sports also teach teamwork and respect for rules.

Other leisure activities also teach values. Visiting art museums promotes respect for beauty and the intellect; it is highly correlated with both trust and membership in voluntary associations. But its effects are limited. Visiting art museums has no independent effect on either trust or joining associations once we take education levels into account. When we go to art museums, we see people very much like ourselves. Playing sports widens our horizons in ways that few other leisure activities can. Sports widen our social contact. They spread tolerance and egalitarian values on the sly. People don't play games to make themselves more moral. Morality lessons are a by-product, not the main event, in athletics.

Even people who doubt our state of malaise point to sports. Lemann (1996: 25) notes that US Youth Soccer now has 2.4 million members, twice as many as a decade ago and almost 200 times as many as twenty years ago. But not everything is soccer. Greeley (1996) finds membership in sports groups flat over the more than twenty years of the General Social Survey.

---

[27] US House Speaker Newt Gingrich (R-GA) noted that 1996 Republican vice presidential candidate and former National Football League quarterback Jack Kemp has showered with more blacks than most Republicans have ever met. We have no direct source for this quote, but Mark Shields, a commentator on PBS and CNN, tells the story regularly on the air.

We must recognize that sports can hardly be a cure-all. We offer three notes of caution. First, sports can be competitive – and cutthroat. El Salvador and Nicaragua fought a war in 1969, ignited by a soccer match. Sherif and his colleagues (1961: 111–12) found that competition between hostile teams only exacerbated bad feelings. And playing sports has costs for student athletes, too. They are *less likely* than other students to take part in other extracurricular activities (Cantor and Prentice 1996: 14). For sports to be an effective conveyer of social capital, they must be a pastime. When they become the source of your identity, you retreat into your world of particularized trust. And sports may consume you so that you can't expand your horizons.

Second, we might be confusing the causal direction with trust. Perhaps more trusting people might be more likely to get involved in sports, especially team sports, in the first place. Then we still would face the problem of how we can make people more trusting. I prefer to be agnostic about the direction of causality now, but I cannot rule out the possibility that these results may be ephemeral. We need longitudinal data (that don't seem to exist now) on whether playing sports may increase participation and social trust, especially among the most impressionable: the young. If sports are more than just another place to meet people – if they really do teach values such as fair play and teamwork – perhaps something as simple as (dare we say) midnight basketball (or, even better, baseball in the daylight) might be an effective moral teacher.

Finally, it would be both remarkable and disturbing if something as simple as playing sports – or, even more unlikely, attending sporting events – is the solution to something as profound as declining participation and trust. Social capital is primarily a moral resource. If our declining social capital reflects a moral crisis, the most we can expect from rounding up both young and old into sports leagues is a jump start in restoring trust in others. It can't provide the bolt of electricity that we need to recharge our spirits. The big answer to how we can restore our declining social capital will lie elsewhere, if anywhere.

In the meantime, it might be worthwhile to start small. Perhaps more people playing sports with others – bowling together – might lead to modest increases in trust and to more people participating in other desirable activities. When I look around at my son's soccer meets, I see few coolers that seem to be stolen (or am I too optimistic?).

REFERENCES

Almond, Gabriel and Verba, Sidney, 1963. *The Civic Culture: Political Attitudes and Democracy in Five Nations*, Princeton: Princeton University Press

Banfield, Edward, 1958. *The Moral Basis of a Backward Society*, New York: Free Press

Bates, Robert H., 1988. Contra contractarianism: Some reflections on the new institutionalism. *Politics and Society* 16, June/September, 387–401

Bendor, Jonathan and Swistak, Piotr, 1991. The evolutionary stability of cooperation. Stanford University Business School, mimeo

Brehm, John and Rahn, Wendy, 1997. Individual-level evidence for the causes and consequences of social capital. *American Journal of Political Science* 41, July, 888–1023

Brody, Richard A., 1978. The puzzle of political participation in America, in Anthony King (ed.), *The New American Political System*, Washington: American Enterprise Institute for Public Policy Research, 287–324

Brudney, Jeffrey L., 1990. The availability of volunteers. *Administration and Society* 21, 413–424

Cantor, Nancy E. and Prentice, Deborah A., 1996. The life of the modern-day student-athlete: Opportunities won and lost. Paper prepared for the Princeton Conference on Higher Education, Princeton University, March

Coleman, James S., 1990. *Foundations of Social Theory*, Cambridge, MA: Harvard University Press

Deutsch, Morton, 1960. The effect of motivational orientation upon trust and suspicion. *Human Relations* 13, 123–139

Forster, E. M., 1965. Two cheers for democracy, in *Two Cheers for Democracy*, New York: Harcourt, Brace and World

Frank, Robert H., 1988. *Passions within Reason: The Strategic Role of the Emotions*, New York: W. W. Norton

Gauthier, David P., 1986. *Morals by Agreement*, Oxford: Clarendon Press

Gerbner, George, Gross, Larry, Morgan, Michael, and Signorelli, Nancy, 1980. The "mainstreaming" of America: Violence profile no. 11. *Journal of Communication* 30, Summer, 10–29

Greeley, Andrew, 1996. Reading to someone else: The strange reappearance of civic America. National Opinion Research Center, University of Chicago, unpublished manuscript

Hamilton, W. D., 1964. The genetical evolution of social behavior, II. *Journal of Theoretical Biology* 7, 17–52

Hardin, Russell, 1992. The street level epistemology of trust. *Analyse & Kritik* 14, 152–176

Hayge, Howard V., 1991. Volunteers in the US: Who donates the time? *Monthly Labor Review* 114, February, 17–23

Helliwell, John F. and Putnam, Robert D., 1996. Correction. *PS: Political Science and Politics*, June, 138

Inglehart, Ronald, 1988. The renaissance of political culture. *American Political Science Review* 82, 1203–1230

Kaiser (Henry J.) Family Foundation, 1996. *Why Don't Americans Trust the Government? The Washington Post/Kaiser Family Foundation/Harvard University Survey Project*, Menlo Park, CA

Knack, Stephen and Keefer, Philip, 1996. Does social capital have an economic payoff? A cross-country investigation. American University, unpublished manuscript

Kohut, Andrew, 1997. *Trust and Civic Engagement in Metropolitan Philadelphia: A Case Study*, Washington, DC: Pew Center for The People and The Press

Lane, Robert E., 1959. *Political Life: Why People Get Involved in Politics*, New York: Free Press

Lemann, Nicholas, 1996. Kicking in groups. *The Atlantic Monthly* 277, April, 22–26

Levi, Margaret. 1996. Social and unsocial capital. *Politics and Society* 24, 45–55

Masters, Roger D., 1989. *The Nature of Politics*, New Haven: Yale University Press

Messick, David M. and Brewer, Marilynn B., 1983. Solving social dilemmas: A review, in Ladd Wheeler and Phillip Shaver (eds.), *Review of Personality and Social Psychology*, vol. 4, Beverly Hills, CA: Sage Publications, 11–44

Meyrowitz, Joshua, 1985. *No Sense of Place: The Impact of Electronic Media on Social Behavior*, New York: Oxford University Press

Mueller, John, 1996. Democracy, capitalism, and the end of transition, in Michael Mandelbaum (ed.), *Postcommunism: Four Perspectives*, New York: Council on Foreign Relations Press, 102–167

Muller, Edward N. and Seligson, Mitchell A., 1994. Civic culture and democracy: The question of causal relationships. *American Political Science Review* 88, 635–652

Putnam, Robert, 1993. *Making Democracy Work: Civic Traditions in Modern Italy*, Princeton: Princeton University Press

1995a. Bowling alone: America's declining social capital. *Journal of Democracy* 6, January, 65–78

1995b. Tuning in, tuning out: The strange disappearance of social capital in America. *PS: Political Science and Politics*, December, 664–683

Rahn, Wendy M., Brehm, John, and Carlson, Neil, 1997. National elections as institutions for generating social capital. Presented at the Annual Meeting of the American Political Science Association, Washington, DC, September

Robinson, John P. and Converse, Philip E., 1972. Social change reflected in the use of time, in Angus Campbell and Philip E. Converse (eds.), *The Human Meaning of Social Change*, New York: Russell Sage, 17–86

Rosenberg, Morris, 1956. Misanthropy and political ideology. *American Sociological Review* 21, 690–695

Rosenstone, Steven J. and Hansen, John Mark, 1993. *Mobilization, Participation, and Democracy in America*, New York: Macmillan

Schor, Juliet B., 1991. *The Overworked American: The Unexpected Decline of Leisure*, New York: Basic Books

Schudson, Michael, 1996. What if civic life didn't die? *American Prospect*, March/April, 17–20

Seligman, Martin E. P., 1991. *Learned Optimism*, New York: Alfred A. Knopf

Sherif, Muzafer, Harvey, O. J., White, B. Jack, Hood, William R., and Sherif, Carolyn W., 1961. *Intergroup Conflict and Cooperation: The Robbers Cave Experiment*, Norman, OK: Institute of Group Relations, University of Oklahoma

Smith, Tom W., 1996. Remarks and tables prepared for panel on trust at the Annual Meeting of the American Association for Public Opinion Research, Salt Lake City, Utah, June

Sullivan, John L., Piereson, James E., and Marcus, George E., 1982. *Political Tolerance and American Democracy*, Chicago: University of Chicago Press

Tocqueville, Alexis de, 1945. *Democracy in America*, vol. II, Henry Reeve (trans.), New York: Alfred A. Knopf

Trivers, Robert L., 1971. The evolution of reciprocal altruism. *Quarterly Review of Biology* 46, 35–57

Tyler, Tom R., 1990. *Why People Obey the Law*, New Haven: Yale University Press

Uslaner, Eric M., 1993. *The Decline of Comity in Congress*, Ann Arbor, MI: University of Michigan Press

   1994. Trends in comity over time. Paper presented at the Wequassett Workshop on Social Capital and Democracy, Chatham, MA, July

   1996. Faith, hope, and charity: Social capital, trust, and collective action. University of Maryland-College Park, manuscript

   1998a. Volunteering and social capital: How trust and religion shape civic participation in the United States, in Paul Dekker (ed.), *Social Capital and Volunteering* (translated into Dutch), The Hague, the Netherlands: Social and Cultural Planning Bureau

   1998b. Social capital, television, and the 'mean world': Trust, optimism and civic participation. *Political Psychology* 19, 441–468

   Forthcoming. Morality plays: Social capital and moral behavior in Anglo-American democracies, in Jan van Deth, Marco Maraffi, Kenneth Newton, and Paul Whiteley (eds.), *Social Capital in European Democracy*, London: Routledge

Whiteley, Paul F., forthcoming. The origins of social capital, in Kenneth Newton and Paul Whiteley (eds.), *Democracy and Social Capital in Europe*, London: Routledge

Wuthnow, Robert, 1991. *Acts of Compassion: Caring for Others and Helping Ourselves*, Princeton: Princeton University Press

   1997. The role of trust in civic renewal, College Park, MD: National Commission on Civic Renewal, Working Paper No. 1

Yamagishi, Toshio and Yamagishi, Midori, 1994. Trust and commitment in the United States and Japan. *Motivation and Emotion* 18, 129–166

6 Liberty against the democratic state: on the historical and contemporary sources of American distrust

Orlando Patterson

As he contemplates his choices, Dole has been getting shriller, reducing some arguments to buzz words and phrases that sound like they've been culled from market-research groups, and repeating them over and over. "The bottom line is trust," Dole shouted at the Fairfeld County Fair Thursday night. "Who do you trust? Who do you trust? Who do you trust? Who do you trust? Who do you trust? Who do you trust? Who do you trust?" . . . Dole's top economic issue, a 15 percent tax cut, has been similarly distilled. "We believe that the federal government is too big, and it spends too much of your money, your money, your money," the candidate says.(Report on the Dole campaign in *The Boston Globe*, October 12, 1996)

I. Introduction

It is now common knowledge among political scientists and comment-ators that America currently faces what Robert Putnam recently called a crisis of "civic engagement." On nearly all indicators of political involve-ment, it has been found that citizens are either not participating or doing so in alarmingly declining percentages.

"By almost every measure," Putnam (1995a) writes, "Americans' direct engagement in politics and government has fallen steadily over the last generation despite the fact that average levels of education – the best predictor of political participation – have risen sharply throughout this period." This decline, he further argues, is part of a broader erosion of "social capital" in which "virtually all segments of society have been affected by this lessening of social connectedness, and this trend, in turn, is strongly correlated with declining social trust."

On the surface, it is hard to disagree with the statement that civic en-gagement is low in America and is at present declining. I part company with Putnam and his colleagues, however, in four respects. First, it is questionable whether this crisis of civic engagement is as recent a develop-ment as is being claimed. One can find evidence of it as far back as the second half of the nineteenth century.

151

Second, the view that this lack of engagement constitutes a crisis of democracy must be sharply qualified. It is a crisis only if one holds to a particular version of democracy. Implicit in the criticism of the present state of affairs is a commitment to one model of democracy – an important model, to be sure, and one, let me hasten to add, I personally adhere to – but *a* model nonetheless. To the degree that this argument assumes that this is the *only* model of democracy either in general or in the American experience in particular, it is demonstrably groundless.

Third, while it is true that on one important measure of self-reported trust – on which I will have much to say later – there has been a serious erosion over the past quarter of a century, the relationship between this decline and the presumed state of democracy in *fin de siècle* America is not self-evident. There is, indeed, an intimate, even constitutive, relationship between trust and democracy. But this relationship is extremely problematic, and it is simplistic in the extreme to assume any simple bivariate relationship between them.

My fourth disagreement flows from the last. In explaining the decline of civic engagement and trust, Putnam relies almost entirely on corresponding socioeconomic changes during the period of purported crisis, "including the movement of women into the paid labor force, rising geographic mobility, and technological change that is 'privatizing' Americans' leisure-time." As a sociologist, my sympathies obviously lean in this direction, and I too will refer to the social behaviors and structures in which democracy and trust are embedded. But here, again, I differ sharply from Putnam and those sharing his position in two critical respects.

One is that *contemporary* socioeconomic developments must be insufficient in any explanation of the present state of democracy and its relation to the problem of trust. If, as I will argue, the observed decline goes back at least a century, the explanandum at issue obviously cannot be sufficiently explained by social changes peculiar to the past quarter of a century.

The other is that contemporary *socioeconomic* factors, in whatever period, can neither sufficiently nor necessarily explain a problem that originates in the political process itself. There is indeed a relationship between socioeconomic factors and the state of democracy, but these factors, I hope to show, largely mediate a more critical causal relationship, this being the behavior of political actors: more precisely, those political actors who determine the kind of democracy that prevails at any given time and, by their actions, critically – though by no means entirely – direct the course of its development.

My objectives, then, are both negative and positive. My negative objectives are to defend the above criticisms of the present description and critique of democracy advocated by the Putnam school of thought. At the same time, however, I hope to present a more positive argument concerning the nature of democracy and its relationship to trust both in general terms and, more particularly, in America.

In doing so, I will draw on two kinds of work: my studies over the past fifteen years on the historical sociology of freedom in the development of Western society and my analysis of the survey data on aspects of trust and democracy reported by the General Social Survey of the National Opinion Research Center.

II.   On the nature of trust

Trust is the condition in which someone, the trustor, commits without security something to the care of another, the trustee, solely on the basis of the trustor's confidence or faith in the trustee's likelihood of fulfilling his obligation. At its core, the condition involves the joint construction of an obligation in which the trustor assumes a risk and the trustee an obligation to justify the taking of that risk.

James Coleman (1990) joins the preponderance of social scientists working on trust in his claim that conditions of trust belong to a subclass of those involving risk, that trusting behavior always entails the trustor placing something – Coleman calls it a "resource" – at the disposal of the trustee, and that there is always a time lag between the placing of trust and the future action of the trustee. However, while his utility model of trust certainly pertains to a large class of trusting behavior – perhaps the predominant one in capitalist societies – it does not exhaust the set of such behavior.

Coleman's trustor is a rational actor who must decide whether he is going to place trust in another with the prospect of gaining something, his expected utility being the probability of the expected gain less the probability of the expected loss should the trustee fail to meet his obligation. A rational actor will risk trust "if the ratio of the chance of gain to the chance of loss is greater than the ratio of the amount of the potential loss to the amount of the potential gain" (Coleman 1990: 99). The problem with this definition is that it neglects the non-rational aspects of trust that most people have in mind when they use the term. The work of Niklas Luhmann (1988) and others such as Diego Gambetta (1988) address some of these issues.

Niklas Luhmann's distinction between familiarity, trust, and confidence is useful, although he confounds the issue by insisting on calling only one of them trust, whereas all three are trust situations, differentiated by the level of risk and the means by which such risk is minimized. The distinction is best seen as that between trust as an established fact, an assumed condition of social interaction; trust as something that does not exist and has to be constructed, to be risked, to use Laumann's term; and trust as something that has been consciously constructed and institutionalized. It is possible not to trust those with whom one is familiar. But it is also clearly the case that one form of trust is, as Diego Gambetta (1988) notes, the spontaneous by-product of familiarity and friendship. It is clearly an abuse of language to declare that the confidence I have in my brother or my wife is not trust because there is no risk in depending on them.

Finally, confidence is clearly a kind of trust and is not to be distinguished from it. Confidence is trust that has already been established or built. It differs from spontaneous trust in having been constructed by parties of trustors and trustees – sometimes acting in both capacities – but shares with it the absence of the preliminary need to decide whether or not to enter into any kind of trust relationship, whatever the probabilities of gain and loss. When my banker hands me a $100 bill, I do not pause to consider whether I want to enter into a trust relationship with the Treasury Department of the federal government.

The following framework of trust relations will inform the remainder of this analysis. First, I distinguish between direct and indirect or systemic trust. Direct trust, at its most elementary, refers to relations of trust between two persons, but exists also where several persons or a large group risks trust on a single, known person such as a chief executive or an elected official. Indirect trust occurs where the trust relation depends on a third party who may be unknown to the trustor. Second, there is the distinction between personal and impersonal trust, to use the terminology proposed by Susan Shapiro (1987). Unlike personal trust, personal qualities of individuals are not critical with impersonal trust. Instead, trust is "a social relationship in which principals – for whatever reason or state of mind – invest resources, authority, or responsibility in another to act on their behalf for some uncertain future return" (Shapiro 1987: 626). It rests on confidence in institutional arrangements, rather than in the individuals involved in these arrangements. Thus, we entrust our children to schools or a school system rather than a particular teacher, our assets to banks and stockbrokers, our life's savings and entire security in retirement to pension funds, and so on.

These two distinctions yield the following fourfold framework of relations of trust:

(1) Affective trust is the classic trust relation that most people have in mind when they use the term. It usually involves one-on-one relations between persons. All the Trustors know or believe they know the trustee.

Trustors rely on wholly personal criteria in deciding the costs and benefits of entering a relation of trust. Where trust is symmetric – both parties being trustors and trustees – elaborate communities of mutual trust can develop, as Coleman notes, and these tend to be reinforced by norms with strong sanctions.

(2) Intermediary trust relies on personal characteristics, not of the trustor but of the trustee, for estimating the costs and benefits of trusting – basically, personal integrity – and does so through known intermediaries. Coleman's (1990: 180–188) analysis of intermediaries in trust is an excellent exploration of such relations. We have here what he calls a "train of trust." One person, A, trusts another, B, who is trusted by a third, C, who, however, has no relation of trust with A. A and C, however, will trust each other if B acts as an intermediary. Intermediaries in trust may be advisers, such as lobbyists and writers of letters of recommendation; guarantors who, unlike advisers risking only their reputation, risk resources in acting as security for another and stand to lose if the trustee betrays trust; or political leaders who elicit support on the basis of their personal integrity and willingness to act as intermediaries between voters and a state that can only be trusted under their leadership.

Mark Granovetter (1985: 491) has observed that this kind of trust is also intimately linked with distrust, since "the more complete the trust, the greater the potential gain from malfeasance."

This linking of trust and distrust cannot be overstated. One special kind of distrust is sometimes generated as a means of creating trust, as we will see shortly. But distrust can emerge from certain conditions without being associated with any kind of trust. It tends to develop where there is economic insecurity and a limited good or a zero-sum view of the world. This is true even in small, intimate rural societies where everyone knows each other, a point forcefully brought home by students of peasant societies. "Peasant communities," wrote Rogers (1969: 26–28) in his summary of this literature, "are characterized by a mentality of mutual distrust, suspiciousness, and evasiveness in interpersonal relations." Because of the limited-good view of the economy, any success on the part of another is viewed with suspicion. This makes cooperation or any kind of civic or communal engagement almost impossible in such societies, since the basic principle of life is that "the claim of any person to be inspired by public interest should be regarded as fraudulent." We will see later that this association between distrust and economic insecurity and a limited-good view of the world is by no means peculiar to peasants.

(3) The third system of trust is collective involves persons with whom we are in frequent direct contact but with whom we either never develop

personal ties or are rejected as trustworthy. This is one of the most neglected, yet important, bases for the construction of trust in societies. As we will see, it was decisive in the invention of democracy itself and has been of special importance in the development of American democracy. Students of trust have failed to recognize its importance because it is best understood only in dialectical terms.

Let me give a few examples of what may be called the familiar stranger: He is the man from whom we buy our newspaper or subway token every working day; she is the janitor who comes every evening to clean the office; and, to take a dramatic example from my own upbringing in Jamaica, it is the Chinese family that owns the grocery, the only people of their kind living amid an island of Afro-Jamaicans.

How do such persons generate trust? In two seemingly opposed ways. First, there is the kind of trust that is rarely discussed in the literature but that may be the most fundamental of all, the *humanistic*: our trust in each other as fellow human beings. We belong to a single species. Our humanness is what is most important to us, yet we almost always take it for granted. To become aware of ourselves as a unique species and of our humanity as a precious source of trust, we need the contradistinctive other to highlight, by their very difference, our uniqueness as humans and our capacity to trust each other simply on this basis. Human societies have used two kinds of otherness in achieving this objective: the otherness of the gods and the otherness of the stranger.

God's otherness defines humanity's uniqueness, especially in the great world religions. Not only does the contemplation of god's otherness bring to the level of consciousness our humanness, but the constant call in many religions to "trust God" inevitably raises the issue of the degree to which fellow human beings, as human beings, can and should be trusted. And, of course, different religions give different answers, but among the great world religions the inherent brotherhood of the faithful, who are defined potentially as all humanity, contribute to such trust.

The stranger in our midst with whom we are in frequent direct contact also plays this role, as Georg Simmel (1971) brilliantly explored in one of his essays. But, alas, there is another way in which the familiar stranger builds trust, this one far less benign. Here trust is generated among the in-group to which the stranger, the outsider, does not belong. Often the main feature, other than their humanness, that in-group members possess is the fact that they are not the stranger. In this way, ties of solidarity are built up between persons and groups who are otherwise antagonistic in their interests. And with these ties comes a bond of solidarity that is a powerful source of trust. The Jew in the heart of Christendom makes possible a bond of solidarity between lord and serf who are together "we Christians"; the Christian and other infidels in an Islamic society become the contradistinctive source of bonding and trust among "we Muslims" who are otherwise often at each other's throats; the black person in white America makes possible the contradistinctive construction of whiteness as a bond of solidarity between white rich and poor, white immigrant and native; and the Chinese grocer in otherwise all-black rural Jamaica creates a consciousness of blackness in a population that otherwise would take its blackness for granted. We may call this sub-type of collective trust solidaristic.

But note, further, that trust also is created among the other in being rejected by the dominant in-group. Frequently, the trust fashioned by being the outsider is often more constructively used in the economic realm. The financial success of the Jews in Europe, of the Chinese merchant class in Jamaica, of the Indians in East Africa, and of the Koreans in America all spring from the trust generated among them not only in their positive commitment to a common tradition, but also in the solidarity arising from their common rejection. Sometimes, tragically, too much rejection by a dominant out-group and too many centuries of being used as the object of distrust so as to generate trust and unity in other groups lead to the adaptive reaction of strong distrust among the persecuted minority.

(4) Finally, we come to the system of trust that is indirect and impersonal – what has been called "*delegated* trust." It is mainly this kind of trust that Shapiro has in mind in her discussion of impersonal trust. This is what Coleman calls "third-party trust." As with intermediary systems of trust, there is a guarantor acting as an intermediary in a trust transaction, but his personal attributes are usually unknown to most trustors. The classic instance is the formal organization. We impersonally trust or mistrust the businesspersons, bureaucrats, journalists, lawyers, and other officers who operate the large organizations upon which so much of our life and livelihood depend. In general, when we speak of confidence in business and in the broader institutions of modern society, it is to such delegated trust that we refer.

III.   On democracy and trust

The problem of understanding just what we mean when we talk about democracy has been approached in three ways. The first is the wholly prescriptive or stipulative approach favored by all political philosophers and some political scientists. The second approach, favored by most current political scientists, is the positivist one of inferring the nature of democracy from generalizations about actual democracies, using either an ideal-typical approach (democracy being exemplified by the best-known cases) or an aggregative approach (democracy being the average properties of all known cases or a random sample of the present population of democracies). The problem with this approach is that it can never isolate those correlates of observed democracies that are necessary for democracy, only those that are sufficient. What is more, as Barry Holden (1974: 8) points out, such an approach can tell us only how democracy works, not what it is. The approach I employ in my own work is sociohistorical. I draw out the "central tendencies" in the meaning of democracy by first analyzing in depth its genesis, the circumstances under which it first emerged, and then observing over time the dialectics of change in the political processes constructed by ordinary persons engaged in the work of democracy.

What I have found so far is, first, the fact that democracy has always meant to ordinary people some form of power-sharing, some experience, however passive and small, of the collective power that constitutes the state in which they live. Central to the idea of the democratic community is the notion of fraternal equality, of being equal, at the very least in the sense of sharing equally in a common political culture with a common heritage, a common present, and a common destiny.

Second, democracy has always entailed some form of participation in the political life of one's society. Sharing power and participation obviously are closely related, but neither necessarily implies the other. It is possible to have power in a society without sharing in its political life: A powerful foreign lobbyist, a king-making plutocrat who disdains the political process, and the wives or mistresses of powerful men in polities that exclude women are some of the cases in point. On the other hand, it is possible to participate in some way in the political life of a polity without sharing any real power in it, a frequent criticism of modern mass democracies in which poorly informed or symbolically manipulated voters choose between candidates whose nomination they have had little to do with and over whom they later have little control. It is striking that from its birth in the fifth century BC ordinary people have always insisted on the joint occurrence of power-sharing and active participation as essential ingredients in whatever it was they called democracy.

A third element of democracy, which has always been one of its central tendencies, is the commitment to and the strong belief in the notion of *isonomia* or legal equality. One must be careful in describing this tendency for the simple reason that, starting with Athens itself, there has always been wide variation in the meanings and experience of the principle of legal equality. At its most elementary, it means simply the rule of law. But equality of laws, equality before the law, and equality under law are not the same, a distinction discussed with great subtlety by Moses Finley (1973). In late republican Rome, for example, Cicero celebrated the principle and practice of the rule of law – it was he who famously said that we are slaves to the law so that we may be free – but he would have been horrified at the thought of complete equality of persons before the law.

Another central tendency in the usage and practice of Western democracy has been the idea of citizenship, of belonging to a special political community that at once includes and excludes. All democracies are conceived of as establishing a special bond of solidarity over against those who are not members of the political community. All democracies have had special rules determining membership, often based on birth, but also on additional qualifications such as gender, age, ethnicity, and race.

Finally, democracy has always been experienced in the West as part of a wider, composite experience: what is called freedom. Until the end of the eighteenth century – things were to change after that – when people spoke of democracy, they always understood it as an aspect of the thing called "freedom." The idea that democracy can be opposed to freedom is largely a nineteenth-century invention. Democracy, for most of its history, was considered inseparable from the other two notes of a cultural chord with which it made a fundamental triad in the Western experience: personal freedom, the absence of constraint on one's capacity to pursue one's desires; and freedom in the sense of being able to do whatever one desired. That is, one was free to the degree that one had power to do what one pleased, including the exercise of power over oneself – self-determination and personal independence – as well as power over others.

Note, finally, that there is a simple yet powerful coherence in the three notes of the chord of freedom. Power gives it its focus. The three freedoms are merely aspects of the experience of power. One is free, first, to the degree that one is not under the power of another. One is free, second, to the degree that one exercises power over oneself, over others, and over property. And one is free to the degree that one shares in the collective power of the community. Each makes possible and guarantees the other. Without democracy, the other two freedoms are constantly at risk; without the other two freedoms, democracy is empty.

Elsewhere I have argued, in line with a few other scholars (Finley 1959, 1980; Raaflaub 1995), that these ideas emerged in the large-scale societies of ancient Greece not in spite of, but because of, the widespread and constitutive presence of slavery. The first democracy emerged in direct relation to the rise of a large slave population and functional dependence on slavery. Democracy was foremost an emerging bond of solidarity between slavemasters and native Greek freemen, in contradistinction to alien slaves, metics, and excluded Greek women. The foundations of the full-blown, primal democracy that culminated in the reforms of Kleisthenes in 507 BC were laid during the course of the sixth century in the long struggles between elites and masses in which the latter were led by aristocratic renegades known by the abusive elite term "tyrants."

That struggle can be seen as the creation of trust between elites and masses, following the crisis of the late seventh century when trust between them had collapsed to the point of imminent mass revolt, which was checked at the last minute by the reforms of Solon. And that trust was not only made possible by, but constructed from, the common bond that emerged between all free male Greeks born in the polis and the distrusted others: slaves, resident aliens (mainly ex-slaves), barbarians, and women.

From democracy's primal premodern roots and medieval adaptations, three kinds of democracies emerged in the modern West. One was the remarkable reinvention of the primal form itself, based on the modern system of slavery; the second was elite capitalist democracy; and the third was inclusive, pluralist democracy. The first is one of the most astonishing cases on record of history repeating itself – primal democracy in modern dress and color. The second kind of democracy is simply the elites' successful attempt to control the egalitarian tendencies of democracy by monopolizing the reins of power and limiting the power of the vote. The third is the opposing form that sought expansion of the franchise, increase in participation, and representation of all interests in the government of the society.

While all three forms advocate the three notes of freedom, each tends to make one fundamental, playing down the other two. Pluralist democracy emphasizes the idea of freedom as political equality and, under the welfare state, as equality in economic security and social citizenship. Elitist capitalist democracy strongly emphasizes personal liberty as the fundamental freedom, even opposing it to equality and, implicitly, democracy. Modern versions of primal democracy have made the notion of freedom as power – the powerful people, the powerful state, the powerful leader – and honor, both individual and collective, the central note in the chord.

Now the remarkable thing about America's political history is that it is here, and here only, that we find the development of all three modern versions of democracy. The enormous complexity and apparent contradictions of modern American politics spring from the fact that its history can be read as a record of the shifting alignments between these three versions of democracy.

IV. Trust and the development of democracies in America

The American colonies were the first part of the modern world to experience anything approaching the constitutive features of democracy that collapsed with Greece in 322 BC. By the late seventeenth century, the majority of free adult males in colonial British America – somewhere between 50 and 80 percent – had the right to vote and, as such, were counted among "the people," the modern name for the *demos*. In practice, the proportion that could actually vote may have been higher, since the only check on eligibility – beyond gender, age, and slave status – was an oath taken at the voting booth. Unlike ancient Athens, however, political participation rarely engaged more than 50 percent of the electorate (Dinkin 1977, 1982).

Despite the relatively low level of inequality and high literacy rates of the Massachusetts colony with its highly developed town-meeting culture, only between 20 and 30 percent of the electorate voted, although this escalated to nearly 100 percent on special occasions when the issues at stake were of great urgency to all. This sounds remarkably like the pattern that prevails in Massachusetts and other parts of America today. In fact, we see here in the very beginning, political behavior very similar to the civic disengagement decried by political scientists as a peculiarity of the past quarter of a century. Ironically, participation rates ran much higher in the slave South: between 40 and 50 percent of the electorate. The middle colonies of the Delaware Valley fell somewhere in between, with between 20 and 45 percent of the electorate voting regularly.

How do we account for America's extraordinary precocity in the emergence of this central element of democracy? It was prompted by aspects of the colonial situation that all the colonies shared: their stubborn belief that they possessed the liberties of "freeborn Englishmen" and their expansive interpretation of these "liberties"; the assembly system of government established with each new colony and the struggles with the governors over sharing power; the English system of representing localities rather than groups taken to its extreme by the exegesis of the colonial situation; the role of charters and fundamental legal codes that soon evolved into proto-constitutions; and the acceptance and institutionalization of religious toleration, largely out of necessity, but long before this was common practice in Europe (Andrews 1934; Rossiter 1953; Morgan 1988).

The Northern proto-democracies were founded on several systems of trust. One was the affective trust of the small face-to-face community. Another, the intermediary trust of the strong, respected leader. Like all such systems, they were reinforced by strongly sanctioned norms, including excommunication, exile, and burnings at the stake. Related to this, but to be considered separately in view of its enormous independent effects, was a system of humanistic trust based on a strong commitment to shared religious beliefs, to an ideology of duties and obligations to other members of the society based on one's duty to and complete trust in God, and to the notion and practice of a compact of freely consenting citizens (Brown 1968).

It was a form of democracy incorporated in a manner very different from that of ancient Athens or Virginia – not the contradistinctive collective ethnic bond induced by a domestic and barbarian enemy, but the contradistinctive bond of the true believer vs. the misguided. It could be as brutal as Athens in the ferocity of its punishment of those found guilty of sin and selfishness, the Puritan version of hubris. But unlike Greece and the US South, it potentially included all who were willing to choose its ideology and faith. The element of choice and the emphasis on belief and ideology as the basis of citizenship are what mark the Northern colonial democracies as unique for their times. It was their most lasting legacy to the modern system of democracy that emerged after the Revolution.

In the old South, there emerged a fundamentally different kind of democracy, founded on a doulotic social order with radically different conceptions of trust and social obligation. Although he never mentions the ancient parallels to the story he tells, making them all the more telling, Edmund Morgan's (1975) seminal study of Virginia portrays one of the rare instances of history repeating itself in broad sociological and cultural terms – which is, of course, the only way history repeats itself. Morgan (1975: 75) begins with the bold assertion that "the rise of liberty and equality in America had been accompanied by the rise of slavery. That two such seemingly contradictory developments were taking place simultaneously . . . is the central paradox of American history."

To prevent any insurrectionary union of white servants and slaves, racism was deliberately reinforced through legal enactments and strong social sanctions aimed at separating the groups. With the growth of this "screen of racial contempt," there was a general raising of the status of lower-class whites. "Partly because of slavery," Morgan (1975: 344) writes, "they were allowed not only to prosper but also to acquire social, psychological and political advantages that turned the thrust of exploitation away from them and aligned them with their exploiters."

The growth of popular government and of a strong local legislature increasingly opposed to the rule of the colonial governors was all of a piece with this association. The Virginian barons had no fear that the populace would vote in people who would then turn against them. To the contrary, they encouraged populist politics, and it was the "union of freedom and slavery" that made this possible. By the second quarter of the eighteenth century, the basic pattern of Southern freedom and democracy and its supporting ingredients were well in place: a large slave-labor force isolated by racism and strong solidarity among all classes of whites who felt a commonality of interests with the dominant slaveholding elite.[1]

What emerged from this system was the strong conviction that there was no inconsistency between liberty and slavery. As William J. Cooper (1983: 39) notes, "The white southern celebration of liberty always included the freedom to preserve black slavery." In the end, even those elite whites who had misgivings about this paired commitment came around to the view that "slaves were property, and the right to hold property was an integral part of liberty" (Cooper 1983: 35; see also Oakes 1982).

Sooner or later these two forms of democracy had to come together. That fateful bonding happened in the great fraternal slaughter of the common father in the American Revolution.

It was the freest and most powerful of the Southern aristocrats who, in leading the colonies to independence from Britain, became the founding fathers of the new nation. Torn from its Southern context in the common war of independence, the aristocratic ideal of freedom as an inherited quality of the individual person – the honorific version of possessive individualism – fused with the borrowed European notion of natural rights to fashion the distinctly American conception of the individual as a bearer of inalienable rights. Forced to accommodate the Northern notion that all men are equal, covenanted children of God, this honorific ideal of freedom was dramatically transformed and democratized, generating the belief that all men are created equal, legally and politically. Inherited privileges and powers of birth for a few became inalienable rights for many through the simple replacement of the earthly aristocratic father by the law-giving godly creator.

The struggles leading up to the political miracle of 1787 need not be summarized here. It is important to emphasize, however, the equally extraordinary compromises that made the Constitution possible. One was that, for all the glorious rhetoric of equality and fundamental human rights, one-fifth of the nation would remain in slavery. This meant, further, that the Southern version of primal democracy based on the *herrenvolk* system of collective trust would continue for another 170 years – 78 of them

---

[1] On eighteenth-century Virginia, see Brown and Brown (1964).

as a slave system – and would powerfully influence the other two forms of democracy with which it formed alignments from one era to the next. The second major compromise had to do with the expansion of the franchise and the degree to which the egalitarian impulse of democracy would be controlled. The elites of both the South and the North dreaded the specter of uncontrolled democracy, of majority rule in which the masses participated fully. From a concern during the revolutionary era of how to protect the ruled from their rulers, the elites of postrevolutionary America became obsessed with the problem of how to protect the ruling class and other powerful minority interests from the ruled. It is now generally agreed that the revolutionary leaders were on the whole wary, even hostile, to the idea of universal suffrage.

Counteracting this was the stormy emergence during the Jacksonian era of forces in favor of a more inclusive democracy and greater participation by nonelite persons in the electoral and governmental process. This would eventually culminate in the form of pluralist democracy. The process, however, was not a simple linear development; it was extremely messy, contradictory, and, in its use of racism and nativism, quite sordid. It involved the collapse of one party system, the Whigs, and the emergence of another. But the development of America's party system is itself a complex and ideologically convoluted process. In no sense can we identify these parties with permanent commitments to one or another of the evolving forms of democracy, given the frequency of their shifting ideological alignments.

In broad terms, the three competing versions of democracy that began to take shape by the mid-nineteenth century differed in the following ways. The *libertarian* democracy of the north was hostile to majority rule and fearful of the power of the masses. It was extensively inclusive, by which I mean that it was willing to embrace all groups of persons, including Afro-Americans and immigrants, partly due to its commitment to market forces and to its hostility to all forms of constraints on individuals, partly to its more legalistic and universalist conception of citizenship – to some extent a secularized heritage of the Puritan past – but mainly because such broad-based citizenship minimized the possibility of solidarity among the masses. At the same time, it resisted any deepening of citizenship, either by expanding opportunities for participation beyond the vote or by extending the notion of political citizenship and equality to the domain of social security. Indeed, it seized every opportunity to demobilize the citizenry and to emasculate the power of the vote. Two powerful weapons were employed toward this end: the ideology of minimal government accompanied by a demonization of state power and the uniquely American legal doctrine of judicial review.

The ideology of minimal government entailed a historic change in the Western conception of freedom. Until the end of the revolutionary era, the chordal nature of freedom prevailed in America and Europe. It was in the early nineteenth century that the chord of freedom was fragmented and the idea emerged that liberty was potentially in conflict with democracy. In America, there was a swift descent from the revolutionary ideal of freedom being, in good part, active citizenship in a virtuous republican state to the mid-century liberal view of the state as a sinister power, the greatest threat to one's liberty. In short, liberty against the state emerged as one of the central themes in the conservative Northern democratic tradition of America. The state, quite simply, could not be trusted, nor could the institutions it required. It was at best a watchman, a policing guardian of national security and personal liberty, at worst a potential monster under the command of corrupt politicians after "your money, your money, your money."

This was reinforced by – indeed joined to – the principle of judicial review. Through the "due process" and "equal protection" doctrines of the Supreme Court, liberty came to be interpreted as a constitutional limitation on the legislative branch of government. This became so entrenched a principle in American law and commercial life that by the early twentieth century it was hard for Americans to grasp the newness and peculiarly American nature of this legalistic twist on the notion of personal freedom. But as Edward Corwin (1948: 182) notes,

In the Ciceronian-Lockian conception of natural law, liberty and equality are not hostile, but friendly conceptions; and in the Declaration of Independence the same amicable relationship holds. . . . In the legalistic tradition, on which judicial review has operated in the past for the most part, "liberty" and "equality" are, on the other hand, apt to appear as opposite values, the former as the peculiar care of the courts, the latter the peculiar care of the legislature.

Finally, the system of intermediary trust was decisive in the libertarian, democratic strategy. The leader is projected as a man of honor who plays the advisory intermediary role, reluctantly taking on the reins of power as a national self-sacrifice and duty. His personal integrity guarantees he will keep his word to keep the state at bay. This is reinforced by the active promotion of distrust of the political system.

Sooner or later this sustained propaganda against the state was bound to taint democracy itself, for, after all, is not democracy quintessentially an act of political life and an involvement with the state? The success of this propaganda also denigrated political parties, which are essential for any well-working modern democracy. As Kleppner (1982: 150) points out, "A deep-seated ambivalence toward political parties has always been a characteristic of American political culture. In the best of times parties have been viewed simply as necessary evils, and at other times as more evil than necessary."

The fact that one of the contending parties chose the name "Democratic" as its title only intensified the tendency to smear democracy by association. Democracy itself was caught up in partisan politics. To be sure, there were limits to which the opposition could go in this tarring of democracy: The American voter never became so befuddled by antidemocratic propaganda that he or she could not tell the difference between the Democratic Party and democracy. For this reason, Republicans have adopted the alternate strategy of insisting on calling the Democratic Party the "Democrat Party," denying it whatever political benefits might accrue from association with the name – a strategy that goes back to Thomas Dewey in the 1940s and that was used extensively by Newt Gingrich and others in Republican radio advertisements in 1996.

Jacksonian democracy championed the common man and actively encouraged the view that ordinary people could participate in government, politics being "a simple thing." Trust in the nation's political institutions was promoted and the electorate mobilized. While there was a strong attack on monopoly power and privilege, *laissez-faire* was strongly supported. Indeed, the advocates of inclusive, pluralist democracy have always emphasized trust in government and in other public and private institutions as a fundamental prerequisite of a good democracy (Watson 1990; esp. chaps. 2 and 4).

Though there were many admirable features in the Jacksonian system, it remained racist and divisive in many respects. Jackson's Southern background was the filter for many of the region's primal influences. The rabidly racist subsequent history of populist democracy had its origins here. The white republic with its expanded franchise learned the Southern primal trick of exclusive inclusiveness, of uniting and expanding the club of democracy by the exclusion and demonization of certain groups (Foner 1995; Saxton 1990: chap. 6; Roediger 1991: Part 2).

The Southern *herrenvolk* democracy thrived on slavery and after the Reconstruction remained "mired in the defense of a totally segregated society" (Black and Black 1987: 75).[2] It shared with the Northern elite a suspicion of majority rule and mass participation. It continued to use collective systems of mutual trust both to provide political solidarity and to divide and discourage participation in the political system. But it dif-

---

[2] On the origins and operation of the *herrenvolk* system during the nineteenth century, see Fredrickson (1981: chap. 4) and Oakes (1990).

fered radically from its Northern conservative counterpart in its lack of hostility to the state and governmental authorities. What the South loathed was, and remains, not big government but centralized, federal government. On the state and city levels, elites see politics as a means of exercising power, not something to be shunned.

This "quintessentially conservative" system, the former Marxist historian Eugene Genovese (1994: 89) wrote in his recent encomium, has "carried on a romance with the land and 'the folk' which has nearly done them in" and is best captured by a passage from M. E. Bradford (1990: 140): "All our social myths presupposed some version of the corporate life – that man is a social being, fulfilled only in the natural associations built upon common experience, upon the ties of blood and friendship, common enterprise, resistance to common enemies, and a common faith."[3] There may be some truth in these interpretations, but they obscure what has been the central feature of Southern democracy, the fact, as Key (1949: 665) stated forcefully, that the "predominant consideration in the architecture of Southern politics has been to assure locally a subordination of the Negro population and, externally, to block threatened interferences from the outside with these local arrangements."

That it was a system frankly acknowledging hierarchy hardly makes it unique, but that it was one explicitly based on social orders of blood and race certainly places it apart from other forms of modern democracy. For, unlike other corporatist systems such as Franco's Spain or predemocratic South America and Mexico, this was a genuine democracy strongly committed to the view that political legitimacy rests on the consent of the people, although the people is defined in *herrenvolk*, inclusively exclusive terms. Its "modernity" when compared with the primal democracy of Athens inhered not only in its agrarian capitalism but also in its rejection of participatory democracy in favor of a representative system manipulable by an oligarchic elite periodically upset by charismatic, populist gadflies who shift the focus from the normal pattern of mutual affective trust within leadership groups and asymmetric collective trust between groups to Coleman-type intermediary trust often of a charismatic character with all its attendant instability.[4]

And precisely because it was based so heavily on these forms of trust, we could expect a great deal of mistrust in them. The opportunities for malfeasance and betrayal were many and rampant – as is true of all honorific cultures – and persons constantly had to be on the alert for those

---

[3] Cited in Genovese (1994: 3).
[4] For the workings of this system, see the classic study by Key (1949).

who would dishonor their personal obligations. The South was the land of the feud and gun duel par excellence, and it is no accident that today it is the region of the country in which nearly every household is armed to the teeth and there is extreme hostility to any form of gun control (see Nisbett 1996; Franklin 1970; Wyatt-Brown 1982). Add to this the collective distrust of the large black minority and the reactive distrust that must inevitably develop within this alienated group, and one ends up with a system characterized by a chronic propensity to distrust (Black and Black 1987: 80).

When viewed from the broad perspective of the nineteenth century to the present, the history of political participation in American elections casts a rather different light on academic claims of a *recent* decline in trust in government and civic engagement. Paul Kleppner's (1982: 13) work clearly demonstrates one of the great anomalies of American political life:

Since the 1840s aggregate turnout rates display an unmistakable trend: a long-term decline in the general level of voter mobilization. That decline has occurred as the measures of the individual and structural factors that mediate turnout have moved at least as decisively in the direction predicting increased participation.

Beneath this broad trend, Kleppner identifies four great turnout eras in American democratic history in the North and three such eras in the South (see Table 6.1). In the North, there was a great era of citizen mobilization between 1840 and 1900; this was followed by the era of electoral demobilization between 1896 and 1928. Then came the New Deal and a new wave of electoral remobilization between 1930 and 1960, followed by what Kleppner calls the era of "demobilization and disillusionment" between 1964 and the present.

There is no space here to summarize Kleppner's many subtle, empirically informed findings. One of them, however, is especially relevant. While citizens' orientations and social-structural factors are no doubt important in explaining these changes, he shows that participation and political competitiveness were not simply outcomes automatically emerging from structural forces and changing attitudes, but rather "required human intervention to develop concrete institutions capable of mobilizing mass opinion." What is more, these interventions can "offset the impact of socioeconomic inequalities and low education" (Kleppner 1982: 30, 43). Conversely, the declining capability of political parties explains the demobilization eras of the North. And in the South, demobilization was the direct result of sustained efforts to disenfranchise the Afro-American and poor Euro-American citizen body. Martin P. Wattenberg (1990: 86) stresses an important aspect of this process: the growing emphasis on candidate centered politics in presidential elections coming at the direct

Table 6.1. *Nonsouthern turnout eras, 1840–1980*

	X̄	σ	Ȳ =	r²
President				
(1) 1840–1900	74.6	7.65	64.31 + 1.215	0.571
1840–1872	68.7	3.95	70.65 − 0.386	0.071
1872–1900	80.7	4.84	75.05 + 1.259	0.405
(2) 1896–1928	71.9	9.53	86.74 − 2.970	0.728
1896–1916	77.1	6.01	86.57 − 2.708	0.710
(3) 1928–1960	68.2	3.22	67.76 + 0.086	0.005
1928–1940	69.2	2.16	65.74 + 1.380	0.675
(4) 1960–1980	62.6	6.58	74.97 − 3.511	0.996
Off-Year Congress				
(1) 1842–1898	61.7	6.74	52.16 + 1.202	0.635
1842–1870	56.7	4.64	55.99 + 0.170	0.008
1870–1898	66.9	3.21	62.16 + 1.060	0.652
(2) 1896–1926	55.3	10.21	73.27 − 3.986	0.914
1898–1918	59.7	7.28	71.88 − 3.477	0.796
(3) 1926–1958	48.7	5.45	44.78 + 0.789	0.157
1926–1938	49.0	7.45	34.89 + 5.650	0.966
(4) 1962–1978	47.1	5.59	56.93 − 3.259	0.850

Table 6.2. *Southern turnout eras, 1840–1980*

	X̄	σ	Ȳ =	r²
President				
(1) 1840–1900	64.3	7.92	75.60 − 1.324	0.633
1840–1872	68.5	4.10	73.57 − 1.015	0.459
1872–1900	60.1	8.30	73.04 − 2.863	0.712
(2) 1896–1948	28.3	10.18	41.84 − 1.795	0.544
1896–1916	36.4	11.28	53.74 − 4.937	0.669
1896–1928	31.4	11.69	49.74 − 3.653	0.731
(3) 1948–1980	41.9	8.09	29.71 + 2.451	0.687
Off-Year Congress				
(1) 1842–1898	52.1	8.79	60.24 − 1.008	0.263
1842–1870	57.4	7.96	46.15 + 2.514	0.598
1870–1898	49.4	9.30	65.17 − 3.375	0.788
(2) 1898–1946	16.3	8.28	29.69 − 1.905	0.802
1898–1918	23.3	7.05	35.44 − 3.451	0.838
1898–1926	20.1	8.45	35.05 − 3.307	0.918
(3) 1946–1978	21.1	8.00	8.01 + 2.634	0.813

Source: Paul Kleppner, *Who Voted?: The Dynamics of Electoral Turnout, 1870–1980* (New York: Praeger Publishers, 1982), pp. 18–19.

expense of the salience of political parties. "As presidential candidates have increasingly come to assume a much larger share of the spotlight on domestic and foreign policy," he found, "the parties have seen much of their base of support erode. A contest for the electorate's attention has taken place throughout the 1952–1980 period between presidential parties and a series of strong candidates have all contributed to the erosion of the electoral salience of parties." This decline, furthermore, is the end result of a "long-term secular trend," preceding 1952 when electoral data were first systematically collected, and therefore has nothing to do with modern "bowling alone" trends.

It is important to add that the emphasis on candidates at the expense of parties has not meant a strengthening of the system of intermediary trust favored by the leaders of the elitist version of democracy. Thus the two best examples of candidate centered politics – Nixon and Clinton – were, not accidentally, politicians whom the electorate did not personally trust. In fact, there is no relationship between trust in government and the decline of party identification. People have not become more cynical about political parities, but rather more neutral and less partisan (Wattenberg 1990: 71–72). Indeed, it may even be that the shift away from party identification toward candidacy politics has been accompanied by growing cynicism about the moral integrity of politicians.

The peculiar features of the Southern version of democracy made it possible to align with either of the Northern parties, as long as its insistence on the *herrenvolk* use of Afro-Americans and its other cherished "traditions" were tolerated. Just such a compromise accounts for the long alliance of both the pluralist and *herrenvolk* versions of democracy within the embrace of the Democratic Party for most of this century up to the 1960s. That alignment collapsed exactly when the Democratic Party came out in favor of the civil-rights movement. This opened the way for the alliance between the elitist Northern system and the *herrenvolk* South, skillfully forged by Nixon with his so-called "wedge" politics.

V.   Toward a sociology of trust in contemporary America: A reanalysis of the GSS data

In the light of all that has been said above, we may now examine the problem of trust in contemporary America. By contemporary America, I refer to the pattern of politics and society over the past quarter of a century or so, roughly the same period as that covered by Putnam in his discussion of the loss of civic engagement. In examining the problem

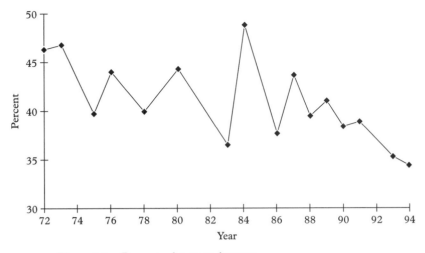

Figure 6.1   Percent who trust, by year

of trust during this period, I will draw mainly on the data base of the General Social Survey.

Trends in trust for selected institutions: 1972–1994

The pattern of change in affective trust over the past quarter of a century is summarized in Figure 6.1, which gives the percent of respondents who answered positively to the question "Can people be trusted?" Overall, trust in general seems to have declined markedly. The oscillations, however, are striking and suggest we must be careful in interpreting the underlying trend. Note that less than half of the population at the start of the period already declared that others could not be trusted. The fact that levels of trust peaked during the heady economic days of the Reagan presidency strongly suggests trust is closely related to perceptions of economic growth.

Figures 6.2 and 6.3 summarize changes in delegated trust, that is, the confidence level of respondents in the federal executive and legislative branches of government. The declines in confidence are striking, going from 29 percent of those saying they had "a great deal" of confidence in the executive and 19 percent responding that they had "hardly any" in 1973, to the respective 1994 levels of 11.5 and 36 percent. This decline of confidence in the executive branch, however, is not as great a *change* as would seem at first sight, as I will explain shortly.

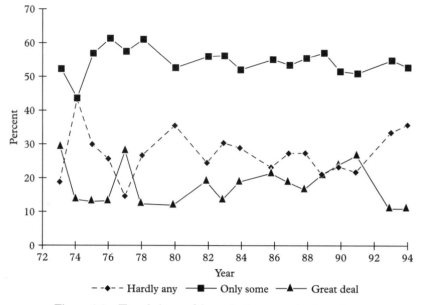

Figure 6.2   Trends in confidence in the executive branch

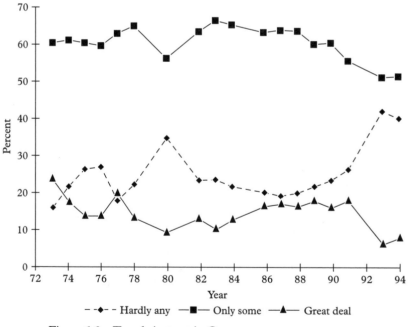

Figure 6.3   Trends in trust in Congress

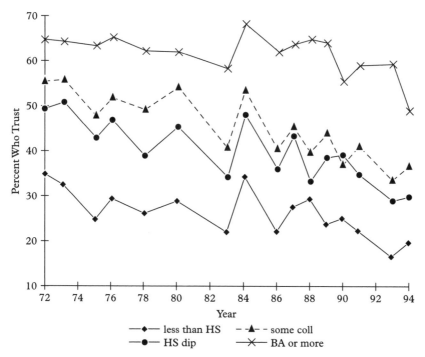

Figure 6.4   Trends in affective trust, by education

The decline in confidence in the legislative branch is seemingly much greater, down from 24 percent of those saying they had "a great deal" of confidence in Congress in 1973 to 8 percent saying the same in 1994. Even more dismaying is the increase in those responding that they had "hardly any" confidence in Congress: from 16 percent in 1973 to 40 percent in 1994 when the Republicans took over the body for the first time in four decades. These figures certainly seem to show a low level of confidence in government. The question with which we are concerned, however, is just how new and important a change these figures represent. Do they indicate some chronic new illness in the democratic process? I think not, for reasons to be discussed in the subsequent sections.

Figure 6.4 demonstrates the close relationship between levels of education and trust. During the entire period, the more educated are more trusting than the less educated. Note, however, that for the three lower educational groups the trend has turned upward from 1993, almost exactly in tandem with the upturn in the economy.

Women are slightly less trusting than men, sometimes significantly more so, as Figure 6.5 shows. We can read in this one source of the much-

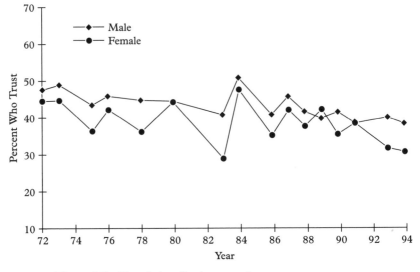

Figure 6.5   Trends in affective trust, by sex

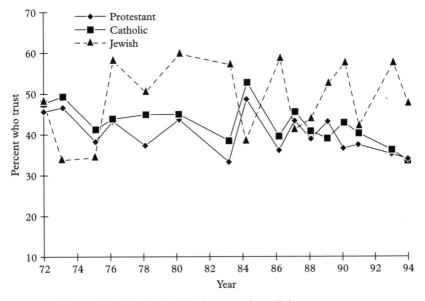

Figure 6.6   Trends in affective trust, by religion
Source: General Social Survey, 1972–1994

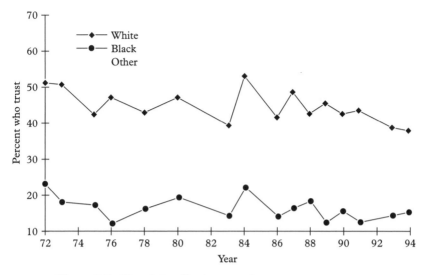

Figure 6.7   Trends in affective trust, by race
Source: General Social Survey, 1972–1994

commented-on gender gap. It strongly suggests that a candidate who can elicit empathic trust will have an advantage over one who cannot, a gap that Clinton effectively exploited after the debacle of 1994.

Figure 6.6 indicates there is relatively little difference between religious groups, except for Jews, who are among the most trusting groups in the population. The racial contrast, on the other hand, is striking. Afro-Americans are among the least trusting groups in America, as Figure 6.7 shows. I will have more to say on this later.

Finally, Figure 6.8 indicates there is more distrust in the South than the North, a finding consistent with our discussion of the differences between the *herrenvolk* democracy of the South and the other two versions of democracy.

In explaining these developments, we must distinguish between two sets of determining factors: cyclical and periodic variables, on the one hand, and structural determinants, on the other. Cyclical and periodic determinants are those factors that arise from long-term changes in the society and polity, and one may further subdivide them into three types: the purely political, the economic, and the demographic. Political effects refer to the present alignment of inherited political forces and the nature of the current voting era, as defined by Kleppner. Economic effects refer to the stage in the long-term cycle of economic growth that prevails during our era and to the nature and growth of inequality.

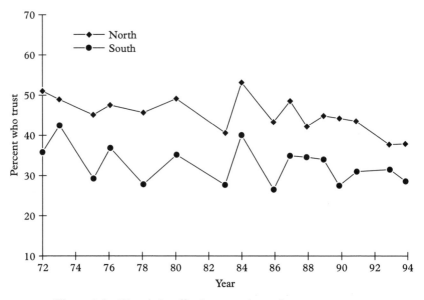

Figure 6.8   Trends in affective trust, by region

Demographic determinants refer to the composition of the population, particularly the operation of cohort and periodic effects, in contrast to life-cycle changes.

Structural determinants are the more familiar social and economic factors used as independent variables in explaining, cross-sectionally, a given pattern of observations.

Cyclical and periodic factors in the decline of trust over the past twenty-five years

Political determinants   As should be clear by now, to understand the American political system during any period, one must first decipher the particular mix of the three versions of democracy that prevails.

The mix in ascendancy over the past quarter of a century has been the "wedge" politics designed by Richard Nixon and successfully carried out by conservatives from the early 1970s through the recent collapse of the Gingrich "conservative revolution." This is the fusion of, on the one hand, Southern conservatism with its antifederalist, states rights, social-interventionist, and *herrenvolk* solidarities, camouflaged under the rhetorical code words of "law and order," "moral majoritarianism," and the attack on "welfare queens" and "urban degeneracy," with, on the other hand, traditional Northern conservatism emphasizing minimal government, tax cuts, the demonization of liberalism, and liberty against the state. The importance of this conception of liberty is reflected in the enormous weight placed on the struggle for the Supreme Court, with the conservative alliance eventually gaining the ascendancy. These developments dovetailed with the emergence of the latest phase in the long-term cycles of Kleppner's voting eras, namely, the active demobilization of the electorate and the encouragement of voter apathy. There even emerged a cheerleading school of political scientists who taught the comforting doctrine that apathy is good for democracy.

The fusion, however, had three contradictions that inevitably led to its undoing, which is what we have just begun to experience. One is the fact, already noted, that Southern antifederalism is not antistatist. The alliance held only so long as Southerners kept their intrusive statism to themselves, with the Northern conservatives willing to turn a blind eye to the notorious intrusiveness and corruption of state-level politics in the South. Closely related to this is the fact that the libertarian impulse in Northern conservatism is grossly at odds with the social and religious interventionism of the Southern version of American conservatism that, precisely because it is not antistatist like its Northern partner, sees no ideological contradiction in legislating morality.

The third contradiction is that, while not actively integrationist or for female or homosexual liberation, Northern conservatism with its libertarian tradition and its extensive, if shallow, "big tent" inclusiveness is inherently uncomfortable with the *herrenvolk* racialism of Southern democracy. Nixon and Reagan themselves were not racists. And Nixon, in his own inimitably perverse way, promoted the interests of Afro-Americans more than any other modern president except Johnson, even as he used those very civil-rights initiatives – especially affirmative action, which he radically transformed – to forge the South–North conservative realignment. (Even Machiavelli must blush in his grave at this. See Skrentny 1996.) And George Bush, the Northern Brahmin, while also no personal racist and from all accounts quite happy with his Mexican daughter-in-law and "little brown ones," as he once innocently described his grandchildren, was badly compromised by his *herrenvolk* use of the notorious Willie Horton campaign ads, a strategy pursued by his Southern campaign director.

What is true of Afro-Americans holds also for women. The already extraordinary level of gender equality, compared with bourgeois Europe, that Tocqueville observed in Jacksonian America actually referred to the position of women among the Northern conservative elite from whom he got much of his distorted view of American equality. It was most certainly not true of the conservative South with its male-bonding, honorific tradition of patriarchy (Fox-Genovese 1998). It is significant that today, it is in the South that we find the strongest evidence of the so-called gender-gap in party identification and voting (Miller and Shanks 1996: 145–146).

The fact that this system has been in ascendancy goes a long way toward explaining the declining level of trust and civic engagement in America over the past quarter of a century. The descent of campaign politics into the vicious use of attack ads is in part the nationalization of the *herrenvolk* strategy of generating loyalty and trust by means of the demonization and distrust of the opposition, the extension northward of the us-vs.-them mentality – we the people, the true Americans, the "moral majority" vs. them, who are the domestic enemy, the unpatriotic, the dishonorable, the untrustworthy – that is classic Southern democratic politics. In essence, this strategy amounted to making niggers of liberals, the identification of the "N" word with the "L" word.

But the alignment is also cyclical in origin. It is the inevitable American reaction against the previous long era of voter mobilization that began with the New Deal and ended in the late 1960s with the enormous increase in the effective electorate after the Voting Rights Act of 1965 and the reenfranchisement of Southern blacks. It is certainly not a new phenomenon, as Putnam seems to suggest. Instead, it is a temporal macro-systemic reaction and adjustment, similar to that which took place between 1896 and 1928 (see Tables 6.1 and 6.2), an adjustment that has already begun to run its course.

Besides these mainly cyclical changes and realignments, there is one powerful periodic political effect of the present era that cannot be over-stated: the crisis of the presidency brought about by the disgrace and resignation of both the vice president and the president of the country. As Figure 6.2 shows, trust in the executive branch collapsed after 1973. Its effects clearly rippled through the last quarter of a century. They were so strong that they counteracted the cyclical turn against the New Deal liberal era that had petered out in the late 1960s, accounting for the anomalous term of Jimmy Carter between 1976 and 1980, during which trust briefly increased but soon collapsed with the economic recession and Iranian hostage crisis. Contrary to what is usually believed, there was no great overall increase in trust in the federal executive during the Reagan years. The mean response of those saying they had a "great deal" of trust in the executive branch remained below 20 percent for his two terms, with only 17 percent expressing such confidence during his last year. There has been a confusion of the high confidence level of the articulate minority who greatly prospered during this period of "yuppie" boom with the general mood of the populace.

The question at issue, however, is whether this and the low levels of confidence expressed in Congress constitute a fundamentally new development in the American democratic system. They do not, for two reasons. First, it is somewhat misleading to use the responses "hardly any" or "a great deal" as measures of how much confidence has changed, for the simple reason that the majority of Americans – on average, 54 percent – have always responded "only some" to the question about confidence in government. When we focus on this category, the interesting thing is that there has been no change in the percent of persons expressing confidence in the federal executive between 1973 and 1994: As Table 6.2 shows, it was 52 percent in 1973 and had inched up slightly to 52.8 percent in 1994.

We find the same pattern for Congress (see Figure 6.3). The extraordinary changes in confidence levels that we reported in the previous section referred to the minority of respondents – 39 percent – who had either "hardly any" or "a great deal" of confidence in Congress. The great majority of Americans – fully 60 percent on average for the entire period – always had "only some" confidence in Congress. That this category had gone down nine points to 51.5 percent in 1994 should not be exaggerated. What is of far greater significance is that for the entire period the average percent of those who had "only some" confidence in Congress is exactly the same as the confidence level reported in 1973 – namely, 60.3 percent.

The majority of Americans, then, have not changed their views about their government, and this sobering fact should always be kept in mind in the following discussion. This, however, does not mean that the changes that have taken place in the other response categories are not important. As we will see shortly, it is only a minority of Americans who have ever been engaged with their government. We strongly suspect, although we cannot prove, this minority tends to respond that it has either "hardly any" or "a great deal" of confidence in its government.

These changes, however, are largely explained by the long-term cyclical changes coinciding with the past quarter of a century as well as the unusual periodic shocks to the political system during this period. They are further explained by the cyclical and periodic changes in the economy during this period.

Economic determinants   The past quarter of a century (up to about 1993) also has coincided with cyclical and periodic shock waves to the economy. The long postwar economic upswing came to an abrupt halt in 1973. "Macroeconomic performance itself has been disappointing," James Tobin (1994: 151–152) writes, summarizing the general trends as follows:

The growth of per capita gross domestic product (GDP) slowed down. The trend growth of productivity per person-hour in the business sector has been about two percentage points lower since 1973 (2.9 percent per year). Not only was the growth of potential output at full employment weaker, but the potential was less frequently and fully realized. Cyclical recessions were more severe after 1973, and the unemployment rate averaged 2.2 points higher.

Accompanying this downturn in the economic cycle has been a series of systemic shocks peculiar to the period, all of which severely eroded confidence. The oil crises reverberated throughout the 1970s, as did the unprecedented economic phenomenon of stagflation. The debt crisis throughout the Third World severely threatened the US banking system during the late 1970s and early 1980s. The reckless and often criminal speculative spree of the junk-bond financial adventure shook confidence in the nation's financial institutions, reflected in the near-catastrophic collapse of the stock market on Black Monday. Most serious of all was the unprecedented deficit growth during the 1980s and early 1990s. Since the early nineties, of course, there has been a sustained upturn in economic growth accompanied by remarkable increases in the value of stocks.

The swings in the percent of persons who trust others shown in figure 6.1 almost exactly correspond to the erratic swings in the economy during this period. Contrary to what is usually thought, there was no great increase in confidence in the business sector during the Reagan era. Although those with "only some" confidence increased slightly between 1980 and 1988, during Reagan's first term the percent of persons who said they had a "great deal" of confidence in the nation's major companies rose from 28 to 32 percent, but fell back to 26 percent at the end of his second term. The figure continued to fall during Bush's term, down to 21 percent by 1991.

Accompanying this poor and erratic economic trend over the past two and a half decades has been a remarkable increase in income inequality. Danziger and Weinberg (1994: 24) sum up the record as follows:

Those in the middle of the income distribution as well as those at the bottom have fared relatively poorly over the past two decades. The income shares of the second and third quintiles were lower in the last few years than in any other year in the post-World War II period. The income share of the second quintile, which was at least 11.9 percent in every year from 1949 to 1973, fell from 12.4 percent in 1969 to 10.5 percent in 1992. Similarly, the share of the third quintile fell from 17.7 percent in 1969 to 16.5 percent in 1992.

One peculiar periodic feature of the present era has been the disappearance of the previous tendency for rising tides to lift all boats. The decade of the 1980s, as Danziger and Weinberg observe, "stands out as a historical anomaly, a period of rising family incomes and rising inequality." The rich grew spectacularly richer during this time, and the poor much poorer, while the middle stagnated. This pattern has persisted during the economic upsurge of the nineties.

All these developments bear directly upon the subject of trust. In an earlier section, we noted the finding of anthropologists of the peasantry that distrust is closely related to economic insecurity and a zero-sum view of the world, realistically induced by a stagnant economic environment. There is no reason to believe that people in advanced economies are any less prone to this tendency. To be sure, this is something to be demonstrated, as will be done shortly with our cross-sectional analysis. In anticipation of that analysis, it can be stated here that both the cyclical and unusual periodic features of the past quarter of a century also account for the trends in distrust observed above.

Demographic determinants In their recently published work, Warren Miller and J. Merrill Shanks (1996: 23–24) offer a fairly persuasive explanation of what they call "the puzzle of declining turnout" in American elections in terms of generational or cohort differences. Such differences, "presumably based on their formative political experiences, are responsible for striking aggregate changes in turnout and party identification." They distinguish between pre-New Deal, New Deal, and post-New Deal generations and place great explanatory weight on "the compositional change of the electorate as the post-New Deal cohorts, who came of age during the turmoil of the 1960s and 1970s, replaced a generation that had come of voting age *before* Franklin Roosevelt and the New Deal."

There is much to be said for the view that the generations who witnessed the triumphs over the Great Depression and Nazism, America's rise to world leadership, and the extraordinary wave of prosperity after World War II would have a different view of the political process from persons who came of age during the political and economic shock waves of the Vietnam War, the Nixon presidential scandal, the oil crises, and the more recent Clinton scandal. But it is not self-evident why the latter should vote less, rather than more. Indeed, it would seem more self-evident that the partisan charge of the 1960s and the outrage induced by the Nixon-Agnew trauma should have created a highly politicized generation more alert to the dangers of political withdrawal. And it could be argued that concern over the prosecutorial tactics of Special Prosecutor Starr might well increase voter turnout from liberal voters as much as outrage over Clinton's behavior might galvanize conservative voters.

Miller and Shanks candidly acknowledge their failure to explain why the shocks of the 1960s and early 1970s had the effects they did. Overall, my own limited analysis does tend to support Miller and Shanks, once the critical intermediary variable of trust is brought into play. Life-cycle effects and cohort effects – with cohorts more narrowly defined – do partly explain the decline in trust and, as such, the declining turnout, assuming they are causally related. I will return to this matter below.

Life-cycle effects. I was very surprised to find that, for all cohorts, the youngest age-groups exhibit the highest percent of untrusting persons. Persons in their 20s have the least percent of the trusting, and this is true for every subperiod in the sample: Only between one-fourth and one-third claimed that others can be trusted. I have no good explanation for why young Americans are so untrusting. This does not seem to be the case in other countries, although I have no hard data to prove this. Still, when Joseph Conrad wrote, "Woe to the man whose heart has not learned while young to hope, to love – and to put its trust in life," he certainly must have thought he was speaking of persons in all Western societies. I have probed the matter with several young Americans, but could get no satisfactory explanation from them.

People mellow out in their 40s and 50s, years that are among the most trusting for all cohorts. As people get older, the percent of the untrusting begins to rise again, although it levels off by about the late 60s. This is all congruent with what we have found about the relationship between trust and economic well-being. People tend to be most economically secure during their 40s and 50s.

Cohort effects. The GSS data indicate that persons born during the 1920s and 1930s are persistently the most trusting, right down to the end of the 1980s (see Figures 6.9A and 6.9B). This is consistent with the findings of Miller and Shanks reported earlier, and the explanation offered seems reasonable. These cohorts came of age either during wartime – which has long been established as a period when societies are most organic, "together," and trusting – and matured during the politically and economically buoyant postwar years. This reinforces the view that trust and economic expansion are positively related. If ever a generation came of age into a world with a prevailing sense of limitless possibilities, it was the generation made of these two cohorts.

Period effects and "the curse of Abbie Hoffman." There seems to be one very interesting period effect that may be called "the curse of Abbie Hoffman," he of the "never-trust-anyone-over-30" fame. Respondents born between 1951 and 1960, the majority of whom were teenagers and college students during the turbulent 1960s and early 1970s, are the least trusting of all cohorts, showing little change in the percent of the distrustful among them with aging. Thus, during 1972–1974, when they were in their late teens and early 20s, 58 percent of them said others

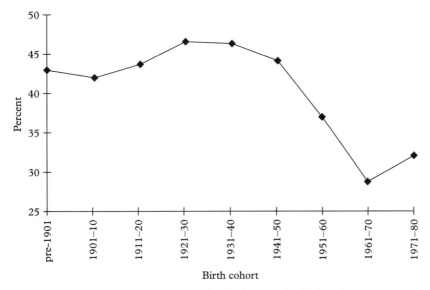

Figure 6.9A   Percent who affectively trust, by birth cohort
Source: General Social Survey, 1972–1994

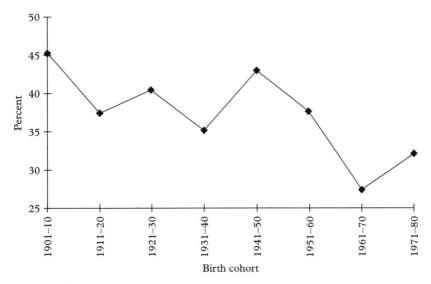

Figure 6.9B   Percent who trust, by birth cohort
Source: General Social Survey, 1990–1994

could not be trusted. Five years later, this figure rose to 63 percent, and it remained roughly at this level during their 30s. They became slightly more trusting as they approached their 40s, but resisted life-cycle effects to a much greater extent than other cohorts, with 57 percent of them still untrusting. During the 1990s, the figure went back to 58 percent, the same as during the untrusting teenage and early-adult years.

Miller and Shanks may be right that this distrustful lot is at least partly responsible for the growth of political apathy, but, as I said earlier, it is hard to see why. This group, it should be noted, formed only a part – the tail end – of the generation coming of age in the 1960s. Nearly half of them were too young to have been caught up in the politically positive events of the first half of the 1960s. The defining events for the vast majority of this cohort were the Vietnam War and the Nixon-Agnew trauma. Any group of persons coming of voting age in the midst of such a national political scandal can be excused for being permanently turned off politics and distrustful of their fellow citizens. They should not, however, be identified with classic 1960s people, the extraordinary generation that came of age in the late 1950s and early 1960s and permanently transformed our attitudes toward race, gender, music, dance, sex, and materialism, resulting in what Ronald Inglehart (1990) has called a cultural shift toward a "postmaterialist" culture in Western societies.

Structural factors in the decline of trust over the past twenty-five years

In this section, I propose to argue for a simple model of the relationship between trust and the political process in contemporary America. This model rests on four positions derived from previous work on the subject.

The first of these is my concurrence with the theoretical assertion of Sidney Verba and Gary Orren (1985: 371) that values are relatively autonomous and that "values and conflict over values play an important part in determining the nature and extent of equality." They no doubt would agree with the extension of this principle: Values are critical in any explanation of social and political behavior. There was a time when such a view was taken for granted in sociology – indeed, was a foundational assumption of the discipline. Alas, with the lemming-like turn toward total structuralism after the reaction against Parsonian functionalism, not only is such a view no longer acceptable in sociology, but it is tantamount to disciplinary heresy. For sociologists reading this paper, I hereby confess my heresy: Values are both causal of, and determined by, social-structural processes, as will be illustrated by what follows.

The second basis of the argument also comes from Verba and Orren; it is their powerful insight that economic and political inequality reinforce each other. Although in America "the norm for politics is more egalitarian," they note, "a significant obstacle to achieving political equality is that economic and political inequality reinforce each other." Economic inequality has both direct and indirect effects on political power, access, and representation.

My third grounding is the finding that American democracy works because it is fundamentally elitist. The argument has been made most persuasively by W. Russell Neuman (1986: 3–4). "The paradox of mass politics," he observes, "is the gap between the expectation of an informed citizenry put forward by democratic theory and the discomforting reality revealed by systematic survey interviewing." What has been revealed, of course, is the fact that "the level of public awareness is disturbingly low." Here is the paradox: "All studies of decision making in Washington indicate that an articulate voice of attentive public opinion is being heard. Where is this voice coming from?"

The reason the system works well, Neuman shows, is that there are really three publics. There is a large middle class of reasonably well-educated persons, constituting about 75 percent of the electorate, who are only passively engaged with the political process. They vote and have a vague idea of the issues, but are not active participants. (I strongly suspect that the "only some" responses to the question on confidence in government come mainly from this group. Indeed, a good name for this semi-engaged majority may well be the "Only-Somes.") Second, there is a significant minority of about 20 percent that knows little about politics and is "profoundly uninterested in the political world." Finally, there is a small group of about 5 percent of the electorate that is extremely attentive to political issues and is very articulate and politically active. This 5 percent accounts for the vibrancy and integrity of the democratic system in America.

While the system is elitist, it is not oligarchic, although there are certainly tendencies and dangers in this direction. However, the fact that the 5 percent of activists who make the system work is still open to nearly anyone with the motivation, time, and energy to participate, plus the high mobility rates between classes, sufficiently works against such oligarchic tendencies.

Fourth, I ground my argument on the established finding that electoral behavior is not simply a product of structural forces or spontaneous action, but the willed result of political action by the dominant political elite. We have already noted this in reference to the historical work of Paul Kleppner. However, many distinguished students of the contemporary political scene have come to the same conclusion. As Huntington and Nelson (1976: 4–10) correctly point out, the "number, attitudes, and behavior of the political professionals, and particularly the political elite, in any political system will often drastically affect the scope and nature of political participation – that is, non-professional activity – in that system." They note further that there is usually a mix of "mobilized and autonomous participation" in all systems and that it is a mistake to distinguish too rigidly between the two since autonomous participation can descend into mindless mobilized party voting and mobilized behavior can become autonomous.

Figure 6.1 summarizes the argument to follow in the most general terms. Cyclical and periodic forces are the critical backdrop to the operation of the interaction between trust and political behavior. Net of these factors, background and current social and economic factors largely determine what I call the socialized propensity to trust. Placed on the same explanatory level, however, is the information to which the person or group in question has been exposed. Education is obviously important, although not nearly as significant as previously thought. Of greater importance are the range of a person's network of contacts and the quality of their media exposure.

There is reason to believe that the kind of media of communication to which persons have been exposed is very important in determining their initial propensity to trust. Many years ago, Richard Hoggart (1992), in his classic study of working-class culture and political behavior in England, showed how the kind of mass literature to which the working classes were exposed in their upbringing and during the course of their adult lives critically influenced their social and political attitudes and their sense of confidence and trust. The same is true of America. The term media quality refers to the level of sophistication of the information sources people use.

Socioeconomic (SES) factors, information exposure and the person's primary identities directly and indirectly influence political trust, participation and outcome, as Figure 6.10 indicates. Control or influence on the political process, finally, has important feed back on the level of political participation and trust.

Willed political action is indicated by the voter mobilization block, the direction of which depends upon the particular voting-era cycle, the past quarter of a century being one of both active and passive demobilization.

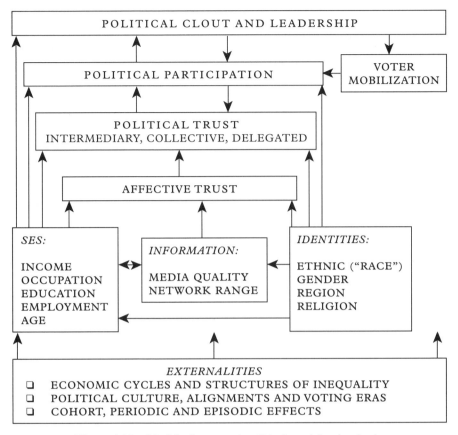

Figure 6.10   Model of trust and political participation in the American democratic system

Class background and trust   Class background is indicated by two income variables: respondents' assessment of the income of their families when they were 16 years old and their statement of the income level of their present household.

As Figure 6.11 shows, during the period between 1972 and 1994 there is a strong positive association between the reported class level and the percentage of those who say that people can be trusted. Thus, in 1972–1974, only 29 percent of those who reported having grown up in families with household incomes far below average said others could be trusted, compared with 46 percent of those from families with above-average income and 46 percent of those with incomes far above average. This

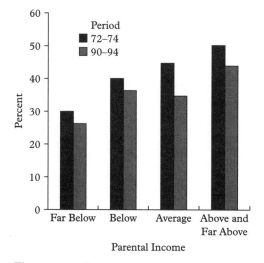

Figure 6.11   Percent who affectively trust, by parental income at age 16 and period

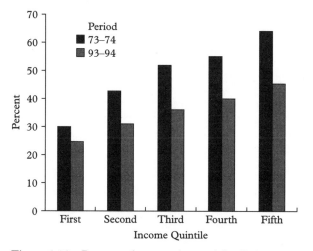

Figure 6.12   Percent who trust, by total family income and period

pattern held for all subperiods until 1990–1994. It should be noted, however, that over the years there is an overall decline in the percent of persons who trust in all income categories of family of origin.

The same relationship holds between trust and reported current household income (see Figure 6.12). Reported family income was divided into quintiles. There was a strong linear relationship between percent of respondents who trusted and quintile level for all subperiods. Again, the overall level of trust declines over the period even though the differences between income groups remain striking. Only 28 percent of the poorest category of persons said others could be trusted in 1972–1974, compared with 67 percent of the wealthiest. By 1990–1994, the proportion of the poorest respondents who believed others could be trusted had declined to 25 percent. During this last period, twice as many rich respondents claimed that others could be trusted, but this marked a decline from 67 to 50 percent.

Other economic background factors   Almost exactly the same pattern holds for all other socioeconomic variables. For the entire period, approximately three-fourths of the unemployed said other persons could not be trusted, compared with one-half of those who worked regularly. One very important change over the past quarter of a century concerns the attitudes of homemakers. Homemakers (nearly all women) were never very trusting, but it is striking that those who believed they could trust others declined from 44.5 percent in 1972 to 28 percent during 1990–1994.

This finding is inconsistent with one of Putnam's explanations for the decline in civic engagement and trust over the same period: the increased labor-force participation of women. Apart from the period of 1975–1979, there was no significant relationship between trust and wife's labor-force status. During 1975–1979, the relationship was significant but, contrary to Putnam's prediction, men whose wives worked had the highest percent of trusting people. For women, the relationship is significant for all periods. Wives with unemployed husbands were very untrusting: Only a quarter of them thought they could trust others. I do not know quite what this says about the relationship between marriage and schooling, but fully 90 percent of women whose husbands are in school found people untrustworthy.

Other economic variables tell exactly the same story. Job anxiety is strongly related to trust. The more people think they are likely to lose their jobs, the less trusting they are, although the difference between the most secure and the least secure declined sharply over the past quarter-century: There was a 21-point difference between them in 1972–1974, but it went down to a 7-point difference by 1990–1994. This could well be a reflection of the general decline in job security among almost all categories of Americans, widely commented on in the mid-1990s. All workers, including those who believe they are least likely to lose their jobs, feel a little insecure at this time.

Anxiety and insecurity are clearly the most powerful forces driving distrust, and this is poignantly brought home by an otherwise odd pattern in the responses to this question. For all subperiods, there was a greater percent of those only "fairly likely" to lose their jobs who were distrustful than those who felt that they were "very likely" to get fired. This suggests that those who had already accepted their economic fates were more trusting than those who were still agonizing over when the ax would fall.

As one would expect, persons with higher levels of job satisfaction and those who reported themselves well satisfied with their financial situation were far more trusting than those who hated what they were doing and were financially dissatisfied.

Social background factors   It has been long established that education and occupational prestige are strongly and positively related to trust, and I found modest support for this relationship for all years, the correlation coefficients being 0.227 and 0.209 respectively.

Married persons are far more trusting than persons in other union statuses, especially the separated and divorced. To the degree, then, that the divorce rate has increased, one would expect an increase in the proportion of persons who distrust others. However, as with other variables, there has been an overall decline in all categories of persons who trust. In 1972–1974, one-half of married persons found their fellow Americans trustworthy, but this was down to 39 percent in 1990–1994.

One thing is certain: The separated are an untrusting bunch, with less than 18 percent of them saying that other people could be trusted. If Marie Edgeworth was right – that "the human heart, at whatever age, opens only to the heart that opens in return" – theirs is a grim lot. In regard to marital status, however, it should be remembered that the trend toward higher divorce rates long preceded the present period of American society.

"Race"   The final social factor to be considered is "race", and what we have found is truly disturbing, although not unexpected. As we saw above (see Figure 6.7), Afro-Americans are the most untrusting ethnic group in the nation. The difference between whites and Afro-Americans is staggering: The mean percent of trusting persons among blacks for the entire period is only 17, compared with 45 percent for whites. As with other measures, there has been a decline in the percent of the trusting over the entire period, with whites declining from 51 to 38 percent, while blacks went down from 23 percent to the present extraordinary level of 15 percent of those who say others could be trusted.

Why is this? I do not have the space here to get into this complex matter. It must be pointed out, however, that while blacks are obviously partly subject to the economic and other forces driving down the numbers of trusting people, the main factors responsible cannot have been the greater levels of poverty and socioeconomic insecurity among them. The reason is that the low percent of the trusting remains true for nearly all groups of blacks – rich or poor, young or old, married or unmarried. Clearly, the distinctive historical experience of Afro-Americans as descendants of a slave population – significant population remnants of whom were still alive and being interviewed as late as the 1930s – and their subjection to *herrenvolk* democracy in the South; post-emancipation semi-serfdom in the share-cropping system; nationwide segregation, racism, and economic discrimination; and the Nixonian "wedge" alliance of the *herrenvolk* and Northern conservative democracies of the last quarter of a century together largely explain the extraordinarily low levels of trust among all classes of the group.

The data make it clear that the mere fact of being an ethnic minority is not inimical to trust. On the contrary, members of ethnic groups no longer persecuted may even have a higher propensity to trust, in view of the greater sense of community they may have experienced growing up. It is significant that the religious group with the highest percent of affectively trusting respondents is the Jews. What is more, the Jews are perhaps the only category of persons who showed almost no overall decline in the percent of trusting persons over the past quarter of a century: 49 percent believed they could trust others in 1972, compared with 48 percent in 1994.

VI.   Trust and the present political system

In light of the above findings, we can reasonably distinguish between persons of upper and lower socioeconomic backgrounds and assume that the former will exhibit a much higher initial propensity to trust than the latter.

Closely related to these structural sources of trust is the communicative system in the society, especially the mass media. James Coleman (1990: 189–94) has emphasized the importance of information in explaining the nature and direction of trust and the building of social capital in modern societies. I have already indicated that the more informed and educated tend to be the more trusting. The mass media, however, are critical, especially for our understanding of the relationship between trust and the political process.

Persons in upper social groups differ from those in lower social groups in two important respects. First, the middle and upper classes get their information not only, or even primarily, from the mass media, but from a range of sources including informed persons in their social networks, professional communicators, and experts on the political process, whereas the masses get almost all their information about politics and society in general from the mass media and often poorly informed personal contacts. Secondly, middle- and upper-class Americans can be more selective in their choice of media: They read more informative newspapers, such as the *New York Times* and *Wall Street Journal*; watch less sensational, more thoughtful news reports on television (when they do watch it), such as "The MacNeil-Lehrer Newshour"; and read books and weekly magazines as well as special newsletters on their social and political world.

One major marker or class status that has emerged in recent years is that between those who read and those who watch. The mass of Americans read less and less and get more and more of their information about society from television and the tabloid press. Coleman (1990: 194) suggests a direct link between TV exposure and the decline in trust in government:

Increasingly, it appears, the mass media constitute the intermediary in whose judgment persons place trust. Along with this acceptance of the media as intermediaries whose judgment is to be trusted has come an aggressive independence on the part of the media where they are not state-controlled. This has sometimes been termed investigative journalism. The mass media can expand their audiences (and perhaps increase the amount of trust placed in them) when they expose defects in the trusted elites; therefore they have an interest in giving selective attention to those defects, leading to withdrawal of public trust in the elites.

This is an interesting argument later emphasized by Putnam but it is based entirely on conventional wisdom. This wisdom, however, has been sharply questioned by many researchers. In a review of where the issue now stands, W. Russell Neuman (1986: 156) argued that the problem of both those who criticize and those who applaud the media for their role in American politics is that they exaggerate the media's power. There are, he claims, "constraints and limitations of the ability of the media to persuade and inform." The media's political information is simply not getting through because the bottom half of the members of the population "continue to ignore and perhaps actively fend off the flow of political communication in their environment, judging it to be both uninteresting and irrelevant." He is not denying that TV news is partly responsible, since his own data suggest a strong relationship between watching TV

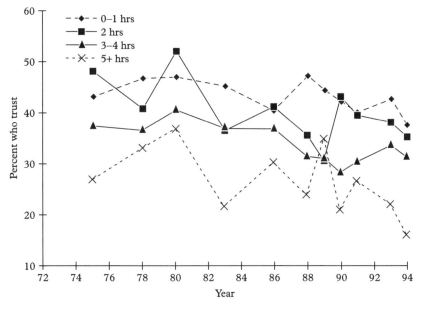

Figure 6.13   Trends in trust, by TV hours
Source: General Social Survey, 1972–1994

news and distrust of politics (1986: 144). His general point, along with those critical of Coleman's and Putnam's position, is that the direct effect of television on the rise of political distrust has been grossly exaggerated.

Neuman and the revisionists are correct in questioning the assertions about television's *direct* role in increasing political distrust and withdrawal. But they are nonetheless wrong in jumping to the conclusion that television is not a major factor in promoting political distrust. What they fail to take account of is that television's corrosive and very strong role is indirect rather than direct. Television promotes voter apathy among the masses not in its direct political newscasts but in the way it socializes those who watch it frequently – whatever it is they watch – into a state of generalized distrust.

This is strongly indicated by Figure 6.13 and the tabular data (not shown). What we see here is, first, that the fewer hours a person watches television, the greater the propensity to trust others: 43 percent of those who watch television less than an hour a day say they trust others. This descends in a direct linear manner down to those who watch five or more hours daily, among whom the mean percent of trusting persons for the entire period is only 28. Note that those who watch more than three hours daily make up almost one-half the population, 49.5 percent, as opposed to the 50.5 who watch only two hours or less. It has long been established by media researchers that there is a strong negative relationship between household income and number of hours watching television: the poorer the household, the more hours. It is safe to conclude, therefore, that TV watching strongly socializes people from lower socioeconomic statuses into a generalized propensity to distrust others.

Second, from Figure 6.13 we also see that the general trend over the past quarter of a century is an intensification of this relationship. Trust is declining among all groups of watchers, but the slope of the descent into generalized distrust is much greater among those who watch more than five hours daily (16 points) than those who watch only one hour or less (six points).

But there is another way in which TV watching indirectly promotes generalized distrust, one that is even more corrosive in its political impact and that dovetails with the racialized "wedge" strategy of the conservative alliance that has dominated the period. This is the mass media's overwhelming emphasis on crime and violence in both their local news reports and fictional programs. There can be no doubt that the greatly increased level of insecurity over crime and violence among Americans has its source in the unrelenting focus of the media on them. This explains why fear of crime has been going up even as the crime rate has gone down.

Naturally, this promotion of distrust in general and fear of violence in particular has played straight into the hands of the "law and order" rhetoric of the dominant "wedge" strategy of the era. Recall that a major factor in George Bush's victory over Michael Dukakis was his use of the notorious Willie Horton ads featuring a black rapist and murderer. And it was television that transformed the O. J. Simpson trial – an otherwise sleazy local event – into the crime of the century and one of the defining racial events of the period. It thus might be wondered whether the emphasis on crime and violence has not promoted the "wedge" strategy in a more direct way, by increasing fear and distrust of the Afro-American minority.

A recent study has demonstrated that this is the case. According to Gilliam and Simon (1996), while it is not true, as some critics have claimed, that local TV news broadcasts report disproportionately more on Afro-American crime than on Euro-American crime, given the actual crime rates of the two groups, the obsessive emphasis on violent crime in these newscasts "means that relatively high rates of black crime are exponentially magnified." In an elegantly designed experiment, they demonstrate that television reporting on crime can alter racial views in a remarkably short period of time. Especially disturbing is their finding that "liberals were more easily dislodged from their [favorable] racial stereotypes when presented with a news story briefly showing a black perpetrator."

A point not made by Gilliam and Simon but that must be added here is that while TV broadcasts do not disproportionately report Afro-American crime in light of the actual amount of violent crimes committed by Afro-Americans, the same cannot be said of crimes in general. Euro-Americans commit a disproportionate number of white-collar crimes in the country. In many cases, these crimes have a far more devastating effect on a much greater number of persons than the black-on-black muggings and killings in the ghetto. The interests of far more people, for example, were permanently damaged by the criminal activities of persons in the financial sector who betrayed the trust placed in them during the 1980s and early 1990s. To take the most dramatic recent case in point, the savings and loan scandal shook the foundations of the nation's banking system and cost the nation's taxpayers incomparably more than all the property crimes committed by Afro-Americans. Yet, astonishingly little attention was paid to this form of criminal activity when compared with the behavior of local underclass criminals.

The TV mass media, then, promote distrust in politics in four ways. First, they do so directly in their tendency to focus not on issues but on investigative debunking of political personalities. This, however, is of limited impact. Second, they do so indirectly by the generalized distrust that frequent TV watching, whatever the content, promotes – a generalized distrust that inevitably spills over into the political realm. Third, they do so indirectly by the relentless emphasis on violence in both dramatic and news programs. And fourth, they do so more specifically in the way they promote racist stereotypes through the overwhelming focus on urban crime, which also happens to be disproportionately Afro-American crime.

To the degree that persons in lower socioeconomic statuses watch more hours of television, then, it is reasonable to conclude that this medium and the tabloid media in general contribute to the disproportionate socialization of the lower classes into a propensity to distrust and reinforce this tendency throughout their adult lives. My analysis, then, supports at least this part of Colemon's and Putnam's argument.

Two trajectories can now be traced from this point. First, the greater generalized trust of the upper SES groups leads directly to greater political trust, while the opposite happens in the lower SES groups. This is not self-evident, as might be thought. Indeed, what is surprising is that a substantial minority of the untrusting do in fact have trust in government. Nonetheless, the gap between those with a socialized propensity to trust and those without remains substantial. Thus, 67 percent of those who affectively trust also expressed delegated trust for local government compared with 57 percent of the generally untrusting. And while the majority of both the trusting and the untrusting distrust the federal government, there is still a significant gap between those who are more affectively trusting (44.5 percent) and those who are untrusting (33 percent).

Political trust, combined with other socioeconomic factors, determines the level of political participation and activism. Three-fourths of trusting people express an interest in politics compared with 57 percent of the untrusting; and one-fourth have attended a political rally, compared with 15 percent of the untrusting. The same striking differences are found in response to the statement that "officials are not interested in the average man." Further, in every subperiod over the past quarter of a century, we find a positive relationship between the number of organizations of which persons are members – a major index of civic engagement – and the percent of persons who say they trust others. Not many Americans join political clubs (only 4 percent for all subperiods), but the few who do – a sure sign of political activism – are disproportionately trusting, always a majority compared with persons who are not members of political clubs.

The remainder of the argument can be stated briefly. Greater political activism means greater access, influence, and control of the political system. This, in turn, means that the well-off gain much more from their political participation. This has immediate feedback effects: Political influence and attendant gains lead to a realistic perception of political effectiveness, which reinforces political trust, and the tendency to be more politically active. The opposite set of linkages operates with persons from lower SES groups.

It is interesting to probe how all this is related to political ideology. At the zero-order level it seems that liberals and moderates, with a mean for the entire period of 41.5 percent who trust, are more trusting than conservatives, with a mean of 39 percent. But this is misleading for several reasons. First, conservatives have shown less of a decline in trust over the past quarter of a century; there is now only a three-point difference from liberals.

Second, and more important, once we control for income and gender we get a more nuanced and altogether different picture. The results are reported in Figure 6.14A–F. What we find is that the higher the quintile, the higher the level of trust among all political orientations and both genders. However, the change across quintiles is most dramatic among conservatives. Lower-class conservative men are generally the least

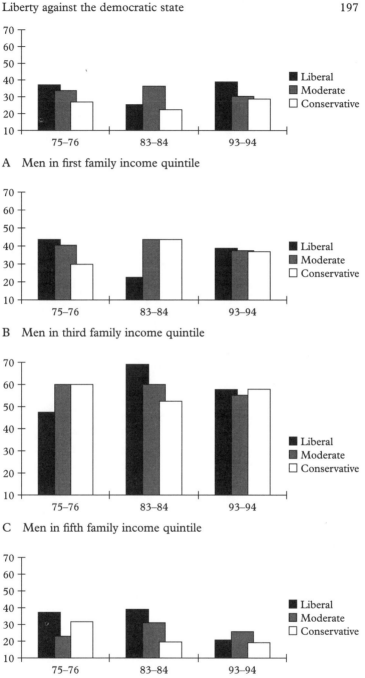

A   Men in first family income quintile

B   Men in third family income quintile

C   Men in fifth family income quintile

D   Women in first family income quintile
Figure 6.14A–F   Percent who trust, by year and political views

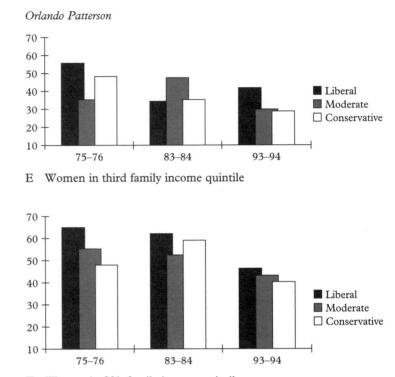

E   Women in third family income quintile

F   Women in fifth family income quintile

trusting for all subperiods. Among the wealthiest men, however, conservative males tend to be the most trusting for the first and last period.

As one might expect, managers have lobbied local officials to a far greater degree than blue-collar workers. But what might come as a surprise is the fact that conservatives exhibit the highest proportion of persons who express delegated trust in the federal government, fully 48 percent, compared with 38 percent of moderates and 27 percent of liberals.

There is, finally, the question of voter mobilization. We have repeatedly noted that the electorate's level of political withdrawal or activism is not wholly a spontaneous product of structural forces, but the result of the decision of political leaders and parties to mobilize or to demobilize. Over the past quarter of a century, the liberal and progressive forces that normally mobilize the electorate have opted out of this role. Given the severe structural constraints on self-mobilization for the mass of the electorate, the decision by the liberal leadership not to act amounts to a decision to demobilize or, at any rate, to accept apathy.

At the same time, conservative forces have been engaged in both kinds of activities. On the one hand, there has been what may be called the

"Phyllis Schlafly strategy" of demobilization. I have called it that because of the seeming paradox of this strategy in which a woman who is highly activist and anything but a quiet homemaker devotes her political ener-gies to persuading women to return to their traditional roles. It is doubt-ful, however, whether this strategy has had any net effects on women's voting turnout since gender differences in turnout had disappeared by the 1984–1988 voting period (Miller and Shanks 1996: 89–90) and the mobilization offort of feminist and other liberal women's advocacy groups would have countered the conservative demobilization strategies. Other forms of demobilization have resulted from conservatives' efforts to keep voter registration difficult for the urban and rural poor and other persons with difficult lives. The motor-voter law, fought to the very end by con-servatives, was a recent change in the opposite direction.

And, of course, there have been old-fashioned attempts to disen-franchise the black vote, the most blatant recent case being the attempt to bribe black preachers to encourage their flocks not to vote during the New Jersey gubernatorial race.

VII.   Conclusion

Has America shifted toward a new era of voter apathy and civic dis-engagement over the past quarter of a century? On the whole, I think not. There certainly has been a decline in expressions of affective trust for other persons and for institutions of government. But, with the im-portant exception of the role of the mass media, to see this as something new or especially threatening to the system of governance is an unwar-ranted rush to judgment. Furthermore, as a recent study of Philadelphia shows, growing levels of affective trust can be found even where civic engagement remains high (Kohut 1997).

What we are witnessing instead are, first, certain cyclical patterns of political behavior in American democracy and, second, the effects of certain systemic shock waves peculiar to the recent past. Both by their very natures are likely to pass away. Indeed, there are already signs that the situation is changing.

I have argued that the American democratic system is the product of a complex, untidy blend of three competing versions of democracy: the liberal, pluralist version; the elitist, libertarian version; and the Southern *herrenvolk* form of primal democracy. Each is distinctive in the nature and systems of trust and distrust it deploys and in the note of the chordal triad of freedom that it emphasizes.

The changing alignments of these three forms of trust and democracy have been the driving force of American political history over the past 170 years. The result has been a quite conservative democratic process that works very well because it depends on the active participation of a vocal and knowledgeable although relatively small section of the electorate. It is, however, an open political elite that now includes Afro-Americans and other once excluded minorities, as well as women, in growing numbers.

Over time, the democratic process also has exhibited a pattern of shifts between eras of activism and egalitarian expansion accompanied by active mobilization of the electorate, followed by reactive eras of de-activism, inegalitarian expansion, and voter demobilization. It is just such an era that we are living through, and it is coming to an end. Paralleling this cyclical political feature of the period has been a cyclical economic pattern of low growth, which also has recently come to a close. Besides these now shifting cyclical patterns, there was a series of unusual political and economic shocks, the most important being the Nixon-Agnew resignations, the oil crises, the erratic patterns of recovery, the enormous growth of the deficit, the extraordinary increase in inequality with stagnant wages for workers, and an increase in the poverty rate.

These developments are always accompanied by the decline of personal trust, as our cross-sectional analysis made clear. When one adds to all these the peculiar one-time, generational effect of the politically traumatized post-1950 generation, the decline in trust and civic engagement is no longer surprising.

But, by the same token, it is not something to be mistaken for a major, permanent shift in political values and behavior. The signs are clear that the cycle of conservative reaction is over. The midterm election of 1994 marked not the beginning but the end of the latest conservative era. Bob Dole's 15 percent tax-cut proposal, antigovernment stand, and personal-trust strategy were strongly rejected by the electorate. Repeated polls demonstrated that the single most important reason for the collapse of the Gingrich "conservative revolution" was the electorate's perception that the Republicans were responsible for shutting down the federal government. Furthermore, that the electorate was willing to re-elect Clinton *despite the fact that the majority of them said they did not trust him personally* speaks volumes for the view that there has been a shift toward the pluralist, liberal emphasis on impersonal trust in governmental institutions. Jack Kemp got to the heart of the difference between the pluralist version of democracy and the Northern elitist approach when he declared in his convention acceptance speech that "they don't have faith in people. They have faith in government." The electorate, by its recent vote, agreed and voted for faith in government.

The recent motor-voter law already has signaled a major shift toward a new era of voter mobilization. And just when everyone had given it up for dead, the labor movement suddenly experienced a renewal of life and leadership and became a major player in the 1996 presidential election. Everywhere there are signs of a new activism. A case in point was the extraordinary teach-in held at the Columbia University in fall 1996 that sought to rebuild ties between the academic and student community and the labor movements. The organizers of the campaign figured that a turnout of 300 or 400 persons would exceed their wildest expectations. A crowd of 1,700 persons showed up, and several hundred had to be turned away!

Finally, it may be asked whether there has been any development over the past quarter of a century that can be seen as a long-term, fundamental shift in the system. I think there are indeed two such changes, and they work in opposite directions. One of them is the role of the mass media, discussed above. Although television now has a history of almost half a century in America, its emergence as a major shaper of attitudes – especially of political attitudes and behavior, both directly and indirectly – is peculiar to the past quarter of a century, and it will remain a permanent feature of the social and political landscape. This development is the only important one that lends support to the view of Putnam and those holding his position that there has been a fundamentally new change toward civic disengagement in America.

But there is a major change working in the other direction. It is perhaps too early to say with any certainty, but there are signs that the *herrenvolk* tradition of democracy may finally be on the way out of American politics. The revival of this system in the "wedge" politics of Nixon and his conservative inheritors may well have been the last hurrah of this pernicious form of primal, racially divisive democracy.

Several developments over the past quarter of a century account for this.[5] One is the urbanization and industrialization of the South. Atlanta, the heart of Dixie, now declares itself a city too busy to hate – too busy making money the Northern way. Agrarian capitalism, the economic foundation of *herrenvolk* democracy, is waning.

Another development during the last quarter of a century also undermines one of the foundations of the *herrenvolk* system: the large influx of

---

[5] On the effect of urbanization, industrialization, and the growth of a new middle class on Southern politics, see Black and Black (1987).

immigrants from Latin America and Asia. The binary conception of race and racial purity with its either- or, us-them, in-group/out-group quality that is so essential for the maintenance of the *herrenvolk* tradition of democracy has been shattered by the emergence of a large new group that is neither black nor white and that refuses to play into the *herrenvolk* primal game by joining the white in-group, achieving in this way a quick path to citizenship and belonging, as did previous generations of white immigrants from Europe (see Saxton 1990: Part 1; Jacobson 1998: Parts 1, 3). Bringing with them different conceptions of race – not necessarily better, but different – and, more importantly, creating a large demographic presence of a group that is not white but not black either, the Latin influx has confounded the traditional racial and social underpinnings of the *herrenvolk* and northern democratic fabrication on social uses of race.

Yet another development that is potentially inimical to *herrenvolk* democracy is, however surprisingly, the fundamentalist movement. In the long run, the growth of Southern fundamentalist Christianity as the most powerful force in the conservative tradition of the region may well hasten the departure of the *herrenvolk* tradition. Contrary to popular conceptions, the Afro-American minority is extremely fundamentalist and as socially conservative as its Euro-American counterpart. The increasing penetration of Hispanic groups by fundamentalist Christianity also works in the same direction: namely, a shift of conservative solidarity and trust from race and personal trust based on mistrust and demonization of others to a return to conservative Christian fellowship, moral activism, trust in God, and a racially neutral demonization of the original devil. I see this, however, as a very long-term development. For the moment, the fundamentalist forces controlling the platform committee of the Republican Party seem hardly uncomfortable with the implicit racialism of the waning "wedge" strategy.

Finally, there has emerged from the South itself a large new class of cosmopolitan leaders strongly committed to the final overthrow of this system. Bill Clinton is a prime example of this new class of Southerners. His southernness, countercultural background, and generational identity all made him the ideal leader to undo the "wedge" politics of Nixon upon which the conservative Republican ascendancy was based. By moving to the center and seizing the law-and-order issue, he robbed the Nixonian strategy of the major tactic used to camouflage its thinly coded racialism. To play the *herrenvolk*, "moral-majority" game now requires calling a spade a spade. And such an openly racist or white-chauvinist strategy the Northern conservative wing of the alliance simply could not stomach or would not abide. The swift and unambiguous rejection of Patrick

Buchanan by established party leaders as well as the electorate in the 1996 election made this very clear. Dole's last-minute, half-hearted use of immigration and affirmative action won him few votes. It badly embarrassed his running mate, Kemp, who is more like Clinton in his capacity to cross the racial divide and empathize with Afro-American voters. The takeover of the party's ideological platform by the Religious Right from the South has simply hastened the disintegration of this alliance.

My conclusion, then, is a cautiously optimistic one. The era of electoral demobilization and conservative "liberty against the state" ascendancy is nearly over, and a new era of pluralist activism is re-emerging. It will remain elitist, because that is the nature of the American democratic system. But there will be more movement in and out of this activist elite, and the electorate's consent will be sought more eagerly and engaged. But above all, it would seem now that one major source of distrust in the system – the cultivated, *herrenvolk* distrust of blacks by whites – might be coming to an end, at least as an active element on the federal level of the democracy.

While the role of television seems currently to work in the opposite direction, it should in all fairness be pointed out that television itself has the capacity to educate, inform, enhance trust, and mobilize voters. Indeed, there already exists a rich variety of quality programs that do just this, although they tend to be watched mainly by the politically active elite. Even so, in a new era of voter mobilization and enhanced participatory democracy, there is no reason to believe that the articulate and activist elite could not pressure the media into playing down their trust-destroying role and, at the same time, use them to increase political education. Even as I write, an encouraging self-scrutiny among journalists and others in the mass media about their role in the promotion of violence and political cynicism is taking place. And the electorate's recent expression of disgust about negative campaigning – especially attack TV ads, which have backfired on the majority of those employing the strategy – augurs well for the view that a new era of voter awareness and participatory democracy is on the horizon.

The present scandal surrounding the Clinton presidency will only hasten these developments. Nothing better demonstrates the end of the elitist, patrician versions of democracy with its emphasis on the intermediary trust of the leader's character and distrust of government than the electorate's response to the scandal. Its continued high support for Clinton's job performance even while deploring his moral failings has perplexed and even disgusted traditionalists. Nonetheless, the electorate's response is consistent with its rejection of Dole's electoral appeal to the issue of character and personal (intermediary) trust, and its election of a candidate already known to be personally flawed. The public's insistence on distinguishing between the the man and the office, and between presidential job performance and presidential character, not only marks the final rejection of elitist democracy, but bodes well for its pluralist, instrumentalist version. It is precisely because the electorate has such profound confidence in the institution of government that it can comfortably make this distinction. A strong democratic government, their actions imply, does not depend upon good men but on a good system effectively managed, which is their view of the Clinton presidency.

This attitude is further demonstrated by other recent responses of the electorate. Its strong disapproval of the Gingrich Republican attempt to "shut down" the state clearly signals its commitment to the view that the state is not a minimalist night watchman but exists to do things for the people. And the extreme unpopularity of Special Prosecutor Kenneth Starr and alarm expressed over his prosecutorial tactics suggests that issues of privacy and personal liberty are not only of great concern but are not viewed as being in any way inconsistent with an activist, well managed democratic state.

In short, not only is the *herrenvolk* version of democracy on the wane, but the century and a half effort of elitist democratic forces to pit liberty against the democratic state has run its course. The effort, which at times seemed so close to success, has in fact failed. Alexander Hamilton, the most brilliant and prescient of the Founding Fathers, saw through the patrician pretensions of liberty when he wrote that "the noble enthusiasm of liberty is too apt to be infected with a spirit of narrow and illiberal distrust." But with equal perspicacity he both anticipated the dangers of *herrenvolk* misuse of "the rights of the people" and recognized the essential tension and complementarity of liberty and government when he wrote that what is arguably the most dazzling passage in *The Federalist Papers* (1961, no. 1): "On the other hand, it will be equally forgotten, that the vigor of government is essential to the security of liberty; that, in the contemplation of a sound and well-informed judgment, their interest can never be separated; and that a dangerous ambition more often lurks behind the special mask of the zeal for rights of the people than, under the forbidding appearance of zeal for the firmness and efficiency of government."

In rejecting the zeal of a moralistic Special Prosecutor, the *herrenvolk* "rights of the people," the distorted view that liberty is antagonistic to the democratic state, and in preferring effective government and governance to morally upright governors and leadership, the electorate has proven

once again, that the morally flawed Hamilton was indeed the most fore-
sighted of the Fathers.

REFERENCES

Andrews, Charles M., 1934. *The Colonial Period of American History*, New Haven:
    Yale University Press
Black, Earl and Black, Merle, 1987. *Politics and Society in the South*, Cambridge,
    Mass.: Harvard University Press
Bradford, M. E., 1990. Is the American experience conservative, in *The Reactionary
    Imperative: Essays Literary and Political*, Peru, Ill.: Sherwood Sugden
Brown, Robert E. and Brown, B. Katherine, 1964. *Virginia, 1705–1786: Demo-
    cracy or Aristocracy*, East Lansing, Mich.: Michigan State University Press
Brown, Robert E., 1968. *Middle-Class Democracy and the Revolution in Massa-
    chusetts, 1691–1780*, New York: Russell and Russell
Coleman, James S., 1990. *Foundations of Social Theory*, Cambridge, Mass.: Harvard
    University Press
Cooper, William J., 1983. *Liberty and Slavery: Southern Politics to 1860*, New York:
    Knopf
Corwin, Edward, 1948. *Liberty Against Government*, Westport, Conn.: Greenwood
    Press
Danziger, Sheldon H. and Weinberg, Daniel H., 1994. The historical record, in
    Sheldon H. Danziger, Gary D. Sandefur, and Daniel H. Weinberg (eds.),
    Confronting Poverty: Prescriptions for Change, Cambridge, Mass.: Harvard
    University Press
Dinkin, Robert J., 1977. *Voting in Provincial America: A Study of Elections in the
    Thirteen Colonies, 1689–1776*, Westport, Conn.: Greenwood Press
    1982. *Voting in Revolutionary America: A Study of Elections in the Original
    Thirteen States, 1776–1789*, Westport, Conn.: Greenwood Press
Finley, Moses I., 1959. Was Greek civilization based on slave labour? *Historia* 8,
    145–164
    1973. *Democracy Ancient and Modern*, New Brunswick, NJ: Rutgers University
    Press
    1980. *Ancient Slavery and Modern Ideology*, London: Penguin
Foner, Eric, 1995. *Free Soil, Free Labor, Free Men: The Ideology of the Republican
    Party Before the Civil War*, New York: Oxford University Press
Fox-Genovese, Elizabeth. 1988. *Within the Plantation Household: Black and
    White Women in the Old South*, Chapel Hill: University of North Carolina
    Press.
Franklin, John Hope, 1970. *The Militant South, 1800–1861*, Cambridge, Mass.:
    Harvard University Press
Fredrickson, George M., 1981. *White Supremacy: A Comparative Study of
    American and South African History*, New York: Oxford University Press
Gambetta, Diego, 1988a. Can we trust trust? in Diego Gambetta (ed.), *Trust:
    Making and Breaking Cooperative Relations*, Oxford: Basil Blackwell

Genovese, Eugene D., 1994. *The Southern Tradition: The Achievement and Limitations of an American Conservatism*, Cambridge, Mass.: Harvard University Press

Gilliam, Franklin, Jr. and Simon, Adam, 1996. Can media cues change thinking about race? An experimental study of television news crime coverage. Paper presented at the Annual Meeting of the American Political Science Association, San Francisco, August–September

Granovetter, Mark, 1985. Economic action and social structure: The problem of embeddedness. *American Journal of Sociology* 91, 481–510

Hamilton, Alexander, Madison, James and John Jay. 1961. *The Federalist*. Edited by Benjamin Fletcher Wright, Cambridge, MA: Harvard University Press

Hoggart, Richard, 1992. *The Uses of Literacy: Changing Patterns in English Mass Culture*, New Brunswick, NJ: Transaction Books

Holden, Barry, 1974. *The Nature of Democracy*, London: Nelson

Huntington, Samuel P. and Nelson, Joan M., 1976. *No Easy Choice: Political Participation in Developing Countries*, Cambridge, Mass.: Harvard University Press

Inglehart, Ronald, 1990. *Culture Shift in Advanced Industrial Society*, Princeton, NJ: Princeton University Press

Jacobson, Matthew F., 1998. *Whiteness of a Different Color*, Cambridge, MA: Harvard University Press

Key, V. O., 1949. *Southern Politics in State and Nation*, New York: Knopf

Kleppner, Paul, 1982. *Who Voted: The Dynamics of Electoral Turnout, 1870–1980*, New York: Praeger Publishers

Kohut, Andrew, 1997. *Trust and Citizen Engagement in Metropolitan Philadelphia: A Case Study*, Washington, DC: Pew Research Center

Luhmann, Niklas, 1979. Trust: A mechanism for the reduction of social complexity, in *Trust and Power: Two Works by Niklas Luhmann*, Chichester: John Wiley and Sons

Miller, Warren E. and Shanks, J. Merrill, 1996. *The New American Voter*, Cambridge, Mass.: Harvard University Press

Morgan, Edmund S., 1975. *American Slavery, American Freedom: The Ordeal of Colonial Virginia*, New York: Norton

1988. *Inventing the People: The Rise of Popular Sovereignty in England and America*, New York: Norton

Neuman, W. Russell, 1986. *The Paradox of Mass Politics: Knowledge and Opinion in the American Electorate*, Cambridge, Mass.: Harvard University Press

Nisbett, Richard E., 1996. *Culture and Honor: The Psychology of Violence in the South*, Boulder, CO: Westview

Oakes, James, 1982. *The Ruling Race: A History of American Slaveholders*, New York: Knopf

1990. *Slavery and Freedom: An Interpretation of the Old South*, New York: Knopf

Putnam, Robert, 1995a. Bowling alone: America's declining social capital. *Journal of Democracy* 6, January, 65–78

Raaflaub, K. A., 1995. *Die Endeckung der Freiheit*, Vestigia

Roediger, David R., 1991. *The Wages of Whiteness: Race and the Making of the American Working Class*, New York: Verso

Rogers, Everett M., 1969. *Modernization Among Peasants: The Impact of Communication*, New York: Holt, Rinehart, and Winston

Rossiter, Clinton, 1953. *Seedtime of the Republic: The Origin of the American Tradition of Political Liberty*, New York: Harcourt

Saxton, Alexander, 1990. *The Rise and Fall of the White Republic: Class Politics and Mass Culture in Nineteenth-Century America*, New York: Verso

Shapiro, Susan, 1987. The social control of impersonal trust. *American Journal of Sociology* 93, 623–658

Simmel, Georg, 1971. The stranger, in Donald Levine (ed.), *On Individuality and Social Forms: Selected Writings*, Chicago: University of Chicago Press

Skrentny, John D., 1996. *The Ironies of Affirmative Action: Politics, Culture and Justice in America*, Chicago: University of Chicago Press

Tobin, James, 1994. Macroeconomic trends, cycles, and policies, in Sheldon H. Danziger, Gary D. Sandefur, and Daniel H. Weinberg (eds.), *Confronting Poverty: Prescriptions for Change*, Cambridge, Mass.: Harvard University Press

Verba, Sidney and Orren, Gary R., 1985. The meaning of equality in America. *Political Science Quarterly* 100, 369–387

Watson, Harry L., 1990. *Liberty and Power: The Politics of Jacksonian America*, New York: Hill and Wang

Wattenberg, Martin P. *The Decline of American Political Parties, 1952–1988*, Cambridge, MA: Harvard University Press

Wyatt-Brown, Bertram, 1982. *Southern Honor: Ethics and Behavior in the Old South*, New York: Oxford University Press

7 Trust, voluntary association and workable democracy: the contemporary American discourse of civil society

Jean Cohen

The relationship between democracy and trust has moved from the periphery to the center of debate among political theorists in recent years. After the "state was brought back in," democratic theorists began to focus on ways to ensure the responsibility and accountability of government officials (Skocpol 1982). Liberals sought protections for the expansion and exercise of rights while debating with conservatives and democrats over the appropriateness of rights rhetoric, litigation and the role of the courts.[1] Paradoxically, the more ubiquitous the administrative and regulatory state became, the more it appeared to trigger entitlement claims that, in turn, seemed to call forth more top-down administrative and judicial "state action." This apparently uncontrollable spiral seemed to threaten both democracy and personal freedoms and to undermine the "habits of the heart" that make liberal democracies work. Small wonder that questions regarding the social and cultural presuppositions of democracy in general and, in particular, the sources of trust in government and in one another on the part of civil actors have now moved to the fore.

In the United States, this conundrum has led in recent years to an intense debate about civil society. The role of civil society in generating social trust, and hence in contributing to social coordination, and its relation to effective and responsive democratic government are the key issues. The guiding idea behind the contemporary American discourse of civil society is that trust is necessary for social integration, for civic engagement, and, hence, for vibrant democratic institutions and that it is generated in voluntary associations. The new concern with social trust and civil society is based on the diagnosis of their precipitous decline in late twentieth-century American life. While there is something to this

---

[1] Rawls' *A Theory of Justice* (1971) was the most influential work reflecting on the importance of rights in the context of the redistributionist welfare state. See also Cass Sunstein's *After the Rights Revolution* (1990). On the other side, see the Trilateral Commission on ungovernability and, more recently, Mary Ann Glendon's *Rights Talk* (1991).

argument, in my view the contemporary American discourse on trust and civil society is both one-sided and politically dangerous. A brief prehistory of the re-emergence of discussions of civil society elsewhere and an in-depth analysis of the hegemonic form of American civil-society talk today will show why.

About 25 years ago, post-Marxist critics of socialist authoritarianism revived the concept of civil society (Cohen and Arato 1992: 1–26). The remarkable historical success of the concept was due to its convergence with a dualist strategy for democratization first in the East and then in Latin America. This strategy was based on the idea of the self-organization of society: the rebuilding of social ties, politically relevant collective action, and independent publics outside state-controlled communication. But it also aimed at creating political publics and institutions that would be responsive and accountable to the electorate.

In Western Europe, the concept also caught on in the post-Marxist milieux of the "new" social movements, which challenged forms of domination within liberal democracies that differed from class oppression, yet persisted and had systematic bases despite formal equality. There the focus was on the further democratization of already existing civil societies and political publics: on the expansion and strengthening of basic rights, on the reduction of social hierarchies, on the modernization of cultural traditions supporting status inequalities, on voice and justice for stigmatized and discriminated-against groups, on the revitalization of civil associations and publics, and on the increase of their access and influence on political society. Theorists such as Bobbio, Habermas, Lefort, Offe, Melucci, Rosanvallon, and Touraine anticipated such a possibility very early, and hopefully Andrew Arato and I were able to contribute to it in our writings during the previous decade (Cohen and Arato 1992: 492–563; Cohen 1982).

Today the political context and projects associated with the discourse of civil society have changed. In the United States, interest in the concept has exploded – a somewhat belated development *vis-à-vis* the European debate, but in certain respects continuous with an earlier indigenous American discussion.

The current American debate has strong affinities with the approach of the pluralist school of the 1950s. Both draw on the sociocultural tradition of political analysis introduced in the nineteenth century by Alexis de Tocqueville's (1969) study of American democracy. The pluralists developed the Tocquevillian concept of a civic culture and focused on the relation of cultural and social factors (including participation in the autonomous associational life of civil society) to responsive and effective democratic government. But the post-war pluralist discourse of civil society was aimed primarily at explaining the "difference" between societies prone to totalitarianism and *stable* democracies.

The intermediary bodies and overlapping forms of plurality and identity characteristic of associations in civil (as distinct from "mass") society were deemed a sign of successful "modernization." When brought together with a universalistic and egalitarian political culture, these allegedly secured cross-cutting solidarities, fostered tolerance, and limited the nature of demands and ideological agendas on the part of elites and social actors (Almond and Verba 1963). Accordingly, a civic culture was believed to protect society against destabilizing mass mobilization and social atomization characteristic of totalitarian movements and states.[2]

The ideological context in the United States is quite different today, as are the stakes of what has become a hotly contested concept open to competing interpretations and political projects. Now it is the crisis of the welfare state – not the threat of a totalitarian state – that is at issue. Now it is dissatisfaction with the cultural and social effects of "successful" and "normal" rather than "failed" modernization that motivates the

---

[2] It also protected against "segmental pluralism," the bad kind of groupness that precludes cooperation across "primordial" or ideological identities. But these pluralists were partisans of the welfare state and of rights despite their critique of mass society. The hostility of the model to movements was aimed at "totalitarian" forms of collective action. This was thus quite different from the later neoconservative discourse of "ungovernability" that emerged in the 1970s. On the other hand, the pluralist model *was* wed to what Ulrich Beck has called the social structure of "traditional" or "simple" modernity. In particular, their approach assumed clear dichotomies between family and work, public and private, state and civil society, male and female gender roles, etc. (Beck 1992). Pluralists never sought to apply the universalist egalitarian principles of the political culture to the family, to the gendered division of labor in and between public and private spheres, or to the status hierarchies that were pervasive in civil society. On the contrary, pluralist political theory presupposed and sought to reinforce traditional modern forms of social integration: the patriarchal nuclear family based on monogamous marriage and the dichotomy between female homemaker and male breadwinner; the vocational understanding of work in the labor market differentiated from "non-work" outside and linked to the gendered division of labor; and the locally based yet nationally organized (from bottom up) associational life (divided on gender and racial lines) this social structure fostered. This institutional/cultural complex of industrial society in the epoch of the welfare state guaranteed a certain amount of civil privatism while channeling participation along specific lines (targeting the national political system for influence) and in (hopefully) predictable ways.

Pluralists also embraced what one can call the assimilationist mode of incorporation of groups into civil society and the polity: Tolerance of difference was based on the expectation that people confine their group identities – religion, ethnicity, sexuality, racial cultures, etc. – to the private sphere. These were to be abstracted away from in public life. Assimilation of formerly excluded and newly arrived groups involved Americanization in public and the privatization of difference. No toleration existed for difference *vis-à-vis* sexual and family mores. Voluntary associations were fitted into a single mode, while ineradicable forms of difference had to be as discreet as possible. This model has been under attack since the 1970s. The discourse of diversity, multiculturalism, and the current contestation over the meaning of civil society must be understood on this terrain.

renewal of the discourse of civil society. And now there is the fear that models of social integration, civic engagement, and associational life, which once were taken for granted and suited industrial society rather well, are being strained by new forms of social diversity, institutional transformation, and economic, scientific, and technological change.

Apparently, neither the centralized state nor the magic of the marketplace can offer effective, liberal, and democratic solutions to the problems of "post-industrial" civil societies in a context of globalization. Confidence in the state's ability to implement its policies, to exercise control over market actors, scientific and technological innovation, or social structural change through direct regulations and top-down administration has waned. Statist correctives, moreover, threaten freedom. But the ever-increasing and unequal social generation of risks and social injustice in such societies are exacerbated when the state completely abandons the field to market forces: Both "reforms" can be socially disintegrative, oppressive, ecologically and medically dangerous, and unjust.[3] Indeed, welfare-state legality has shifted emphasis toward the administration and the courts and triggered calls for revitalizing and protecting both democracy and community. Given the political and social impossibility of continuing industrial society and the welfare-state model in the old way and the undesirability of returning to market magic, it is understandable that the discourse of civil society has become so widespread and contentious.

To be sure, much of this was already true in the 1980s (Cohen and Arato 1992). But what strikes us today is the ubiquity with which the term "civil society" is invoked in response. No longer an arcane concept deployed by a select group of political and social theorists, the term has entered the speech of politicians, journalists, and public intellectuals on all sides of the political spectrum, from Pat Buchanan and Newt Gingrich to Bill Clinton and Bill Bradley (Bradley 1995; Coats 1996a; Coats 1996b; Skocpol 1996). "Civil society" has become a slogan for the 1990s in part because it appears to offer an alternative center for political and economic initiatives. But the idealized, backward-looking, one-dimensional version of the concept that is being revived is hardly up to the task, in my view.

This paper addresses the contemporary American discourses of civil society with an eye to the politics of theory and the political effects of rhetoric. I focus on two of the most prominent recent interventions in the civil society debate: the neorepublican stance of Robert Putnam and his school, and the communitarian version of the political theorists who gather

---

[3] On the social creation of risks to health, ecology, safety, and psychological well-being inherent in late modernity, see Ulrich Beck (1992).

around the journal *The Responsive Community*.[4] "Civil society" in these approaches has become so reduced and so romanticized that the normative thrust of the concept, along with its relevance to contemporary problems, is being obscured. Nearly everyone in the current discussion has come to equate civil society with traditional forms of voluntary association (including "the" family). And nearly everyone assumes that the "intermediary bodies" created by voluntary association, the alleged sources of social trust, the guarantor of responsive government, and the key to civic virtue, are in decline in contemporary America. The debate is over the causes of the decline and what to do about it.

This conceptualization of civil society is theoretically impoverished and politically suspect. When combined with the discourse of civic and moral decline, it undermines democracy instead of making it work, threatens personal liberty instead of enhancing it, and blocks social justice and social solidarity instead of furthering them. Why? I will try to show that because they focus exclusively on how *traditional* but now waning and anachronistic models of civil association generated social trust and facilitated civic engagement and influence on the political system, Putnam and his school divert analysts from reflecting on ways to foster the reflexive continuation of democracy and effective forms of participation. I will also show that the neocommunitarian focus on an equally anachronistic conception of family, associational life, and the value consensus an intact civil society allegedly requires and reinforces, entails a repressive response to the pluralization of forms of life inherent in post-industrial society and to the rights required not only for purposes of "self-realization" but also for the generation of social trust and effective democratic participation.

Unless these backward-looking models are challenged, the current revival of the discourse of civil society in the United States will play into the hands of political elitists seeking to narrow the scope of democratic politics and/or social conservatives who aim to retraditionalize civil life and to substitute local "volunteerism" for the public services and redistributive efforts of the welfare state, as if these are our only options. Far too many political theorists and actors pretend that we can have a vital, well-integrated, and just civil society without states constitutionally guaranteeing that universalistic egalitarian principles (open to critique and

---

[4] The main figures of the neocommunitarian movement are Amitai Etzioni, a professor of sociology at George Washington University; William Galston, political philosopher, former professor at the University of Maryland, and now a domestic policy adviser to President Clinton; Mary Ann Glendon, Harvard law professor; and Michael Sandel, Harvard professor of political science. Their journal, *The Responsive Community: Rights and Responsibilities*, which is edited by Etzioni, is seen as the voice of a new movement for communitarian values.

revision) inform social policy regardless of which social institution or level of government carries it out. If civil-society discourse is left in this form, we will not be able to articulate, much less resolve, the critical problems facing democratic polities in the coming century. My claim is that it matters very much, both politically and theoretically, which concept of civil society and which understanding of the concept and sources of trust we use and seek to foster.

The concept of civil society

Whether we take Hegel or Tocqueville as our starting point, the concept of civil society made available to us by nineteenth-century theorists was rich and multileveled. "Civil society" was understood as a sphere of social interaction distinct from the economy and state, characterized by voluntary association, civil publics, the media of communication (at that time, print), and sets of subjective legal rights. The rule of law and the autonomous administration of justice were central to civil society because, although the latter creates itself spontaneously, it cannot on its own institutionalize or generalize its norms and orientations ("habits of the heart"). A legal system and a legal culture committing practitioners to the norms of impartiality are crucial to the process by which the particularistic goals and projects of associated individuals within civil society could be informed by, made compatible with, or generalized into the universalistic principles of modern constitutional democracies (Hegel 1969: 83–116; Habermas 1996).[5] These dimensions of civil society reciprocally influenced or mediated the institutionalized political publics (parliaments as well as parties and political organizations) and legal publics (courts and juries) of the political system proper.

Twentieth-century European analysts civil society added three crucial components to this understanding. The first, stressed by Gramsci (1971: 206–277; see also Anderson 1977 and Cohen and Arato 1992: 142–159),

---

[5] Law has a foot in both civil society and the state. It institutionalizes generalized norms of the public sphere that constrain state (as well as individual) action. It is also the carrier of state (or class) imperatives. The basic rights established in constitutional liberal democracies construct the terrain of civil society on which social actors clash over cultural evaluations and interpretations of norms, identities, modes of inclusion/exclusion, etc. But states also construct privileged or stigmatized group identities through legalization and classification according to their own imperatives or the imperatives of powerful private actors. Thus, legalization can be highly ambiguous. On the liberal paradigm of civil society, law must be formal, general, abstract, and neutral. Legal formalism allegedly protects against privilege and bias. The defenders of the liberal paradigm of law and the liberal conception of civil society are thus blind to the role of private power in undermining the worth of liberty of those formally entitled to rights.

was an emphasis on the cultural and symbolic dimension of civil society and the role it plays in generating consent (hegemony) and, hence, in integrating society. Gramsci was the first and most important Marxist to abandon the economistic reduction of civil society to political economy and to insist on its autonomy and distinctiveness from the state (political society). While his conception is presented in a notoriously confusing terminology, the idea that runs through all his attempts at a definition is that the reproduction of the existing system occurs through a combination of two practices: hegemony and domination, consent and coercion. These operate through two sets of institutional frameworks: the cultural and associational forms of civil society, and the legal, bureaucratic, police, and military apparatus of the state. Indeed his most important category, hegemony – referring to the dominant action-orienting symbols, beliefs, values, identifications, and social constructions of reality – is meaningless without its corollary concept, civil society.

Thus, Gramsci's key contribution to the conceptualization of civil society was his emphasis on its politically relevant cultural dimension: Civil society is construed both as a symbolic field and as a network of institutions and practices that is the locus for the formation of values, action-orienting norms, meanings, and collective identities. But the cultural dimension of civil society is not given or natural. Rather, it is a stake of social contestation: Its associations and networks are a terrain to be struggled over and an arena wherein collective identities, ethical values, and alliances are forged. Indeed, competing conceptions of civil society are deployed in a continual struggle either to maintain cultural hegemony by dominant groups or to attain counter-hegemony on the part of subordinate collective actors. Accordingly, no conception of civil society, including Gramsci's own, is neutral. Each is part of a project to shape the social relations, cultural forms, and modes of thought of society. In short, Gramsci has shown us that the discourses and culture of civil society are politically relevant and multiple.

Both the second and third crucial twentieth-century contributions by Europeans to the theory of civil society take up the threads of Gramsci's analysis while dispensing with his exclusive focus on class hegemony and with his rather functionalist and monistic approach to civil society's cultural and associational institutions as the expression of one or another class' hegemony. In short, they retain the importance of the cultural and dynamic aspects of civil society stressed by Gramsci while insisting that the abstract norms and organizational principles of modern civil society – from the idea of rights to the principles of autonomous association and free horizontal communication (publicity) – have intrinsic value and are not simply functional to the reproduction of capitalist or any other class hegemony. The structures of civil society allow the contestation over hegemony to occur.

One major contribution on this terrain, made by Touraine (1981), Melucci (1980, 1985), and others (see Cohen and Arato 1992: 492–564), was the emphasis on the dynamic, creative, and contestatory side of civil society: informal networks, initiatives, and social movements as distinct from the more formalized voluntary associations and institutions and from class organizations (parties and unions). Recognition of this dimension allows one to articulate and shift between two perspectives: civil society as a dynamic, innovative source for thematizing new concerns, articulating new projects, and generating new values and new collective identities; and civil society as institutionalized civic autonomy. It also allows one to see how, in its dynamic capacity (collective action), the institutional shape of civil society as well as the polity can be targeted in struggles over democratization.

The other key contribution I have in mind is the communicative, deliberative conception of the public sphere developed primarily by Jurgen Habermas (1989) and his followers (see Calhoun 1992; Cohen and Arato 1992). The category of the public sphere was already present in eighteenth- and nineteenth-century understandings of civil society, but its normative weight and its role in mediating between the particular and the general were not clarified until relatively recently.

In civil publics, people can discuss matters of mutual concern as peers and learn about facts, events, and others' opinions, interests, and perspectives. Discourse on values, norms, laws, and policies generates politically relevant public opinion. Moreover, through its generalized media of communication, the public sphere can mediate among the myriad mini-publics that emerge within and across associations, movements, religious organizations, clubs, local organizations of concerned citizens, and simple socializing. There are, of course, differentiated and institutionalized civil and political publics, weak and strong.[6] But on the normative idea of the liberal public sphere, discursively generated

---

[6] On the distinction between civil and political publics, see Cohen and Arato (1992). On "weak" and "strong," see Nancy Fraser (1992). One must think of the distinction between civil, weak, political, and strong publics as a continuum. Weak publics are, relatively speaking, more deliberative and open to fewer constraints on deliberations. Strong decisional publics are more constrained both qualitatively and quantitatively (i.e. time for deliberation is shorter). A consciousness-raising group in a feminist movement is an example of a weak, uninstitutionalized civil public open to all sorts of statements and reasoning. A jury is an example of an institutionalized civil public that is "strong" in the sense that its deliberations lead to politically binding decisions. A parliament is an even stronger institutionalized political public, legislating for the whole society. For another way of distinguishing among the various constraints on different sorts of publics, see Rawls (1993: 212–254).

public opinion is meant to influence the debates within political and legal publics proper (legislatures and constitutional courts) and to bring under informal control the actions and decisions of rulers and lawmakers (the principle of responsiveness), while remaining autonomous of censorship and manipulation by state officials.

The normative conception of the public sphere also has a democratic-theoretical component: Openness of access, free discursive contestation and debate, and parity of participation (equal voice) are at its core. All citizens affected by public policy and laws should have the right to articulate their views and to influence and the relevant deliberations, and all participants should be able to do so on equal terms. The democratization of civil society entails the reflexive application of the normative conception of the public sphere to itself: Processes of deliberation, negotiation, and accommodation developed in informal civil publics must be provided for in the important non-state institutional arenas – in professional associations, in science, and in "economic" society – and open to general discussion as well.

The concept of the public sphere thus brings together the normative and the empirical, the universal and the particular.[7] It is, in my view, the normative core of the idea of civil society and the heart of any conception of democracy. Indeed, the political legitimacy of modern constitutional democracies rests on the principle that action-orienting norms, practices, policies, and claims to authority can be contested by citizens, are open to their input and revision, and must be discursively redeemed. As Claus Offe (this volume) argues, unconstrained critical discourse in the public sphere (secured by rights) is the form of institutionalized "distrust" that is crucial to maintaining trust – belief in legitimacy – in constitutional democracies.

I would defend an even stronger claim: The deliberative genesis and justification of public policies or decisions deeply affecting the public in political and civil public spaces respectively must be seen as *constitutive* of the modern form of democracy. This means that wherever important decisions, or developments are occurring – be it in the scientific, corporate, media, or educational establishments – public spaces involving criticism, articulation of alternatives, and counterpowers must be provided for and protected. This, in my view, is the *sine qua non* for trust and confidence in institutions to be maintainable and warranted.

As already indicated, voluntary association is an important aspect of a vital civil society. But focusing exclusively on this dimension is impover-

---

[7] This way of conceptualizing the public sphere precludes granting legitimacy to any group or institution simply on the basis of a claim to embody or represent the public.

ishing, to say the least. So is the degeneration of civil-society talk into rhetoric about the decline of morals and civic virtue. It is also backward-looking and politically dangerous.

Voluntary association, social capital, and workable democracy

Robert Putnam's claim in his extraordinarily influential book *Making Democracy Work* that democratic government is more responsive and effective when it faces a vigorous civil society is, of course, one that I embrace. He argues convincingly that horizontally organized voluntary associations that cut across social cleavages are more likely to nourish wider social cooperation, to reinforce norms of reciprocity, and thus to "make democracy work" than hierarchical segmental organizations or clientelistic structures (Putnam 1993: 173–175).[8] A civic culture of "generalized trust" and social solidarity, peopled by citizens willing and able to cooperate in joint ventures, *is* an important societal prerequisite of a vital democracy.

Nevertheless, Putnam's approach is unsatisfactory, in part for methodological reasons. He reduces civil society to the dimension of voluntary association and construes the latter as the *sole* source of what he calls social capital. The feature of the social context that matters most to the performance of democratic institutions, on Putnam's analysis, is the presence or absence of a civic culture. The indicators of civicness that he cites are similar to those mentioned in the civic culture studies of the 1950s: the number of voluntary associations, the incidence of newspaper readership (a sign of interest in and being informed about community affairs), electoral turnout, and a range of civic attitudes including law-abidingness, interpersonal trust, and general cooperativeness. So far so good.

Indeed, Putnam's historical chapters provide a rich description of the emergence of civicness and what it needed to take root, at least in the north of Italy. Here, in addition to the dense network of associational life and the oaths of mutual assistance sworn by members of associations in the early Communes, Putnam mentions the importance of institutions and institutionalized norms, such as the professionalization of public

---

[8] Putnam knows that all networks and associations mix the horizontal and the vertical but insists nonetheless that the basic contrasts between horizontal and vertical linkages, between web-like and maypole-like networks, is reasonably clear. But isn't it possible for people to belong to both sorts of organizations? Does Putnam insist on full congruence between civil and political institutions? For a critique of this idea, see Rosenblum (1994).

administration and credible state impartiality in the enforcement of laws, for the maintenance of social trust. Strong and autonomous courts, reliable administrative state structures, and *confidence* that the administration of justice, enforcement of contracts, and legislation would be impartial seemed to be a *sine qua non* for the networks of civic associations to succeed in generating solidarity outside the bonds of kinship (Putnam 1993: 128, 147).[9] Thus, on the descriptive level, at least, the charge of reductionism seems inappropriate.

The important concluding theoretical chapter of the book, "Social Capital and Institutional Success," however, *is* open to such a charge. For there, history, tradition, culture, normative orientations, and their transmission over time are analyzed in terms of the concept of inherited "social capital" – defined as the social stock of trust, norms, and networks that facilitate coordinated actions – whereas the *source* of social capital and of its generalization is narrowed down to involvement in secondary associations. We are left with a weak theoretical framework and an unconvincing analysis. Unfortunately, this framework is greatly influencing the American civil-society debate.

The crucial chapter on social capital asks how "virtuous circles" generate, generalize, and transmit traditions of civic engagement through centuries of radical social, economic, and political change. Putnam dismisses the classic Hobbesian solution, "third-party enforcement." If cooperation for the common good requires trust in everyone's willingness to contribute equally, a "third-party enforcer" such as the state should enable subjects to do what they cannot do on their own: namely, trust one another. But apparently the use of force is expensive, and impartial enforcement is itself a public good subject to the same dilemma it aims to solve: What power could ensure that the sovereign does not defect? Nor, as the new institutionalists suggest, will the best institutional design ensure impartiality even if it entails the participation of the affected parties in defining the rules, the subjection of violators to sanctions, and low-cost mechanisms for resolving conflicts. For the same dilemma apparently obtains *vis-à-vis* the institutionalist understanding of the state

---

[9] I use the word "confidence" advisedly. What is at stake is analytically distinct from interpersonal trust, i.e. the trust of concrete individuals. Confidence that the administration of justice will be impartial or that the legislative process is fair, responsive, and representative rests on the shared understanding that the principles of impartiality, fairness, equal concern and respect, etc. have been institutionalized as norms and that these are internalized by the institutional actors as well as those subject to these institutions. It is thus possible to lose trust in a particular lawmaker or judge without the loss of confidence in the legal system or the legislative process as a whole. Their legitimacy rests on the belief that generally they function in a manner appropriate to their institutionalized norms.

as impartial lawgiver that confronted the state as Hobbesian sovereign, namely, the problem of infinite regress: Trust and generalized reciprocity are presupposed for the establishment of the institutions in the first place. Putnam accordingly turns away from state structures to "soft" socio-cultural solutions. Dense networks of civic involvement are both a sign and a source of social capital. Participating in horizontal voluntary associations lubricates cooperation and generates social trust, thus allowing dilemmas of collective action to be resolved (Putnam 1993: 165–166; Putnam 1995: 67. Apparently, such participation produces "moral resources" that can be transmitted over generations (inherited) and whose supply increases through use: Stocks of social capital tend to be self-reinforcing and cumulative. Inheritance of a stock of social capital renders voluntary cooperation in a community easier and thus makes democracy work (Putnam 1993: 167, 176–177, 182).

Although Putnam does say that trust has two sources – norms of reciprocity and networks of civic engagement – the first is primarily a function of the second (Levi 1996: 47; see also Putnam 1993: 171–174). Dense networks of associations entail repeated exchanges of what he calls "short-term altruism" and "long-term self-interest": I help you now in the expectation that you will help me in the future. These rational exchanges and the direct experience of reliability, repeated over time, encourage the development of a norm of generalized reciprocity.

That voluntary association is *evidence* of social cooperation and trust is both undeniable and almost tautological, but why is it construed as the only significant source of social capital? Why are democratic political institutions, the public sphere, and law absent from the theoretical analysis of how social trust is developed? The answer is obvious: Once the state is defined and dismissed as a third-party enforcer, once law is turned into sanctions that provide for a certain level of social order but no more, once institutions are dismissed as irrelevant to social trust because their genesis already presupposes social trust, and once a vital civil society is reduced to the presence or absence of intermediate voluntary associations, no other source of social trust is conceivable.

As others have pointed out, the theory has many flaws.[10] One of the most serious is the failure to say just what generalizes the social trust produced within voluntary associations. How does intragroup trust

---

[10] Portes and Landolt (1996) stress the circularity of the argument, while Tarrow (1996) points to the confusion of the indicators with causes of civicness. Levi (1996) notes the sloppiness of the definitions, which makes it almost impossible to differentiate among social capital, interpersonal trust, and generalized reciprocity, as well as the absence of a definition of trust in Putnam's work. Skocpol (1996) notes the one-sidedness of the

become trust of strangers outside the group? Why does the willingness to act together for mutual benefit in a small group such as a choral society translate into willingness to act for the common good or to become politically engaged at all? Indeed, *is the interpersonal trust generated in face-to-face interactions the same thing as "generalized trust"?* I don't think so.

Let me be clear here. I don't doubt that trust lubricates cooperation or, more important, that general abstract *norms* of reciprocity allow the reconciliation of self-interest and solidarity. I am not convinced, however, that the trust that emerges within particular associations is sufficient for producing "generalized trust" or, in the language I prefer, belief in the legitimacy of institutionalized norms, acceptance of the universalistic principles of reciprocity and societywide social solidarity, and confidence that these will orient the action of both powerful elites and average citizens. What is very odd is that Putnam offers no mechanism for explaining how these emerge.

I believe that the use made of the concept of social capital is at fault. Obscuring more than it illuminates, this concept allows one to avoid the difficult task of showing that the particular trust built up between specific individuals in one context can be transferred without further ado to other contexts, to strangers, or to society at large. In short, before the issue of what generalizes social capital is the question of whether "inherited social capital" is the right concept to use for *six* rather different things: interpersonal trust, social solidarity, general norms of reciprocity, belief in the legitimacy of institutionalized norms, confidence that these will motivate the action of institutional actors and ordinary citizens (social solidarity), and the transmission of cultural traditions, patterns, and values.

The metaphor of social "capital" allows the theorist to finesse the generalization issue and to blur these distinctions by suggesting a false analogy between direct interpersonal social relations and economic exchanges on the market. Capital accumulated in one context of course can be invested in another place: It can be saved, inherited, and exchanged regardless of its particular form because there is a universal equivalent for it – money – and an institutional framework for exchange – the market economy. As the medium of exchange and the universal equivalent for all forms of wealth, money solves the generalization issue. Impersonal contractual

society-centered analysis to the neglect of other important actors – most notably, government – and factors such as the structure and nature of the state. Although I agree with these criticisms, we must beware of overcorrecting here. The society-centered analysis itself is a corrective to one-sided, state-centered approaches. What we need is a model broad enough to capture both dimensions.

market relations are possible because money in a market system substitutes for direct communications in the coordination and integration of actions (see Habermas 1981: 113–199). Of course, even the market presupposes *confidence* that the value of money is backed up by the banking system and that contractual obligations are recognized and enforced by states.

Interpersonal trust, on the other hand, is by definition specific and contextual: One trusts *particular* people because of repeated interactions with them in specific contexts in which reciprocity is directly experienced. Interpersonal trust generated in face-to-face relationships is not an instance of a more general impersonal phenomenon. Nor can it simply be transferred to others or to other contexts. Indeed, it is entirely possible that without other mechanisms for the "generalization" of trust, participation in associations and membership in social networks could foster particularism, localism, intolerance, exclusion, and generalized mistrust of outsiders, of the law, and of government. Without other mediations, there is no reason to expect that the forms of reciprocity or trust generated within small groups would extend beyond the group or, for that matter, that group demands would be anything other than particularistic.

The argument that repeated interaction games within small-scale, face-to-face groups of strategic calculators can generate universal norms of law-abidingness or reciprocity is unconvincing. Repeated interaction within a group may help generate local norms of reciprocity between members, because each learns gradually to expect that the other will cooperate (Coleman 1990: 251, 273).[11] Interpersonal trust involves not only the experience of the other's reliability but also the moral obligation of the trusted person to honor the trust bestowed upon her and the mutual expectation that each understands this principle and will be motivated internally to act accordingly.

For interpersonal trust to turn into generalized reciprocity or to foster general law-abidingness, however, the universalistic normative expectation itself would have to be presupposed *as a norm* in a wide variety of contexts. The *obligatoriness* of reciprocity and law-abidingness and the motivation to act accordingly, over and above the experience and hence expectation of the regularity of behavior of particular others and in distinction from simply contingent prudent behavior, require something more

---

[11] Coleman (1990) shows that under the assumption of rational action, norms can arise, but he gives no argument about the emergence of norms in general. Nor does he address the deeper issue of how values (standards used to evaluate evaluative standards) emerge. I don't believe this can be answered within a rational-choice framework. Putnam's work suffers from the same deficiency.

than the repetition of sets of strategic interactions. In short, for impersonal, general trust of strangers to be conceivable and warranted, other factors would have to mediate.[12] The principle of reciprocity would have to be institutionalized on the one side, and the aspiration/motivation to be trustworthy would have to become part of one's identity, as it were, on the other. Thus, the analysis does not escape the problem of infinite regress.

Indeed, I submit that what is called "trust in government" is not the result of "generalized" interpersonal trust at all but derives from something rather different. To see what role institutions play here, one would have to understand law and the state not just as a third-party enforcer. At the very least, the two-sidedness of law – law as sanction *and* law as institutionalized cultural values, norms, rules, and rights – would have to be theorized. Only then would it be possible to reflect on the role of law and rights in substituting *universalistic* norms as functional equivalents for personalized trust and substituting confidence in institutions (backed up by sanctions) and belief in their legitimacy and purpose for direct interpersonal ties. For example, legal norms of procedural fairness, impartiality, and justice that give structure to the state and some civil institutions, limit favoritism and arbitrariness, and protect merit are the *sine qua non* for societywide "general trust," at least in a modern social structure. So is the expectation that institutional actors will live up to and enforce the norms of the institutional setting in which they interact. Rights, on the other hand, ensure that trust is warranted insofar as they provide individuals the opportunity to demand that violations of legitimate reciprocal expectations be sanctioned.

It makes little sense to use the category of generalized trust to describe one's attitude toward law or government. One can trust only people because only people can fulfill obligations. But institutions (legal and other) can provide functional equivalents for interpersonal trust in impersonal settings involving interactions with strangers because they institutionalize action-orienting norms and the expectation that these will be honored.

What Durkheim (1958) once called "professional ethics" does indeed affect "civic morals". If one knows one can expect impartiality from a judge, care and concern from a doctor, protection from police, concern for the common good from legislators, and so on, then one can develop confidence (instead of cynicism) that shared norms and cultural values will orient the action of powerful others. But confidence of this sort also presupposes public spaces in which the validity of such norms and the

---

[12] On the concept of warranted trust, see Warren (1996) and this volume.

fairness of procedures can be challenged, revised, redeemed, or reinforced through critique.[13] Democracy goes with trust and civic initiative or engagement to the degree to which institutions (political and otherwise) exist that are receptive to the influence and/or input of collective actors in an appropriate way.

The point here is that Putnam's narrow theoretical framework prevents him from articulating these complex interrelations. Nevertheless, even with its flaws, *Making Democracy Work* was open to a more sophisticated interpretation. After all, the book traces the effects of institutional reform in Italy: the devolution of important powers from a centralized state to newly created regional political public spaces, closer to the populace and open to their influence. Moreover, many of the vital elements of a richer society-centered analysis were at least mentioned in the text. Though Putnam misinterprets his own data, his research suggests that well-designed political institutions are crucial to fostering civic spirit because they provide enabling conditions – a political opportunity structure – that could become an incentive to civil actors to emerge and a target of influence for them once they do (see Urbinati 1993: 573). The path not taken in the theoretical chapter of this book was nonetheless made available.

The recent work on civil society in the United States is all the more disappointing in this regard. Far from broadening the analytical framework, the new research is guided exclusively by the methods and categories of that final chapter. "Civil society" is cast in very narrow terms. As I already indicated, the linking of the reductionist conception of civil society to the discourse of civic decline makes this approach prone to ideological misuse.

Social decapitalization in America?

In a series of recent articles, Putnam and his associates have argued that low electoral turnout and declining membership in political parties in the United States are part of a much wider phenomenon: the gradual disappearance of American "social capital" (Putnam 1995a, 1995b, 1996). Given the alleged centrality of social capital to civic engagement and effective, democratic government, its erosion is presented as a serious cause for alarm.

---

[13] As Claus Offe (this volume) puts it, democratic citizens build "generalized" trust on the basis of what they know about institutions, institutionalized norms (and sanctions), and their ability to orient action, not on the basis of what they know about political elites (whom they in fact do not know).

The startling discovery of "social decapitalization" emerged out of the application of the method and concepts of Putnam's work on Italian civic culture to the American context. Accordingly, the presence of secondary associations, deemed the most reliable empirical indicator of social capital, is *the* independent variable used to test the vitality of American civil society. And the research indeed does show a drastic decline of membership in such associations, beginning in the second half of the twentieth century.[14]

These findings would not be so alarming if functional equivalents for the old groups were emerging. But, according to the research, they have not. "Counter-trends," such as the emergence of new mass-membership organizations such as the National Organization for Women and the explosion of interest groups represented in Washington such as the American Association of Retired People are only apparent, for these groups are really "tertiary," "mailing-list" organizations rather than "secondary" associations. The latter are characterized by face-to-face interactions and direct horizontal interpersonal ties of people who actually meet one another, whereas the former involve abstract impersonal ties of people to common symbols, texts, leaders, and ideals and not to one another (Putnam 1995a: 71, 1996: 35). According to the theory of social capital, associational membership should increase social trust. But apparently membership in tertiary groups does not yield the kind of social connectedness that generates social capital.

Compared to the civic generation born between 1910 and 1940, the post-war baby boom generation that matured in the 1960s and all those who followed are disturbingly "post-civic." Indeed, the phenomenon of decline is generational, all other factors having been controlled for (Putnam 1996: 35–43). What caused this decline, if we assume that it is real?

Putnam's thesis is that the decline was caused by the arrival of television, a new medium of communication that became prevalent while the 1960s generation was maturing. Television viewing is the only leisure activity that inhibits participation outside the home, coming at the expense of nearly every social activity. Analyzing General Social Survey data from 1974 to 1994 and controlling for factors such as education, age, and income, Putnam found that TV viewing is negatively correlated to social trust, group membership, and voting turnout (Putnam 1996: 46–48). People who watch too much television are no longer neighborly; they don't socialize, join clubs, or form the sorts of secondary associations that foster civic orientations. Apparently, the culture industry is

[14] Putnam (1996: 35–36) indicates an erosion of roughly 25 to 50 percent of membership over the last three decades. See also Putnam (1995a: 67–70).

finally having the effect so feared by its critics: the transformation of American civil society into a mass society.[15] I do not find this account persuasive. First, other analysts show that not all the data on civicness point to decline. In a recent major study, Sidney Verba and his colleagues (Verba, Schlozman, and Brady 1995: 68–91) do not find that the falloff in voter turnout is part of a general erosion in voluntary activity or political participation. They report increases in certain forms of civic activism such as membership in community problem-solving organizations. Some older types of associational membership and activities have even been expanding both numerically and qualitatively. Moreover, different loci and sorts of social activity may serve purposes similar to those of traditional forms of secondary association (Schudson 1996: 17–18). Putnam's research screens out such innovations in social connectedness.

Equally important is the phenomenon of "shifting involvements" noted many years ago by Albert O. Hirschman (1982). The political engagement of contemporary citizens is episodic and increasingly issue-oriented. Membership in political parties, labor unions, and traditional voluntary associations may have declined, but the willingness of Americans to mobilize periodically on local and national levels around concerns that affect them cannot be deduced from this fact. The new action repertoires invented by civic and political actors cannot be assessed adequately by criteria derived from older forms.[16]

[15] It is bizarre to present the adult generation in the 1950s as the paragon of civicness or the 1950s and early 1960s as an era of the generalized social trust that makes democracy work. This period was the heyday of McCarthyism (hardly noteworthy for generalized trust), institutionalized racial segregation, exclusion of women from a wide range of economic and political institutions and associations (hardly a model of cross-cutting pluralism), and a pervasive ideological (and economic) movement to push women out of the labor force and into the housewife role with all its attendant "volunteerism" (something that did not exactly foster egalitarian gender norms or undermine familialism). Civil privatism, authoritarian cultural and social conservatism would seem a more apt characterization of that period than civic virtue. Indeed, if voluntary association was alive and well in the 1950s, this is proof that it does not suffice to render a political culture civic or to generate generalized trust or active egalitarian participation in public life. Moreover, I suspect that economic expansion and the impact of the New Deal had a good deal more to do with the effectiveness of government than the vitality of the Elks Club.

[16] Indeed, if one's theoretical framework did not screen out the existence of new action repertoires and new modes of association (such as networks), one could begin to reflect on complementary (or even prior) changes in the political system and in the economy that trigger, facilitate, and/or block appropriate forms of participation in public life. Tarrow (1994) and others have argued that social movements can produce lasting effects on political culture by legitimating new forms of collective action and by establishing a permanent place on the public agenda for issues that remain alive even in a general context of demobilization. See also Cohen (1985). For an interesting albeit controversial recent discussion of the relation between movements and state forms, see Dryzek (1996).

Indeed, to discount the new types of association, mobilization, and public engagement of the 1960s and 1970s simply because they differ from traditional secondary associations makes little sense. These allegedly uncivic generations and their successors created the first consumers' movement since the 1930s, the first environmental movement since the turn of the century, public health movements, grassroots activism and community organizing, the most important feminist movement since the pre-World War I period, the civil rights movement, and innumerable transnational nongovernmental organizations and civic movements, all of which have led to unprecedented advances in rights and social justice (Schudson 1996: 20).

This highly civic activism is not the product of disassociated individuals mobilized by direct mailings or glib leaders. It draws instead on myriad small-scale groups and networks different in kind from Putnam's preferred intermediary organizations but most certainly involving face-to-face interpersonal interaction and oppositional public spheres, *as well as* more generalized forms of communication. In other words, the forms of association out of which mass mobilizations emerge nowadays might not involve groups organized with official membership lists, but they can and often do involve discussion networks, consciousness-raising groups, self-help groups, and the like that are continuously cropping up and disappearing but surely are signs of the ability to connect and act in concert. Moreover, top-down and bottom-up forms of political mobilization are not incompatible.[17]

Why is all of this dismissed or ignored? If one starts from the assumption that only a certain form of secondary association is the source of "social capital," then obviously if it wanes, the conclusion of overall decline is unavoidable: It is an artifact of the method. But one cannot measure the vitality of civil society by comparing only one indicator (statistics on membership in secondary associations) over time. The normative structure and identity of society have different manifestations in different contexts and epochs. The real question is why certain forms of civic activity appear when they do. Surely the "political opportunity structure" afforded by constititutional design, state institutions, "political society," legal developments, the level and type of organization of economic life and the nature of other dimensions of civil society, including the form and impact of the mass media, would have to be analyzed in order to arrive at an answer (Skocpol 1996: 23).

---

[17] Nor are direct and more mediated forms of communication. Ties to common leaders, texts, symbols, and ideals can inform and foster horizontal styles of association and interpersonal interaction by providing points of reference for discussion and for mobilization when the time comes. Skocpol (1996: 25) points to the Christian Coalition as a successful example of a secondary association that melds top-down and bottom-up styles of political mobilization.

If one does not screen out "functional equivalents" for traditional forms of voluntary association at the outset, then the relationship of new media of communication to new forms of collective action and new types of publicity and public engagement could be analyzed along with their (alleged) potential to undermine old ones.

Indeed, if the analyst had the normative concept of the public sphere at his disposal, the "two-sidedness" of all mass media would be apparent. Generalized forms of communication, from the printed word to radio, television, and now cyberspace, do not necessarily displace or degrade interpersonal communication.[18] Nor do they perforce "privatize" or block civic engagement. They even could foster it by enabling the extension of communications and networks beyond local contexts (Norris 1996: 475–476).[19] The public media of communication, along with law, are an important mechanism by which the "particular" and the "universal," the local, the national, and the international (meanings, norms, and issues) are interrelated. Even media that have little claim to be interactive, such as television, might foster discussion about the content of what is broadcast despite the fact that reception initially may be private. Of course, interactive media can do more. The new media of communication do raise new issues *vis-à-vis* access, influence, participation, and the effects of the respective technologies for democratic theory, as did the development of print and the emergence of the "bourgeois" public sphere in the beginning epochs of modernity. But these have to be addressed in nuanced ways and not bemoaned as disintegrative simply because they displace an earlier form of communication. In short, there is no zero-sum relation between deliberation and mass media, between direct face-to-face discussion and indirect communication.

Moreover, generalized media of communication are themselves institutions subject to the norms of the public sphere and hence are open to critique if access to them or their functioning violates these norms. Indeed, one might note that today the autonomy and integrity of civil

---

[18] Pippa Norris (1996) convincingly shows that the data do not permit one to claim that civic and political disagreement vary unambiguously and positively with the sheer amount of television that one watches. What matters more is the content of what one watches. Given the diversity of channels, programs, and choices – from Nightline, 60 Minutes, CNN World News, NPR, Meet the Press, and C-Span to the information available on the Internet – it might even be the case that Americans as a whole are better informed about national and international issues than ever before.

[19] The problem of disentangling the direction of causality that plagues all cross-sectional survey analysis is not resolved regardless of how one comes down on this issue. It is not clear whether those who are already actively involved in public life turn to the news networks for more information or whether tuning into TV news or reading about public affairs encourages people to become more active in public affairs or civic life. Either way, the charge that television is the root cause of the lack of trust in American democracy is unproven and implausible.

publics and personal communication are explicitly asserted and institutionalized as public norms, and they are better protected by law and courts than ever before. Certainly compared to the 1950s, First Amendment protections for public, political, and personal expression are incomparably stronger, as are legal protections of personal autonomy rights. To focus only on aspects of the media that privatize and trivialize, to conclude that the amount of time spent with such media is both a sign and a cause of the erosion of social capital, is thus highly misleading.

I do not doubt that the old sorts of associations that fostered civicness for certain segments of the population are disappearing. Nor do I want to claim that functional equivalents are flourishing and that there is nothing to think about. Assuredly, some social, economic, technical, and structural changes have undermined the traditional shape of civil society and rendered some of the old avenues of participation and influence obsolete. We may well be in a political context in which *institutional redesign* of various aspects of the political system is necessary to strengthen new sorts of civil sociality. It is not necessary to choose between an institutionalist and an associationalist path to the creation of social trust, as Putnam seems to imply. These can be mutually interdependent and reinforcing. But where to look and what is to be done will only be obscured by backward-looking analyses focused on reviving old forms of association that may no longer be appropriate. Indeed, the focus on the allegedly privatizing effects of television viewing steers the theorist away from analyzing the structural, technological, and political causes for the changes in action repertoires and modes of civic association. Even worse, such an approach plays into the hands of those who are far more concerned with pushing back the achievements of the welfare state than with its "reflexive continuation" and with reviving traditional and authoritarian forms of civil society than with its further democratization (Cohen and Arato 1992; Beck 1992; Beck, Giddens, Lash 1994).

Strange bedfellows: the rhetoric of decline and suspect agendas

The two groups that deploy the discourse of civil society most effectively are the Republican right and the neocommunitarian movement associated with the journal *The Responsive Community*.[20] Both define civil society

[20] My remarks here regarding "neocommunitarians" reference primarily the works of communitarians associated with Amitai Etzioni's journal, *The Responsive Community*. For a representative sampling of their work, see Etzioni (1995). I do not address the far more complex theoretical and political positions of theorists such as Michael Walzer and Charles Taylor, who are not part of this movement although they are labeled communitarians.

in terms of traditional forms of voluntary association, and both lament their decline. Unlike Putnam and his associates, however, the former explicitly target the welfare state and the latter blame the rise of an amoral culture of expressive (and secular) individualism and a legalistic focus on individual rights for the alleged disintegration of social capital. I will comment briefly on the first as it is not particularly new and then turn to the more nuanced analysis of the second.

The civil-society discourse of the Republican right is straightforward: It argues, in Newt Gingrich's words, for "replacing the welfare state with an opportunity society" (see Skocpol 1996: 20–21). Market incentives, volunteerism, and localism are presented as the alternative to big government and the best way to revitalize initiative and independence in America. Centralized national "interventionist" government is blamed for both economic stagnation and social disintegration: It displaces voluntary association and creates dependence, undermining both individual initiative and the sense of personal and civic responsibility.

This discourse conflates the market and business with civil society, placing local self-help and charity in a zero-sum opposition to national public policy. It is hardly a project for a "reflexive continuation of the welfare state."[21] Its proponents do not seek to honor universalistic principles of social justice by means less obtrusive than top-down legal ordering, which might avoid the administrative penetration and fragmentation of social life, a real concern in my view. Instead, the discourse functions as a thinly veiled cover for dismantling public services and redistributing wealth to the top – already a highly successful project in the United States. In the current context of corporate internationalization, globalization of labor markets, downsizing, out-sourcing, capital flight, growing economic disparity, and the corresponding decline of secure or career-oriented jobs, not to mention the veritable disappearance of work in certain communities, this discourse is both disingenuous and destructive (Wilson 1996, 1997). It obscures the fact that, when unregulated, the capitalist economy itself has corrosive effects on community, solidarity, and family that scarcely can be mitigated by volunteerism or moral exhortation.

The latest communitarian version of the discourse of civil society seems to be aware of this problem. As Michael Sandel (1996) puts it in his recent book, *Democracy's Discontent*, not only big government but also "big economy" undermines responsibility, virtue, and character. On closer inspection, however, it turns out that it is above all the misguided focus of public policy since the 1970s on growth, redistribution, and rights

---

[21] See Cohen and Arato (1992: 11–15, 468–491) for a critique of neoconservative critiques of the welfare state and for a discussion of its reflexive continuation.

without regard for moral concerns that has undermined civil society. This policy orientation is both effect and cause of a deeper disintegrative development: the triumph of a culture of expressive individualism, a corresponding fragmentation of social life, and moral impoverishment of our public discourse. The "procedural republic," with its neutrality toward substantive values and its rights orientation, has not only missed the moral boat but also actively contributes to moral decay.

The communitarians thus choose a *values* discourse predicated on the premise that only good people make good citizens. Their central thesis is that we are facing a potentially disastrous decline of good values in the United States. Accordingly, the emphasis is on reviving substantive ethical (and religious) discussion in the public sphere to arrive at a new consensus on core values (Sandel 1996: 21, 318–351). "Formative" public policies guided by an explicitly articulated, shared substantive conception of the good, oriented toward inculcating the proper values and shaping preferences in the right direction, are needed to reintroduce an ethic of responsibility, social solidarity, and virtue into the worldview of citizens. They assume that in order to be well integrated, society requires a "thick," extensive, nationally articulated substantive value consensus on a wide range of "public" *and* "private" issues. Strengthening civil society's institutions is the first priority of such "soulcraft," for these are the primary agents of character formation. The state and law are important, but instead of granting rights and entitlements they should encourage talk about virtue and ethics, institutionalize the right values, and foster strong civil institutions that will help integrate people into what will be, in effect, a refurbished American civil religion.

This assessment of the problem (and the proposed solution) is deeply misleading. It is based on four misconceptions. The first is the assumption that a thick, substantive, societywide value consensus is necessary for social integration in modern societies. The second is the equation of open, public pluralization of life forms with social fragmentation and disintegration. Communitarians, third, also tend to construe the concern for self-realization and social responsibility as mutually exclusive, misunderstanding the structural imperatives of individualization in late modern society as a matter of personal choice and egoism (Beck 1992). Finally, they assume that the rights orientation of contemporary Americans undermines our sense of community, our moral impulses, and the democratic legitimacy of our political system.[22]

It is not difficult to articulate theoretically what is wrong with each of these notions. Since Durkheim (1933; see also Habermas 1984,

---

[22] For two critiques, see Cohen (1992: 66–98) and McClain (1994).

1987), social theorists have known that social integration in modern differentiated societies does not depend on a nationwide, substantive, comprehensive value consensus. Although a general acceptance of the abstract moral principles undergirding America's (and every) constitutional democracy *is* important, these are compatible with a variety of cultural systems of evaluation (Rawls 1993). They are, moreover, open to different institutionalizations that vary with the prevailing conception of the cultural and ethical identity of the society.[23] An "overlapping consensus" among comprehensive views on a particular substantive conception of justice is desirable and necessary for a stable, well-ordered, well-integrated (modern) society. Such a consensus involves more than acceptance of the general moral principles of constitutional democracy. But, as John Rawls notes, this is predicated on the assumption that diversity among ways of life and a plurality of comprehensive worldviews within civil society are tolerated and even fostered, providing they are "reasonable" – i.e. compatible with a general conception of justice and the use of public reason. It is thus not necessary to have a comprehensive, society-wide consensus on values and on a value hierarchy for society to be well ordered.

Contestation over past institutionalizations and struggles over cultural hegemony – over the power to name, signify, and interpret norms and national identity – are not necessarily signs of social disintegration or moral decay. Instead, open, public, even conflictual pluralization and individuation of forms of life can be a response to change that has the potential to realize these principles in less exclusionary, less hierarchical ways. A relatively thin conception of national identity, together with political processes that accommodate diversity and acknowledge the equal claim of all to participate and to live openly according to their evaluations, could foster rather than undermine social inclusion, trust, and social solidarity.[24]

The communitarian thesis of value decline and social fragmentation is neither self-evidently true nor politically innocent. Social contestation over institutionalized public values and cultural models *is* evidence that a once-hegemonic conception of the American way of life is being challenged and decentered. But to call this a sign of corruption is a rhetorical ploy that positions one particular set of values and identities as "the moral"

---

[23] On the general abstract principles informing every constitutional democracy, see Habermas (1996: 82–132).

[24] Just how thick or thin a national consensus or identity must be is a matter of heated debate. Among those who claim a thin consensus suffices are Rawls (1993) and Habermas (1995). But see also Hollinger (1995) and Lind (1995) for arguments for a thick national identity in the United States.

and all others as deviant. In short, it conflates one conception of the good with the morally right.

The four "misconceptions" are, in my view, elements of a political project aimed at retraditionalizing civil society, at homogenizing our social and cultural life, and at re-imposing a particular conception of American national identity on our political and civil institutions, to which citizens would have to assimilate or risk stigma and exclusion. Under the guise of reviving republican civic virtue, neocommunitarian rhetoric effaces the elective affinity between the universalistic principles undergirding modern civil society and plurality. Let me turn to a concrete example, their analysis of "the" family, to make my point.

Although they vary on whether the intermediary associations of civil society include primarily churches, neighborhood groups, and the usual list of locally based voluntary associations, or additionally unions and social movements, all communitarians agree that the family is *the* institutional core of a modern and civil society. Indeed, "the" family is now deemed the most important "voluntary" association because it is the place where the capacity for collaborating in other secondary intermediary associations emerges. It is here that competence and character are first formed, solidarity and trust first experienced, values first learned. Only in well-functioning families do children develop the healthy self-confidence and independence of mind crucial to citizenship along with the civic virtues of cooperation, self-restraint, and concern for the common good (Glendon 1991: 115; Sandel 1996: 104–118; Galston 1991: 222; Galston 1995; Whitehead 1992: 1–2; Elshtain and Buell 1991; Struening 1996). Of course, the other mediating institutions of civil society matter. But it is from the family that we first inherit social capital! Social connectedness and the ability to participate constructively in the other associations of civil society presuppose the health of this core institution. "Family values" and the values produced in "the" family are thus at the center of the communitarians' civil-society discourse.

They also argue that the sort of family that imparts the virtues necessary to a vital civil society and a democratic polity has been in decline for the past thirty years. Why else would we need a family-values discourse? The well-known statistics on increasing divorce rates, out-of-wedlock births, single-parent families, teen pregnancy, female-headed households, the postponement of marriage, the increasing incidence of premarital sex, and so on are cited in all of their works as evidence of an alarming moral decline and a dangerous unraveling of community (Glendon 1991: 133–134; Sandel 1996: 112–115; Galston 1995: 140–141, note 1; Elshtain 1995: 3–8). Among the alleged consequences of these trends is the failure of children to learn the virtues that make for responsible, self-reliant,

self-controlled, independent, productive, cooperative, and civically virtuous citizens. Apparently only one family form can generate the proper
values and social capital necessary to a vital civil society: the intact two-
parent heterosexual nuclear family with children, based on a companionate marriage construed as a lifetime commitment of love, solidarity, fidelity,
and responsibility. In short, the communitarians' family-values discourse
places the blame for poverty, drug use, and civil privatism on cultural
developments and on family composition rather than on structural factors in economics and politics. They have successfully shifted public-policy
debate away from asking how to ensure that all households can attain an
adequate standard of living, health care, and housing toward how to for-
tify the two-parent family. This argument revives the American tradition
of blaming poverty on the moral failings of the poor, especially women.[25]
    But why has this family form along with the other institutions of civil
society so drastically declined? Instead of pointing to the impact of new
technologies as Putnam does, the communitarian movement blames a
huge shift in cultural values. We are reaping the bitter harvest of the per-
missive culture of the 1960s, Putnam's first "post-civic" generation. The
rise of a new self-indulgent and irresponsible "expressive" individualism
and the triumph of the "voluntarist" conception of the self are the chief
culprits here.
    Echoing the story told by Robert Bellah et al. (1985) in *Habits of the
Heart*, neocommunitarians insist that the focus on self-realization initiated by 1960s radicals leads people to view intimate relationships and
all other associations solely as contexts for self-fulfillment and hence as
temporary or endlessly renegotiable (cf. Giddens 1992). An older American culture of individualism based on self-control and a willingness to
assume responsibility for oneself, one's family, and one's community used
to reinforce the citizen's sense of civicness. But this ascetic individualism
has been replaced by an ideal that emphasizes personal happiness over
all other concerns. This ideology undermines individuals' capacity for
exhibiting civic virtue or social solidarity, both of which require commitment and self-restraint. Strong, inner-directed people striving for
independence, yet sharing the same family values and work ethic, have
given way to narcissists whose only value is their own self-fulfillment.

[25] This discourse has not gone unchallenged. Many analysts have questioned the claim
that it is the wrong family composition or divorce that causes poverty and disfunctional-
ity. See Stacey (1994), Skolnick and Rosencrantz (1994), and Young (1995: 536–542).
Others (Morone 1996) have noted that the halcyon days of stable marriage featured
dependent women without significant career options and thus argue that the low divorce
rates of the past do not necessarily reflect an earlier generation's greater commitment
to family and virtue, but rather women's lack of the means and rights to mobility and
independence.

The new voluntarist conception of moral obligation fostered by contemporary liberal theory also has played its destructive part. Taking
their cues from Michael Sandel's jeremiad against the liberal ideal of the
"unencumbered self" and the "procedural republic," communitarians
insist that a widespread contractualist conception of morality has weakened
Americans' sense of obligation to family and local and national community. We are obligated to fulfill only those ends that we have chosen (Sandel
1996: 11–14). The image of the sovereign authentic self, recognizing
obligations only if they are voluntarily assumed by the moral agent, mis-
construes and erodes the moral fabric of that all important community
– the family – with important consequences for the rest of social and civic
life. The thin consensus on procedural principles touted by liberal
contractualists, which goes with the voluntarist conception of the self, is
deemed insufficient for civic virtue, especially given our increasing diversity in ethnic, religious, and moral makeup. It cannot provide the shared
understandings necessary for a well-integrated polity.

It is to the development of liberal jurisprudence, however, that we
must look for an explanation of how the cultural orientation of a relatively small minority spread to the population at large. According to the
communitarian analysis, the "rights revolution" begun in the 1950s and
consolidated in the 1960s and 1970s is the culprit. The "legalization" of
American society and the saturation of political discourse with "rights
talk" began with the civil rights movement and accelerated when the
Warren Court decided vigorously to exercise the power of judicial review
as a means of protecting individual rights from state injustice (Glendon
1991: 1–30).

The tendency (instigated by lawyers) of collective actors to articulate
social and political issues as rights-based claims fostered and was in turn
reinforced by the vast expansion of the role of courts and judges in the
political system. Legalistic rights talk with its emphasis on personal liberty and entitlement has had a "colonizing effect" on our moral intuitions and discourses.[26] By turning almost every political issue and passing
desire into a claim for rights, the ever-expanding process of legalization
generalized egoism and undermined alternative moral discourses along
with the institutions in which these are generated (Glendon 1991: 4–5,
77). It also allegedly undermined common values and exacerbated

---

[26] According to Mary Ann Glendon (1991: 4), this introduced an entirely new focus to
constitutional law. Before that time, the principal emphasis of constitutional jurisprudence was not on personal liberty as such, but on the division of authority between the
states and the federal government and the allocation of powers among the branches of
the central government. "Today the bulk of the Court's constitutional work involves
claims that individual rights have been violated."

tendencies toward fragmentation by encouraging entitlement claims and identity politics on behalf of particularistic groups that aggressively assert their interests with no thought to the common good.[27] Post-1950s liberal jurisprudence, in short, brought the expressivist conception of the self along with a contractualist, legalistic model of obligation and association to the population at large.

Small wonder that the rights revolution is considered most destructive in the domain of "intimate association." The constitutionalization of key aspects of family law that began in the 1960s, in particular the discovery of "fundamental" *individual* privacy rights in this domain, allegedly has had deleterious effects on the associational life of civil society because it has privileged individualistic over community values.[28] It transposes contractualist assumptions from the market to spheres of life with which they are incompatible. The rights revolution in family law thus introduced a destructive atomization and an adversarial relationship into otherwise solidary family communities, pitting one member's rights against another's and undermining the bases of social trust and cohesion. This disruption has undermined social capital by destroying the individual's ability to conceive oneself as responsible for the effect of one's actions on others or as concerned with the well-being of community members.

Given this diagnosis of American civil society's decline, the solution is obvious: replacement of the rights-oriented policy with a responsibility-based family and social policy, and replacement of entitlement talk with a discourse of duty in the political and legal public spheres. Alongside a good deal of moral exhortation, communitarian journals are filled with authoritarian policy proposals geared toward reinforcing the two-parent family; discouraging divorce, out-of-wedlock sex, and (unmarried!) teen pregnancy; refurbishing the work ethic; and undoing various allegedly destructive, individualizing rights in the domain of intimate association. The discourse of reinvigorating the most important of civil associations, "the" family, is thus linked to a clear, socially authoritarian project of retraditionalization and uniformity. In short, what is at work here is, in my view, a doomed yet destructive effort to return us to the social,

---

[27] What the communitarians have in mind is affirmative action, demanded not only by African-Americans, but also by a variety of ethno-racial and "special interest" groups, all in the name of redressing past discrimination and/or protecting the value of diversity. These claims raise thorny issues that I cannot address here. One thing is clear, however: Incantations about civic virtue and common values will redress neither wrongs and injustices caused by discrimination nor the harms caused by misrecognition.

[28] The Supreme Court privacy decisions from Griswold v. Connecticut, Eisenstadt v. Baird, and Roe v. Wade down to Casey v. Pennsylvania are at issue here. See Sandel (1996: 94–119) for a recent restatement of this position. See also Cohen (1992) for a discussion and critique of these arguments.

structural, and cultural world of industrial society. What is yearned for are the cultural certainties and clear boundaries between roles and spheres of life typical of industrial society (as well as its status hierarchies): in particular, its gendered division of labor; its neat separation between family and paid work, complemented by the care ethic for women and the work ethic for men; and its overall strategy of distinguishing between public and private in order to handle contentious issues. For such a reactionary and rear-guard project to succeed, extremely repressive, authoritarian measures would be required that would contradict the discourse of reviving the autonomy and integrity of civil society, family values, and trust.[29]

It is not hard to see who are the targets of this discourse nor to challenge some of the empirical claims and their meaning. For example, although it is true that Americans have a high divorce rate, 79 percent of households include a married couple, according to the 1990 census, down undramatically from 82.5 percent a decade earlier (Morone 1996: 37).[30] Marriage has hardly become a minority lifestyle.[31]

The figures on marriage, divorce, single parenthood, and sexual standards do indicate ethical change, but this change cannot be understood as the demise of "the family." Only one particular family form is losing ground: the 1950s model of the patriarchal nuclear family composed of a heterosexual couple married for life – a male breadwinner, a female homemaker, and children – and this for complex economic, structural, cultural, and political reasons.[32] Indeed, what has disintegrated is not "the family" but the consensus on what a proper family is, on what form a

---

[29] State power would have to repress the pluralization of life forms, suppress individual choices and efforts at self-realization that individualization processes nevertheless force upon the individual, and revoke the advances toward gender equality in both the workplace and the home. This hardly reinforces the autonomy, integrity, or solidarity of civil society. An example of such a contradictory approach is the claim that welfare violates the work ethic and hence that people (i.e. women with small children) on welfare should enter the labor market and the simultaneous claim that mothers should stay home and care for their children. When applied to mothers of young children, the universal worker model urged here conflicts directly with the family-values discourse.

[30] People divorce and then remarry, creating "blended families" with children from more than one marriage, ex-spouses, step-parents, half siblings, and several sets of grandparents (Cherlin 1992).

[31] Divorce rates have not increased since the late 1970s. Moreover, the claim of a general decline of moral values with the weakening of religiosity is also unconvincing. According to recent surveys, 95 percent of Americans profess a faith in God, 87 per cent say adultery is "always wrong," and 75 percent belong to a church. Rates of church attendance have increased as much as 30 percent in the past two decades. These are not only the highest figures in the Western world, but they indicate no decline in the United States over time (Morone 1996: 31–32). Even if divorce rates are high and even if marriage were to decline, one should avoid identifying marriage with family.

[32] One of the most important of these is the entry of women, and especially young mothers, into the labor force. For an interesting analysis and overview, see Beck (1992: 87–150).

good intimate relationship must take, and, more precisely, about the nature of women's (and men's) roles and gender/sexual identity.[33] Pluralization of forms of intimacy, however, is not the same as the disintegration of family values. There *is* conflict and uncertainty over how best to realize the general values appropriate to the domain of intimacy: love, care, loyalty, mutuality, trust, equality, and reciprocity. Communitarian rhetoric steers us away from reflection on these important issues by miscasting the dissolution of the cultural hegemony of one form of intimate life as a phenomenon of moral decline, positioning one ethical model as the moral norm against which every other form appears morally suspect.

This rhetoric must be understood for what it is: a political intervention in the battle between those who insist there is only one right way (to be backed up by law) to conduct intimate relations and those who argue that a plurality of types of intimate association can realize the relevant values as long as they do not violate the moral principles that regulate interaction generally.

The more general theoretical claim that the expansion of individual rights in the domain of intimate association undermines community and mutual responsibility is also profoundly misleading, politically motivated, and based on flawed premises. The relevant personal rights protect individuals if and when the solidarity of the love community breaks down and against the unjust use of power and force by the stronger party; they are not the cause of the breakdown. Such rights do not pretend to substitute for the ethical forms of love and commitment that are "beyond justice." They do, however, protect a relationship of respect that the law will enforce when all else fails. Moreover, equal rights for women and men in the domain of intimacy foster relations of reciprocity by mitigating differences in power and opportunity. Protecting against the terrible effects of unwarranted trust, they facilitate warranted trust.

The criminalization of spousal violence and marital rape, decisional autonomy regarding sexual and reproductive decisions for women, equal voice over familial affairs, equal access to marital property, legal regulation of family support, egalitarian exit options for both genders when the ethical substance of the family dissolves and the like do not turn marriage into a contractual economic exchange relationship. But legalization of this sort does bring moral principles of justice to bear on intimate

---

[33] The demographic data refer to the decentering of marriage vis-à-vis intimacy. Functions and events that were fused on the old hegemonic model of the nuclear family – marriage, domesticity, parenthood, childrearing, love, and sex – have become disaggregated and recombined in a variety of intimate and kin relationships. Furstenberg (1995) sums up the situation by stating that marriage is no longer the master event that orchestrates the onset of sexual relations, parenthood, departure from the home, or even the establishment of a household.

relations by acknowledging the individuality, legal standing, personal autonomy, and claims to self-realization of all adult family members. It thereby provides the minimal basis for a companionate marriage to live up to its own egalitarian ideal.

Indeed, the companionate ideal of the family construed as a voluntary association based on love, mutuality, reciprocity, esteem, and care among members presupposes, under contemporary conditions, the norm of equality and the value of happiness in intimate relations. It *is* easier to ensure the *stability* of marriage when one member of the couple is subordinate and dependent without any meaningful exit option. But modern companionate marriage is not supposed to rest on such things.

The communitarian wants it both ways: The family is somehow to be *in* but not *of* civil society. When cast as the most important voluntary association mediating between the individual and the state, the family must be located within and not, as Hegel had it, outside civil society in the realm of nature. This means that the principles of justice must also apply to it. But, like Hegel, the communitarian discourse also constructs the family as based on a "contract to transcend contract" – as a natural association and an affective community innocent of the conflicts of self-interest, power dynamics, and egoism characteristic of contractual voluntary relations generally. Contractual relations and rights allegedly destroy this community. The family is thus "beyond justice," not subject to the principles or risks of civil society.

The trick is to pretend that full legal standing and protections for intimate associates and the ability consensually to order the terms of one's intimate association on the basis of gender equality turn families into contractual business relationships with no ethical content beyond the rights of their members. By implication, we must return to the old status understanding of the family with its internal hierarchies.

The choice, however, is not between status and contract, for as any serious student of civil society knows, most forms of civil association elude this dichotomy.[34] Moreover, the very idea of voluntary association entails the free creation, entry, and maintenance of the group because of the solidarity, support, recognition, or happiness it affords to its members. Of course, responsibilities and duties arise in all such association. It is ludicrous to allege that rights (especially those according equal status to both genders) undermine responsibilities because every right and every relationship carry with them reciprocal duties.[35] There is no reason why

---

[34] Legal marriage and legally acknowledged family forms involve a range of legally acknowledged statuses with attendant rights and duties: husband, wife, father, mother, grandparent, etc.

[35] See McClain (1994) for an excellent critique.

the ethical content that is "beyond justice" cannot inform such associations along with the principles of justice. Nor is there any reason to revive the Kantian dichotomy between duty and happiness, as if the only choice we have regarding failed intimate relationships is "moral" renunciation (self-denial of a life of love and happiness) or "immoral" narcissism. To trot out "the best interests of the child" as an argument for restricting rights in the domain of intimacy is utterly polemical and counterproductive.

I do not want to be misunderstood. There has been real and radical change in the domain of intimacy over the past three decades and families *are* under enormous stress today. The application of the ideal of self-realization to this domain *is* new, but it does not indicate immoral egoism or the decline of values. Instead, it heightens expectations for intimate relations (especially for marriage and family) and an equalization of these between the genders. Happiness, trust, and being there for others are not opposites, as the simplistic dichotomous thinking revived in communitarian rhetoric implies; they belong together.

The problems and insecurities plaguing intimate among other forms of associational life today are not due to cultural (or ethnic) diversity, value dissensus, vice, or the pluralization of family forms. Institutional change, individualization, economic uncertainty, and dislocation on the one side, and greater gender equality, expanded mobility, and opportunities on the other render all associational forms looser and more fragile. These raise many complex theoretical and legal issues. How to regulate intimate associations once the old "consensus" on "the" patriarchal nuclear family has broken down, and on what legal paradigm, are two of them.

I cannot address these here. But I can say that moralizing, backward-looking rhetoric or policy proposals do not help. One should beware of reviving a bad old American tradition of sowing moral panic and scapegoating relatively powerless groups in times of economic stress and social change. The very rights that constitute civil society, protect plurality and civic and personal autonomy, and allow voluntary associations including intimate ones to emerge may be sacrificed to an authoritarian cultural populism in the name of virtue and social solidarity. The discourse of declining family values and disintegration of civil society diverts us from the real issues by constructing our policy problems as moral meltdowns, making them more difficult to address.[36]

---

[36] I am paraphrasing Morone (1996: 36–37). The quality of intimate relationships, not their particular structure, is what matters. Instead of a moralizing discourse that stigmatizes a variety of forms of intimacy outside "traditional" marriage, one should think about the ethical quality of relationships – are they reciprocal, egalitarian, fair, solidary, caring, fulfilling, and just? – and about ways to help ease the demands and strains on working parents, married or single.

Conclusion

What connection does this sort of jeremiad, or the discourse of the Republican right, with Robert Putnam's approach to civil society? One cannot accuse him of advocating the demise of the welfare state or blaming the expansion of civil rights and declining personal morals for social decapitalization.

Indeed, in *Making Democracy Work*, the family was dismissed as a primitive substitute for social capital, not a source of it. Strong kinship ties were actually found to hinder strong civic traditions and to block the generalization of social trust. But there is a revealing shift in Putnam's views on the family in the texts where the discourse of decline dominates. In "Bowling Alone," we suddenly are told that "the most fundamental form of social capital is the family." We also are told that the "massive evidence" of loosened family bonds "may help to explain" the theme of social decapitalization. By the time he wrote "Strange Disappearance" (1996), Putnam was citing the increase in divorce rates, single-parent families, teen pregnancies, and the like as "unequivocal" evidence of family decline. His new claim is that successful marriage is statistically associated with greater social trust and civic engagement! Although not "the" main cause of social decapitalization, the "disintegration of the family" is now deemed to be an important accessory to the crime.[37]

This remains so far a minor strain in Putnam's work. But it derives from an analytic approach that offers no conceptual counterweight to the main theoretical claim of conservative communitarians who, as we have seen, already have appropriated his core concept, social capital. Because law, rights, and the public sphere play no theoretical role in his analysis, Putnam has no conceptual means to counter the thesis that legalization itself – in particular, the expansion of personal individual rights and entitlement claims – actually causes the disintegration of civil society and civic capacities.[38] The step from here to the moralizing values discourse of social conservatives is not a large one. But it takes us further from the real issues that a civil-society discourse can and should raise.

[37] If we combine these claims with the strong relationship noted between the decline in traditional (gender-segregated) associational memberships such as the PTA, which relied heavily on the volunteer work of housewives, and the increase in working mothers since the 1960s, a very conservative message does seem to be implied in the recent texts. It is hard to avoid the impression that, despite disclaimers, the changing role of women plays a large part in the apparent decline of civicness. See Levi (1996: 52).
[38] Given his too narrow conception of the sources of social trust (face-to-face relationships), he has no other place to turn for an explanation of the apparent "decline" of social capital. The TV explanation on its own is simply too weak – hence the tendency to place more and more weight on the family.

I have argued in this paper that a narrow conception of civil society obscures and miscasts important problems, not that these problems do not exist. There is no question that the welfare-state paradigm, corresponding forms of legalization, and established modes of civic engagement, political participation, and social integration are all in crisis today. But the dichotomous thinking that counterposes civil society to the state, duties to rights, custom to code, informal to formal sociation (as the source of trust), culturalist to institutionalist approaches, and status to contract leads to an overly hasty conclusion of social decapitalization and a set of false policy choices.

If we had a richer concept of civil society and a more abstract understanding of its cultural presuppositions, the discovery of the erosion of one type of civic institution would not have to lead to a claim of general civic decline. Given different methods, functional equivalents for older forms of associationalism could become visible, along with new types of civic action targeting an altered environment of civil, economic and political institutions. The question of whether the existing political public spheres including the party and electoral systems are sufficiently receptive to new forms of civil engagement of citizens aimed at influencing them could then be addressed. How these block or channel participation and reforms required by late modern society in ways that would enhance both trust and democracy could be researched. This in turn could point to consideration of the role of government in encouraging or discouraging civic participation. It could also direct attention to the institutional structure of the state and its impact on and receptivity to organizational initiatives in civil society.

A richer conception would also allow one to consider the role of various paradigms of law, conceptions of rights, and designs of political institutions not only in establishing and protecting civil society and public spaces, but also in opening up key institutional arenas to multiple voices, projects, critical contestation. Instead of the ad hoc policy proposals that abound today in response to analyses of declining trust and disappearing social capital that are at once too substantive and too abstract, the prior and deeper question of the effects of the existing institutional arrangement of the US could be addressed. In other words, issues of constitutional design and redesign – the deepest level of institutionalization at stake in any theory or project of civil society – could move to the center of concerns where they should be when important structural change is occurring.

Such considerations do not replace a societalist analysis with a state-oriented one. Rather if we had a rich conception of civil society that included the civil public spheres, we could fruitfully consider the reciprocal lines of influence between it, the state, political publics and the economy. This perspective could point us to an important range of questions begging for serious research. For it is incontestable that the shape of the four key domains of civil society – plurality, publicity, legality and privacy – are undergoing important changes today. Theoretical and practical interventions into these transformations suggest research agendas premised on the constructed as opposed to natural character of contemporary civil society. Only a civil society perspective that is informed by issues of institutional design and is geared to its reflexive modernization and democratization will do in the current context. I close with a short list of research areas that would help to analytically differentiate the dimensions of the study of civil society, trust and workable democracy.

The problem of democratic legitimacy

Certainly we need to study the difference between the democratic legitimacy provided by the legal, procedural preconditions of electoral legislative politics, and the wider "procedures" of a democratic public sphere in which a rich network of associations are capable of participating. We need to be able to distinguish empirically between the types, levels, and duration of support for and trust in governments on the basis of the narrower procedures of political society, and the more open democratic ones of civil publics.

Issues of constitutionalism

It is time to explore seriously the role of civil society, its associations and publics in constitution making, and in the development of constitutional patriotism. We also need to examine whether constitutions can foster a healthy civil society by (a) explicitly providing for channels of participation and (b) facilitating the emergence of politically relevant civil associations by regulating their internal life and limiting the forms in which they pursue political influence. What should/could a multicultural constitutionalism entail?

The problem of the machinery of democracy

We know that representative democracy exists in different forms. Yet we know much too little about the relationship between consensus, pluralist and majoritarian varieties of democracy, presidentialism and parliamentarianism, federalist and unitary states, and the development of associations and publics as active components of will formation. What are the consequences of various combinations for civil society? There is much room here for both empirical comparison, and creative proposals of design. At present there are few really convincing normative arguments for preferring different types and combinations of democracy. There is reason to hope that the point of view of civil society might supply such arguments.

The relationship between political and civil society

What is the effect on civil society of different models of local government and different party systems? In the case of local government it will be important to document the political opportunities presented to associational life by decentralization. But we need to also consider whether extreme localism might provincialize civil institutions whose teleology today is trans-local or even trans-national. In the case of party systems we must examine the effect of the number of parties, the level and type of polarization, and their organizational structure on different models of associational life.

The problem of the media and the public sphere

The issue raised by Putnam but inadequately addressed as to how new media of communication impact on civil society is of course crucial. Just as Habermas once inquired into the effects of the new media of print on the emergence of a new type of public sphere so must we now look into the electronic media: their technological effects, their institutional structuration and mode of control and their relation to perhaps differently conceptualized civil publics. This is a preeminent issue for theorists of civil society interested in a democratic public sphere. We have to address anew the problems that commodification and commercialization as well as governmental control present for free critical communication. How can the legal and monetary inputs of state and economy be absorbed in a manner that does not destroy of the very idea of civil publics?

Privacy and intimacy

If the neo-communitarian claim that expansion of individual personal rights in the domain of intimacy destroys the ethical content of families is unconvincing, it is nevertheless true that certain forms of juridification can have destructive and polarizing effects. Excessive reliance on courts and legalisms to discover fundamental personal rights and adjudicate disputes in this domain is disturbing. Yet it is no longer possible to conceptualize intimate relationships as existing in a pre-political natural private sphere immune from legal construction, regulation, intervention, and shielded from the demands of justice. How then can we conceptualize the privacy needed for intimate relationships to flourish and the personal autonomy that we want and need in and for such relations? What legal mode of regulation and which forms of constitutionalism could protect the plurality of modes of life within civil society including intimate relations from intolerant majorities while avoiding both the disintegrative effects of over-legalization and the unjust effects of "non-intervention"? How in short are we to think privacy and its relation to public virtues, morals, institutional structures, discourses?

The relationship of civil society and social solidarity

We must take a new look at the problem of the reconstruction and decentralization of the welfare state. What institutional reforms or redesigns are necessary to accomplish the substantive goals (justice) of the welfare state without threatening the personal autonomy, associational solidarities and incentives for individual and group initiative and responsibility? The negative side-effects of bureaucratic interventionism, including the weakening of the rule of law, have been justly called to our attention by the critics of the welfare state. But marketization and privatization of social services cannot satisfy existing social needs in a sufficiently egalitarian manner. What shape can the reflexive continuation of the welfare state take? Which forms of inequality undermine the key norms of the public sphere along with the bases of interpersonal trust and confidence in institutions and what can government do about it? How does the idea of reflexive law help here? How can government contribute to the autonomy, vigor, and responsibility civil actors and help to institutionalize mutuality, solidarity, justice and fairness?

The problem of the globalization of civil society

Many of the most important civil society organizations are now global in nature. This is true of NGOs and of human rights organizations dedicated to the establishment of the basic parameters of civil society in democratizing countries. Similarly civil publics are today of an international character. What are the relationships of global associations and publics to local societies and cultures as well as to both national states and international governmental organizations?

These areas of research can help turn the theory of civil society into a differentiated set of analytical instruments, more intellectually plausible for the decades ahead then simply focusing on defining and redefining the concept. But they also help to challenge one-sided and ideological conceptions. I believe that favorable results in these areas alone would go a long way toward legitimating the concept of civil society in social science discussions and clarifying the relationship between voluntary association and trust in government. Indeed, positive results in any of them would be a great contribution to those who already are engaged in the politics of civil society, and wish to better understand the meaning of their own action. It would also steer those interested in the question of what makes democracy work in the right direction.

REFERENCES

Almond, Gabriel and Verba, Sidney, 1963. *The Civic Culture: Political Attitudes and Democracy in Five Nations*, Princeton: Princeton University Press

Anderson, Perry, 1977. The Antimonies of Antonio Gramsci. *New Left Review* 100, November/January, 5–78

Beck, Ulrich, 1992. *Risk Society: Towards a New Modernity*, Mark Ritter (trans.), London: Sage Publications

Beck, Ulrich, Giddens, Anthony, and Lash, Scott, 1994. *Reflexive Modernization: Politics, Tradition and Aesthetics in the Modern Social Order*, Stanford, Calif.: Stanford University Press

Bellah, Robert N., Madsen, Richard, Sullivan, William M., Swidler, Ann, and Tipton, Steven M., 1985. *Habits of the Heart: Individualism and Commitment in American Life*, New York: Harper & Row

Bradley, Bill, 1995. America's challenge: Revitalizing our national community. *National Civic Review* 84, Spring, 94–100

Calhoun, Craig, ed., 1992. *Habermas and the Public Sphere*, Cambridge, Mass.: MIT Press

Cherlin, Andrew J., 1992. *Marriage, Divorce, Remarriage*, Cambridge, Mass.: Harvard University Press

Coats, Dan, 1996. Re-funding our "little platoons." *Policy Review: The Journal of American Citizenship* 75, January/February, 25–28

Cohen, Jean L., 1982. *Class and Civil Society: The Limits of Marxian Critical Theory*, Amherst, Mass.: University of Massachusetts Press

1985. Strategy or identity: New theoretical paradigms and contemporary social movements. *Social Research* 52, Winter, 663–716

1992. Redescribing privacy: Identity, difference and the abortion controversy. *Columbia Journal of Gender and Law* 3, 43–117

Cohen, Jean L. and Arato, Andrew, 1992. *Civil Society and Political Theory*, Cambridge, Mass.: MIT Press

Coleman, James S., 1990. *Foundations of Social Theory*, Cambridge, Mass.: Harvard University Press

Dryzek, John S., 1996. Political inclusion and the dynamics of democratization. *American Political Science Review* 90, September, 475–487

Durkheim, Emile, 1933. *The Division of Labor in Society*, New York: Macmillan

1958. *Professional Ethics and Civic Morals*, Glencoe, IL: The Free Press

Elshtain, Jean Bethke, 1995. *Democracy on Trial*, New York: Basic Books

Elshtain, Jean Bethke and Buell, John, 1991. Families in trouble. *Dissent* 38, Spring, 262–266

Etzioni, Amitai, 1995. *Rights and the Common Good: The Communitarian Perspective*, New York: St. Martin's Press

Fraser, Nancy, 1992. Rethinking the public sphere: A contribution to the critique of actually existing democracy, in Craig Calhoun (ed.), *Habermas and the Public Sphere*, Cambridge, Mass.: MIT Press, 109–142

Furstenberg, Frank F. Jr., 1995. Family change and the welfare of children: What do we know and what can we do about it? in Karen Oppenheim Mason and An-Magritt Jensen (eds.), *Gender and Family Change in Industrialized Countries*, Oxford: Clarendon Press, 245–257

Galston, William A., 1991. *Liberal Purposes: Goods, Virtues, and Diversity in the Liberal State*, Cambridge: Cambridge University Press

1995. A liberal-democratic case for the two-parent family, in Amitai Etzioni (ed.), *Rights and the Common Good: The Communitarian Perspective*, New York: St. Martin's Press, 139–149

Giddens, Anthony, 1992. *The Transformation of Intimacy: Sexuality, Love and Eroticism in Modern Societies*, Stanford, Calif.: Stanford University Press

Glendon, Mary Ann, 1991. *Rights Talk: The Impoverishment of Political Discourse*, New York: Free Press

Gramsci, Antonio, 1971. State and civil society, in Quintin Hoare and Geoffrey Nowell Smith (eds. and trans.), *Selections from the Prison Notebooks of Antonio Gramsci*, New York: International Publishers, 206–277

Habermas, Jürgen, 1984. *The Theory of Communicative Action*, vol. I, Thomas McCarthy (trans.), Boston: Beacon Press

1987. *The Theory of Communicative Action*, vol. II, Thomas McCarthy (trans.), Boston: Beacon Press

1989. *The Structural Transformation of the Public Sphere*, Cambridge, Mass.: MIT Press

1995. Citizenship and national identity: Some reflections on the future of Europe, in Ronald Beiner (ed.), *Theorizing Citizenship*, New York: SUNY Press, 255–281

1996. *Between Facts and Norms: Contributions to a Discourse Theory of Law and Democracy*, William Rehg (trans.), Cambridge, Mass.: MIT Press

Hegel, Georg Wilhelm, 1969. *Hegel's Philosophy of Right*, T.M. Knox (trans.), New York: Oxford University Press

Hirschman, Albert O., 1982. *Shifting Involvements*, Princeton, NJ: Princeton University Press

Hollinger, David A., 1995. *Postethnic America: Beyond Multiculturalism*, New York: Basic Books

Levi, Margaret, 1996. Social and unsocial capital: A review essay of Robert Putnam's *Making Democracy Work. Politics and Society* 24, March, 45–55

Lind, Michael, 1995. *The Next American Nation: The New Nationalism and the Fourth American Revolution*, New York: Free Press

McClain, Linda C., 1994. Rights and irresponsibilities. *Duke Law Journal* 43, 989–1037

Melucci, Alberto, 1980. The new social movements: A theoretical approach. *Social Science Information* 19, 199–226

1985. The symbolic challenge of contemporary movements. *Social Research* 52, Winter, 789–816

Morone, James A., 1996. The corrosive politics of virtue. *The American Prospect* 26, May/June, 30–39

Norris, Pippa, 1996. Does television erode social capital? A reply to Putnam. *PS: Political Science & Politics* 29, September, 474–480

Portes, Alejandro and Landolt, Patricia, 1996. The downside of social capital. *The American Prospect* 26, May/June, 18–21, 94

Putnam, Robert, 1993. *Making Democracy Work: Civic Traditions in Modern Italy*, Princeton: Princeton University Press

1995a. Bowling alone: America's declining social capital. *Journal of Democracy* 6, January, 65–78

1995b. Bowling alone, revisited. *The Responsive Community* 5, 18–33

1996. The strange disappearance of civic America. *The American Prospect* 24, 34–48

Rawls, John, 1971. *A Theory of Justice*, Cambridge, Mass.: Harvard University Press

1993. *Political Liberalism*, New York: Columbia University Press

Rosenblum, Nancy L., 1994. Democratic character and community: The logic of congruence? *Journal of Political Philosophy* 2, March, 67–97

Sandel, Michael J., 1996. *Democracy's Discontent: America in Search of a Public Philosophy*, Cambridge, Mass.: Harvard University Press

Schudson, Michael, 1996. What if civic life didn't die? *The American Prospect* 25, March/April, 17–20

Skocpol, Theda, 1982. Bringing the state back in. *Items* 36, 1–8; reprinted 1990, in Roy C. Macridis and Bernard E. Brown (eds.), *Comparative Politics: Notes and Readings*, 7th ed., Pacific Grove, Calif.: Brooks-Cole Publishing

1996. Unravelling from above. *The American Prospect* 25, March/April, 20–25

Skolnick, Arlene and Rosencrantz, Stacey, 1994. The new crusade for the old family. *American Prospect*, Summer, 59–65

Struening, Karen, 1996. Feminist challenges to the new familialism: Lifestyle experimentation and the freedom of intimate association. *Hypatia* 11, Winter, 135–154

Sunstein, Cass R., 1990. *After the Rights Revolution: Reconceiving the Regulatory State*, Cambridge, Mass.: Harvard University Press

Tarrow, Sidney G., 1994. *Power in Movement: Social Movements, Collective Action and Politics*, Cambridge: Cambridge University Press

1996. Making social science work across space and time: A critical reflection on Robert Putnam's *Making Democracy Work*. *American Political Science Review* 90, June, 389–397

Tocqueville, Alexis de, 1969. *Democracy in America*, George Lawrence (trans.), J. P. Mayer (ed.), Garden City, NY: Doubleday

Touraine, Alain, 1981. *The Voice and the Eye*, Alan Duff (trans.), Cambridge: Cambridge University Press

Urbinati, Nadia, 1993. The art of tolerance. *Dissent* 40, Fall, 572–573

Verba, Sidney, Schlozman, Kay Lehman, and Brady, Henry E., 1995. *Voice and Equality: Civic Voluntarism in American Politics*, Cambridge, Mass.: Harvard University Press

Warren, Mark E., 1996. Deliberative democracy and authority. *American Political Science Review* 90, 46–60

Whitehead, Barbara Dafoe, 1992. A new familism? *Family Affairs* 5, 1–2

Wilson, William Julius, 1997. *When Work Disappears: The World of the New Urban Poor*, New York: Knopf

1996. When work disappears. *The New York Times Magazine*, August 18, 1996, 28–52

Young, Iris Marion, 1995. Mothers, citizenship and independence: A critique of pure family values. *Ethics* 105, April, 535–556

8 Trust and its surrogates: psychological foundations of political process

Rom Harré

Part one: A semantics for "trust" in the context of democracy

Well-defined questions need sharply articulated concepts. The investigation of the role of interpersonal trust in that loose cluster of social-psychological phenomena we call "the democratic process," definitive of those democratic institutions that define, for us, a democratic society, requires some well-defined questions about the social-psychological phenomena that we observe, which in their turn require sharply focused concepts. Analytical philosophy grew up as the very instrument that, by making finer and finer distinctions, would provide psychologists, lawyers, political scientists, physicists, and so on with the conceptual armory they needed, but protected against the fallacies and mistakes that come from too superficial a use of characteristic vocabularies. My argument is aimed at substantiating two main intuitions: that the concept of "trust" in most contexts points to a personal relationship, and that the post-Enlightenment shift from governance by custom to governance by code enhances trust in one dimension while weakening it another.

The concepts of "politics" and "democracy" to be deployed in what follows

In developing my analysis, I shall be taking the idea of a "political process" rather broadly, including any procedure by which differences of opinion with respect to the future of some more or less loosely bounded group are resolved. The scale of such processes ranges from departmental (and family) politics (universities offering wonderful examples) to the deliberations of the rulers and managers of collectives of millions of human beings. Among the myriad ways that resolutions of difference are achieved, I shall single out for the accolade "democratic" just those in which the resolving process is discursive. The received wisdom on how to single out democratic from other forms of governance is certainly better known to most of the contributors to this volume than it is to me. However, since I am hoping to make some points about the role of trust relationships in and conditional for "democratic processes and institutions," it would be wise to rough out how I understand the concept. In sum, then, I take a process to be "political" if differences of opinion, conflicts of interest, and so on are to be reconciled by means of it, and that it is to be accounted "democratic" insofar as these differences are resolved discursively, with some conditions in place to ensure equity of "voice."

Beginning modestly with a look at politics in the small, there are plainly two quite different procedures of resolution of dissent, difference of opinion, and/or conflict of interest in use, both exemplified in those aspects of the governance of universities we would unhesitatingly call "democratic" and both implemented discursively. There is the idea of arriving at decisions, plans, and so on about what to do by evolving consensus. It is generally accounted a failure of proper process in an Oxford college if the Governing Body is forced by the intransigence of some members, by entrenched opinions, or both to resolve an impasse by resort to a vote. However, in large matters of policy when Congregation – the entire teaching faculty of Oxford, its governing body – is convened, decision-making by majority vote is perhaps not customary but fairly common. Let us call the former "consensual democracy" and the latter "parliamentary democracy."

Though these modes of achieving resolution of oppositions of various kinds are logically polarized, real institutions display all sorts of variations, combinations, and hierarchical patterns of these modes. They do not represent an exclusive disjunction, but more the defining poles of a continuum of practices.

Mark Warren has pointed out to me the necessity of distinguishing politics from other social relations and practices. However, distinguishing cooperative from adversarial or agonistic social practices, and identifying only the latter as "political," seems to me too specific. Resolutions of difference can be achieved by a "due process" such as voting or by the incorporation of the dissenting voices in the ultimate resolution. For that reason, I find the distinctions in Mansbridge (1980) between consensual and adversarial processes too stark, if related too neatly to differences in the degree or importance of dissent or difference of opinion. The most interesting cases to me are those in which there is a sharp conflict of interest and/or opinion, but it is resolved consensually. Consensual resolution in the contexts we have in mind is resolution by discursive means. But it may take all sorts of forms from discussion to meditating together. The practice of voting, thereby formalizing and even in some cases creating a majority/minority distinction, is also a discursive practice having its own "grammar" and procedural modes.

Clearly, trusting relationships, using this notion preanalytically and informally, enter into these institutional decision-making styles in different ways, or rather with respect to different matters. Thus, consensus works if, amongst other necessary conditions, the members of the consensual group can trust other members not to go back on the consensus that has already been achieved. As Baker (1985) has pointed out, there is no requirement on the use of the word "trust" in situations like these that the trust-relation is formulated explicitly. If it is majority voting that is in question, then in addition to the implied acceptance by the minority of the majority decision, the minority must trust the majority not to abuse its power, while the majority must trust the minority not to engage in subversion, but to wait its turn at the ballot box. It seems to me that even within this rather crude analysis two of the problems with the understanding of the variety of trust relations are clearly visible.

Are trusting relations predominantly pragmatic or predominantly moral, or both? How is the everyday usage that refers to trust between individuals and institutions related to its root usage in describing certain interpersonal relations?

"Trust" in the "political" context

Part of the context for our deliberations on the deep questions of trust and democracy is the confluence of personal intuitions that trust is not what it used to be, with the results of large-scale surveys of national attitudes toward other people and toward institutions that seem to show the same thing. Before I turn to a close examination of the concept of trust in the language games of everyday life, it will be useful to draw some distinctions between the research objects of different kinds of "trust" studies to see how our intuitions and our surveys relate to one another.

Discourses of trust and practices of trust The important, indeed fascinating, results of the large-scale surveys described by Ronald Inglehart (see this volume, chapter 4) and Orlando Patterson (see this volume, chapter 6) are much more difficult to interpret than one might think from the rapidity with which both investigators moved from macrolexicography to social analysis. The results were obtained by asking people questions such as "Do you generally trust people?" By what were the answers determined? I would be inclined to say by the discursive conventions of this or that social group or linguistic culture for talking about people. The difference between the statistics of the answers given in Protestant Europe from those obtained in Catholic Europe might be put down almost wholly to different conventions as to how one talks about other people in these regions. Without attention to the local *practices* of trust and distrust, it is not clear to me how the results of large-scale lexicography, fascinating though they are, home in on the infinitely variable fine grain of the micro-interactions that make up the political process.

Let me illustrate what I mean by "practices of trust and distrust."[1] In the Christ Child Opportunity Shop in Georgetown, there is a prominently displayed notice that declares that checks will be accepted only if the address and telephone number of the purchaser is printed on them and if they are accompanied by two independent photo IDs. The implementation of that set of rules I shall call a "practice of distrust." Contrast this: Last year I was visiting at the University of Canterbury in Christchurch, New Zealand (a country where there are no security checks on boarding internal flights!), and I needed a transformer for my laptop. I went to the nearest computer shop and, finding the very thing I needed, proposed to pay by check. Using my new checkbook for an account opened the day before I wrote my check, I was asked neither to identify myself nor to give an address or phone number. I call this a "practice of trust."

I have no idea how the prevalence of practices of trust correlates with the results of surveys of the discourses of "trust." I would like to see a thorough cross-cultural, cross-epoch,[2] and cross-social class exploration of practices of trust integrated with the lexical surveys that have been the traditional resort of those engaged in "trust" studies. The assumption that the lexical survey is a fully adequate guide to the culture in which it has been carried out presumes a very strong version of the Sapir-Whorf hypothesis, a version that is not now widely accepted even by those who, like myself, would regard language use as the prime medium of sociality. It is quite possible that the conventions governing discourses of trust might be different in various ways from those governing practices of trust and distrust.

Words and their uses   Sometimes one hears social scientists adopting the principle that the caterpillar enunciated to Alice: "Words mean what I decide they mean." However, while physicists can raid ordinary

---

[1] Throughout this paper, I make use of examples of "distrusting practices" culled from my experience of life in the United States. My choice of examples is dictated by the American setting of our discussions rather than by any vulgar assumptions that Americans are more or less trustworthy than other folk!

[2] I overheard one of the visitors to the Conference on Democracy and Trust at Georgetown declare that there were no data on trust before 1960 or thereabouts. But the practices of trust and distrust can be traced back through documentary sources as far as you like, to Governor Winthrop and beyond.

language for a vocabulary, creating neologisms such as "potential and kinetic energy" with impunity, social scientists must be more circumspect. The reason for this caution is simple but profound. The behavior of electrons owes nothing to the semantics of the words physicists use to talk about them, but the behavior of people is largely influenced by the language they use and that is used of them. Even the distinction I have drawn between "discourses of trust" and "practices of trust" is not independent of this point, since "practices of trust" are Wittgensteinian language games, practical activities interwoven intimately with the uses of words. As I remarked in the previous section, we do not have a great deal of knowledge of how, in the whole gamut of language games of trust, the discursive and the practical conventions are interwoven.

The two main problems as I see them   Is it the case that the context and occasion of the assumptions of interpersonal trust lead to differences in what that trust is taken to be? To pursue this question further, it will be necessary to look closely at the semantic field within which the everyday uses of the word "trust" are embedded.

If, in each of the cases distinguished above, trust is an asymmetrical relation, what is its reciprocal? Does each of the above cases reveal a different reciprocal relation? Is the possibility of failure to acknowledge or implement the relevant reciprocal relationship the same in each case?

Even at this early stage of the discussion, a distinction quickly stands out. In consensual democracy the trust relation is between individuals, while in parliamentary democracy the trust relation is between groups, for example, between members of the minority party and of the majority party, Socialists and Christian Democrats. Using departmental politics as a working model, we might find that there are those for and those against a new master's program. Immediately we are presented with a familiar philosophical problem, a problem that repeatedly surfaces in social psychology: namely, how far is the sense of a term used commonly to describe a relationship that obtains between individuals preserved when that term is used for a relationship between groups? In many cases of the displacement of concepts, we would be inclined to call the displaced usage metaphorical, resting for its main semantic force on our use of it in its context of origin. Some have argued that there is a radical semantic gulf between the uses of the word "trust" in the interpersonal and the intergroup contexts. It might be thought that the polysemy of "trust" discloses a radical ontological gulf between relations between individuals, say owners of adjoining apartments, and those between groups, say the personnel of two rival departments or agencies in an institution, say the State Department and the CIA. It may even be, as Claus Offe (see this volume, chapter 3) argues, that trust between people is disjoint in meaning from trust between a person and his bicycle, and both are disjoint in meaning from trust between a person and the government. The last is offered as a paradigm case of trust or lack of it between individuals and institutions. I shall return to explore this issue in more detail in what follows.

Aspects of the semantic "space" of the word "trust"

Semantic preliminaries　It will be helpful in managing the analysis of the use of a term such as "trust," which has a variety of uses in a variety of contexts, to borrow a "term of art" from Wittgenstein. Drawing on earlier authors, he took over the expression "language game" for any practical activity in which words play an essential part. He thought that the meanings of words are established in paradigmatic language games, for example, those activities in which children are introduced to new words. He mounted a thoroughgoing attack on the traditional semantic theory that words acquire their meaning by the teacher pointing to exemplary objects or situations. For many important words, there are no such objects or situations. Words are picked up mostly in the course of learning to perform practical activities. For instance, number words are picked up in language games of counting and comparing sets of objects and so on, not by any kind of pointing to different-sized aggregates. So our attempts to understand words of great import to some aspect of our lives must be referred to the language games within which they have a part to play. I shall also make use of another important Wittgensteinian insight: that the fact that a certain *word*, as a lexical item, has a range of diverse uses does not imply that there is a covert common essence accounting for the different overt meanings. Instead, we should think of a field of "family resemblances," multiple linkages of similarities and differences of use, to be studied in detail with no preconceptions as to the existence of any common semantic core. Of course, at some level of generality, there may be such a core, but it is for the analyst to reveal it. It may not be presumed.

These insights led him to suggest that there are two interconnected and pervasive sources of errors in our thinking. The first is the tendency to think there must be an entity corresponding to every meaningful word, thus populating the universe with a plethora of redundant abstract objects. The second is the assumption that the use of every word in all its contexts of employment is governed by a common essence. The two errors come together when that mythical essence is thought to be an abstract or unobservable entity, a cognitive procedure entirely proper in mathematics and the physical sciences but often out of place in human studies. If no essence or abstract entity is easily imagined, then there is a complementary tendency to declare that a word with multiple applications and uses is vague or indeterminate. I have heard it said that the word "democracy" is vague and indeterminate. On the contrary, I believe it is a word the uses of which form a complex field of family resemblances, uses that have their force in many different language games. But, relative to the discursive task in hand, none that I come across is vague.

I shall try to describe a field of family resemblances in the use of the word "trust," offering no speculative presumptions as to "the essence of trust" and grounding these descriptions in examples of concrete language games with which we are all familiar. However, I will suggest that there is a thematic unity to the uses of the trust vocabulary in that in most of its contexts of use the notion of reliability has a place.

Trust relations between individuals   Hardin (1993) is right to remind us that the word "trust" is usually used to describe or query a certain kind of interpersonal relation rather than to express or display it. He is also right, if I have understood him, to advocate a logical form for "trust" relations that I lay out in the following double schema:

A trusts in B in respect of X
B is trusted by A in respect of X

In this section, I shall be concerned only with "A trusts in B" and "B is trusted by A" relations implied by the general formula, leaving a discussion of the nature of X to what I shall call "boundaries of trust." Ordinary language uses of "trust" for describing such relations require that A be a person, but B can be a person, animal, or material thing (such as my neighbor's ladder or Claus Offe's bicycle). So we must ask what are the characteristics – cognitive, affective, moral, and material – of the people who trust and of the people, animals, and things in which they trust, in case the trusting is warranted. Of course, A may be a bona fide truster and B a two-timer or a shill. That A trusts B is no absolute guarantee that B is trustworthy. But what A has to know or believe, as we shall see, does provide some evidence for favorable attributions to B.

(1) *A person and a thing*: We are discussing a mountaineering trip. Talking over the equipment, I ask my very experienced companion, "Would you trust that kind of piton?" What sort of answer would be expected? Either "It's a good make" or "It's well-designed" or "Most of my friends have used them and they never fracture" would make sense. All three answers imply reliability, a future-directed generic dispositional

property. The first two answers refer the judgment to something *a priori* and distance the focus of trust elsewhere than the object being examined. The third answer refers the judgment to something *a posteriori*, the fact of successful empirical tests.

(2) *A person and a person*: We pass on to discuss the Sherpas. "What do you think of Lin Po?" "I'd trust him anywhere." I press you for your grounds for the judgment: "Why?" There seem to be at least two possible kinds of answer. An answer such as "He is a grandson of Tensing" makes reference to something given in the nature of the person concerned, his ancestry, and sometimes his role. For a contemporary example, we can cite "Colin Powell is a good family man." This answer type refers to something *a priori*. We take him on to the team, on trust, without having seen him in action. However, we might offer experiential, *a posteriori* grounds for our confidence, such as "Well, he was with Roger Finnis on K2, and he did very well" or "The Smiths say Michelle is a fine baby-sitter!" Here we have the basis of an inductive judgment.

In these examples, we have two clusters of language games, one thing-directed, the other person-directed. In both some individual person is the anchor, but in the one case the target is a material thing and in the other, another person. In both we find sub-clusters of judgments depending on the kinds of grounds that are invoked in justification of that trust. In one the trust is ascribed *a priori* on the basis of some (perhaps "necessary") pre-given property of the target entity, and in the other *a posteriori* on the basis of experience either of the being in question or of another sufficiently similar to it. We could call the former "ascribed trust" and the latter "earned trust." Luhmann (1979), in an extensive study of the concept of "trust," does not distinguish so sharply between the *a priori* and the *a posteriori* in trusting relations, since he takes trust to have to do with confidence in expectations derived from beliefs about the nature of things and persons trusted from whatever source these beliefs may be derived. This seems to me to brush over matters of considerable concern when we turn to the origins of trust, to its loss and decay, and to the sources and grounds of mistrust.

Wittgenstein's strictures on wastefully chasing after mythical essences do not forbid anyone from asking whether, in any given case and at some level of abstraction, there is one. In this case, the question does have some point: "Is there something common to all these ascriptions of trust and the generic future-directed dispositional properties they ascribe to people and to things in support of the confidence that trust engenders?" We might be inclined to answer that the matter of reliability is at issue. Here we have the heart of an issue to be discussed below: that is, the relation between a root idea in the concept of "trust" – namely, confidence in something or someone, the psychological correlate of a belief in the reliability of the target – and the psychological thesis that as a matter of fact those who trust a person or a thing have confidence in it. To trust something *is* to have a belief in its reliability, that is, that it will perform according to specification or, if it is a person, to what we believe he or she is committed. The studies by Yamagishi and Yamagishi (1994) show that, at least in Japan, the "trusting in" relation has both a pragmatic and a moral version. It might be expressed in the attitude of the one who is trusted, on which the truster bases an expectation of the other's "good-will" – that is, a moral or affective commitment to the truster. Or it might be expressed in the dispositions of the one who is trusted, on which the truster bases an expectation of benign behavior – that is, a pragmatic commitment to the truster.

The concept of "reliability," too, is a family-resemblance notion and covers a broad semantic field. What "reliability" amounts to, be it ascribed to a person or a thing, is made overt when we express a belief that the person or thing will continue to behave as it has always behaved, as things very like it have behaved, or as things of that sort should behave: "If that thing's a saw it should cut wood." The concept will shift and change with context and with the kinds of things concerned and the characters and roles of the people to whom we are inclined to give our trust. Luhmann (1979) anticipates this point in seeing that trust as an anticipation of the future implies a "theory of time" or at least, if not so grand, a sense of the temporal dimensions and future-directedness of personal dispositions.

There is a Polish Jewish parable in which a father sits his son high on the top of a dresser. "Jump!" he says. "Will you catch me?" asks the child. "Of course, I'm your father," says the man. The child jumps, and the father lets him fall. The moral of the story is "Trust no one, not even your own father."

Reflecting on this disturbing little tale uncovers two further features of "trust" language games. This story is meant to teach a young person to trust no one by undermining trust where it is most to be taken for granted, in roles that are definitive of the moral basis of a culture. Trust is not related to expectations of behavior in general, but to what is to be expected of someone in their role relative to the person who trusts, or according to their type relevant to the action in question if they are mere material things.[3] In the mountaineering dialogue, a relevant range of

---

[3] There is an interesting question here about trusting animals, say dogs *qua* "man's best friend." What exactly is brought into question when you are threatened by the next door's Rottweiler?

behaviors and uses was taken for granted by both parties to the discussion. This range excluded such questions as "Is this make of piton any good for opening cans?"[4] or "Is the Sherpa likely to be any good as a counsel for the defense?" Opening up trust talk, explicit or implicit, requires attention to a presumed range of behaviors, since it may not always be the case that the same range is assumed by all parties to the discussion. Contextual distinctions enter the discussion at this point, since what is to constitute the Hardin X can never, I believe, be specified in advance and in general for any two human beings, dogs, or ice axes. These are the boundaries of trust, shifting context by context. Trust, I believe, is never unlimited.

The second point I want to draw from the disturbing Polish parable is that the *a priori* ascription of those reliabilities that serve trust in the case of trusting people are role-related. But these trust relations are between individuals.

So far I have been concerned with the mix of cognitive and affective attributes that characterize the one who trusts. What of the person who is trusted? Trusted ones must share with things and animals a certain reliability and consistency in their relations with the truster, but – and here both Offe (see this volume, chapter 3) and Jane Mansbridge (see this volume, chapter 10) seem to be right – they must also take on an obligation to fulfill the expectations of the truster, to be true to the love, respect, deference, or whatever is the affective motor of the trusting relation. They may even, for all sorts of reasons, open themselves up to this obligation. Material things cannot take on obligations, but they do have natures that serve as surrogates for moral commitments – at least we hope that the alloy of which the piton is made endows it with a material reliability parallel to the human reliability that we hope stems from the taking on of an obligation or the adoption of a pragmatic strategy that will so benefit the one trusted that the truster can rely on it. "Hope" is, of course, a necessary component of the psychological makeup of the person who trusts, be it in the piton or in the dean.

Looking back now to the attributes of the person who trusts, I am obliged to take issue with Hardin's claim that trusting is wholly (largely) cognitive, a matter of belief. To take an everyday example: It seems to me that love is not a reason for trusting someone. To love someone is to trust them, *inter alia*. Where Hardin is, I am sure, largely right, is in emphasizing that the decay or loss of trust is the upshot of cognitive activities. It is because beliefs are subverted and expectations unfulfilled

---

[4] Once I was obliged to use an ice ax to open cans on a mountain, but this possibility had not occurred to me in making my initial selection amongst brands.

that A ceases to trust B in the matter at issue. And that is because the *a priori* assumption or *a posteriori* inference of reliability is called into question by evidence to the contrary.

Trust between individuals and institutions   What is involved in trusting an institution? Does the shift of the concept "trust" to this context transform its meaning in any serious way? Is "trust in the law" more like "trust in the rope" or like "trust in the leader of the team"? Is it based on some *a priori* understanding of the target of the trust, or is it arrived at inductively through experience of the workings of the institution in question? Or is it *sui generis*? In which case, what are the similarities and differences in use that account for the adoption of the very same word, "trust," in this new context?

First of all, it is not obvious to me that trust in the government (or one of its agencies) or trust in my bank is not a special case of trust in persons. Why do I trust the Federal Aviation Administration in the matter of judgments of airworthiness? I think it is because I believe this government agency is staffed by experts. In a similar mood, I trust my bank because I believe, without perhaps ever having formulated the thought explicitly, that it is staffed by honest and competent people. The difference is that these people are not known to me personally. This is a case of the relation that Orlando Patterson (see this volume, chapter 6) calls "indirect personal trust." It would follow that a decline in my trust would follow the same pattern as a decline in my personal direct trust in someone known to me. So when it comes to government, some of the members of which *seem* to be known to me through the activities of the media in portraying them this way and that, we have at least the illusion of person-to-person trust and distrust. In Britain, the current "discourse of distrust" has been exacerbated by the almost continuous revelations of the allegedly shady characters of various ministers of the Crown.

Basing our trust in the rope on the nature of the rope (such and such a weight of nylon) and basing our trust in the leader of our party on our assessment of his character leave us vulnerable to the fact that there is greater difficulty in making the latter than the former assessment. The duties and so the degree of trust that attach to the role of leader may be *a priori*, but the occupant of the role is a vulnerable human being subject to the vagaries of daily life that beset all of us. Napoleon's gall bladder troubles probably accounted for his betraying the trust of the Old Guard when he sent them headlong into the sunken road at Waterloo. Much depends on just what sort of institution we are putting our trust in. For instance, is it an institution that is rule-ordered, people-ordered, or some blend of the two? I would put my trust in a constitutional democracy rather than an Oriental despot on the grounds that rules, though vulnerable to human frailty and inconstancy in their interpretation and application, do provide something that stands outside the whims of individuals. In a way, "the government of Pol Pot" is not an institution at all, considered from the point of view of the concept of "trust." Trusting or distrusting the "government of Pol Pot," since it is a despotism, amounts to trusting or distrusting the despot, and he is an individual.

Zucker (1986: 57–58) makes a somewhat different analysis of the "trust" concept, appropriate for trust between persons and institutions. She offers two root notions. Both are psychological, and both are, we might say, trust-engendering conditions rather than analyses of the trust relation. There are background expectations, rooted in unexamined assumptions of a common frame or form of life. Then there are "constitutive expectations, the rules defining the context or situation." Though this phrase could do with some refinement, it is easy to see the import. Both, it seems to me, would more properly be called "social representations" (as the Parisian school of social psychology would say) than individual psychological characteristics. They might not reside as tacit knowledge in the "head" of any individual but might be immanent in the practices of an institution, practices inculcated perhaps by means of training programs that explicitly acknowledged neither background nor constitutive expectations. Wittgenstein thought it was very important to be clear about the distinction between "following a rule," where the rule was consciously attended to and our personal conformities self-monitored, and "acting in accordance with a rule" in which, sometimes, the rule could be extracted from the practice only retrospectively.

In summary, then, I am not convinced that trusting in an institution is a species of that kind of trust that obtains between a person and an inanimate object of use, such as a ladder or a bicycle. On the contrary, I would cite the above reasons as supporting the conclusion that the trust relation between a person and an institution is a species of the person-to-person relation, at least insofar as we are looking at it from the point of view of the one who trusts. Our beliefs about, as well as our affective and social relations to, the personnel account for standing in a trust relation to the institution they staff. However, it still remains for me an open question how far the characteristics of an institution as the recipient of our trust parallel those of individuals. They are certainly much more like those where the target of trust is a person than when it is a thing, since unlike things and like persons, institutions are subject to moral demands and are often self-disciplined by their internal rules. Nevertheless, I think there are considerations that help to make clear that there is a preponderance of similarities. An institution is constituted by a loosely bounded set of rules and customs that constrain its personnel. These have the effect of making the vagaries of its staff less evident in their institutional behavior. But in the everyday noninstitutional settings in which trust relations come to exist there is also a background of shared conventions (what Wittgenstein called a "form of life") within which individual vagaries are constrained. Trust in an institution is no more open-ended in matters germane to the relation than is simple interpersonal trust. Both are context-bounded and differentiated.

Trust between groups   In our reflection upon the institutional structure of social entities that work by "parliamentary" practices, they appeared, when closely examined, to be cemented together by trusting relations between groups. The most salient would be the group that at a certain time was a majority and those who were a minority. Again, taking our cue from the thesis that interpersonal inter-individual relations are the home territory for the concept of trust, what is the nature of the trusting relation as displaced to this territory?

I am skeptical of the psychological plausibility of such expressions as "The minority must trust the majority in a democracy," "the people's trust in Parliament," and so on, taken in a collective sense. Warren (1996: 48) uses the pronoun "we" in his hortatory remark: "We simply must count on most decisions being well made. . . . trust is pervasive and essential in modern societies . . ." "We" has a variety of uses, prominent being the collective "all of us" and the distributive "each of us." If we adopt the collective reading, then we have run headlong into the problem of what the trust relation as it obtains between groups might be. But if we stick to the distributive, then we have reduced this case to the complex but unproblematic case of the individual in relation to an institution. I do not think it makes much sense to take the source term in a trust relationship as anything other than a person. Group expressions simply serve to provide a shorthand for a criterion for picking out any individual person of the right sort. The arguable point concerns the target.

I have suggested that trusting the institution is shorthand for trusting the personnel. Mark Warren (1996: 49) has argued, rightly, that democratic procedures "serve to constitute and reproduce the boundaries of authority, and in so doing they help generate the terms of trust and authority." We trust a democratic institution because, he believes, that very institutional form is the best guarantee against abuse. Here the locus of trust has moved from persons to codes. There is a further implication in Warren's remark, namely, that the existence of a "loyal opposition" is yet another institutional device to keep the group in power morally up to scratch. But the character of the individuals and national traditions can hardly be ignored in the giving of trust, since it is not unknown for all kinds of wheeling and dealing to go on between those we presume are institutionally serving to discipline each other. There is a radical difference between the trust that is given, unearned, and that survives – as Luhmann points out – even in the face of some degree of failure of our expectations, and the trust that is earned and that can be readily forfeited by failure.

However, with the target in mind, the question of the reciprocal to trust must be addressed in more detail than in the paragraph above. The reciprocal concept to "trust in . . ." is, as I have argued, some contextually specified form of reliability. The problem with trusting individual people is not only the difficulty of making good inductive assessments of the character of the one we trust – even if the notion of "character" were less labile than it is – but also, in the absence of constraining rules accepted as such by the individual in question, our vulnerability to whim. There are those who give lip service to the rules and privately (and secretly) violate them and those we rule out of our circle of the trusted on grounds of corruption. The whimsical, the inconstant, and the corrupt are equally threats to trust. They are threats just because those character traits undermine attributions of responsibility. So far as I can see, there is no formal procedure, no code, by the use of which these uncertainties can be resolved.

Part two: surrogates for trust

A paradox of individualism

My question is this: Given that we can everywhere (except in New Zealand) observe a shift from a customary regulation of daily life to a growing resort to codes – explicit sets of rules – is this a sign of a growth of distrusting practices? At first sight, it would seem obvious that it is, or even must be. Surely the Christ Child Opportunity Shop has shifted from a custom to a code for dealing with checks because the managers of the shop believe that people who shop there are no longer trustworthy. That was the intended implication of my introduction of the example above. But now I want to query that slick conclusion and look for something deeper.[5] My conclusion will be that as rules become surrogates

---

[5] In the course of discussion at the Conference on Democracy and Trust, I came to see that there was another influence tending to shift practices from customs to codes, namely the bringing together of persons from different communities by immigration, the weakening of class barriers, and so on. Such people simply do not share a repertoire of customary ways with the dominant social group.

for trust – and I will look at the reasons for this shift in what follows – a paradoxical situation with respect to the foundations of democracy (in the most general sense, that is, resolution of conflict by discursive means) comes to be. In the shift from customs to codes, there is a strengthening of the moral conditions for individualism, but in so doing we weaken the moral conditions for trust. And this is a paradox, since democracy in whatever form we find it requires of its participants both individual responsibility in the exercise of their democratic rights and, falling in with that, a degree of interpersonal trust that makes possible the working of institutions of management that rely on discursive rather than authoritarian means for the resolution of differences.

"Thick" and "thin" democracy

There is another way in which rule-following and trust interact that brings out a further feature of the social psychology of democratic practices. This has the effect of enriching our understanding of the varieties of practice that fall within the general conception of "the democratic way" and of the contrast between customs and codes.

The Canadian and the cop

European newspaper coverage of the Atlanta Olympics quickly became markedly hostile to the meta-Olympic performance of the city itself and its officials and managers. The London *Times*, rounding off its unfavorable string of stories, gave front-page prominence on August 2, 1996, to an account of the arrest of Mrs. Julie Pound, the wife of one of the senior Olympic officials. It resulted from a clash between consensual common sense and authoritarian rule-obedience or code-following. Mrs. Pound, seeing there was, for the moment, no traffic in the street, crossed while the pedestrian light was red. A local cop, Officer Browning, ordered her back, applying the rule "Thou shalt not cross against the red light" independently of the circumstances. Mrs. Pound pointed out that there was no traffic at that moment, initiating a situated negotiation that she took for granted would have been appropriate in the context. Officer Browning then laid hands on Mrs. Pound and arrested her. This story illustrates an important distinction in democratic practices in which rule-following, interpersonal trust, and subtle differences in political ideology interact. To see the point, we need to bring to light a root dichotomy in the conception of a democratic practice (society).

In a *thin* democracy, an elected assembly, without further reference to the citizens by referendum or poll, institutes a law or rule. An official or factotum, usually appointed rather than elected, applies the rule regardless of the particularities of individual cases. Debate, negotiation, or discussion of the rule and its conditions of application is reserved to the members of the elected assembly. This democracy is "thin" because it consists of an overlay of parliamentary democracy over an essentially authoritarian life-form. In a *thick* democracy, an elected assembly institutes a rule, but the officials charged with implementing it negotiate its application with the citizens on a case-by-case basis, the outcomes of which will depend on the situation. This democracy is "thick" because it consists of a thin layer of parliamentary democracy over an essentially consensual and democratic life-form "below." The case of Mrs. Pound vs. Officer Browning is an example of a person who takes for granted that everyday life is a thick democracy in conflict with someone whose conception of and training in democracy inclines her to the thin life-form.

Trust in integrity of officials

This distinction is one of large psychological import, for on it hangs the quality of the relationship between the government, as executive and legislature, and the citizens. The discussion of grounds of trust above left a crucial structural property of that relation unanalyzed. I had in mind citizens and governments, but there is a middle layer in every complex society, ancient or modern. There are officials and bureaucrats, and they face two ways. Facing one way, it is with these people that the citizen touches government. But they also face another way, in that at their higher reaches they are in direct contact with the government itself. The relationship between the government and the people governed, vis-à-vis the relation of trust, depends on whether there is trust between the lawmakers and those whose job it is to implement the laws, and whether there is trust between these officials, bureaucrats, and petty officeholders and the citizens with whom they have daily contact.

In a thin democracy, trust between the government and its agents is low, so officials are trained to "mindless" implementations of laws and ordinances. In a thick democracy, that trust is high, so officials are, so to say, licensed to negotiate the applications case by case. It would have been nice to be able to claim that in a thin democracy the citizens do not trust the officials as much as they do in a thick democracy, but, alas, theoretical symmetry must give way to what I believe actually to be the case: that there is no correlation of this sort. The investigation of the origins of thin and thick democratic practices would take us into a study of historical, anthropological, and psychological matters of great complexity and, to my mind, of great interest, but for which I am certainly not qualified. However, I am ready to claim that the more diverse the population in social origins and in cultural background, the more codes will replace customs. And, as I argued above, this may – whether it suits our sentiments or not – be an advance in social justice. The tension arises just because the shift to codes opens the way for the petty tyranny of the officeholder.

Where trust is not rules shall be

I turn now to a more careful investigation of the custom-to-code transition that I have identified as a salient feature of contemporary democratic practices.

The decay of trusting relations

"Trust" is such a central concept for deliberations in the nature of governance and of society partly, I think, because of its double connotation as a psychological and as an ethical concept. We have already seen it tied in with the double connotation of "reliability." Human reliability is both a psychological concept, highlighting a certain steadiness of character in those to whom it is ascribed, and a moral concept, highlighting a certain attitude toward the fulfillment of duties. No doubt dutifulness and steadiness of character go regularly together in the Puritan world we all have inherited, whatever our sectarian affiliations or which prophet in whose footsteps we follow.

Following the advice of J.L. Austin for studying the uses of "trousers words" (a famous, but no doubt politically incorrect, coinage) – that is, words the negative of which "wears the trousers" – let us look once again at some of the situations in which trust would be lost. What leads to a lack of trust? What is the nature of the "betrayal of trust?" Clearly, one type of occasion that would be properly called a case of betrayal, a moral falling-down, and so an occasion for a loss of trust, a psychological consequence, would be the failure to fulfill an expectation held by the one who trusts with respect to the being that is trusted. This failure could be in respect of either an *a priori* or an *a posteriori* expectation – that is, one that in the human case was either role- or experience-based – in a situation in which it would be expected to be fulfilled. For example, trust is betrayed and confidence lost when one discovers that someone one trusts to tell the truth, perhaps by virtue of his or her place in society, has been lying. Another morally milder response to betrayal of a more venal kind might be disappointment, say, in not getting the quality of service that the advertisement for a garage had led one to expect. However, the disappointment of one who has been let down is still a moral disappointment.

The moral tone of post-letdown accusations suggests that one who is trusted has an obligation thrust upon him or her, perhaps even a moral obligation to fulfill the expectations of the one who trusts. Is it a duty? And is it exactly commensurate to the actual trust, that is, not supererogatory? I think it is neither supererogatory nor exactly commensurate to the actual trust. I do not find out my obligations to one who trusts me – say, a business partner or a graduate student – by interrogating them as to the fine details of their trust. Both trustor and trustee depend on something transcendental to the immediate relationship, something immanent in the culture. This might be explicitly defined in some cases in roles, such as priests and presidents. Then there is, or perhaps I should say "was," a vast corpus of implicit foundations of trust, as in our common understanding of what was demanded of role-holders such as fathers, professors, and the like. The decay of a common culture of trust and reciprocal duties is displayed in the writing and publishing of what should be the redundant statutes of a code of conduct to guard against such derelictions of duty and betrayals of trust as sexual harassment and plagiarism. The norms of behavior that the codes explicitly incorporate ought to have been immanent in the role of teacher or employer. This tendency to make the immanent explicit has shifted the meaning of "trust" in many human contexts toward the *a posteriori* grounds of experience and away from the *a priori* grounds of role expectations. So an employee gains trust in an employer who, it is implied by the existence of an explicit code of conduct, will sexually harass her unless experience proves the contrary. The only thing standing between civilized behavior and a Hobbesian state of nature is a code.

Rules and individual responsibility

I have yet to establish a strong relation between individualism and the shift from customs to codes. Let me begin my analysis of the role of rules as surrogates for interpersonal trust with another anecdote. At the Baltimore Opera House, there is a drinks bar, open at the intervals. I asked the young person (a volunteer, I believe, since the bar is run by a supporters group) for a club soda. She fetched a can, opened it, and began to pour it carefully into a glass. Lots of people were waiting their turn, so I said, "Give it to me. I'll pour it out and you can serve the others." "I can't do that," she said. "We are not supposed to let people take the cans away."

Why did this intelligent and personable young lady refuse to take an initiative that would have saved the thirsty clients a few seconds' wait? The anecdote touches a very deep aspect of a particular form of democratic culture; it has to do with the diffusion of responsibility. Insofar as the server kept to the rules, the responsibility for any untoward consequences of the sale of drinks to opera patrons would not fall on her shoulders. This points to a sharp line of demarcation between individual and institution. The institution is immanent in the rules, but the server is not, in her own eyes, an integral part of that institution. Nor, I suppose, would the institution so regard her. It would not take responsibility for actions outside the rules in which it is immanent, however intelligent and beneficial the initial innovation might have been.

In this example we have in miniature a display of a deep and distinctive feature of societies in which individualism involves the metaphysical separation of persons and institutions, of roles and role-holders. How could such a powerful set of customary practices have come about? Mr. Jefferson, Mr. Madison, Mr. Hamilton, and the other wise persons who spent that long summer in Philadelphia did not, I believe, envisage the reign of rules as surrogates for trust. Among the gentlemen of Virginia and Maryland, interpersonal trust was taken for granted and required neither rules to preserve it nor tests to establish it. But there are always new members in the club. As the social diversity and cultural heterogeneity of the citizens have expanded, and the overall maintenance of democratic forms has remained a prime imperative, so codes must of necessity displace customs, even when it is customs that they codify.

Systematizing the three distinctions

The parliamentary and the consensual distinction in modes of decision-making and the thin and thick democracy distinction do seem to fit neatly to one another. If we add to this pairing the distinction between trust rooted in implicit norms of behavior and trust surrogation by rule control, we complete a neat dichotomy of mutually mapping triads.

Rules and rule-following are practiced more rigidly in the United States than in any other of the guardian cultures of individualism. The strict separation of role from role-holder is one of the unintended consequences of the surge to individualism that began in the Renaissance and flowered in the Enlightenment. In the United States, more than in any other Western democracy, there have been a powerful and sustained practical need and a more fluctuating but nevertheless often acknowledged moral imperative to incorporate new and diverse members into the "club." This has led to a pragmatic shift from customs to codes as the dominant mode of social control that consists in following the rules for conduct of some authorized practice. At the same time, this very mode achieves that external attachment of person to institution that protects the individual whose necessary but vulnerable independence would have seemed incomprehensible to the medieval mind. Pragmatic necessity has engendered a moral transformation, in keeping with the powerful founding tradition of moral individualism.

The analysis offered here, of changing practices of trust, depends on the claim that there has been a massive shift from custom to code in the management of everyday life. The same contrast underlies the distinction between thin and thick democracies. I have sketched the outlines of an explanation for the shift by reference to two yet more fundamental phenomena: strong individualism and the mixing rather than the mutual absorption of different cultures. These explanatory proposals recommend themselves in the light of the observation that the shift from custom to code has progressed further in the United States than elsewhere, while American cultural practices and rhetorics display a strong individualism within a social framework that makes possible a common form of life for people of very diverse cultural origins.

However, there are other matters that could be remarked upon, either as alternative explanations or as supplementary to those I have already cited. Popular rhetoric would have it that in recent times traditional hierarchical structures have lost their authority. The examples of shifts from custom to code that I have used to illustrate my argument could be accounted for by a shift, not merely in rhetoric, but in practices, from hierarchical to egalitarian modes of life. Thus Officer Browning's altercation with Mrs. Pound could be taken to illustrate the subsumption of everyone, regardless of notional status, within a common framework of rules. Whereas thick democracies leave space for the exercise of hierarchical social influence, thin democracies protect egalitarian relationships. If Jack is as good as his master, Joan as her mistress and Joan is as good as Jack, then a common code serves as some measure of guarantee that the practices of everyday life will express these claims. Rather than serving as an alternative explanation of the shift from customs to codes, I would be inclined to recruit the shift from a hierarchical to an egalitarian rhetoric, with the spread of practices to match, as yet another influence on the deep relations between trust and democracy with which this discussion has been concerned. Since there is an obvious tie between strong individualism and egalitarianism, the inclusion of another influence in the explanatory package makes sense. And there may be yet other influences to be identified in the origins of so vast a change in the management of everyday life.

From parliaments to courts: "entitlement" and the shift from democracy

However, there is more to the shift from trusting persons to trusting codes than I have yet brought out. I now turn to a much more difficult issue than those I have tackled so far. This issue arises from reflection on the central dilemma of contemporary social orders, the problem of striking a balance between rights and duties. The problem is deep in that it arises at the intersection of two features of the concepts of "duty" and "right." Rights and duties are morally asymmetrical in the sense that while a right entails a moral imperative on action *toward* the person whose claim to a right is recognized *from* some other person or institution, a duty entails a moral imperative on action *from* the person to whom an assignment of a duty has been recognized *toward* some person or institution. This means that while conflicts of rights have to be sorted out by an external authority, usually the courts, conflicts of duties have to be sorted out by the conscience of those to whom duties have been assigned. Though conflicts are resolved in very different ways, it does not follow that duties may and often are imposed and enforced by external authority. An academic contract is a case in point. The duties of a post-holder are spelled out in more or less detail. Failures to fulfill one's duties are not only a matter of one's own conscience but may incur the wrath of the institution. Conflict of duties cannot be so resolved.

The asymmetry of direction between rights and duties is a feature of the moral structure of rights and duties and leads to their possessing profoundly different psychological characteristics. In asserting one's rights, one's attention is focused on the good of oneself, while in accepting and fulfilling one's duties, one's attention is focused on the good of someone else. In a predominantly hedonically oriented society, people will surely pay more attention to their rights than to their duties. But if the shift from customs to codes as the basis of trust tends to separate individuals from their roles, the moral aspect of the reciprocal of trust – namely, duty – would seem to weaken. My adherence to a code may be, and I suspect usually is, just pragmatic: "Keep your nose clean, your head down, and your job is safe."

In the context of this discussion, I do not intend to try to resolve the evident paradox of this analysis – namely, that if there are rights, there are correlative duties that someone must assume – except for one very important consequence of this paradox. If people are more willing to assert their rights than to accept their duties as anything other than a pragmatic adherence to codes, and if this comes to be true of nearly everyone, then how are the duties correlative to the rights, the fulfillment of which is a necessary condition for the realization of rights-based claims, to be activated? The answer surely must be either by codes and rule systems for which sanctions for failure are well-known and readily available, such as minimal merit raises for those who teach badly, or by regulation by an independent – that is, a judicial – authority. So we slip step by step into government by the courts. Neither in a parliamentary nor in a consensual democracy could a recalcitrant and ego-oriented public be brought to an unforced resolution of the self-created paradox. The steadily enlarging domain in which the legal system, rather than the local moral order, assigns duties is emblematic of so-called "entitlement societies." Already we can see how the growth of the domain of rights erodes the scope for democratic decision-making as to the identification and distribution of rights.[6]

A further development of the psychological contrasts between rights-based and duties-based societies can be worked out by making use of the general principle that rights are grounded in vulnerabilities and duties in powers. It makes no sense to assign a duty to someone who, for a huge variety of possible kinds of reasons, cannot fulfill it. Furthermore, as Robinson and I (1995) have argued, there are duties to beings for which even a vicarious claim to rights seems ungroundable. But there is a further consequence to be drawn, in the context of the discussion of the conditions for democracy and the concept of "trust." It is the disparity in scale between the scope of rights and the scope of duties. Duties are derived from the actual powers inherent in the nature of human beings. The scope of duties is finite. Rights are derived from the *actual and possible* vulnerabilities of human beings. The scope of rights is indefinite, since what is a possible vulnerability does not depend wholly on the nature of human beings, but also on the environment and historical circumstances in which they live. No one in Europe could have a right to a nonsmoking workplace before Sir Walter Raleigh brought back tobacco. No legislative program could possibly enact a real Bill of Rights, except in respect of rights so anodyne and generic as to leave everything yet to be done or ones so local and specific as to be rapidly overtaken by history. Insofar as human nature is more or less invariant under transformation of environments (and that may not be so in the very long run), an assignment of duties via an *a priori* analysis of human powers, with escape clauses and *ceteris paribus* reservations to accommodate the Gaussian curve that describes anything human, including human powers, is feasible.

---

[6] I personally have a distaste for rights-based societies and favor those that are duties-based. But I acknowledge that in coupling this preference with a regard for regulation by custom I am revealing myself as a sentimentalist at best and a fuddy-duddy at worst.

The addition and deletion of rights by judicial proceedings is surely endless. But in a duties-based society in which there is trust in those whose dutiful actions we encounter, there is no need for rights, even when the catalogue of duties attaching to any social or institutional place is determined by ordinance or convention. It is worth rereading the order of service of marriage in any Christian book of common prayer, predating the revisions of the last couple of decades. Husbands and wives need no rights because there is a well-defined catalogue of duties derived *a priori* from what was then thought to be an exhaustive analysis of the natures of men and women. Insofar as those natures are thought to have changed or our analyses of them to be subject to revision, the catalogue of duties will be different. For example, the shift from authoritarian to consensual family structures can be seen as reflected in the differences in the promises at the core of the ceremony. Just so far as these no longer express a taken-for-granted catalogue of duties, the way is opened for contests of rights, premarital "contracts" spelling out not only duties but explicit lists of rights. But a marriage culture based predominantly on rights is fragile, and its demands are open-ended just because of the impossibility of creating a finite catalogue of rights. An entitlement society is impossible, but in our efforts to create the impossible we have shifted the center of gravity of our governance from parliaments to courts.

Summary and conclusions

Our analyses of the semantic field of the concept of "trust," in the context of the discussion of the conditions for the establishment and preservation of a form of human association we could roughly call "democratic," has brought out the double-sidedness of the notion. To trust someone and to be trusted by someone constitute both a pattern of psychological dispositions and beliefs of an essentially pragmatic character and a pattern of moral obligations, of which duty to those who trust is the paramount one. This conclusion came through strongly from the way that the concept of "reliability," in a variety of variants, emerged from the analyses. But added complexity was forced on our attention through the need to take account of the fundamental distinction between parliamentary and consensual democracy. Trust is needed in both, but works differently in each. The trusting relation as an interrelated pattern of psychological dispositions and moral imperatives is not the same in the two major democratic forms. Complication mounts when we take into account the possibility of combinations of parliamentary and consensual democratic forms in looking at examples of thin and thick democracies. Thin democracies provided examples of the important contemporary solution to the decay of interpersonal trust as a cement of society, namely, the rise of a culture of rules. But that turned out to be paradoxical. Is the shift from customs to codes the result of a decay of trust, or it is among the causes of that decay? I have suggested that one of the driving forces of the shift is the need to protect the individual whose moral independence leads to a vulnerability that can be protected only by adherence to a code. But then it is the code and not the individual that is the guarantor of reliability, and interpersonal trust no longer plays a central role. But is the decay real? In drawing a distinction between discourse of distrust and practices of distrust, I hoped to open a space for the question. Perhaps the shift from customs to codes has made room for a discursive convention by which we express ourselves as distrustful of government, just because when life is codified the presumption is that we cannot trust those with whom we deal. But perhaps when we look more closely into trusting practices the picture may look somewhat different.

REFERENCES

Baker, J., 1985. An analysis of the concept of "trust." Paper presented at the International University Centre, Dubrovnik

Hardin, Russell, 1993. The street-level epistemology of trust. *Politics and Society* 21, 505–29

Harré, R. and Robinson, Daniel N., 1995. On the primacy of duties. *Philosophy* 70, 513–32

Luhmann, Niklas, 1979. Trust: A mechanism for the reduction of social complexity, in *Trust and Power: Two Works by Niklas Luhmann*, Chichester: John Wiley and Sons

Mansbridge, Jane, 1980. *Beyond Adversary Democracy*, New York: Basic Books

Warren, Mark E., 1996. Deliberative democracy and authority. *American Political Science Review* 90, 46–60

Yamagishi, Toshio and Yamagishi, Midori, 1994. Trust and commitment in the United States and Japan. *Motivation and Emotion* 18, 129–66.

Zucker, Lynne G., 1986. Production of trust: Institutional sources of economic structure, 1840–1920. *Research in Organizational Behavior* 8, 53–111

9 Geographies of trust, geographies of hierarchy

James C. Scott

Introduction

Why have so many huge development schemes, designed to improve the human condition in poor countries, so tragically failed? In the course of addressing this question I have, I believe, stumbled across the rudiments of what might be called a "geography of trust." Put crudely and briefly, authoritarian high-modernist development schemes replace thick, complex, quasi-autonomous social orders (and natural orders too) with thin, simplified, mechanical orders that function badly, even for the limited purposes for which they are designed. Such thin simplifications, if they survive at all, do so by virtue of their unacknowledged dependence on improvised "order" outside the scheme.

The sort of improvised order I have in mind has a lot to do with the "mutuality without hierarchy" celebrated by anarchist thinkers and practitioners. Such mutuality, I believe, rests on relations of trust analogous to those examined by the literature on democracy and trust, except for the fact that I will be examining it exclusively in its informal, nonorganizational forms.

Lest this description remain too cryptic, let me specify briefly the phenomenon I have in mind. It is captured in the labor tradition of the "work-to-rule" strike (*grève du zèle*). The premise of such a strike is that the formal rules and regulations governing work are never an adequate guide to the actual practice of work. To follow the rules mindlessly and to the letter is, in fact, to bring the work to a virtual standstill. Thus, Parisian taxi drivers, in their protests against municipal authorities, had only to obey the provisions of the *code routier* meticulously to bring traffic in the city to a halt. For our purposes, they were calling attention to the fact that traffic circulation in Paris depended on a host of informal practices – some of which were strictly illegal – that could never be codified formally.

The small but powerful insight embodied by the work-to-rule strike can be applied to many large development schemes whose planned simplicities are underwritten by unplanned, outside-the-scheme improvisation. Thus, the high-modernist, planned city of Brasilia, for all its human inadequacies, survives by virtue of an "unplanned Brasilia" that now constitutes two-thirds of its population. Official Brasilia would not last a week without its "dark twin." Similarly, the centrally planned collective farms in Russia survived only by virtue of the desperate improvisations of their inhabitants, growing illegal crops on the side, hiding private land, engaging in informal trade and barter, and "stealing" time, machinery use, and fodder from the collective to ensure their own subsistence. Such anomalies – often winked at – both sustained the collective farm sector and provided much of the diet of the urban population as well. Much the same logic could be applied to the planned *ujamaa* villages of Nyerere's Tanzania or to the way in which the vulnerabilities of industrial agriculture (a heroic floral simplification) are mitigated by the great variety of open-pollinated land-races that it is bent on extirpating (see Scott 1998).

Readers following contemporary debates will note that my argument bears a similar structure to the argument made recently by John Gray: namely, that liberal democracy is a self-liquidating project in the sense that its survival rests on social processes that it cannot reproduce and that, in fact, it is eroding by virtue of the logic of its operating assumptions. I shall not pursue that argument directly here. Rather, I will examine the way in which informal social order necessary to a satisfactory social life and to production is undermined by the thin simplicities of high-modernist planning. The "discovery of trust" in Gray's case and the discovery of informal social order in my own analysis are nearly classical cases of the owl of Minerva flying at dusk. That is to say, they tend to remain undiscovered or taken for granted until the moment when their erosion begins to have massive, discontinuous effects. Only the effects of their absence, like that of the background music that is noticed only when it is turned off, alert us to their importance.

A just so story

The Ministry of the Interior in Brazil, as in many "settler colonies," has had a grisly record in its treatment of indigenous peoples. In much of its early history, its function was to drive native peoples away from the frontier, a process that included concentration camps, poisoning, and murder. The point, for our purposes, is that many native peoples came justifiably to regard state officials as a scourge and fled deeper into the interior to avoid contact. Later, in the 1960s, a more humane officialdom in the ministry wanted to reestablish contact with such groups but found that the legacy of total distrust and fear apparently had made it impossible. Intermediaries failed, as did direct contact; whenever bands knew they had been sighted, they fled.

An anthropologist suggested a new strategy. Officials of the ministry went to a clearing where a band had been seen recently and strung a clothesline between trees on which they hung objects they imagined the band members might want: knife and ax blades, penknives, plastic bowls and cups, cloth, rope, paints, waterproof matches. Then they left. When they returned a few weeks later, all the objects they had left had been removed; in their place were hung objects one imagines band members might have thought their "gift-leaving visitors" would want: necklaces, plumage, traps, flutes, scrapers, knife handles. They were reciprocating the gift and, at the same time, opening the possibility of continuing barter relations. The officials took these gifts-in-trade and left other goods; the band returned the favor. As the intervals diminished, the two groups were gradually in sight of one another and eventually close enough to exchange greetings. Thanks to the anthropologist's faith in the unspoken but universal etiquette of barter and reciprocity, enough wary trust had been created to open other lines of communication.

Substrata of cooperation and exchange

The example cited above is surely a limiting case of mutuality and coordination. Even this minimal "vocabulary" of cooperation, however, requires some basis in reciprocity and exchange. If these are the irreducible "elementary forms" of social coordination, one may imagine that more complex, elaborate forms of social coordination require correspondingly higher levels of reciprocity and exchange – forms of reciprocity and exchange that extend beyond the trading of pots and knives in the bazaar and to the exchange of hospitality, civility, kinship (as in marriage alliances), and elements of culture.

For the sake of argument, I am prepared here to treat social trust, in the sense of mutually reinforcing expectations about reciprocity, as a kind of all-purpose social "glue." It represents a kind of abstract capacity for joint action that may or may not be deployed. Above all, it leaves two vital questions unanswered. First, it says nothing about the nobility or worthiness of the purposes of such joint action. As Barrington Moore has noted in the case of peasants and workers, a capacity for joint action (solidarity?) is the *sine qua non* of any social action at all; without it we have atomization and passivity. This, he and others have persuasively claimed, is the reason why radical mobilization is more likely to emanate from damaged, but intact, "older" classes "over whom the waves of history are about to roll" (e.g. artisans and peasants) than from a newly urbanized proletariat with only thin and historically shallow networks of mutuality. Such networks of mutuality are, of course, as necessary to antidemocratic mobilization as to democratic mobilization. Surely we need a taxonomy of forms of trust to attack this issue – a job I will not take up here but that has been begun well by Mark Warren and Orlando Patterson in this volume.

The second, and related, issue is the extent to which a high degree of trust within one group necessarily implies a corresponding distrust of that "other" against which any cohesive identity is always formed. When Fukuyama (1995) designates Germany and Japan as "high-trust societies," it is hard not to speculate about the role this "high trust" may have played in the mobilized anti-Semitism of the former or the insularity vis-à-vis other ethnic groups of the latter. In this respect, there is something to be said for certain forms of healthy mistrust. One striking example is Francois Rochat's insightful examination of the social processes within the French village that managed to save some 6,000 Jews and other opponents of Nazism and of Franco from the Vichy regime. In this village, a Huguenot tradition had fostered local solidarity, a lively distrust of a potentially persecutory state, and a corresponding fellow feeling toward its victims. If skepticism is the antonym of trust, then certain forms of civic courage that have their origin in a calculated distrust of authority are valuable democratic resources.

The argument that follows, therefore, should not be read as a blanket endorsement of all forms of social trust. Viewed instrumentally – like furniture glue – social trust of the kind I am examining facilitates the building of all kinds of social products. How we judge the activities that this social glue makes possible is another matter. My objective is more limited: to show how a certain genre of generalized trust underlies functioning civic order.

A geography of trust

Let me return to the informal patterns of sociability that undergird civic life and safety. They are the rudiments of a life in common without which democracy is unthinkable. I think of them as the elementary forms of civic life. Here I want to emphasize the adjective "informal." What I have in mind are not the civic groups and formal associational life to which Robert Putnam (1993) points in northern Italy. Such organized activities may well be a logical outgrowth of the elementary forms I have in mind. But the elementary forms considered here are not organized activities in any formal sense. Their very essence (and their "efficiency"[1]) lies in the fact that they have no formal existence: no name, no office-bearers, no meetings, no table of organization, no banners. And yet they do palpable social work.

In the American context, I believe Jane Jacobs (1961), in her criticism of urban planning, has best understood phenomena of this kind. We may take as a diagnostic example her treatment of successful and safe neighborhoods (many of them quite poor) in Boston, New York, Chicago, and Philadelphia. The phrase that best captures the process is her own: "eyes on the street." In the course of trying to understand why some neighborhoods were desirable, animated, and safe, Jacobs realized that it was not the police that made a neighborhood safe. Far from it, the presence of policemen in any substantial number was evidence of the breakdown of other social processes. Order was maintained instead by "eyes on the street": the curiosity, presence, and vigilance of hundreds of people throughout the day doing the "unpaid" work of sustaining public order. They were small shopkeepers, news vendors, fruit sellers, and butchers who tended their enterprises all day, elderly men and women looking at the passing scene from their windows, local shoppers, women pushing baby-carriages, strollers:

> ... the public peace – the sidewalk and street peace – of cities is not kept primarily by the police, necessary as the police are. It is kept by an intricate, almost unconscious, network of voluntary controls and standards among the people themselves, and enforced by the people themselves. ... No amount of police can enforce civilization where the normal, casual enforcement of it has broken down. (Jacobs 1961: 31)

The "enforcers" in question were not organized in "block-watch associations" (another sign that informal order has failed). At best, they had what Jacobs called "street acquaintance," a recognition that this was also someone from the neighborhood, though they might not know anything more about them. For the most part, these "eyes on the street" were simply going about their own daily rounds and/or observing the animated, passing scene. When, however, a child seemed lost, a fight started to develop, or a passer-by seemed ill or was injured, they stepped in to inquire what the matter was or to offer or seek assistance. At a more banal but no less vital level, they made the small reciprocities of public life possible (e.g. "would you please . . . keep an eye on my bike . . . hold my place in line . . . watch my briefcase . . . etc."). Their very presence was more instrumental to "social order in the street" than anything they

[1] In the unpardonable utilitarian parlance of rational-choice analysis, "their efficiency in terms of minimizing transaction costs."

did; their presence helped make the neighborhood safe, even for the local panhandlers.

> Most of it [small exchanges and conversations] is ostensibly utterly trivial but the sum is not trivial at all. The sum of each casual, public contact at a local level – most of it fortuitous, most of it associated with errands, all of it metered by the person concerned and not thrust upon him by anyone – is a feeling for the public identity of a people, a web of public respect and trust, and a recourse in time of personal or neighborhood need. The absence of this trust is a disaster to a city street. *Its cultivation cannot be institutionalized.* And, above all, it implies no private commitments. (Jacobs 1961: 56)[2]

Jacobs distinguishes "being on sidewalk terms" with others from friendship. People are frequently on "sidewalk terms" for years, even decades, with others quite different from themselves – others with whom friendship is all but precluded. Public acquaintance of this kind is possible, Jacobs argues, precisely because there is a sharp line between these public civilities and actual friendship.

The chief value of Jacobs' analysis is her close, ethnographic account of how public order is sustained by the informal, unpaid activities of thousands of citizens. Her description of the way in which each block in a functioning neighborhood has one or more shopkeepers who hold apartment keys for relatives and friends of nearby residents who are temporarily away is a classic case of the public services informally provided by private citizens. The shopkeepers who perform this service surely thereby strengthen their ties to customers, but the service they provide could not conceivably be provided by a public bureaucracy.

Jacobs regards this informal web of public trust as the necessary condition of collective public action. Unless a neighborhood has an informal public life – what in Durkheimian terms we might call "the elementary forms of public life" – that provides the integument, formal voluntary organizations fail to take hold. In a real sense, such practices of daily trust are also an "elementary form of self-government." Jacobs tends to reverse the planners' logic. Instead of asking how the correct design of decent housing, schools, and parks could create a strong neighborhood, she presumes that a strong neighborhood could create and maintain the housing, schools, and parks it needs by mobilizing and fighting for them. In Hirschman's terms, the informal infrastructure of trust is the precondition of democratic voice.

Accepting the gist of Jacobs' argument, what are the local, urban conditions necessary to this street-level trust? The *creation* of informal trust,

---

[2] I have changed the emphasis. In Jacobs' text, only the last sentence was italicized.

as distinct from its maintenance, remains, self-consciously, something of a mystery to Jacobs. What is clear to her is that a successful neighborhood is the result of "spontaneous self-diversification" and the vector-sum of multitudes of particular initiatives over time; it cannot be planned from above as part of a deliberate scheme. She approvingly quotes a city planner of rare modesty: "We will have to admit that it is beyond the scope of anyone's imagination to create a community. We must learn to cherish the communities we have; they are hard to come by" (1961: 336–337). Planning a city is a little like trying to legislate a living language. No one can possibly foresee the variety of uses to which language or urban space might be put, and to pretend to engineer either is an exercise in arrogance and what Jacobs calls "social taxidermy."

On the other hand, planners can play a small role in maintaining street-level trust. Jacobs' suggestions are particular and detailed since her book is a point-by-point indictment of contemporary urban-planning doctrines. The principles behind her analysis, however, are instructive.

A certain concentration of population in densities well beyond what standard urban-planning doctrine of the time allowed was necessary. A modicum of stability was also vital. Very rapid turnover in residence was a disaster for "street-acquaintance" and for "eyes-on-the-street" safety. Above all, the successful urban neighborhood required an animated street-scene of foot traffic throughout the day that, in turn, was underwritten by great diversity in housing, commerce, and occupations. It was the complex mixture of shops of all kinds, bars, restaurants, kiosks, residences, studios, public offices, laundromats, small manufacturing, and small white-collar firms that provided the traffic, the stability, and the animated street-scene necessary to informal trust relations.

What is important for our purposes is that these rudimentary principles of street-level trust flew directly in the face of the urban-planning doctrines of the time. Those doctrines emphasized either social engineering from above (so many square feet of dwelling space per resident, so much commercial frontage and shelf space per thousand inhabitants, so many school rooms, etc.) and/or the city as a disciplined work of art, meant to be admired for its sculptural properties. In the case of social engineering, planning was the implacable enemy of complexity and mixed use. The logic of large-scale urban planning was strict separation of functions reinforced by zoning: residences in one zone, commercial establishments in another, entertainment in another, public offices in another, and museums and theaters in still another. Planning was vastly easier and, in the short run more efficient, when each function was separate and treated as a single variable. Where this logic was applied rigorously, the results were the sterile housing towers, such as the Pruitt-Igoe award-winning project in

St. Louis, subsequently dynamited, and single-use districts that are empty and frequently dangerous for much of the day.

The city designed from scratch as a "work of art," such as Le Corbusier-inspired Brasilia or Chandigarh, also proved unsatisfactory to the great majority of its inhabitants. Not only did it replicate the spatial segregation of functions, but it also confused visual order from above and outside with the "actual-functioning" order for real inhabitants living at "ground level." A thin, mandated, hierarchical, socially engineered, urban social order failed to create the necessary conditions for informal social order. Here it is instructive to remember that the planners of these urbanscapes were often visionary professionals dedicated to providing the basic needs (affordable shelter, clean water and air, open space, and other amenities), particularly for poorer citizens. Their planning, however, was for an abstract, standardized citizen – much like the "unmarked" citizen of liberal democratic theory – and not for real citizens with distinctive histories, tastes, values, customs, ideas, traditions, and attachments to place and space. The thin planning simplifications devised to serve them not only effaced a previous social order that often functioned tolerably well; they also replaced it with an engineered social order that typically militated against the creation of informal, street-level order.

The political conditions of Jacobs' street-level trust

If we grant the importance of uninstitutionalized, uncodified habits of street-level trust in the production of civic order, what can we say about the political conditions for this particular form of mutuality? The sort of civic order we are examining, it is worth emphasizing again, is supplied from below as a skein of behavior and habits. Similar results in terms of safety and order might be achieved institutionally by police forces, block-watch patrols, vigilantes, organized crime, or armed religious forces (e.g. the Taliban on the streets of Kabul, Afghanistan). The difference is that Jacobs' civic conduct is the collective, if radically informal, achievement of many community members who constitute, in their unsupervised severalty, much of "the force of public order."

Because she takes for granted the background conditions of American liberal democracy, Jacobs does not inquire directly into the background conditions for street-level trust. The fish don't talk about the water! It is not difficult, however, to tease out some of the major facilitating conditions. Perhaps the most obvious precondition is small property. Many of the unpaid "eyes-on-the-street" are those of vendors, butchers, bar keepers, and grocers who depend on neighborhood trade, who may live nearby, and who therefore have a vital stake in the health of the neighborhood. The smallness of the property in question is crucial: Jacobs is indirectly making a case for the public value of the petty bourgeoisie. Large, bureaucratized enterprises with scores of employees would not play the same role, she reasons.[3] In this respect, Jacobs' case for the petty bourgeoisie is not a generic appeal to untrammeled market forces. On the contrary, the public functions served as a by-product of small proprietorship are so important (when aggregated) that they may merit protection against large competitors in zoning ordinances.[4] Jacobs recognizes as well that, given the large turnover characterizing the petty bourgeoisie everywhere, a modicum of stability is a condition of street acquaintance and local citizenship. In this respect also, she would favor restraints on market forces.[5]

Permeating Jacobs' account of a "working" neighborhood is, in addition, the assumption of a robust sense of local citizenship and liberal democratic rights. The citizen who tries to break up a fight-in-the-making or help someone apparently in trouble must have the confidence that he or she is acting with public approval and will not be victimized for acting.[6] And, as noted earlier, the skein of nodding acquaintanceship and mutuality of practice in a successful neighborhood is, for Jacobs, the foundation of effective, formal political action of a collective sort.

Mutuality of the kind Jacobs examines is, I believe, dependent not only on an equality of abstract citizenship rights but also on some rough equality of status and wealth. At the very least, the existence of a substantial marginalized and/or exploited population would seem to militate against street-level civic order from below. First, the mutual recognition and reciprocities that typify such order require that individuals stand, vis-à-vis one another, on relatively equal terms, at least publicly. Great

---

[3] A small illustration: When I am lost and require local directions in a city, I always choose to enter a small shop that looks like a family enterprise. I have found that personnel in chain stores are typically less knowledgeable about the neighborhood as well as less solicitous of a stranger's query.

[4] One could, in this sense, make a principled case for serving the public weal by preventing large "mega-stores" from displacing a host of smaller shops, despite the fact that the prices of the latter might be higher. While Gaullist governments in France may have discriminated against les grandes surfaces in Paris and elsewhere because small shopkeepers often voted for them, there were other public-spirited reasons that would justify such a policy.

[5] The conditions for a Jacobs-style neighborhood may, in fact, by maximized when the degree of physical mobility is somewhat limited. That is, small shopkeepers typically have a lot of sunk investment in their enterprise that they are unlikely to recover completely if they move. Being relatively immobile, they may be more inclined to fight actively for their neighborhood's quality than a haute bourgeoisie and professional classes, which can more easily shift their residence and business to another locale if the neighborhood declines.

[6] So-called "Good Samaritan" laws attempt to institutionalize this when it can no longer be taken for granted.

and obvious disparities in sort and condition are likely to thwart the easy assumptions of mutuality that are required. A homeless person is unlikely to ask a man in a three-piece suit to watch his bag while he buys a cup of coffee; the businessman is unlikely, by the same token, to ask the homeless man to hold his place in line while he hangs up his camel's hair coat.[7]

Why, in a larger sense, should one expect those who benefit least – or who are actually disadvantaged – by a particular "public order" to contribute to its daily maintenance? The principle is captured at a nearly metaphysical level by an experience Alice Walker (1982) once reported. She was going door-to-door in an inner-city neighborhood soliciting signatures for a "nuclear disarmament" petition. To her dismay, few African-Americans were willing to sign. In talking with them, she realized many regarded the nuclear balance-of-terror as a state of affairs white elites had brought on themselves. Their sense of alienation was such that they looked on the prospect of nuclear destruction with a certain equanimity if not malevolent pleasure: "Serves them right . . ." In any case, they were unwilling to take even a small hand in trying to undo a situation that they had no role in creating and that, for them, was a social order filled with daily injustices and humiliations. We might infer somewhat speculatively that street-level trust, like responsible citizenship, requires a community in which most members believe, legitimately, that the preservation of civic order is in their interest.

Geographies of appropriation, control, and hierarchy

If we shift our gaze from its hitherto parochial, North American focus to much of the Third World, the situation is radically different. For all the failures and inhumanities that can be laid at the feet of high-modernist urban planning in liberal democracies, this record looks rather benign when read against the twentieth-century forms of authoritarian social engineering. There are two striking differences. The first is that the micro-level social order that planners have confronted may have been historically deep and effective in terms of public safety, but it typically was not democratic. The second difference, which goes a long way toward explaining many disastrous outcomes, is that planners had the full weight of state power behind them and ignored any informal local practices that contributed to local order.

Let me state in rather crude and stark terms, the case I believe I could convincingly make at greater length – book-length to be exact (see Scott

---

[7] Ethnic or linguistic disparities pose barriers as well, but ones that can be overcome more easily by familiarity.

1998[8]) – had I the latitude and your forbearance. That case is that much of the social planning embedded in the great development schemes of the erstwhile "Second" and "Third Worlds" (both colonial and post-colonial) can be read as attempts to replace a local social order that was quasi-autonomous, resistant, and "illegible" with a planned social order that was, by contrast, designed to be dependent, compliant, hierarchical, and "legible" from the center. The purpose, often quite conscious, was to create a social landscape of residence and production that would facilitate control, appropriation, and manipulation from above. Such plans required the systematic dismantling of existing social networks that were, at the same time, hard to penetrate and a potential source of resistance to state plans. In other words, the creation of a social landscape legible to state authorities implied the destruction of informal, nonstate structures of trust and cooperation. It should be emphasized that such structures were not typically either egalitarian or democratic; they often embodied hierarchies of caste, gender, and lineage that were profoundly disabling of real citizenship. They were ordinarily replaced, however, by even more hierarchical and centralized state plans that had the further disadvantage of being thin and schematic as well as authoritarian. The most ambitious of such plans typically miscarried badly, sometimes tragically, but the immanent logic of their implementation was evident.

In sketching the bare bones of a more elaborate argument, I will concentrate on rural development schemes, although the reasoning could be as easily applied to the re-construction of Paris by Baron Haussmann under Louis Napoleon or the building of Brasilia.

Much of the history of classical imperial conquest and early colonial rule was an attempt to establish, by force if necessary, new patterns of residence more amenable to control and appropriation. States have nearly always been the enemy of people who moved around (autonomously), whether the offenders were gypsies, nomads, slash-and-burn cultivators, vagrants, or peddlers. The concentration of a dispersed and mobile population, often to the point of what we would recognize as "concentration camps," was at the center of early imperial policy. Any system of taxation, conscription, and political control requires a "legible" population. The Spanish *reducciones* in the New World or the friar estates and *ecomiendas* they established in the Philippines are a striking case in point. Fixing a population in space was at the very center of any system of unfree labor: A majority of Tsarist decrees dealt with the problem of runaway serfs; the Thai monarchy tattooed commoners with the mark of their

---

[8] The extended subtitle of the book is "How Certain Schemes to Improve the Human Condition Have Failed."

owner and paid bounty hunters to return them; and in the antebellum US South, returning "fugitive" slaves from the North was big business. A great many of the twentieth-century's experiments in massive rural social engineering, I believe, can be viewed through much the same lens. Collectivization in the Soviet Union and *ujamaa* villagization in Tanzania under Nyerere can serve as brief diagnostic examples. In each case, the ambition of the social engineers was far greater than earlier empires or absolutist kings. Two new circumstances underwrote their ambition. The first was an authoritarian state with a level of power and knowledge that was far greater than its predecessors (e.g. censuses, population registers, maps, currency, and a relatively modern military and security apparatus). The second was an ideology of "high-modernism." By high-modernism, I mean a belief in the capacity of technicians and engineers to design and implement comprehensive new forms of living and production that would be superior – that is, more "progressive," productive, healthy, and humane – to anything thus far devised. The comprehensiveness of this faith in a designer-society (one shared across much of the political spectrum in the early twentieth century), its disdain for existing practice and for the knowledge and values of citizens, and the temptation to impose a rationally designed future by force if necessary (by persuasion if possible) made it qualitatively different from the more limited ambitions of its predecessors.

Upon assuming power, the Bolsheviks faced a civil war, a resistant rural population subjected to arbitrary seizures of grain and men since 1914, and an "illegible countryside" in terms of population movements, landholdings, and production. Unable to appropriate the grain necessary for its industrialization plans and faced, in the 1920s, with growing resistance to its requisitions, the regime (Stalin) chose to return to its collectivization plans, this time with the full coercive power of the state.

For our purposes, what is significant is the replacement of an existing (often quite ancient) community that was illegible to the center with a collective farm the uniformity and simplicity of which was ideal for central control. The Bolsheviks decided not to base the new *kolkhoz* on earlier villages; they wanted to start from zero with a demobilized population shorn of much of its social capital – social capital that could be a potent source of resistance. The fields and residences (typically apartment buildings in place of individual houses) were created anew. The administrative structure of each *kolkhoz* was nearly identical: Where possible it produced a single specialized crop, its farming equipment was standardized, and, of course, its crops and production plans were derived from the Five-Year Plan. Rather like the Roman military camp, it allowed the central official to follow a standardized routine; the layout and operating procedures of each collective farm were similar. Above all, the new design of agriculture was ideal from the point of view of production control, appropriation of grain and livestock, and the social control of the population itself. The great achievement of the Soviet state in the agriculture sector was to take a social and economic terrain singularly unfavorable to appropriation and control and to create institutional forms and production units far better adapted to monitoring, appropriation, and central direction. All of these plans accorded not only with the Bolsheviks' aspiration to state control but also with a Leninist vision of electrification and of large-scale, specialized, industrial agriculture that would abolish the difference between the countryside and the city and transform the peasant (*narod* = dark) into an enlightened modern worker and socialist.

In practice, as we know, the Soviet agricultural sector had more of the facade of modern agriculture than the reality. Its highly touted yields of some grains were achieved at preposterous costs in terms of inputs of fertilizer, labor, and machinery. It nevertheless failed to provision the cities adequately and, instead of creating a new Soviet rural worker, provoked demoralization and illegal flight to the cities. That it survived at all was a tribute to the informal improvisations, many of them illegal, of the *kolkhozniki*: their illegal barter trade, their work on their private plots, their private sales of fruits, vegetables, poultry, etc. Ironically, it was the local knowledge and informal social networks that the Bolsheviks had set out to replace that, in their reconstituted and fragmentary form, proved to be the saving grace of the *kolkhoz*.

The rather more benign, but compulsory, resettlement of some five million Tanzanians in new villages, called *ujamaa* villages, bears a family resemblance to the Soviet case. President Julius Nyerere was convinced that a better future for rural Tanzanians depended on their resettlement into planned villages where state services such as piped water, health clinics, electricity, and education could be more easily provided to them and where they also could take advantage of scientific agriculture and mechanization, preferably by communal farming. Though influenced by his visits to model collective farms in Russia and China, Nyerere also believed that living in "proper" (his term) villages was an important step in bringing his people into the modern world.

When the campaign for villagization became compulsory in 1976, villages were laid out by surveyors on new terrain according to a standard grid pattern. The members of the population, their previous residences often having been razed if they protested, were transported to the new location. The immanent logic of the *ujamaa* campaign was that all Tanzanians would live in villages, that these villages would resemble one another, that they would grow specified cash crops on communal fields, and that they would be governed by officials of the party-state (TANU). Had the scheme been successful, Tanzania would have become a dispersed but centrally administered plantation; its population would be residing in standard villages, planting designated crops on communal fields according to state specifications. As in Russia, it would have replaced an illegible, small-holding (and nomadic, in the case of Tanzania) population planting mixed subsistence crops with a population whose residence, social organization, and production was far more amenable to central coordination and control.

In fact, *ujamaa* villages were generally failures as satisfactory human communities and, above all, as units of production. What the high-modernist planners of the Tanzanian state failed to realize was that the prior dispersion and movement of the population was a finely-tuned and long-practiced response to a very stingy semi-arid environment. Similarly, the complex forms of poly-cropping they practiced were generally quite productive and ecologically sound, despite having been judged, partly on aesthetic grounds, to be "backward" by agricultural planners. The mono-cropping mandated in its place typically failed. As the failures of the *ujamaa* became more manifest and the fiscal capacity of the regime to subsidize them weakened, communal production was abandoned and many of the villages broke up altogether. Where the new villages persisted it was due more to the improvisational skills and kinship networks of those resettled than to the logic of the planners' design.

Like the Soviet state, the Tanzanian state had replaced an independent, migratory, and illegible rural population with a regimented, fixed peasantry. In the process it damaged, if not destroyed, a preexisting human capital of working knowledge and social connective tissue. By making an abstraction of the peasant farmer and insisting on a vastly simplified, mono-cropping regimen, its own scheme proved a recipe for failure.

The mystery of social and natural capital

No designated social order can remotely match the complexity and intricacy of an actually functioning social order of some historical depth. However sophisticated their models, social planners are reduced to mapping the requirements of, and tradeoffs between, a comparatively small number of variables. Their problem is rather like the Newtonian problem of predicting the future position of heavenly bodies. Given accurate measurements of distance and mass, the formula for only two bodies is simple. The more bodies, the more complex the interaction effects (which increase geometrically), such that when nine or ten bodies are interacting, it is impossible to predict the state of the system far in advance. The point is that social planning on a large scale affecting the daily routines of many people – who themselves are an active part of the system being erected – must necessarily ignore variables and interaction effects that such exercises have no means of assessing. I suspect that informal social "capital" represents a good part of what is missing in the planners' calculations. The larger the planning exercise, the more tenuous the order "within the brackets" and the more likely that unforeseen "rogue" variables and interaction effects will upset the artificial order. It is perhaps for this reason that so many "pilot" projects and "model development schemes," carefully engineered to minimize such interference, miscarry when they are applied on a larger scale.

The more obvious analogy for the difference between a planned, schematic order and a more complex, decentralized order is the distinction between grammar, on the one hand, and speech practices on the other. This distinction is evident in the paper in this volume by Rom Harré (see this volume, chapter 8). Grammar by itself cannot generate speech; we do not learn to speak by learning the rules of grammar and then following those rules to produce speech. Grammar codifies the rules of thumb that can be abstracted from the regularities of acceptable speech practice; it is, in a real sense, parasitic on speech. Grammar is thin, while the spoken language is thick. The thickness of spoken language derives from its cumulative history of literature, allusion, invention, imported expressions, and idioms constantly being enlarged by practice. One can, of course, invent a language from scratch; Esperanto and many technical languages are just such creations. The result, however, is necessarily a very thin language, precise for some specified purposes but utterly lacking in the richness, texture, and range of expression of a historical language.[9]

Here, I think, it is helpful to see the parallels between high-modernist social engineering and intervention into complex natural systems with a view to simplifying them radically for utilitarian (e.g. revenue or profit) ends. One classic example is the effort to replace complex, mixed-species forests with mono-cropped industrial forests designed to maximize the output of lumber or wood pulp. The result was the single-species (Norway spruce in the nineteenth century), straight-row, same-age, production-forest created throughout Europe in the nineteenth century. For a time it worked brilliantly, making German forestry techniques the hegemonic world-model for commercial forestry. Soon it became apparent that this new "simplified" forest had courted disaster by ignoring all

[9] The purpose of inventing Esperanto was precisely to create a (European-based) language that belonged to no one national culture in the hopes that it would transcend the deadly nationalisms of the continent. It has remained, largely for that reason, no one's language except for a small and dwindling avant-garde of intellectuals and linguists.

other species of flora, insects, birds, and mammals. In time, the lack of diversity made the industrial forest so epidemic-prone that even the limited production goals for which it had been devised could no longer be obtained. The ironic "solution," itself fraught with difficulty, was the attempt at restoration forestry, of trying to reintroduce the absent birds, insects, and small mammals by creating artificial habitats for them without going so far as to abandon mono-cropping. The result, was an expensive "virtual-forest" that was still unsuccessful.

Other examples of the radical simplification of natural ecosystems redesigned for human management and production could be examined through the same lens. The creation of shrimp farms by radically modifying mangrove swamps was successful for a time as a commercial matter. After a few years, however, the shrimp grounds became so polluted by fertilizer and wastes that their production plummeted. The industry has prospered only by moving on to fresh, unspoiled marine environments and exploiting them until they are no longer profitable. Herman Daly (1996: 13ff.) has called these engineered production systems "cultivated natural capital" and has analyzed how they are less redundant, resilient, stable, and sustainable than "natural capital" by virtue of their lack of diversity. His premise is that the complexity of even rather simple ecosystems is so daunting as to preclude the specification of a working model describing how they operate. In replacing that complexity with a stripped-down, man-made order specifying only a few variables, vital elements of a sustainable order are inadvertently violated. The resulting system typically fails at some point or is kept going by ever more heroic interventions.

Authoritarian high-modernist schemes to improve the human condition have failed in an analogous way, I believe. They have, often purposely, violated complex human arrangements of sustainable social order that they have no means of understanding. In their place they have erected "virtual social environments" that are unsatisfactory for those who live in them and rarely achieve even the limited purposes for which they were originally designed. If the crude analogy I have drawn between natural systems and social systems makes any sense, it suggests that we adopt a radical modesty about our capacity to predict the consequences of any major social intervention into a tolerably functioning, complex social or natural order.

REFERENCES

Daly, Herman, 1996. Polities for sustainable development. Paper for the Program in Agrarian Studies, Yale University

Fukuyama, Francis, 1995. *Trust: The Social Virtues and the Creation of Prosperity*, New York: Free Press

Jacobs, Jane, 1961. *The Death and Life of Great American Cities*, New York: Vintage

Putnam, Robert, 1993. *Making Democracy Work: Civic Traditions in Modern Italy*, Princeton: Princeton University Press

Scott, James C., 1998. *Seeing Like a State: How Certain Schemes to Improve the Human Condition Have Failed*, New Haven: Yale University Press

Walker, Alice, 1982. Nuclear exorcism. *Mother Jones*, September/October

10   Altruistic trust

Jane Mansbridge

A modicum of trust greases the wheels of commerce, politics and social life. Large-scale economies and polities must generate this modicum of trust among strangers. Stranger-to-stranger transactions are most efficient if they can draw on reliable sources of situation-specific and more generalized trust, secured by social and institutional sanctions that punish breaches of that trust and by a moral basis for trustworthiness in individual consciences.

All this is well known. In this chapter I will argue that in addition to trustworthiness, systems of trust work better when members in the system adopt the moral stance of "altruistic trust." In altruistic trust, one trusts the other more than is warranted by the available evidence, as a gift, for the good of both the other and the community.

Predictive versus altruistic trust

Everyday English suggests at least two meanings for trust. The first is a matter of rational, probabilistic expectation, in regard to either some specific matter (situation-specific trust) or a large set of matters (more generalized trust). Trust in this sense involves prediction. I trust you in this matter up to the point at which my best estimate tells me you are trustworthy, and no more. In this definition, trust itself is not praiseworthy. It is an "unmoralized notion" (Hardin 1993: 512). Because trust is a probabilistic expectation, it is a belief. We do not in general consider beliefs moral or immoral. Therefore trust is neither moral nor immoral. In an interaction in which trust means only prediction, the moral virtue is trustworthiness, not trust.[1]

---

[1] In this volume (see also 1998), Hardin definitively separates trust from altruism, defining trust as belief and not act. He further defines "trust" as a subset of predictive beliefs, namely those that are grounded in the truster's expectations of the trustee's interests (trust as "encapsulated interest" Hardin 1990: 187, 1993: 505, and this volume). In his first treatment of trust, however, Hardin also included what I call "altruistic trust" in his

A second, less dominant, meaning also colors the contemporary use of the word, at least in the United States. In this usage, "trust" includes a stance toward one's probabilistic expectations in which one gives the other "the benefit of the doubt." That stance commits one to making, in either one instance or a large number of instances, a leap of faith beyond (perhaps only slightly beyond) that warranted by pure prediction. I call this second meaning "altruistic trust." Altruistic trust runs the spectrum from acting as if one trusted more than one's actual predictions warrant, through giving the other the benefit of the doubt in translating one's belief into action, all the way to coming to believe predictions about others that are more optimistic than realism would warrant. In this analysis I will call trust "altruistic" when it results from empathy or from a principle intended to benefit others or uphold an ideal that usually benefits others.[2]

understanding of trust when he described "normative commitments to be more decent than is rational" (1990: 187). Noting the Japanese precept of perfect hospitality, "We meet but once" (discussed in Shizuko Go's *Requiem*, a novel on social relationships in Japan in the last months of World War II), Hardin pointed out that meeting only once precludes understanding hospitality to mean encapsulating one's "interest in reciprocity over the long run. It is purely a gift or an expression of my hospitable character" (191). He concluded then that this kind of behavior "may simply be normative outright," and could apply to trust as well as to hospitality (192). Referring to Elster's (1976: 146) categorization of trust with altruism, he suggested that "In many of our relationships, trust is perhaps a bit like altruism. . . . My trust is virtually a gift" (196).

[2] In this chapter I stipulatively use the words "altruistic" and "altruism" to refer both to empathetic behavior and to principled behavior intended either to benefit another or to uphold a prosocial ideal that the actor believes is right. Many writers reasonably want to reserve the term "altruism" for *empathetic* behavior intended to benefit another (Batson 1991). This definition has the two great advantages of comporting well with the ordinary language connotations of the word and with the intentions of Comte ([1851] 1875), who coined the term. If we reserve the term for this usage, we then need a broader term, such as "prosocial nonegoism" or "unselfishness" to describe not only empathetic but also principled behavior that either is intended to benefit another or (in the case of prosocial principles) has long run consequences that benefit others. I have argued elsewhere (Mansbridge 1990, 1995) that both empathetic and principled behavior (behavior driven by nonegoist prosocial commitments) are worthy of moral approbation. Debates on which of the two is most worthy, or most deserves the implicitly approving label "altruistic" or "nonegoist" (e.g. Dawes et al. 1990, Sen [1978] 1990), do not further the analytic enterprise of contrasting both sets of behaviors with behavior that is narrowly self-interested. Readers should feel free to substitute mentally for "altruism" in this essay the broader word "unselfishness" (which I have rejected because of its nonactive connotation) or the phrase "prosocial nonegoism" (which I have rejected because of its rarity in ordinary language).

The concept of intention is critical for this definition of altruistic behavior. That intention however, need not require a fully conscious thought process (Monroe 1995). As will become clearer later, developing rules of thumb, or a character that habitually acts in a certain way, falls within this definition of "intention."

It is, of course, always possible to define every form of action, including empathetic and principled action, as being in one's "interest" or even "self-interest." For problems with this tautological terminology, see Mansbridge (1990) and Monroe (1995).

This secondary meaning, captured in some forms of ordinary usage, gives trust a tinge of moral coloring, making it worthy of approval. This positive moral evaluation is justified only when an individual's trust involves altruism, acting for the benefit of another. Altruistic trust is also morally praiseworthy only so long as the ends to which it is directed are not morally condemnable. Like all forms of altruism, altruistic trust can be used to bad ends. But when the ends are good or morally neutral, altruism deserves praise.

There are at least three altruistic, and morally praiseworthy, reasons for trusting more than is warranted by the objective probabilities. First, trusting expresses respect for the other, treating the other as one would oneself wish to be treated. Second, trusting expresses positive concern for the relationship between self and other. One may be willing to sacrifice oneself – or take an unwarranted risk of sacrifice – for the possibility of turning a potentially hostile interaction into a potentially cooperative one, either because regardless of material payoffs one considers cooperative relations better than competitive ones, or because one has made the other's good one's own. Third and least important (because parasitic on the first two), trusting may serve as a model to others, making them more likely to trust in similar circumstances.

To clarify the distinction between predictive trust and altruistic trust, it helps to describe both forms of trust in the context of an iterated prisoners' dilemma game. In this game, the potential payoffs are arranged so that no matter what the other player does, each player will gain most by "defecting" (making a move that produces major gains for oneself at the cost of losses to the other) rather than cooperating (adopting a move that produces smaller gains for oneself but also some gains for the other). The payoffs are also arranged so that if both players defect, as it is individually rational for them to do, they will both lose. When the game is played many times in succession by the same players, both players will gain most if they can sustain a run of mutual cooperation (piling up a series of small gains).

In such an iterated game, a high payoff strategy is "generous Tit for Tat," which begins with a cooperative move and subsequently duplicates the move of the other player. After a run of mutual defection, generous Tit for Tat throws in a cooperative move to see if this move will trigger cooperation on the part of the other player. By contrast, in pure Tit for Tat (which, after beginning with cooperation, always duplicates the other player's last move), a defecting move by either player ends the run of cooperation. In either generous or pure Tit for Tat, when the players know that the game has a finite end, the incentives are for any cooperative run to "unravel," as each player, wanting to gain the rewards of defecting at the end, tries to preempt the final defection of the other.

In a single-play situation it pays each player to defect rather than cooperate. An iterated play starting with a cooperative move is rational so long as there is a sufficient probability that the other player will also respond cooperatively (for example, if the other player is also using the strategy of Tit for Tat). At three points – at the beginning of the game, at the moment during the game when a "generous" cooperative move may end a run of mutual defection, and when the game has a finite end – the strategic task for each player is to determine how likely the other is to react cooperatively. If at any of these points one player is certain to defect, it will pay the other to defect first.

When trust means no more than predictive trust, my risky cooperative behavior ("trust") in such a game – by cooperating on the first move with the hope that this will start a run of mutual cooperation, by throwing in a generous cooperative move in the midst of a run of defection, or by continuing to cooperate toward the end of the game, when it looks as if the game might unravel – is based solely on my estimate of my partner's likely behavior. That estimate in turn is based on my estimates of my partner's material incentives, social incentives, and internal (characterological) incentives both before and after experiencing my trusting behavior.

The results of trusting too much in this situation are vivid. The word "sucker" is traditionally used to describe this position. Margolis's (1984) word "exploited" also captures the angry self-blame and potential derision that flow from being duped. Absent a moral norm to the contrary, however, the results of trusting too little (and defecting preemptively before it is necessary) are indistinguishable from cleverness. If self-interest is the logic of the game, defecting is rational.

Introducing moral behavior into this game makes a great difference in the outcome. The first and most important moral behavior is trustworthiness (Hardin 1996). If my partner can promise me that she will cooperate, and if she is completely trustworthy for internal moral reasons, I can make an accurate prediction that she is very likely to cooperate. (It is not certain that she will cooperate, because events beyond her control may make her cooperation impossible.) When she is less than completely trustworthy, my predictive trust in her will vary with the indicators I receive about the likelihood that she will cooperate.

With altruistic trust, a second form of moral behavior enters the picture. If I practice altruistic trust, my risky cooperative behavior will be based not only on my probability estimate of my partner's behavior but also on altruistic considerations that may influence my behavior, my estimate of my partner's likely behavior, or some combination of the two. We may think of this altruistic trust as a gift. An individual willing, for altruistic reasons, to risk the relatively high penalty attached to cooperating when the other defects (the "sucker's payoff") is able to begin more interactions with cooperation. Doing so will produce more cooperative interchanges and more interchanges ending in the other's defection than if one trusted only as much as the evidence warranted.

To qualify as altruistic trust my move must pass two tests. First, it must require a degree of trust (as some combination of belief and action) exceeding that justified by the available evidence. Second, it must be motivated by a conscious or unconscious intent to benefit the other (e.g. by respecting him or her) or by an intent to uphold a principle that in the long run usually benefits others (e.g. "Do as you would be done by"). It is the intent that is moral.[3]

Imagine walking down the street on a dark night alone. A young Black man turns the corner and, begins to catch up with you. A calculus of probabilities floods your mind, including Jesse Jackson's point that he would worry more with a Black young man behind him than with a young White,[4] and the recent statistics on rape in your neighborhood released by your university, which include many more rapes by Black men than White. On the basis of the best evidence you have, you reach the predictive conclusion that even though the probability of anything bad happening is low, the magnitude of the potential bad is great enough to warrant crossing the street. You want very much to cross the street, but you restrain yourself, thinking of the times you have heard Black men friends speak of their humiliation in situations like this, when women acted as if they were rapists simply on the grounds of their sex and race. In this instance, you are practicing altruistic trust, deriving from the intention to do good to another. Part of your action may derive from empathy, as you give the other the gift of respecting the persona he presents to the world. Another part may derive from duty, as you try to act justly, not judging an individual on the basis of statistical correlations.[5]

In a more everyday example of altruistic trust in social interaction, one person may reveal to another a vulnerable area of herself as a way of creating intimacy. That gesture opens her to potential costs, such as ridicule or the use against her of the information she has proffered. By being willing to risk those costs, the person revealing vulnerability makes an implicit statement of trust in the other. She pays a moral compliment

---

[3] I therefore disagree with Karen Jones's conclusion (1996: 15) that one of the "fairly obvious facts" about trust is that "trust cannot be willed." Altruistically trusting acts can be willed, an altruistically trusting disposition can be cultivated (as Jones concedes, 1996: 22), and intent, as I argue here, can even influence belief.

[4] Quoted in Richard Cohen, "Common Ground on Crime," *Washington Post* December 21, 1993, A23.

[5] Sabini and Silver (1982: 37) point out that "action may involve reproach." One may altruistically avoid a nontrusting action based on an appropriate statistical prediction in order not to inflict reproach on another person.

by saying, in effect, "I consider you trustworthy." Pleased at being so valued, the other may respond in kind. But not always. The strategy is indeed risky. Practiced in circumstances in which the payoff to the actor, discounted by the risk, is less than the probability of higher costs, this strategy involves either stupidity, over-optimism, or altruism, that is, potentially costly behavior intended to benefit others.

In these and other comparable circumstances, there are valid independent grounds for considering greater trust than is warranted by the predictive evidence a moral good. Such altruistic trust expresses respect for others, catalyses cooperation, and creates even more altruistic trust through modelling the behavior to others. Altruistic trust thus differs from Hardin's "optimistic trust" (1993: 508ff., 513ff., 519ff.; also Jones 1996) in its cause. An optimistic person, in Hardin's depiction, overestimates the probabilities of trustworthiness for various nonmoral reasons. Such optimistic overestimates, like altruistic overestimates, precipitate greater cooperation in social dilemmas.[6]

What Hardin calls "optimistic trust" Toshio and Midori Yamagishi (1994) call "cognitive bias." In 1988, Toshio Yamagishi demonstrated that, contrary to what many would expect, American students at the University of Washington in Seattle were more likely than Japanese students at Tokyo University to cooperate in one-shot anonymous prisoners' dilemma-like experiments.[7] The Yamagishis believe that this somewhat

[6] Hardin (1993) points out that learning from one's mistakes should make the overly optimistic more accurately less optimistic over time. This is undoubtedly the case. It is also true, however, that human beings with "normal" mental health are, at least in the United States in the 1980s and 1990s, slightly overoptimistic. They overpredict, for example, how many people will like them in a given group. Depressed people predict more accurately (Seligman 1990). Consciously or unconsciously recognizing that slightly overoptimistic people are happier, the overoptimistic may not want to exchange greater realism for greater unhappiness and so may be less likely than predicted to become more accurately less optimistic over time.

[7] In other studies reported by Yamagishi and Yamagishi (1994), representative samples of the US population were almost twice as likely as representative samples of the Japanese population to say, "you can put your trust in most people" (e.g. 47 and 26 percent respectively). These relationships may have changed recently. The 1995–97 World Values survey (reported in Inglehart, this volume) shows levels of interpersonal trust in Japan surpassing those in the United States by more than 5 percentage points (Inglehart, this volume, chapter 4, Figure 4.3) or at least falling not less than 10 percentage points behind (Inglehart, this volume, chapter 4, Figure 4.1). Yamagishi and Yamagishi also report that items on what they call a "General Trust" scale (composed of questions such as "Most people are basically honest," most of which begin "Most people") factor differently from items on what they call a "Caution Scale" (composed of questions such as "People are always interested only in their own welfare"). Congruently with Kelley and Stahelski's finding that "cooperators believe others are heterogeneous as to their cooperativeness versus competitiveness, whereas competitors will believe other persons are uniformly competitive" (1970: 66), the Yamagishis show that most low trusters are also cautious, but some high trusters are cautious and some are not (1994: 150). In the Yamagishi's study, Americans scored significantly higher than Japanese on the General Trust scale, but about the same on the Caution Scale.

generalized trust (extended to other unknown students who meet in a university setting with no reputational markers beyond their clothes and demeanor) is highly functional for what I call a stranger-to-stranger society. They attribute the greater trust in the United States not to the greater trustworthiness of the strangers with whom individuals in the United States interact, but rather to a "cognitive bias," that is, to "*a bias in the processing of imperfect information* about the partner's intentions. [A person with this bias] overestimates the benignity of the partner's intentions beyond the level warranted by the prudent assessment of the available information" (1994: 136, emphasis in original). Because we have few studies of trustworthiness, it is not yet possible to test how much of the difference between the US and Japan derives from cognitive bias, how much from accurate predictions of the behavior of others in one's society, and how much from decisions to perform an altruistic act. To ascertain how much was cognitive bias, one would need independent measures of the trustworthiness of others in the society, the trusters' predictive abilities, and the trusters' moral codes.

Let us assume, however, that the Yamagishis are right, and that at least some part of the American students' greater cooperative behavior results from a cognitive error in their beliefs about others. It is easy to see how such an error might arise without any altruistic intent. One handy rule of thumb, appropriate for a "cognitive miser" who wants to understand the world reasonably well without engaging in costly information-seeking, is to assume until demonstrated otherwise that others are like oneself. In the absence of other information, many quite reasonably adopt this rule of thumb. Orbell and Dawes (1991, 1993) have shown, for instance, that those who themselves plan to cooperate in a prisoners' dilemma-like situation are likely to overestimate the number of other cooperators among those with whom they interact. For the same reason, trustworthy people would be likely to overestimate the number of trustworthy others. This is a cognitive mistake.

In everyday speech we give the label "trust" to many kinds of overly optimistic and altruistically motivated beliefs and acts. Hardin (1998 and this volume) usefully suggests confining the meaning of "trust" for analytic purposes to matters of belief rather than action. If we define trust as belief and not action, acts in which one cooperates more frequently than one's best assessment of the other's future behavior warrants are best thought of, in Hardin's words, as "acts beyond trust." Such acts help create the fabric of mutually trusting relations in a particular context.

Both ordinary language and several thoughtful philosophers and social scientists (see Hardin 1998) often slip from belief to act in the use of the word "trust." That slippage is not due solely to stupidity or inattention.

One reason for the slippage is that we often want a single word that means "the entire fabric of mutually trusting relations". That fabric includes the trustworthiness of actors in the particular context, the beliefs those actors hold about one another's trustworthiness, and the willingness of those actors to "act beyond trust" in a set of matters or more generally. This is one current usage of the word "trust."

A second reason for the slippage between belief and act in ordinary language and previous philosophical analysis is that the dichotomy between belief and act is not absolute. Although acts are usually driven by beliefs, beliefs are also driven by the intention to act in particular ways. Individuals allow their intended acts to make their calculations of probability less realistic.

Altruistic trust, as I understand it, thus comprises a spectrum that includes various combinations of belief and action. One end of this spectrum is anchored by an "act beyond trust." In an act beyond trust, one acts as if one believed in the other's benign intent, although one's actual belief is not strong enough to lead one to act in this manner without altruistic intent toward the other. In the pure case of act beyond trust, belief and act are clearly separate in the mind of the actor, although the act is designed to mimic a belief that is in fact not present.

Farther along the spectrum, intention to act begins to affect belief. Assume, as is often the case, that the other's future act is dichotomous. The friend will or will not use your volunteered information to hurt you; the stranger's story about needing $20 to "get to the airport" is or is not a con. Assume that your own action is also dichotomous. You will or will not tell your friend about your illegal abortion; you will or will not give the stranger $20. The belief structure that intervenes between these two dichotomies, however, is probabilistic, not dichotomous. In translating a probability, often with a high degree of uncertainty, into a (dichotomous) choice, one may stress in one's mind the factors that favor the other. One gives the other "the benefit of the doubt" in the already conceptually difficult translation from belief to action.

Many people in everyday situations make their decision on how to act in these instances in an instant, without thinking through the calculations. Such people develop a "standing decision," a "stance" toward these probabilities that becomes part of their self-image and identity. Just as some cultivate an altruistic stance toward many parts of collective life, which leads them, say, occasionally to pick up litter or let a car in ahead of them in traffic "automatically," without "thinking," so too some cultivate an altruistic stance toward others' self-presentations.

If such a standing decision, stance, or "automatic" action has its origins in the intent to help others, that standing decision deserves moral praise. On a purely will-based account, such as the one offered by Immanuel Kant, an act or intent to act has moral worth only if it derives from an act of will. You might act or intend to act in a trusting way toward me beyond the point that available evidence warranted in order, through a conscious act of will, to further my good or (unselfishly) to further the good of our relationship. The critical feature is that of will. On a more character-based account, you could over time have created a character for yourself that was trusting, in order to help others and create good relationships around you. You would then, without a conscious exercise of will, often act beyond trust and translate beliefs into action in a way that gave others the benefit of the doubt. As a result, you would consistently engage in actions that mimicked cognitive mistakes. If derived originally from altruistic intent, those acts would deserve moral praise.[8]

We can now distinguish between the optimistic truster who makes a cognitive mistake, whom we may want as a friend but do not have grounds for praising morally, and the altruistic truster whose acts mimic the optimistic truster's cognitive mistake.

Most troubling analytically is the point farther down the spectrum at which one may even block contrary evidence from one's consciousness, encouraging in oneself beliefs about others that are unrealistically optimistic. We know that people acting on moral grounds can sometimes convince themselves incorrectly that they are at the same time acting prudentially. In a recent study, Neil Pinney and John Scholz (1992) discovered that US taxpayers who were committed for independent moral reasons to not cheating on their income tax systematically overestimated the likelihood of their being caught if they evaded their taxes. At least in the United States many people prefer to explain their own behavior, to themselves and others, as self-interested rather than altruistic, even when their motives actually derive from the intent to help others (Miller, Downs and Prentice 1998).

Those who are committed for moral reasons to various forms of altruistic trust may similarly refuse to face the true probabilities of being deceived. If they convince themselves inaccurately that their trust is well

---

[8] Character-based accounts are usually associated with Hume, will-based accounts with Kant. See Baier (1986) and discussion in Mansbridge (1993: 357–9). Character-based accounts of morality, however, run into the problem that many character traits seem to have a partial genetic base. Altruism, for example, seems to be about 50 percent heritable. That is, half the variation among individuals (at least in Canada and Sweden) seems due to genes, half to other factors (Rushton 1986). To the degree that altruism is inherited, that provenance undermines its candidacy for moral praise. As Bernard Williams puts it, there is a "feeling of ultimate and outrageous absurdity in the idea that the achievement of the highest kind of moral worth should depend on natural capacities, unequally and fortuitously distributed as they are" (1962: 116).

placed, we could say no more than that by this act they transform themselves into over-optimistic trusters, who usually deserve no moral credit.
To deprive them of moral credit would, however, be too quick a move.
For unlike the usual optimistic truster, whose overestimation of others'
trustworthiness derives, say, from growing up with loving parents or in a
small Midwestern town, the altruistic truster's overestimation derives in
the end from the altruistic intention. Because of its derivation, this "belief
beyond realism" may be morally praiseworthy even though it is indistinguishable on its face from the cognitive mistake of the optimistic truster.

In Holyoke, Massachusetts, every year for more than 40 years the Irish
community has chosen a Grand Colleen to preside over the town's annual
St. Patrick's Day Parade. The young women competing for the honor
are asked, among other things, about "the quality that equipped them to
be good Colleens." On a recent occasion, the first positive quality suggested was "their trust" (Blais 1995). Some positive valuation, probably
a moral valuation, made trust appear first in a list of desirable attributes
in this contest.

It does not require a great stretch of the imagination to picture a society that encourage some subset of actors to trust unrealistically in the
benignity of others. Even the more realistic subset would usually approve
of these actors and their character. The holders of those beliefs themselves might also feel they deserved approbation for holding beliefs that
they sensed posed some danger to their personal security. These more
trusting members of the society would be particularly useful in a societal
division of labor. They would also serve well as models to young children, who as they grew up would be encouraged either to develop more
realistic beliefs or to remain in the less realistic subgroup. Other members of the society would have a duty to protect those whom they had
encouraged to develop and maintain these unrealistic beliefs, and this
protection would be easiest if the more trusting subgroup were segregated in a relatively protected environment.

Would such protected creatures – let us call them "Colleens" – be
worthy of genuine moral approbation? As innocents, they would be
worthy of love and protection. They would deserve moral approbation
only to the degree that as they grew up they recognized realistically the
dangers of a stance that habitually overestimated others' benignity, and,
with this knowledge and altruistic intent, claimed this character as their
own. They might consciously take the risk of developing this character
because they knew from experience that such a character "brought out
the best" in many others (although it might also bring out the worst
in those with a strong predatory streak). Stupidity is not praiseworthy
(indeed, one ought to warn one's children against it). Optimism is morally

neutral (although most people like to be around optimistic others). But, when it is to some degree deliberately chosen, building and maintaining a character that habitually acts with overly-trusting belief deserves some moral praise.[9]

I do not want to derive an argument for the morality of altruistically based unrealistic belief simply from existing social praise for such belief. A positive moral valuation of "trust" as trusting belief, in, say, the selection of Colleens, might derive both from the advantage to onself of others being trusting or from one or two simple mistakes.

The first possible mistake results from a kind of "magical thinking" by which we sometimes make the unconscious assumption that our acting in a certain way will make others act that way (Quattrone and Tversky 1976). Magical thinking differs from the effects of modelling a behavior, in which one's acting in a certain way actually makes others more likely to act that way. If I want others to be trusting, and I conclude through magical thinking (not through correctly understanding the effects of modelling) that therefore I ought to be more trusting, this is a mistake.

The second, probably more common, mistake is to think that an individual's trustingness is causally, as opposed to only associationally, related to that individual's trustworthiness. If trustworthiness is morally valued (as it is everywhere), and if the kinds of people who are trustworthy are also more likely to be trusting (as is also the case), one might erroneously conclude that being trusting causes one to become trustworthy. Being trusting would then seem to have moral value as a cause of another moral good. Trusting behavior and trustworthiness are correlated in most (perhaps all) existing societies (see Yamagishi and Yamagishi 1994: 140 for the existing studies). The main reason for this correlation is undoubtedly that widespread trustworthiness creates widespread trust. If one grows up in an environment where most people are taught to be trustworthy, one is then likely both to be taught to be trustworthy oneself and to interact with a large number of trustworthy others, thereby acquiring a justified tendency to trust others. Here the causal arrow runs from trustworthiness to trust, not the other way round. An additional reason for the correlation might be that the same parents who teach one to be trustworthy

---

[9] When one subgroup is historically dominant and wields more political, social and economic power than the other (as in the case of gender and therefore of Colleens), moral praise for subordinate traits can become a significant instrument of domination. For this reason, in current discussions of "women's voice," Catharine MacKinnon rightly concludes, "Take your foot off our necks, then we will hear in what tongue women speak" (1987: 45). The fact that a pattern of behavior has traditionally been typical of subordinates does not, however, disqualify it for general adoption. Although the powerful may prefer it if only subordinates act in a way that furthers the general good, universal adoption of such actions and stances may further that good to an even greater extent.

may also teach one to practice altruistic trust. Here the causal arrow runs from an external cause to two separate outcomes – being trusting and being trustworthy. In neither of these cases does being trusting cause trustworthiness. Deriving the moral worth of having trusting beliefs from the assumption that such beliefs cause the moral value of trustworthiness is simply a mistake.

In short, the fact that many people value trusting beliefs in others does not necessarily mean that such beliefs deserve moral approbation. We may value and praise trustingness in others simply because we are likely to benefit from it. Or the value we place on trusting beliefs may derive from incorrectly assuming that trusting beliefs cause trustworthiness. My argument that acts beyond trust and acts driven by one or more forms of intentionally over-trusting belief are morally praiseworthy when they derive from the intent to help others cannot depend on the fact that such people often give moral praise to those who perform such acts and even to those who hold such unrealistic beliefs.

The consequential benefits of morally praiseworthy trust

As Robert Frank (1988, 1990) has pointed out, trustworthy individuals can succeed in competition with the untrustworthy when the interaction is voluntary and when the trustworthy have some reasonably accurate way of identifying other trustworthy individuals with whom to cooperate. In most societies, trustworthiness is guaranteed by sanctions, first social and then governmental. Without easily available sanctions, the search for trustworthy partners requires reputational or other markers by which those who are trustworthy for internal reasons can identify one another.

To parse out the logic of the mutual search by the trustworthy, let us imagine five societies in increasing order of "modernization." The first has no established government for remedying what Locke ([1679–89] 1963) called the "inconveniences" of having one's property stolen by others. Nor are violations of contract easily punishable by kin or social sanction. In this society, exchange relations must be of a barter or bazaar form, in which payment and delivery of product take place at once, on the spot.

A second society has no established government, but an extensive system of kin networks in which kin sanctions can be applied if a contractor reneges on a promise. These kin networks allow exchange relationships at a distance. To carry on overseas trade, shippers rely on the sanctions and personal commitments involved in family networks to make it more likely that the family member entrusted with the surplus value of the work of hundreds of others does not take the ship to a faraway port, debark, and live happily ever after on the proceeds. In a situation with no established government, where agents are made accountable to their principals only by kin sanctions, the most extensive shipping and long-distance banking relations will be carried on by close knit families, such as the Rothschilds, or extended kinship networks, such as the Maghribi in the twelfth century Near East (Greif 1993, 1994).

A third society, such as Genoa in the twelfth century, also cannot depend on established government for long-distance enforcement, but invents a system in which good long-distance traders are overpaid relative to what they could get in other work. Overpayment gives them a long-run incentive to act honestly as agents to their principals, returning with all the goods received in trade for the goods with which they were entrusted, in order to receive another order. A society with this system is likely to win in competition with the purely kin-based society, because it will have far greater flexibility in recruiting trading talent. It is also likely to develop formal organizations (such as the permanent partnership with unlimited and joint liability), proto-governmental legal institutions (such as courts) and legal instruments (such as the bill of lading) appropriate to monitoring relations with strangers (Greif 1993, 1994). This society, however, will pay a premium in the overpayment of trustworthy traders.

A fourth society has an established government supplemented by intensive and dense reputational networks. The London merchant banker who can make a £200,000 loan over the telephone on no more substantial basis than the ship owner's intention to repay (Wechsburg 1966, also Coleman 1990: 92; see Hardin 1993: 524 for the governmental context) can act effectively with few transaction costs in this context, as can networks of manufacturers and suppliers in Japan. Governments are expensive, however, and dense reputational networks can be inflexible.

A fifth society has established government and weak reputational networks supplemented by a moral code that includes two commands: 1) act in a trustworthy manner to strangers; 2) begin interactions with strangers with a trusting act. If these two moral commands were sufficiently internalized, the society would be able to conduct many transactions without a costly apparatus of monitoring and sanctions. This society would do best of all in competition with the others, so long as the two internalized moral commands were combined with sufficient legitimate external coercion to control the few defectors who attempted to exploit those who acted morally.

What kind of moral code could produce this last society? Suppose that human beings are in some way hardwired, innately cathected, to the "group." We attach ourselves to sports teams for fun, we give up our lives for the tribe or nation, and we distribute money unequally to favor our group even when this distribution reduces overall output and we have only been made members of this "group" a few minutes ago by a coin toss (see the "minimal group experiments" of Tajfel 1982, Brewer and Kramer 1986). Such group cathection can produce stranger-trust within a group, say the "chosen people," even if the members of that group have never met one another and do not know one another by reputation. Traditionally, such groups are kin or tribally based. But if a religion specifies that the chosen people, the group with which one is supposed to cathect, is potentially all humanity so long as the individuals have signed on to a particular moral code, the potential catchement area is huge.

To be most effective, such a code would focus not on action but on character. It would have to inculcate a belief that it was better to create and retain a good character, to be a good person, than to have material possessions (or, in extremis, to live at all). Such a code might advocate "turning the other cheek" (e.g. cooperating a second time in Tit for Tat), even when the material outcomes to such behavior were strongly negative.[10] The formal code might urge an extreme form of this conduct, but street-level morality would surely moderate the norm of good conduct to whatever could be sustained against extinction in a given social environment.

Street-level morality further ensures that the higher the costs of moral action, the less it will be practiced. In this respect morality is like any other good. Holding constant commitment to the same moral code, one would therefore expect more trustworthy and trusting behavior in environments such as the American Midwest in the wake of the Homestead Act, where relative opportunity and equality gave almost everyone a reasonable subsistence, than in fourteenth-century Europe, where subsistence was often hard to come by. The high proportion of both trustworthy and trusting individuals in the nineteenth-century Midwest probably reflects at least three conditions: an ethos of hospitality to strangers (mandated not only on the Midwest farming plains but also in traditional Icelandic, Homeric and Japanese societies); a Judeo-Christian norm that urged treating all humanity like oneself regardless of consequences; and widespread material non-scarcity.

If Christianity preached a message of trust among believers, based on the expectation that Christians would forgo material reward to maintain the Judeo-Christian morality of "love thy neighbor as thyself" and the

---

[10] See Baier, drawing on Luhmann 1979: "If a trust relationship is to continue, some tact and willingness to forgive on the part of the truster and some willingness on the part of the trusted both to be forgiven and to forgive unfair criticisms, seem essential" (1986: 238).

more specifically Christian morality of "turn the other cheek," and if that message could nevertheless not take hold effectively until security in material well being made a high level of trustworthiness sustainable, then the combination of Judeo-Christian morality and reasonable material security might, along with other factors, help produce a culture of relatively high stranger-to-stranger trust.[11] As several studies reveal, by the 1990s, about 35 percent of American college students (increasing to 85 percent or 100 percent after discussion and mutual promises) were willing to cooperate with relative strangers in a one-shot, anonymous prisoners' dilemma-like situation, against their narrow self-interest (Mansbridge 1990). Fukuyama (1995) describes both Japan and the United States as "high trust" societies, but as the Yamagishis point out, the American trust is more likely to apply with strangers. Similar processes might also have helped generate the even higher rates of interpersonal trust that all the Scandinavian countries report on surveys. Experiments with prisoners' dilemmas in these countries would test the degree to which this is stranger-to-stranger trust.

In order to avoid the penetration of its system by defectors, a society that brought up its young to be both trustworthy and trusting to strangers would need to supplement this socialization with social and governmental sanctions that were widely perceived as fair (Zucker 1986). It would probably also require social support for moral outrage and revenge against transgressors. Although such outrage is not easily reconciled with the moral code of Christianity, it seems to exist nevertheless in most and possibly all societies, Christian or otherwise. Individuals often seem willing to suffer considerable material deprivation to revenge an injustice (Frank 1988, 1990), although the conditions in which this is the case

[11] The combination of causes that I have suggested is highly speculative, particularly regarding the role of Christianity. Widespread democracy, even when limited to White males, may also have had a major impact not only by generating relatively legitimate formal sanctions but also by helping produce relatively widespread feelings of community and shared fate. Whatever the causes, nineteenth-century European travellers such as Martineau, Butler, Bryce, and Trollope reported high levels of law-abiding behavior, even in US cities, far higher than in European contexts with equally high rates of stranger-to-stranger interaction (see Mansbridge 1997). High levels of trust would presumably follow from, and possibly interact positively with, such high levels of trustworthiness. In addition, as Uslaner (this volume) argues, trust is strongly related to optimism, and if for most of US history the culture has been optimistic, that optimism alone could account for a major part of the culture's high degree of stranger-to-stranger trust. Finally, some anthropologists suggest that markets are associated with positive-sum thinking based on the creation of value through exchange (making it possible to see others as potential creators of value), whereas settled agriculture and the relative absence of trade is associated with zero-sum thinking, based on fixed amounts of land (in which one individual's gain can derive only from another's loss). If this is so, the combination of open frontiers and markets might make it easier to see others as potential cooperators rather than inevitable competitors (Mansbridge 1997).

have not yet been mapped out. Revenge is costly for the avenger, but impulses to revenge might not be extinguished in the course of cultural evolution because the positive side-effects of having others fear one's revenge reactions might be fairly large.

When the trustworthiness of a population is too low to sustain a general stance of initials trust, and when geographic and social mobility make reputational, kin and local sanctions less viable, the trustworthy members of a given population will benefit from finding ways of distinguishing themselves and other trustworthy individuals from the untrustworthy. These distinguishing marks would make it easier to seek one another out for voluntary cooperation. Such individuals might, for example, create a class of "gentlefolk" committed to a "sense of honor," who would be sanctioned, even by strangers within the class, if they did not live up to the appropriate standards of trustworthiness. If increasing geographical and social mobility made such sanctioning uneven and the system relatively permeable by defectors, the trustworthy would find it useful to train themselves to recognize subtle signs of trustworthiness in others and also to develop in themselves signs that could not easily be mimicked. One part of the fascination of the novels of Jane Austen and Trollope, I believe, is that they function in part as "how-to" manuals for deciphering trustworthiness in an increasingly mobile society in which local reputation and the more general markers of class no longer suffice to predict trustworthiness. The readers of these novels, then and now, may enjoy them not only for their subtle portrayal of character but also for their embedded lessons on the crucial matter of whom and when to trust when one's own moral code prescribes trustworthiness.

After ethnic prejudice began to come under attack in England, several plays and novels began to rehabilitate the figure of the "Jew." From Sir Walter Scott's *Ivanhoe* to other less-well-known works, these new plots stressed the altruistic acts of individual Jews toward Christians, often at great cost to the Jew (see Herzog 1998). The underlying message advocated trust, on the basis of character rather than ascription, beyond the boundaries of those who subscribed to the Christian code.

Stranger-to-stranger trust relations are relatively fragile. Those relations can be maintained easily in an environment in which most of the population is trustworthy, because trusting predictions will usually be accurate, creating opportunities for cooperation in which the accumulated benefits will typically exceed the costs of the few inaccurate predictions (in which one is taken for a sucker). The problem for a society where most people are trustworthy is to prevent an invasion by nontrustworthy individuals seeking to exploit the majority's potential gullibility. Fair and effective institutions of justice and social control, cultural practices of retaliation for betrayal and strategies for the mutual recognition of the trustworthy all undoubtedly play a role in this effort. Recognition based on marks of inner character, for which I speculate that in England Trollope, Austen, Scott and others may also have served as guides, may also have been served in the Great Plains of the United States in part by the scrutiny of self-presentation and even facial features. "Honest Abe" Lincoln's integrity was thought to have shone through on his face. Illustrations in books for teenage boys also portrayed the square-jawed, frank and open faces of young male heros, some actually named "Frank." Styles of speech emphasizing frankness and directness ("dugri" speech in Israel or Midwestern openness in the United States) might be hard to mimic accurately. A subtle societal system based on such deeply socialized features of self-presentation could be cracked by superb mimics, such as Robert Redford and Paul Newman in *"The Sting,"* but in practice most non-altruists find such mimicry hard to pull off. In their non-acting lives both Redford and Newman give far higher percentages of their incomes to good works than most actors do. It is just conceivable that the altruistic characters of Redford and Newman do show upon their faces, making it easier for them to play believable con-men but harder for con-men who are not Redford or Newman to fool the public.

If societal systems based on such subtle uses of language and demeanor do help create mutually protective signals among trustworthy strangers, such signals are likely also to exclude or disadvantage those who have not learned the cultural code or who cannot, for ascriptive reasons such as race or gender, accurately mimic that code. The challenge is to rearticulate the system of mutual trust to admit new players while retaining signalling mechanisms sufficiently reliable to protect the trustworthy and trusting against invasion.

Conclusion

I have made two linked arguments in this paper. The first argument is that trust comes in both predictive and altruistic forms. Altruistic trust, deriving from the intent to help another, is morally praiseworthy. We should therefore add to the "unmoralized notion" of predictive trust the "moralized notion" of altruistic trust.

The second argument, which is far more speculative, points out that a society in which large numbers of individuals have internalized both the morality of trustworthiness and the morality of altruistic trust will usually succeed in competition with other societies once stranger-to-stranger economic relations become potentially fruitful and some solution can be found to the problem of predatory actors invading the cooperative system.

A combination of social sanctioning institutions that are perceived as fair, moralistic retaliation, and the development of hard to mimic signals can help solve the invasion problem. The analysis suggests further, and highly speculatively, that the combination of Judeo-Christian morality and a standard of living that makes practicing some of that morality relatively feasible may have produced, in some parts of the world, systems of internal commitment – to both trustworthiness and altruistic trust – that make stranger-to-stranger relations based on a modicum of trust economically productive.

If this account has any plausibility, the phenomenon it describes depends heavily on trustworthiness being perceived as moral, applauded, and internalized. It may not depend so heavily on altruistic trust being perceived as moral, applauded, and internalized. But it does not seem a good idea (particularly from a utilitarian perspective) to "unmoralize" descriptions of either behavior or beliefs based on unrealistically optimistic assessments of others' goodwill, when such acts and beliefs contribute – even if not dispositively – to a larger climate of mutually trustworthy interaction.

REFERENCES

Batson, C. Daniel, 1991. *The Altruism Question: Towards a Social-Psychological Answer*. Hillsdale, NJ: Lawrence Earlbaum Associates
Baier, Annette, 1986. Trust and antitrust. *Ethics* 96, 231–260
    1987. Hume, the women's moral theorist? in Eva Kittay and Diana Meyers (eds.), *Women and Moral Theory*, Totowa, N.J.: Powman and Littlefield
    1994. *Moral Prejudices: Essays on Ethics*, Cambridge, Mass.: Harvard University Press
Blais, Madelaine, 1995. The queen of the green. *New York Times Magazine* (March 26), 58ff.
Brewer, Marilyn B. and Kramer, Roderick M., 1986. Choice behavior in social dilemmas: effects of social identity, group size, and decision framing. *Journal of Personality and Social Psychology* 50, 543–549
Buss, David M., 1994. *The Evolution of Desire*, New York: Basic Books
Coleman, James S., 1990. *Foundations of Social Theory*, Cambridge, Mass.: Harvard University Press
Comte, Isidore Auguste [1851] 1875. *System of Positive Polity*, vol. 1, London: Longmans, Green
Dawes, Robyn, Van de Kragt, Alphons J. C., and Orbell, John M., 1990. Cooperation for the benefit of us – not me, or my conscience, in Jane Mansbridge (ed.), *Beyond Self-Interest*, Chicago: University of Chicago Press
Dover, Kenneth, 1974. *Greek Popular Morality in the Time of Plato and Aristotle*, Berkeley: University of California Press
Elster, Jon, 1979. *Ulysses and the Sirens: Studies in Rationality and Irrationality*, Cambridge: Cambridge University Press

Frank, Robert, 1988. *Passions Within Reason: The Strategic Role of the Emotions*, New York: W.W. Norton

1990. A theory of moral sentiments, in Jane Mansbridge (ed.), *Beyond Self-Interest*, Chicago: University of Chicago Press

Fukuyama, Francis, 1995. *Trust: The Social Virtues and the Creation of Prosperity*, New York: Free Press

Greif, Avner, 1993. Contract enforceability and economic institutions in early trade: The Maghiribi traders' coalition. *American Economic Review* 83: 525–548

1994. Cultural beliefs and the organization of society. *Journal of Political Economy* 102: 912–950

Hardin, Russell, 1990. Trusting persons, trusting institutions, in Richard J. Zeckhauser (ed.), *Strategy and Choice*. Cambridge, Mass.: MIT Press

1993. On the street-level epistemology of trust. *Politics and Society* 21: 505–529

1996. Trustworthiness. *Ethics* 107: 26–42

1998. Conceptions and explanations of trust. Russell Sage Working Paper #129, New York: Russell Sage Foundation

Herzog, Don, 1997. *Poisoning the Minds of the Lower Orders*, Princeton University Press

Jones, Karen, 1996. Trust as an affective attitude. *Ethics* 107: 4–25

Locke, John, [1679–89] 1963. *Two Treatises of Government*, Peter Laslett (ed.), Cambridge: Cambridge Unversity Press

Luhmann, Niklas, 1979. Trust: A mechanism for the reduction of social complexity, in *Trust and Power: Two Works by Niklas Luhmann*, Chichester: John Wiley and Sons

MacKinnon, Catharine A., 1987. *Feminism Unmodified*, Cambridge, Mass.: Harvard University Press

Mansbridge, Jane, 1990. On the relation between altruism and self-interest, in Jane Mansbridge (ed.), *Beyond Self-Interest*, Chicago: University of Chicago Press

1993. Feminism and democratic community, in John W. Chapman and Ian Shapiro (eds.), *Democratic Community: NOMOS XXXV*, New York: New York University Press

1995. Rational choice gains by losing. *Political Psychology* 16: 137–155

1997. The moral uses of the "Prisoners' Dilemma." Presented at the conference, "Twenty-five years: Social Science and Social Change," at the Institute for Advanced Study, Princeton, N.J., May 8–11

Margolis, Howard, 1984. *Selfishness, Altruism and Rationality*, Chicago: University of Chicago Press

Miller, Dale, Downs, Julie, and Prentice, Deborah. 1998. Minimal conditions for the creation of the unit relationship: The social bond between birthday mates. *European Journal of Social Psychology* 28: 475–481

Monroe, Kristen, 1996. *The Heart of Altruism*, Princeton: Princeton University Press.

Orbell, John M. and Dawes, Robyn, 1991. A "cognitive miser" theory of co-operators' advantage, *American Political Science Review* 85: 515–528

1993. Social welfare, cooperators' advantage, and the option of not playing the game. *American Sociological Review* 58: 787–800

Pinney, Neil and Scholz, John, 1992. Can cognitive consistency cure collective dilemmas? Self-interest versus duty to pay taxes. Russell Sage Working Paper #28, New York: Russell Sage Foundation

Sabini, John, and Silver, Maury, 1982. *Moralities of Everyday Life*, Oxford: Oxford University Press

Seligman, Martin E., 1990. *Learned Optimism*, New York: Knopf

Sen, Amartya, [1978] 1990. Rational fools, in Jane Mansbridge (ed.), *Beyond Self-Interest*, Chicago: University of Chicago Press

Tajfel, Henri, 1982. *Social Identity and Intergroup Relations*, Cambridge: Cambridge University Press

Quattrone, George A. and Tversky, Amos, 1976. Self-deception and the voter's illusion, in Jon Elster (ed.), *The Multiple Self*, Cambridge: Cambridge University Press

Wechsburg, Joseph, 1966. *The Merchant Bankers*, Boston: Little, Brown

Williams, Bernard, 1962. The idea of equality, in Peter Laslett and W. G. Runciman (eds.), *Philosophy, Politics and Society*. Oxford: Basil Blackwell

Yamagishi, Toshio, 1988. The provision of a sanctioning system in the United States and Japan. *Social Psychology Quarterly* 51: 265–271

Yamagishi, Toshio, and Yamagishi, Midori, 1994. Trust and commitment in the United States and Japan. *Motivation and Emotion* 18: 129–166

Zucker, Lynne G., 1986. Production of trust: Institutional sources of economic structure, 1840–1920. *Research in Organizational Behavior* 8: 53–111

11   Democratic theory and trust

Mark E. Warren

It is not obvious that trust should be of interest to theorists of democracy
– except, perhaps, as an undesirable or unavoidable residue of undemo-
cratic modes of governing and decision-making. After all, democratic
progress is most often sparked by distrust of authorities. Innovations in
democratic institutions usually involve new ways of monitoring and controlling those in power, on the assumption that, as a rule, those with
power cannot or ought not to be trusted. In the first instance, democracy
is about controlling, limiting, and distributing power. And democracy
in this sense seems most necessary precisely when those who claim they
are trustworthy are found to have abused their trust.[1] Clearly, distrust is
essential not only to democratic progress but also, we might think, to the
healthy suspicion of power upon which the vitality of democracy depends.[2]

As the essays in this volume suggest, although not all kinds of trust are
good for democracy, it is increasingly clear that certain kinds are necessary to its stability, viability, and vitality. So the problem for democratic
theory is to conceive of those kinds of trust that are good and necessary
for democracy, as well as the ways that democratic institutions might
protect, support, or generate those kinds of trust relations that are good
in themselves. My aim in this chapter is to outline a democratic theory of
trust. I shall proceed as follows. In the first section, I discuss generic
reasons for the tense and often hostile relations between relations of trust
and political relations. These relations, I suggest, give us a first appropriation of how we ought to conceive of the paradoxical place of trust
within democracy. In the second and third sections, I reconstruct and
assess neoconservative and rational choice approaches to relating trust
and democracy. In the final section, I put the case for a third approach
evolving out of deliberative conceptions of democracy.

---

[1] Survey data indicate that democratic transitions are accompanied by increasing distrust
– especially of the state. Cf. Inglehart, this volume, chapter 4.
[2] Cf. Hardin, this volume, chapter 2.

The ambivalent relationship between trust and politics

Since we do not have a well-developed theoretical account of the relationship between democracy and trust, we shall need to begin with some basics: Whatever place trust has or should have within democratic politics needs to be understood in terms of generic relationships between trust and political life. Trust, as I suggested in the introduction, involves *a judgment, however tacit or habitual, to accept vulnerability to the potential ill will of others by granting them discretionary power over some good.* When one trusts, one accepts some amount of risk for potential harm in exchange for the benefits of cooperation – whether these benefits come directly from other persons or from reliance on abstract systems that coordinate efforts over distances of time and space.[3] If I extend trust, I am also judging – however habitually or tacitly – that my trust will not be abused. And this implies that there is no essential conflict of interest between myself and the person, institution, or abstract system to which I extend trust, or at least no conflict of interest that is not mitigated by other relationships, securities, or protections. Alternatively, as Mansbridge suggests (this volume, chapter 10), it may imply that I am extending a moral recognition to another, treating him as if he were trustworthy while accepting the risk that he may not, in fact, be so. Even if I perceive potential abuses, I may extend trust as a way of generating normative expectations that hold these potentials at bay.

Clearly, the generic problem is that *political* relationships would seem to throw the very conditions of trust into question. As I shall conceive them here, *political relationships are those social relationships characterized by conflicts over goods in the face of pressure to associate for collective action, where at least one party to the conflict seeks collectively binding decisions and seeks to sanction decisions by means of power.*[4] From the individual's

---

[3] Cf. Anthony Giddens's (1990: 34) definition of trust: "Trust may be defined as confidence in the reliability of a person or system, regarding a given set of outcomes or events, where that confidence expresses a faith in the probity or love of another, or in the correctness of abstract principles (technical knowledge)." While Giddens is correct to emphasize that in modernity trust can be displaced onto abstract principles, confidence in their *correctness* is not sufficient for trust. One must also judge that the agents of abstract principles share interests or, minimally, lack malice. This point is key to conceptualizing trust in political circumstances.

[4] Somewhat more formally, politics occurs when a social relationship is simultaneously characterized by conflict and power. With respect to the dimension of *conflict*, politics is the subset of social relationships subject to pressures to associate for purposes of collective action, in the presence of conflict over the means, goals, or domain of collective action. With respect to the dimension of *power*, politics involves social relationships in which at least one of the parties seeks a binding resolution to a problem sanctioned by power, where power originates in control over means of physical coercion, means of livelihood and well-being, or symbolic means of identity. For analysis of the concept, see Warren (1999).

perspective, politics is a distinctive kind of social relationship, emerging when the habitual routines of everyday life break down, often under the pressures of power relations, injustices, or systems that shift the para-meters of everyday contingencies. When social relations become political, this means that one or more of the goods of everyday life have become problematic in ways that are not addressed, or no longer addressed, by the relatively automatic coordinations of social relationships – relation-ships that form the horizons within which individuals take securities, iden-tities, routines, and habits more or less for granted. When social relations become political, social points of reference are contested, threatened, or challenged. Relations can become *socially groundless: groundless* not in any metaphysical sense, but rather in the existential sense that social rela-tions lose their taken-for-granted status, the qualities that provided for secure social locations (Warren 1996b). Where there is politics, then, the conditions of trust are weak: the convergence of interests between truster and trusted cannot be taken for granted. Likewise, the powers of norma-tive attribution often depend on shared role expectations and other, sta-ble forms of familiarity. Political contexts imply that at least some of these everyday normative expectations cannot be taken for granted. Conceiv-ing politics in this way does not mean, of course, that trust is absent among partisans. In fact, conflict with other groups often strengthens the bonds of trust within a group – although the *kind* of trust so strengthened may be particularistic in nature, cemented by the fact that conflict pro-duces a line of demarcation between friend and enemy. Particularistic trust heightens distrust between adversaries (cf. Patterson, this volume).

Under these circumstances, two often contradictory elements emerge within individuals' horizons. When social relations are no longer taken for granted – when they enter a domain marked by challenge and conflict – new horizons of possibility emerge. Politics provides opportunities for breaking with inherited, perhaps unjust, social relations and thus can usher in change and newness – *natality*, in Hannah Arendt's (1958) terms. Pol-itics is inherently *future–oriented*. But the emergence of possibility also brings uncertainties and risks. The risks that come with politics are not only that one might choose badly in the face of uncertainty, but also – and perhaps more importantly – that *political* uncertainty is never benign. Parties to a conflict bring with them resources – coercive, economic, and symbolic – that they may try to use to impose a solution. The terms of possibility often are given by the field of forces that come to bear upon an issue, a fact that heightens the risks of losing. For this reason, political relationships heighten one's sense of contingency. They can heighten anxieties; they can overgrow social relationships in ways that cause potentially containable conflicts to infect all other interdependencies. Political relationships, in other words, are characterized by a distinctive tension between possibility and risk. Thus, despite the fact that the conditions of trust are at their most problematic in politics, it is precisely because of the natality of the political that trust is potentially desirable and productive, in contrast to secure situations of routine predictability within which the conditions of trust are fully secure, but for precisely this reason there is less need for trust.

The structure of trust is *homologous* to politics in that individuals extend trust to expand their horizons of possibility, but they do so by accepting risks. As Niklas Luhmann (1979; cf. Seligman 1997) has noted, trust extends beyond the familiar – the everyday relations in which one has confidence – to the unfamiliar and in so doing breaks with the inherently conservative bias of familiarity. In this sense, then, the judgment to trust is a judgment oriented toward future possibilities. But because the risks include uncertainties that fall beyond the capacities of individuals to assess, let alone control, trust leaves individuals vulnerable to the trusted and thus exposes them to new, perhaps exploitive, relations of power. There is, as Anthony Giddens (1990: 89) remarks, "an ambivalence that lies at the core of all trust relations . . . For trust is demanded where there is ignorance – either of the knowledge claims of technical experts or of the thoughts and intentions of intimates upon whom a person relies. Yet ignorance always provides the grounds for skepticism or at least caution." While ambivalence lies at the core of all trust relations, political relations heighten this ambivalence owing to the (often warranted) suspicion that here, at any rate, not all interests and motives are shared and that it would be imprudent to rely on the moral force of trustworthiness alone.

For these reasons, the structural homology between trust and politics is at the same time a structural tension, suggesting that whatever else democratic institutions do, they ought to balance (1) the fact that trust is desirable in politics because it is one, perhaps necessary, way of cultivating the natality inherent in politics, and (2) the fact that the relations of vulnerability inherent in trust are more visible, delicate, and problematic in political situations.

But we lack an account of this tension because, I think, our theories of trust tend to be sociological rather than political in nature. To be sure, this is understandable: We often conceptualize trust as arising in face-to-face interactions between people who share interests or dependencies or who are tied together by attachments of culture. "Pristine" trust, as Adam Seligman suggests (1997: 97–98), is modeled on relations between friends, who share expectations and situations in ways that are not political in the sense that I am conceptualizing politics here. The sociological basis for trust exists where

the participants are both living in a system which is familiar to both, and so requires no further information about it but tacitly provides an everyday basis for mutual understanding. In such circumstances the participants know that they are bound to encounter one another again and that they are bound to become dependent on one another in situations which cannot be exactly foreseeable, and which sometimes favour one of them and sometimes the other. They also know, each of them, that his partner assesses the situation in those terms. Trust relationships find a favourable soil in social contexts with the same kind of structure, i.e. are characterized by the relative persistence of the relationship, by reciprocal dependencies, and a certain quality of the unforeseen. (Luhmann 1979: 37)

Situations with such a structure do not in themselves generate trust. But, importantly, they minimize the risks of trust because (1) interests and/or identities (with their associated values and ethical commitments) converge so that the trusted does not have a motive to exploit the relationship, and (2) the shared social circumstances provide the truster with important knowledge about the reliability of the trusted. Together, these factors constitute a domain within which trust can be extended and sheltered.

Even without the second condition, however, the first condition can produce what Allan Silver (1997) has identified as the uniquely modern phenomenon of trusting strangers: When societies begin to depersonalize necessary social functions (through markets, legal structures and protections, etc.), personal encounters are relieved of the suspicion of malign interest connected to these functions. One is less fearful of enslavement, robbery, and trickery when institutions secure against these possibilities, which in turn allows individuals to extend trust without the suspicion that they might, as a consequence, become victims. As Smith, Hume, and Ferguson argued, it is only when strangers are no longer treated as bearers of malign intent that the possibilities of extensive commerce can develop (Silver 1997: 52–53). By extension, we might speculate that trust in strangers is at least one condition of mitigating problems of collective action.

It is characteristic of *political* situations, however, that these two conditions are weak or missing, so that, all other things being equal, the bias or lean of political relationships will be toward distrust. We can see these distinctive tensions between politics and trust exemplified in a number of ways in the American political system. To take a familiar example, consider the difficulties involved in the trust that a voter may hope to place in an elected representative – and that a representative might hope to

receive. In our complex and pluralistic society, representation by territorial district does not correspond to natural communities of interest or
identity and so lacks the "thick" social context defined by background
assumptions about shared interests, identities, and mutual understandings.
For this reason, the trust that the representative seeks will come to depend,
to a greater or lesser degree, upon "political entrepreneurship," that is,
evoking communities of interest sufficient for a majority coalition. In many
cases these communities of interest may be beyond suspicion: They are,
perhaps, broad but latent, as with many environmental concerns, requiring political organization to transform them into a political force. In other
cases, the communities are manufactured by evoking principles that are
broad enough to evoke widespread identification, but so abstract that
they dissimulate real conflicts of interest and identity. And in still other
cases, communities are manufactured by evoking threats to identity and
creating particularized trust based on race, ethnicity, lifestyle, moral identity, or religion.

But the trust manufactured within contexts where there are, in fact,
conflicts of identity and interest is prone to disillusionment, precisely
because – as I shall argue below – one of the conditions of *warranted*
trust – namely, shared interests or identities between the truster and
the trusted – is ambiguous, fragile, or simply missing. In the dynamic of
trust between representative and constituency, for example, the fragility
of trust exists for two reasons.

First, governing is different than campaigning. Once in office, a representative finds that the trust of those who voted for him may be hard to
keep as broad values and abstract principles meet with policies that now
evoke the conflicts of interest that were always there. Because it focuses
upon *public* policy, politics tends to evoke and focus contentious issues,
while other institutions (markets, scientific establishments, etc.) tend to
decentralize and defuse decisions (Luhmann 1979: 54). The focused
quality of the voters' commitments demands criteria of trust that are linked
to broad conceptions of public good, and these are inevitably disappointed
by the disintegration of the focus into the detail of policy-making and
governance, as well as by the conflicting interests that come to the surface with every policy-specific decision. As Luhmann (1979: 54) puts it,
in politics the

lack of clarity in the mechanisms for the formation of trust is based, first of all, on
the fact that . . . the impetus towards commitment – the investment beforehand
– by the person trusting, and whatever he is putting his trust in, both evaporate
into a cloud of uncertainty. The metaphor of the "social contract," according to
which the people (in terms of free natural man) undertake to trust each other or
the established sovereign has no counterpart in real life. Certainly, the citizen

casts his vote. But to vote is not to mandate someone to represent one's interests. What is declared as the main aim of this institution is for the elected representatives of the people to reach decisions according to criteria of the public good. But they demand sovereign power to take decisions, and one cannot trust a sovereign.

Trust is vulnerable, in other words, because the representative's mandate to represent the public good obscures the reality that interests and identities conflict making power dangerous. Without a secure social basis, it remains unclear whether the trust that exists is warranted and – lacking clear warrant – when interests are subsequently clarified, trust easily dissolves into betrayal. As Hardin (this volume, chapter 2) argues, it is questionable whether trust belongs in such relationships at all. And yet for individuals distant from government, the complexities of issues, the impossibilities of knowing, and the personalization of political campaigns create strong incentives to extend trust beyond its "natural" domain within thick social relationships.

Second, to the extent that a competitive campaign places a premium upon manufacturing trust by evoking the distrust of other communities of interest (particularized trust), a winner assumes office having cultivated the distrust of a significant number of constituents. Often a representative finds that he or she must now reach out to these constituencies, if only to neutralize their potentials for mobilization and obstruction. A political representative must, inevitably, compromise, but reaching out to distrusting constituencies blurs the boundary between friend and enemy that had initially served as the social-psychological basis of particularized trust. In such cases, compromise necessarily evokes the affect of betrayed identity, which in turn is expressed in the language of betrayed principles.

This familiar kind of example is, I think, only one instance of the more general dynamics of betrayal foreshadowed by any political domain defined by conflicting identities, the compromise of which will appear as unprincipled action. The movement from trust to betrayal is heightened within an atmosphere that is morally charged, that is, where the public discourse focuses on conflicts between lifestyles, moral duties, and right and wrong. The dynamic is especially evident in cases of groups that are relatively enclosed within their moral universes: Because they expect their moral identities to be represented at the level of the whole – and free of other influences – any political compromise of the trust bestowed on a representative to represent this moral identity will be judged a betrayal, *even* for those representatives who seek to act in good faith.[5]

---

[5] Peter Johnson (1993: 11), the only author who has considered this tension, notes a related but different issue. Those who are morally trustworthy in the private sense are those who are likely to be politically ineffective at achieving morally desirable ends. So we are faced with having to place trust in those with "dirty hands." What he does not note is that

In short, without political mechanisms that can alter and mediate the constraints, political representatives are caught between the promise of politics to look toward collective futures – an element of every campaign – and the fact of conflicting interests/identities and competing powers. No wonder American voters often seem almost obsessively concerned with the "sincerity" and "character" of candidates. Unable to follow the enormous complexities of public policy and political strategy and faced with institutions that are not transparent in any case, individuals often must choose between trust in their representatives or withdrawal. But because of the fragile nature of trust in politics, their expectations are often disappointed, fueling the generalized cynicism that is becoming characteristic of the American political landscape.

Considered in this way, then, a central problem for democratic theory is to conceive how, under contemporary conditions, tensions between politics and trust might be mitigated, diffused, or transformed. The tension between politics and trust, while inevitable, does admit of a number of institutional responses that can make the difference between a politics that generates a vicious circle of distrust and one that transforms political conflict into social relations of trust. These possibilities have not, however, been adequately articulated within democratic theory. In part, the difficulty is that the concept of trust covers a number of distinct relationships and phenomena. While many of these have been distinguished in the literature of sociology (e.g. Barber 1983; Giddens 1990; Luhmann 1979; Seligman 1997) and management (e.g. McAllister 1995), the distinctions have not been absorbed into political theory generally or democratic theory specifically.

Nonetheless, there are three kinds of approaches to trust and politics emerging within the literature, approaches I shall refer to as *neoconservative, rational choice,* and *deliberative.* The approaches are distinguished by the ways they locate sources of trust, respectively, within culture, within the rational monitoring of risks by individuals, and within discursive processes. In terms of political programs, the approaches correspond to neoconservatism (withdrawal of demands from the state in favor of social and economic modes of organization), traditional liberal-democracy (interest-based monitoring of the state), and deliberative democracy (guidance of economic and political systems by deliberative publics). In the next several sections, I shall elaborate the possibilities and dilemmas of trust in politics within the context of assessing these three approaches.

any principled position in politics will lead to the charge of "dirty hands." If, however, some dimensions of politics are defined by the absence of an agreed moral ground, then the charge has less substance, and a politician is much closer to being a creator than a violator of morality if he seeks to compromise conflicting moralities.

The neoconservative approach

What is perhaps most striking about the emerging neoconservative approach is that the essential tension between trust and politics is mitigated by conceiving them as attributes of distinctive spheres: society and state. It is precisely because "one doesn't trust a sovereign" that trust ought to be conceived as essential to social and economic life where, ultimately, the work of collective decision-making and action ought to be centered. Politics, centered in the state, is at best corrosive of trust and the "social capital" it engenders, and for this reason the demands of collective action, which are best served where there are "reserves" of social capital, ought to be kept out of the realm of state decision-making and action whenever possible. As Jean Cohen (this volume, chapter 7) notes, this emerging "discourse of civil society" is primarily a values discourse since social organization is, ultimately, conceived as an effect of moral commitments.

Nowhere are the difficulties with the neoconservative approach to trust better exemplified than in Francis Fukuyama's *Trust: The Social Virtues and the Creation of Prosperity* (1995). While the book is focused primarily upon economic performance, there are enough comments on democracy, liberalism, and the state to discern the outlines of a political theory of trust – one that is especially important because it resonates with neoconservative concern about the decline of trust, especially in authorities, institutions, and inherited communities. Fukuyama's thesis is that many of the differences in economic success among countries can be explained by whether or not communities defined by their shared ethical horizons bind people into networks of trust. "Trust," he writes, "is the expectation that arises within a community of regular, honest, cooperative behavior, based on communally shared norms, on the part of other members of that community" (26). For Fukuyama, trust is primarily cultural in nature and is inherited from "preexisting communities of shared moral norms or values" (336).

Importantly, there are two key kinds of cultural trust: One kind of trust extends to strangers (referred to in this volume as "generalized" trust; see chaps. 5 and 6); the other kind extends only to members of the same family, clan, or group (in this volume, "particularized" trust) and is often combined with generalized distrust of strangers. The importance of generalized trust from an economic perspective is that it enables actions to be coordinated across time and space without requiring laws, contracts, and explicit rules, which tend to be cumbersome and costly defenses against risk (26). Because shared ethical horizons facilitate economic exchanges by enabling very low "transaction costs" (36), high-trust societies can extend economic networks beyond families and kinship groups, enable the construction of large-scale economic institutions, and encompass societywide divisions of labor. This is why the relatively high-trust societies of Japan, Germany, and the United States have been economically successful, while those societies that combine low social trust with strong extended families – such as Korea, China, and southern Italy – have been less so. Both kinds of trust are an effect of the moral communities, and their differing qualities explain the differing amounts of "social capital" within these countries upon which capitalism can draw.

Fukuyama's analysis of democracy follows much the same lines: Both capitalism and democracy draw on "stores of social capital" for their effective functioning (1995: 356–357). Echoing Tocqueville, he notes that a key requirement of democracy is the ability to associate, so that if "the institutions of democracy and capitalism are to work properly, they must coexist with certain premodern cultural habits that ensure their proper functioning" (11). What is happening in America today, in Fukuyama's view, is that our inherited stores of social capital are eroding, owing primarily to the "'rights revolution' in the second half of the twentieth century. This revolution has provided a moral and political basis for the promotion of individualistic behavior, with the consequent weakening of many earlier tendencies of group life" (284–285; cf. 10, 314). Thus, America today "presents a contradictory picture of a society living off a great fund of previously accumulated social capital that gives it a rich and dynamic associational life, while at the same time manifesting extremes of distrust and asocial individualism that tend to isolate and atomize its members" (51). The rise of the "strong state" with its inherent tendencies to step into the vacuum is both a result of the dissipation of trust and a further cause of its decline.

Interpersonal and institutional forms of trust

While Fukuyama's comparative economic thesis involves an important insight into the social embeddedness of market relations, his conception of trust is inadequate to the basic demands of democratic theory. Some of the inadequacies follow from his premodern conception of trust: the trust that stems from "*inherited ethical habit*" (1995: 34), which is "the product of preexisting communities of shared moral norms or values" (336).[6] It is correct and important that trust stemming from shared ethical habits is pervasive in everyday interactions. But this is not the only

---

[6] Fukuyama's formulations evoke Hegel's conception of *Sittlichkeit*, but lack Hegel's attention to distinctions among spheres and their distinctive ethical criteria.

kind or source of trust. It is, however, the only kind of trust that cannot be produced by *artifice* – and so there is little point asking whether or not democratic institutions might enable it. But there are ways of creating trust, some of which are distinctively modern. And wherever trust can be encouraged by institutional artifice, we have a form of trust of interest to democratic theory.

The limits of Fukuyama's conception of trust are visible even within his sociological history of economics. In a now classic article, for example, Lynne Zucker (1986) convincingly argues that the American economy began to grow rapidly when it was able to detach trust from the kinds of characteristics Fukuyama identifies with community (cf. Silver 1997). There are, Zucker argues, at least three ways trust may be produced, only two of which appear in Fukuyama's analysis. Trust may be "(1) process-based, where trust is tied to past or expected exchange such as in reputation or gift-exchange; (2) characteristic-based, where trust is tied to person, depending on characteristics such as family background or ethnicity; and (3) institutional-based, where trust is tied to formal societal structures, depending on individual or firm-specific attributes (e.g. certification as an accountant) or on intermediary mechanisms (e.g. use of escrow accounts)" (1986: 53).[7] Thus, on Zucker's account, the American economy began to develop institutionalized means of "producing trust" during the latter part of the nineteenth century, a time that correlates with the emergence of the United States as an economic power (cf. Silver 1997). The development of institutionalized trust is a causal factor, for as long as exchanges depend upon community-based moral sanctions for trustworthy behavior – as, for example, in the networks of Baptist businessmen in the American frontier that intrigued Max Weber (1946) – economic exchange will be limited, in part owing to the limits of the community, but in part owing to the difficulties inherent in gaining information at a distance about who is a trustworthy member of the community (and thus about who is or is not subject to the sanctions of the community). Fukuyama focuses on the limitations that family-based trust imposes on economic exchanges. But the same limits apply to "moral communities," albeit on a larger scale, as well as to those kinds of trust, however important, based on reputation or confidence-building exchanges, since these kinds also require face-to-face, "lifeworld" experiences.

---

[7] Barbara Misztal (1996) develops a similar set of distinctions between three types of social order (stable, cohesive, and collaborative), each of which depends on a different source of trust – habits, passion, and policy, which in turn involve three sets of factors: cultural rules, common values, and bonds created for cooperative purposes. Cf. Giddens' (1990: 100–2) distinctions between premodern and modern forms of trust.

The differences between interpersonal and institutional trust are analyzed in detail by Luhmann (1979, 1988), who notes that social systems
can gain the advantages of complexity only when exchanges can be
secured in ways that become semi-autonomous of face-to-face relations
(cf. Habermas 1984, 1987; Giddens 1990). This does not mean that semi-
autonomous institutions (such as the institutions of law) do not rely upon
interpersonal forms of trust for their functioning (cf. Habermas 1996;
Giddens 1990: 83–88; Seligman 1997), but that institutionalized forms
of trust provide forms of assurance that relieve interpersonal and cultur-
ally sanctioned forms of trust of the full burden of facilitating social and
economic exchange.[8] Thus, a key problem with Fukuyama's analysis is
that he models the economic successes of modern societies by using a
premodern conception of trust, one that fails to distinguish those modes
of trust that depend upon interpersonal relations sanctioned by cultural
norms from those that become institutionalized.

This limitation in turn results in two kinds of difficulties for working
out the conceptual relations between democracy and trust. First, because
political relationships are in part distinguished from other social relationships by the fact that shared moral, communal, or reputational horizons
cannot be taken for granted, Fukuyama's conception of trust provides no
guidance for the most difficult problems of trust: those that arise between
communities. It may be that trust is especially difficult between communities marked by differing ethical habits. And it is likely that similarities of ethnicity, class, race, religion, occupation, and the like – that is,
those factors that are, sociologically speaking, most closely associated
with existing communities – do make trust within communities more
automatic. This is because communities provide three requisites of trust:
(a) Communities facilitate the interpretation of the motives of others
through shared language and culture; (b) communities provide sanction;
and (c) communities provide common identities that often override conflicting interests. Yet because we cannot take these factors for granted in
many, even most, contemporary political situations, it is even more important for democratic theorists to conceptualize how political processes
that might facilitate trust might be built between different communities,

[8] S. N. Eisenstadt and L. Roniger (1984) make this point in comparative analyses of Southern
Europe, the Muslim Middle East, Latin America, Asia, Israel, the United States, and the
USSR. They focus on the relationship between interpersonal and institutionalized trust,
noting that societies with weakly institutionalized trust depend on relatively rigid relations between personal identity and culture to maintain exchange relations and thus are
less able to tolerate the zones of individual discretion. Societies that institutionalize trust
free individuals from the rigid behavioral demands of societies that are integrated primarily by culture. When freed from cultural demands, individuals become more creative
and social relations more dynamic. Allan Silver (1997) makes a parallel point.

as well as between communities and institutions (cf. Earle and Cvetkovich 1995).

Second, owing to his association of trust with premodern origins, Fukuyama assumes that trust cannot be generated anew by the means available to governments. The only policy recommendation that can follow from Fukuyama's conception of trust is that we ought to avoid destroying whatever inherited social capital remains: "Social capital is like a ratchet that is more easily turned in one direction than another; it can be dissipated by the actions of governments much more readily than those governments can build it up again" (1995: 362). If the social capital associated with trust can be generated, it is only by virtue of a "mysterious cultural process" within civil society (11). That is, political processes that rely upon government action, democratic or otherwise, can only damage trust. Such generalizations obscure democratic possibilities by conceptually limiting the domain of collective responses to political problems.

Trust, familiarity, and risk

Fukuyama's faith in inherited cultural dispositions is related to the fact that he defines trust without reference to risk: Trust is "the expectation that arises within a community of regular, honest, cooperative behavior . . ." (1995: 26).[9] To be sure, expectations of such behavior are important factors in limiting the risks of trust. But sociologists today rightly are interested in trust as a response to risks that result from the high degrees of interdependency and complexity in modern societies, combined with a relatively high degree of change.

One reason Fukuyama misses the link between trust and risk is that he confuses trust with something more like *familiarity*, a way of interacting with others that depends upon projecting knowledge of the past onto future interactions. This backward-looking confidence is the key element of Fukuyama's location of trust in inherited expectations sanctioned by communities. As Luhmann and others (Earle and Cvetkovich 1995; Giddens 1990) have emphasized, however, trust and risk increasingly complement familiarity and danger in orienting social actions. Familiarity and the kinds of confidence that comes with it imply that we have a certain amount of knowledge of the possibilities and dangers to which we are subject, in part because they are relatively close at hand. From a cognitive

---

[9] Fukuyama shares this failing with others who focus on trust in economic institutions, where the emphasis upon the regularity of expectations deflects from a more political emphasis upon risk and power. Cf. Zucker (1986: 54): "trust is defined as a set of expectations shared by all those involved in an exchange."

perspective, we are able to generalize to the future on the basis of past knowledge. But, as Luhmann puts it, as

a social order becomes more complex and variable, it tends on the whole to lose its matter-of-fact character, its taken-for-granted familiarity, because daily experience can only envisage or recall it in a fragmentary way. Yet the very complexity of the social order creates a greater need for coordination and hence a need to determine the future – i.e. a need for trust, a need which is now decreasingly met by familiarity. In these circumstances, familiarity and trust must seek a new mutually stabilizing relationship which is no longer grounded in a world which is immediately experienced, assured by tradition, close at hand. (1979: 20)

On slightly different but complementary grounds, Adam Seligman (1997: chaps. 1–2) argues that trust is a distinctively *modern* phenomenon, linked to the emergence of individuality. Individuality is the element of agency that is not exhausted by the roles one inhabits and that therefore inserts into social relations an element of choice, discretion, and freedom. It is when individual agency emerges that it makes sense to connect risk and trust, for one kind of risk to which trust (and trustworthiness) respond is precisely that generated by the potential unpredictability of the actions of others. The point is analogous to Kant's view that actions can acquire moral significance only when humans possess capacities to choose. By analogy, capacities for reflexive choice generate the kinds of risk to which trust is an appropriate response; and it is only here that trustworthiness goes beyond externally imposed role expectations to become a moral virtue.

The emergence of both modern phenomena – increasing complexity and individuation – means that decisions based on familiarity are no longer sufficient with respect to engaging future possibilities. Familiarity and trust are distinct ways of orienting toward time. In a situation of confidence based on familiarity, "one is exposed to dangers, but no thought is normally given to them because they are familiar and fall within one's realm of competence to manage. In a situation of trust, in contrast, one must decide between alternative futures, each of which may or may not turn out to be manageable" (Earle and Cvetkovich 1995: 62). Familiarity orients individuals to the past, while trust is extended toward the future, suggesting that modes of security and complexity reduction located in familiarity are inherently conservative. Familiarity, writes Luhmann (1979: 20), provides a basis for judgment in which

the past prevails over the present and the future. The past does not contain any "other possibilities": complexity is reduced from the outset. Thus an orientation to things past can simplify the world and render it harmless. One can assume that the familiar will remain, that the trustworthy will stand the test once more and that the familiar world will continue into the future. . . . As against this, there is the future orientation of trust. Of course, trust is only possible in a familiar world; it needs history as a reliable background. . . . But rather than being just an inference from the past, trust goes beyond the information it receives and risks defining the future. . . . The actor binds his future-in-the-present to his present-in-the-future. In this way he offers other people a determinate future, a common future, which does not emerge directly from the past they have in common but which contains something comparatively new.

Because Fukuyama confuses trust with familiarity, he defines trust in such a way that it must, of logical necessity, underwrite a politics that elevates the past over the future.[10]

Trust and power

That Fukuyama fails to include risk in his conception of trust is closely related to a failure to conceptualize the close relationship between trust and power – another key conceptual relation between trust, politics, and democracy. As Baier (1986: 240) and Hardin (1993: 506) have noted, because trust involves a three-way relationship between truster, trusted, and a valued good, it sets up a potential power relation. The trusted (A) gains the potential to exercise power over the truster (B), owing to A's control over resources needed or valued by B. It is important, however, that vulnerability to power is a *risk* of trust and not a necessity, because trust and power differ: In the case of *trust*, B normally assumes that A has his interests in view (including, where appropriate, identity interests), whereas a *power* relation involves a situation in which A can cause B to act in A's interest against B's interests, typically because A controls some resource (means of livelihood, cultural sources of identity, means of security, etc.) that B needs or desires. Because trust involves accepting a relationship with a parallel structure, the risk is that A will use his control over the good against B's interest, potentially to influence B's future actions to serve A's interests. *This* is the relationship that renders

---

[10] While Luhmann's analysis is purely conceptual, it does help to make sense of certain apparent anomalies in American politics. Although trust in political institutions is low and in decline, Americans do not appear to want radical change, and there remains a high level of "diffuse support" for the political system. What Luhmann's analysis suggests is that trust and familiarity are now trading off against one another, as functional equivalents. The fate of President Clinton's 1993 health-care initiative suggested that although our current health-care delivery system is bad, its dangers are familiar, and Americans do not trust their politicians to change the system owing to the risk that they will become worse off. And although polls before the 1996 presidential campaign showed that most Americans did not trust Clinton, they nonetheless preferred him to his challengers. The message seemed to be that although Clinton was judged untrustworthy, he represented the familiar option as compared to a Republican Congress that represented change. With respect to the federal government, Americans seem to be forgoing trust for familiarity and the predictability it entails.

relations of trust risky, and it is why the background of interests and potential power relations is central to understanding the durability of trust relationships. It should come as no surprise that individuals will distrust when they perceive a conflict of interest, withholding what they can to mitigate the potential for a power relation. We *should* expect disillusioned withdrawal of trust where conflicts of interest between the truster and the trusted are exposed.

Put in these terms, we should be able to see quite clearly why an analysis of trust in terms of the moral dispositions of a community is inadequate not only to democratic political theory but to any political theory. Although we should never discount the impact of ethical dispositions on temptations to abuse trust, focusing on these dispositions alone deflects attention from the context of power and conflict of interest that may, in fact, be managed and altered in ways that also contain the risks of trust – and empower ethical dispositions – a point I discuss below.[11]

Trust and rights

It is because of the homologous relationship between trust and power that we should look closely at the functions of rights in generating trust. Fukuyama places the blame for the dissipation of trust and the "social capital" it represents on the development of a "liberal rights culture" in the latter half of this century. Rights, in Fukuyama's (1995: 316) view, are primarily matters of advancing individual interests against the authority of group norms, in effect pitting the powers of the state against the ability of groups to sanction deviant behavior.

---

[11] Certain of Fukuyama's examples go beyond and contradict his analysis. Thus, he is impressed with the "lean production" model, which relies on trusting low-level workers to make decisions (1995: 342): "Lean manufacturing is perhaps the clearest example of the efficiency gains that can come about from the proliferation of network structures in the context of a high-trust society. Lean production decentralizes decision-making authority down to the lowest of the factory floor and replaces centralized, rule-based cooperation with a more informal sense of workplace community." Fukuyama (1995: 255–259) notes, interestingly, that owing to the division of the workplace into a manager-oriented, bureaucratic hierarchy, and with the adoption of Taylor's model of mass production in the United States, unions came to focus on limiting chances of exploitation by means of detailed job descriptions while bargaining primarily for economic gain – both symptoms of low-trust workplaces in which the worker is merely a cog in the machine. When American corporations have tried to adopt lean production, however, they often fail to understand that trust requires an "ethical bargain": In exchange for trust from workers, employers need to guarantee job security (Fukuyama 1995: 317). One could learn something by analyzing this example as a situation beset by risks related to vulnerabilities and relevant to the ways that securities can be organized to provide an environment within which trust can be generated. Likewise, Fukuyama's (1995: 302–303) interesting analysis of slavery in the United States as "deculturation" implicitly grants the centrality of power relations to trust and distrust.

It is certainly true, especially in the United States, that individual rights claims often corrode common goods. This is especially true of property rights – although never criticized by Fukuyama[12] – which have been used historically to support slavery, exploit labor, avoid responsibility for environmental degradation, and more generally externalize the costs of private activities onto others. Nonetheless, it is a misnomer, both conceptually and historically, to assert as Fukuyama does that "liberal rights" produce, with monocausal logic, a society of atomized individuals.

Fukuyama misses key supportive relationships between rights and trust in part because he fails to distinguish among the many classes of rights: rights of property, rights of intimacy, rights of association, rights of political participation, and rights of welfare and security. Many of these rights have functioned, and do function, to reduce vulnerabilities to power by limiting its reach, in this way enabling voluntaristic, solidaristic, and public modes of association (Cohen and Arato 1992: 345–491; Habermas 1996: 118–131; Preuss 1995; Lefort 1986: 245–259; Teubner 1983). Rights can and do alter principles of association, stemming coercive organization in favor of voluntary association, enabling broader participation in politics and policy-making, as well as mitigating the economic power of firms over their employees. In case after case, from the guarantees of freedom of conscience in the eighteenth century to the economic securities that even Fukuyama asserts are necessary for "lean production," expansions of rights have produced sheltered spaces within civil society and the economy within which relations of trust can grow (Silver 1997).[13]

The general point here is straightforward: Fukuyama is certainly right that it is difficult for states to create relations of trust directly via enforcements of rights. But liberal states can use their powers, usually by means of rights underwritten by the powers of an independent judiciary, to protect spaces within society from the power relations that destroy trust or

---

[12] Fukuyama's (1995: 316) targets include freedom of speech (because it protects pornography) and the right to bear arms.

[13] This point is missed by Adam Seligman (1992), who argues that trust and rights trade off against one another. He notes, correctly, that the existence of rights depends upon the capacity to promise, which in turn requires a background of trust. Here, however, "we see the paradox of modern society, rooted in abstract and generalized trust, which in the political sphere is represented by the universalization of citizenship (the guarantee of moral agency in the public arena secured by the State). The very universalization of trust in citizenship however undermines that concrete mutuality and shared components of the moral community, upon which trust is based" (Seligman 1992: 10–11; cf. 1997: 6). Like Fukuyama, Seligman fails to disaggregate rights and so fails to grasp the ways in which they enable, protect, and facilitate association and discourse within civil society – all preconditions of promising and trust.

keep it from ever developing. Certain kinds of rights – in particular, rights of association, speech, political participation, and security – shift modes of problem-solving from coercive to discursive relations (Habermas 1996). These shifts do not produce or guarantee trust in themselves, but without these protections, what trust exists is likely to be corroded by power. Moreover, without rights, a society will lack the means to distinguish relations of trust that are warranted from those that are not, since so many power relations within society and between society and state will be safe from challenge.[14]

The ethics of trust

A final deficit in Fukuyama's approach is ethical in nature, a deficit to which I have been alluding by distinguishing *warranted* from *unwarranted* trust. Despite his claim that trust depends upon the ethical regulations of a community, Fukuyama (1995: 25) has little to say about how we might think of trust relationships themselves as ethical or unethical, sliding easily from the notion of an inherited community to ethics and assimilating the kinds of virtues that make individuals trustworthy to inherited community norms.

But a community's moral precepts will generate *warranted* trust under only two conditions: (1) There are no empowered conflicts of interest within the community of trust relations; and (2) the moral precepts and ethical regulations of the community are in fact ethical – a more difficult judgment I shall not address here.[15] The first condition requires attention to the backgrounds of powers, interests, and vulnerabilities within which trust operates. Trust may or may not be warranted in any given case, and this will have much to do with whether the trusted is trustworthy: that is, whether the trusted uses her discretion for the good of the truster and without detriment to the larger community. This does not exclude, of course, the common possibility that the trusted serves herself as well. Rather, what is important is that there is a community of interest that causes trust to work to mutual benefit. Trust is warranted

---

[14] Cf. parallel points by Ayres and Braithwaite (1992).
[15] Clearly, the "ethical habits" of some kinds of communities – of slaveholders, the Mafia, etc. – cannot be said to be ethical under any account of ethical judgment. Although I do not address the issue, the judgments implied by discourse ethics are consistent with the account of trust I develop here. See Habermas (1990, 1996). Addressing condition (1), however, implies an ethical community will maintain conditions of warranted trust within the community, which in turn implies many of the conditions suggested by discourse theories of ethics.

when it does not, in fact, conceal relationships of exploitation, domination, or conspiracy against others.[16]

But how would the truster know? Inherent in a trust relationship is that the truster *does not* monitor the background of interests and conditions. When one trusts another, one forgoes whatever opportunities one has for monitoring – although it is important that the opportunities exist and may even sometimes be used. But if one monitors continually, not only would the advantages of trust in terms of existential security, reduction of complexity, and extensive divisions of labor be lost, but the one who is monitored would herself feel untrustworthy, subject to a suspicion corrosive of trust (cf. Mansbridge, this volume, chapter 10). And yet, there is nothing more corrosive of social relations than trust that is abused, typically arousing in the victim a moral bitterness that not only damages future relations with an individual or institution but also reflects upon all other potential relations of vulnerability, producing a downward spiral in trust.

It is because of the vulnerability of trust relations that the ethical robustness of trust is so important. Annette Baier suggests that trust be tested for its ethical qualities at one remove, a test worth notice because it suggests an indirect but supportive relationship between trust and deliberative democracy, a topic to which I return in the final section. Trust, Baier (1986: 259–60) writes,

> is morally decent only if, in addition to whatever else is entrusted, knowledge of each party's reasons for confident reliance on the other to continue the relationship could also be entrusted – since mutual knowledge of the conditions for mutual trust would be itself a good, not a threat to other goods. To the extent that mutual reliance can be accompanied by mutual knowledge of the conditions for that reliance, trust is above suspicion, and trustworthiness a nonsuspect virtue.

What is noteworthy about Baier's "expressibility test" is that it recognizes that a virtue of trust is that *one does not have to know* and yet recognizes the vulnerabilities inherent in such a relation by introducing a hypothetical monitoring: If one *did* know the conditions of the trust relationship and would *nonetheless* remain in the relationship, then trust is "morally decent." What I shall suggest in the following sections is that desirable forms of trust are facilitated by political contexts that provide *actual* recourse to monitoring, specifically through institutional devices that (1) align the interests of truster and trusted, thus limiting the risks of trust, and (2) enable and facilitate democratic deliberation and challenge.

---

[16] Thus, the trust exhibited among members of the Mafia is unethical because it conceals conspiracy (Gambetta 1988). Cf. Dennis Thompson's (1993) analysis of corruption in the American political system.

Both sets of devices make it more likely that trust will not be abused in political situations and that, if abused, the damage will be found out and limited.

Rational choice and legal/liberal devices

We can learn more about (1), aligning the interests of truster and trusted, by looking at an approach to trust rooted in rational choice theory, the most developed of which is Russell Hardin's (1991, 1993, 1995; cf. Bianco 1994; Coleman 1990; Williams 1988). In contrast to Fukuyama, who focuses on the close relationship between social embeddedness within a community and stable expectations, rational choice theory emphasizes the vulnerability inherent in trust relations. In part, the emphasis stems from rational choice axioms: Individuals seek to maximize (self-interested) preferences; knowledge about what will maximize preferences is a cost, so individuals will weigh the costs of additional information against the expected utilities of information.

From the rational choice perspective, then, trust is paradoxical. On the one hand, relations of trust decrease the cost of information while increasing the utilities of cooperation. On the other hand, because individuals are self-interested, those who trust would seem to be choosing, irrationally, to increase their vulnerability to others. No doubt some dimensions of this paradoxical situation can be accounted for by those aspects of rational choice assumptions about the self that are of questionable sociological or psychological validity (Green and Shapiro 1994; Warren 1990). Nonetheless, if we are interested in *political* relationships (as compared to social relations more generally), a politicized context will tend to select for traits that make rational choice assumptions somewhat more illuminating. As I have suggested here and argued elsewhere (Warren 1996b), this is because political relationships often represent the breakdown of the routine coordinations of social relationships. In a political environment, commonalities of interests and identities may exist, but they cannot be taken for granted, so that individuals and groups are more likely to think and act in strategic ways. In such situations, rational choice axioms help to focus on interests and judgments in contexts that combine potential vulnerabilities with apparently insufficient information – contexts typical of politics.

Hardin's aim is to show why we might consider trust to be rational for individuals (owing to its benefits), despite its apparently paradoxical nature. Most importantly, he notes that trust turns on the truster's judgments of the interests of the trusted: "you trust someone if you have adequate reason to believe it will be in that person's interest to be trustworthy in the relevant way at the relevant time. One's trust turns not on one's own interests but on the interests of the trusted. It is encapsulated in one's judgment of those interests" (1993: 505). There are two aspects of Hardin's description of trust that are of particular relevance to political situations: (a) Trust is a *judgment* with cognitive content (as opposed to a habit or affect); and (b) trust involves judgments of the trusted's *interests*, *not* a judgment of the information, knowledge, or skills of the trusted relevant to the trust relationship. I shall consider these two points in turn.

Cognitive vs. affective trust

The literature on the psychology of trust typically distinguishes trust that has cognitive origins – that is, origins in individuals' judgments about the circumstances surrounding a trust relation – from trust that has affective origins in love, friendship, relations between children and parents, or other such attachments (Earle and Cvetkovich 1995; McAllister 1995). While affective trust almost always has a cognitive component – a child learns from experience that his parents are trustworthy, for example – it is important that the *affective relationship itself* is often a shared interest that merges with a shared identity between truster and trusted, parent and child, marriage partners, etc. Such shared identities mitigate the chances that the vulnerabilities of trust will be exploited by the trusted. For the same reason, trust with cognitive origins (what some call "rational trust") is more appropriate for relationships that occur at a distance and lack this affective coincidence of interests, such as when one trusts professionals, authorities, political representatives, or institutions. Affective trust can, of course, spill over onto strangers. Many claimed to have trusted Ronald Reagan despite the fact that they were not part of his constituency of interests. His media images were replete with the kinds of interpersonal cues and assurances typical of interpersonal attachments. What is risked in cases lacking common interests is that the vulnerabilities of truster are easily exploited. When trust is cognitive, however, the assurances are of a different sort: Professionals are certified, past performances give some indication of future performances, business relations are built, and so on. Typically, even cognitively based trust tends to settle into a set of habitual dispositions and relationships. Thus, Hardin writes, a decision to trust is not like a decision to gamble on taking a risk.

It is, of course, risky to put myself in a position to be harmed or benefited by another. But I do not calculate the risk and then additionally decide to trust you; my estimation of the risk is my degree of trust in you. Again, I do not typically choose to trust and therefore act; rather, I do trust and therefore choose to act.

The degree of trust I have for you is just the expected probability of the dependency working out well. (1993: 516)

Trust need not be purposive to be cognitive; its cognitive component recedes into social relations and learned dispositions that can come to stand in for judgment. This is why, Hardin argues, "the correct way to see the role of thick relationships is as one possible source of knowledge for the truster about the trustworthiness of another and one possible source of incentives to the trusted to be trustworthy" (1993: 510, emphases removed).

Hardin overdraws the cognitive nature of trust, assimilating affective elements that work quite independently to the kind of (cognitive) confidence that is built from pragmatic experience and recedes into a dispositional background. For example, in an affective relation of trust, it is not that the social relationship operates as an "incentive" for the trusted to be trustworthy which the truster judges the trusted to have, but rather that the relationship comes to constitute part of the identity of each. In an affective relationship, the truster does not think to check up on the trusted, not because the trusted has proved trustworthy in the past, but because there is a coincidence of interests that would be best described as mutually defining moments of personal identity. Thus, for example, in marriage or other intimate relationships of mutual dependency and identity, trust may initially follow affect rather than experience. The cognitive correctives (one's mate is found to have cheated or proved incompetent with joint finances) come later and will often diminish the domain of affective trust. Alternatively, cognitive confidence may complement and strengthen affective trust.

Nonetheless, with this qualifier, Hardin's emphasis on the cognitive bases for trust is especially relevant to trust relations with institutions, strangers, business associates, and political representatives, since here affective relations of trust are, at best, foolhardy – reminiscent, perhaps, of the love of a people for their monarch. In democratic relations, trust *ought* to have cognitive origins because individuals ought to be able to assess their vulnerabilities as one dimension of self-government.[17]

Judging interests

What is definitive of *political* relationships, I have argued, is that common interests and identities cannot be taken for granted. The apparent paradox

---

[17] This is not, of course, Hardin's position (this volume, chapter 2). He argues that because these cognitive demands are impossible to satisfy, one ought not to trust government at all. I am, of course, broadening the applicability of Hardin's cognitive focus since I am interested in trust within political relations beyond the domain of government.

is that avoiding the vulnerabilities introduced by conflicts of interest/ identities would appear to require the kind of continuous monitoring that defeats its purpose. Hardin's focus upon interests suggests, however, that the paradox is not as stark as it would first appear – although, as I shall argue, mitigating the paradox requires robust forms of democracy that he does not consider.

On Hardin's formulation, the truster needs to be able to judge the *interests* of the trusted, not his knowledge, skills, or competencies. For the individual, many advantages of trust stem from being able to rely upon the trusted's knowledge, skills, and competencies. While there are, to be sure, vulnerabilities that attach to incompetence exercised in good faith, there are numerous mechanisms having to do with the discourses and checks internal to specialized disciplines and their concerned publics that can serve to check these risks (Warren 1996a). More importantly, in politics the vulnerabilities of trust have to do with conflicts of interest. That vested interests, parties, and authorities often cloak their aims in the rhetoric of the common good provides fertile ground for the growth of distrust, cynicism, and the bitterness of betrayal – possibilities that stem from the truster's initially mistaken acceptance of the rhetoric of commonality when, in fact, conflicts of interest exist. So we need to ask how it is possible for trusters to judge the interests of the trusted without losing the advantages of trust: the benefits of cooperation, the possibilities for new kinds of collective action, the securities of reduced complexity for the individual, and the advantages of increased complexity for society as a whole.

Hardin's focus on interests suggests two interrelated strategies. First, it is a less complex matter to judge the configuration of interests that motivate a trusted individual or institution than it is to judge the information, knowledge, and competencies upon which the truster relies when he trusts. In part, this is because capacities to assess interests do not require specialized discourses with their high entry requirements. I may not understand why my doctor is prescribing a particular drug, let alone the biochemistry of its actions. But I assume he shares with me an interest in my health, *until* I learn that he receives favors from the company that makes the drug. Understanding that my trust was misplaced requires no special learning; it requires only institutional designs that make the relevant information available. Similarly, if my elected representative claims that lowering the capital gains tax will stimulate the economy for the public good, I have no reason not to take him at his word (especially if I understand little about economics) *until* I discover that his election was funded by bundled contributions from brokerage firms.

Second, even in the absence of necessary information, it is relatively easy to design institutions to facilitate commonalities of interest and block conflicts of interest. If I no longer trust my doctor (or any doctor for that matter) because of systematic conflicts of interest, my best bet is *not* to learn about medicine, but rather to lobby for institutional structures that oversee conflicts of interest and realign the interests of doctors and patients. From this perspective, we can see how the devices associated with the rule of law and liberal democracy can, and often do, provide environments that facilitate trust by limiting vulnerabilities and risks – within civil society as well as within the economy and political system.[18] Making trust less risky by traditional legal and liberal means, however, is necessary but not sufficient to mitigate the paradoxes of trust in political situations, a point I develop below.

Legal devices: mitigating risks of trust

It follows from the rational choice emphasis upon the vulnerabilities of trust that a number of familiar institutional designs, created by law, can indirectly create environments in which relations of trust are more likely to grow. Although this point is noted by Hardin (1993: 522–524; cf. Silver 1997: 48), Luhmann (1979: 34) is much more explicit about the ways in which law answers to the fact that trust stands in for information that individuals cannot have: "Legal arrangements which lend special assurance to particular expectations, and make them sanctionable, are an indispensable basis for any long-term considerations of this nature; thus, they lessen the risk of conferring trust." As Luhmann points out, law and trust are quite different in their operations: For reasons of tact and complexity in everyday relations of trust, the sanctions of law cannot and do not work explicitly. The sanctions that operate within social relations are of a different sort: the probability of repeat encounters, shared interests, identities, interdependencies, and the like (cf. Hardin 1993: 524). Nonetheless, Luhmann (1979: 37) argues, "possibilities of sanction produce a generalizing effect in the context not only of hierarchical relations, but also of those between equals. They stabilize interaction through the anticipation of extreme contingencies," which in turn makes it easier to extend trust.[19] This point is especially relevant in political

[18] Keohane, Haas, and Levy (1993: 22–23) note that international environmental regimes that enable monitoring can be "vital to the ability of states to make and keep agreements. Wherever states have reason to fear the consequences of being cheated, monitoring can help reassure them that such cheating will be detected in time to make appropriate adjustments. Monitoring makes state commitments more credible, thereby increasing the value of such commitments."

[19] Cf. Zucker (1986), who notes the numerous institutional devices that enable trust in the world of business transactions, including escrow accounts, professional certification, consumer protection and fraud laws, laws regulating contracts, and so on. Although

relations, which tend to operate at the margins of sociologically stable relations and tend to produce resolutions that are, in the first instance, legal rather than sociological in nature.

At the most basic level of security, for example, laws make it easier to develop relations of trust with strangers, especially if we can count on them not to be violent (Hardin 1993: 524). High rates of crime dampen the spontaneous generosity of people with respect to their assessments of the motivations of others, which in turn corrodes the capacities of a society to generate relations of trust.[20] Similarly, the rule of law with its rights of equal protection and due process decreases the risks of creating new associations and forms of organization – a point especially relevant to emerging and transitional democracies.

Likewise, the differentiation of society tends to limit vulnerabilities by pluralizing their sources. If one's job, physical security, salvation, food, housing, retirement portfolio, and information do not depend upon the same source (as they might in a company town or under totalitarian regimes), then each decision to trust becomes relatively less risky. Some amount of security stems from broad, sociological processes of differentiation. And some significant amount of security is economic in origin, which may explain Inglehart's (this volume, chapter 4; cf. Patterson, this volume, chapter 6) findings that the wealth of a nation correlates with interpersonal trust. But a significant amount of differentiation is a matter of institutional design, as when liberal constitutions distinguished the proper realm of the state from civil society and put the powers of the state (especially the courts) behind enforcing the separations (Preuss 1995).[21] Likewise, welfare securities, regulations affecting work hours and conditions, and other rights can limit the ability of employers to control

---

Zucker refers to such institutions as *productive* of trust, I do not think we should see such institutions as generative of trust in themselves. They work indirectly by making trust less risky and therefore more likely to be extended.

[20] In the United States, the percentage of people who respond that "most people can be trusted" to the survey question "Would you say that most people can be trusted or that you can't be too careful in dealing with people?" has fallen from 54 percent in 1964 to 35 percent in 1995. Data compiled from the General Social Survey, the American National Election Studies, and a survey jointly conducted by *The Washington Post*, the Kaiser Family Foundation, and Harvard University, and reported in *The Washington Post* (Morin and Balz 1996). A 1996 survey finds higher levels of interpersonal trust (45 percent) but finds that trust in neighbors drops significantly in neighborhoods with high rates of crime: from 57 percent in low-crime neighborhoods to 25 percent in high-crime neighborhoods (Pew Research Center 1997: 18, 67). It is likely that some amount of the decline in interpersonal trust is driven by the increasingly cosmopolitan nature of society: We are increasingly likely to encounter strangers in daily life, and so individuals are more likely to be cautious. What is of concern is not increasing cautiousness as such, but rather situations in which encounters with strangers immediately evoke threats to physical security.

[21] Cf. Michael Walzer's (1983) conception of "blocked exchanges."

the totality of workers' lives. In most Western nations, rights and laws now limit the economic dependence of wives upon their husbands. In each case, institutional artifice can contribute indirectly to warranted kinds of trust by limiting vulnerabilities and risks. But it is also clear that trust will be highly risky when vulnerabilities overlap, as is often the case with individuals dependent upon state welfare agencies or – as with many African-Americans – when vulnerabilities of race coincide with those of jobs, housing, and physical security.[22]

Finally, trust in political representatives and government is somewhat easier when risks are mitigated. Many political devices seek to align the interests of representative and constituents, or at least to limit the conflicts. Voting, for example, can be interpreted as a device that aligns a representative's interest in his job with the interests of his constituents. Ideally, the vote is a small piece of political power that can be leveraged against the representative's discretion as a policy-maker. In addition, the need for individuals to monitor conflicts of interest can be limited by conflict-of-interest laws and by campaign-finance reform – the lack of which in the United States is a continuing source of warranted distrust (Thompson 1993).

Limits of rational choice

Although the rational choice focus on interests helps illuminate institutional contributions to trust, the approach has inherent limits with respect to democratic theory. These can best be understood if we focus on the nature and conditions of cognitive judgment, which from a rational choice perspective is inherently backward-looking and therefore biased against future-oriented trust (Earle and Cvetkovich 1995: 62–64; Mansbridge, this volume, chapter 10). Hardin himself is quite clear about the problem. Judgments made on the basis of cognitive assessments of experience are inherently subjective in the following sense: "*What is sensible for a given individual depends heavily on what* that individual *knows, both about the past and the future of the person and the other party to be trusted.* . . . The problem with the Bayesian individual [i.e. the individual who generalizes probability from past experience] is that past experiences may have little bearing on future possibilities. . . . To break the hold of a bad and misleading past, the Bayesian requires a lot of new experience or a bit of theory that runs counter to prior experience." Correcting "the pessimistic Bayesian estimates of trustworthiness merely by amassing better

---

[22] In fact, race is one of the most important predictors of trust. See Patterson, this volume, chapter 10, and the Pew Research Center survey (1997).

experience may be slow, so that these misestimates produce a long string of lost opportunities" (Hardin 1993: 525–26). We are, Hardin argues, more or less stuck with these biases in the case of institutions that operate at a distance. They may explain why many people do not trust government, but they are nonetheless concerned about its predictability, which, Hardin suggests, may be all we can expect (1995: 26–27; this volume, chapter 2).

While predictable government may be sufficient – especially for those whose lives and securities are located elsewhere – it suggests a truncated vision of what politics ought to be able to achieve by democratic means, or what it must achieve in times of change or crisis. It is not just that the "cognitive bias" of generalization from the past will cause individuals to forgo opportunities, but also that it will tend to support stalemates of competing, plural interests, causing societies to forgo the potential benefits of collective actions.

Although it may be that, as an empirical matter, predictability has replaced trust for a decisive number of people in the United States,[23] we shall need to look more closely at the nature of political judgment to be able to ask how much of this replacement is inevitable and how much results from existing institutional configurations. I have already suggested that even in rational choice terms our institutions fail to provide the protections sufficient to trust – in particular, with regard to necessary securities (for example, against workers being treated merely as commodities by a firm) and conflicts of interest (for example, campaign finance and the potential blackmail effects of mobile capital over public policy). But there are also possibilities that remain unnoticed owing to the fact that cognitive judgment is, in rational choice terms, limited to individuals' subjective horizons. In particular, we should think about how institutions might alter the nature of political judgment, by focusing upon how institutions structure processes of judgment. What stands out in the American political system is the extent to which individuals make judgments isolated from deliberative contexts, contexts that may hold out possibilities for overcoming the bias of *subjective* cognitive judgment by introducing an *intersubjective* element.

Deliberative democracy

Advocates of deliberative democracy have not, for the most part, focused on problems of trust, in part because they fail to emphasize the risks of political interaction, a problem I detail elsewhere (Warren 1996b). None-

[23] As far as I am aware, there are no surveys that distinguish trust from predictability.

theless, there exist possibilities within this approach that deserve to be explored. This is not the place to focus on the theory of deliberative democracy, which has become quite nuanced and sophisticated in locating its institutional possibilities (Habermas 1996; Cohen and Arato 1992; Cohen and Rogers 1995). Rather, my aim is to clarify and elaborate two possibilities: (1) that trust complements and supports deliberative resolutions of political conflict; and (2) that deliberative approaches to political conflict can generate trust, both among individuals and between individuals and institutions.

Complementarity and deliberative challenge

Trust and deliberative democracy are different ways of making collective decisions and organizing collective actions. Trust can stand in for participation, particularly when one has reason to believe there exists a community of interests or identities. On the other hand, deliberative participation and challenge make sense in political situations: when there exist conflicts about things that matter. The discretion one permits the trusted is not appropriate in such situations because one of the conditions of *warranted* trust – a commonality of interests – cannot be taken for granted. Here, one ought to be calling others to account and arguing about what to do. In such cases, participation in deliberative processes will matter.

Although trust and deliberation are distinct, they are also complementary. One important complement is that where there are high levels of warranted trust within society and between individuals and authorities, deliberative democracy is easier to conceive and organize. A key problem for theories of deliberative democracy is that deliberative ways of making decisions are relatively time-consuming and cumbersome, as well as demanding of cognitive resources. The time available to participants, the mechanics of mass inclusion, and the limited capacities of individuals to learn what they need to know about complex issues all suggest that deliberative decision-making will, of necessity, be the exception within the totality of collective decisions, especially at higher levels of organization (cf. Hardin, this volume, chapter 2). For these reasons, deliberative mechanisms ought to be reserved for highly politicized decisions where the benefits of deliberation outweigh the cost, a point I have argued elsewhere (Warren 1996a).

An important political function of trust is that it can mitigate these constraints upon deliberation. *If* I can trust food inspectors to do their jobs and scientists to set appropriate standards, *then* I can minimize my worries about the risks of food and turn whatever deliberative resources

I have (time, security, expertise, etc.) to other issues: the quality of public schools, US involvement in eradicating cocaine in Peru, or whatever seems most worthy of my attention.

But the boundary between trust and politicized issues is fluid, and the relationship delicate. A stable background of trust upon which I can depend while my political attention is elsewhere is unlikely if there are consistent and pervasive conflicts of interest within society. Where these conflicts are stabilized by power, limitations on speech, or an unreflective and deferential political culture, then the background may be predictable, but trust will be weak. What maintains a background of trust, rather, is my knowledge that I *could* monitor and challenge authorities or trusted others, as well as the *others'* knowledge that I can do so. One of the ironies of *modern* forms of trust – a point missed entirely by the neoconservative approach – is that they are more robust when they can be challenged because the atmosphere of possible challenge tends to hold relations of trust to their appropriate goods. Thus, the potential for challenge can help to stabilize warranted trust, even while it disillusions unwarranted trust (cf. Braithwaite 1998). Luhmann, who is no advocate of deliberative democracy, nonetheless makes this point in identifying the crucial role of communication in underwriting trust. Although trust can be extended into impersonal institutions and systems,

one must bear in mind that – with trust in generalized media of communication as with trust in general – a minimum of real foundation is required. The pillars of trust must be built on solid ground. . . . [T]he supports of trust are mainly found in opportunities for effective communication: in the possibility of exchanging money for things of real and lasting value, in the possibility of reaching a definite agreement in the kinds of statement in which truth is demanded, in the possibility of activating the means of coercion which belong to the state on the basis of set rules. Given these opportunities for communication, the person who gives his trust is in possession of enough reality to be able usually to opt out of using them. Thus he places twofold trust in two different levels of generalization: he trusts in the effectiveness of certain opportunities for communication as a safety valve, should it become necessary, and he trusts in the general functioning of the system, which enormously increases the effectiveness of these opportunities. (Luhmann 1979: 55–56)

The point of particular relevance here is that trust thrives when institutions are structured so as to respond to communication. This requires (a) access to information and institutions structured so as to provide the necessary transparency, and (b) institutional means for challenging authorities, institutions, and trusted individuals (Warren 1996a; Braithwaite 1998). When these circumstances are in place, the trust I place in authorities and experts may be warranted, but quite indirect: Whatever trust

I have in the Environmental Protection Agency depends, in part, on the interested publics and public spheres that surround an agency's function. I know that Greenpeace and the Sierra Club are watching, and I know that I share interests and identities with these organizations or, more accurately, with the activist individuals who disclose their interests and identities through their membership. They represent me, and I trust them to do so (*because* I am convinced that I share interests or identities), which allows me to direct my own limited resources to other issues.

Public spheres are the institutional parallel to Annette Baier's expressibility test. Recall that the test distinguishes warranted from unwarranted trust by means of the hypothetical possibility that the truster would agree to the relationship of trust could he know all of its conditions, including the interests of the trusted. We might call a politicized version a *publicity test*: By analogy to the expressibility test, *an institutional relationship of trust is warranted if the truster would agree to the relationship with full knowledge of its conditions.*[24] While such knowledge will remain hypothetical most of the time, the constant possibility of public scrutiny will limit the temptations of trusted authorities to exploit the relationship. For individuals, when these conditions exist, the risks of trust will be, most of the time, *unknown but not unknowable.* In "real world" situations, of course, individuals know something of the institutions they trust, and may decide that in some respects the institution is trustworthy, and in other respects not, leaving them to extend trust selectively or to know that they are doing so in the face of some risk. As a generalization, however, where the possibilities for public challenge are present and the institutions responsive, trust will tend to be warranted and robust. Where these conditions do not exist, trust will be fragile and prone to disillusion. In such cases, individuals will lack the means to monitor trust, if they should think it necessary. Lacking these means, suspicions of betrayal can abound, corrupting even warranted relations of trust.

Deliberative generation of trust

As I have constructed the issue, institutions that encourage conflict resolution, bargaining, consensus-building, and/or discovery of common interests should work to settle issues into warranted social relations of trust, easing political conflict back into social routines with their presumed solidarities, minor conflicts, and benign differences. Where this kind of complementarity between trust and politics exists, we also might

---

[24] I owe this suggestion to Alisa Carse. As stated, the publicity test is complementary to Habermas's Discourse Principle: "Just those action norms are valid to which all possibly affected persons could agree as participants in rational discourses" (1996: 107).

expect that trust would *directly* enable deliberation in at least two ways. First, when warranted relations of trust become characteristic of a society, they should function to contain issues that become politicized, which in turn will make it easier for participants to extend trust in political situations. Second, robust social relations of trust indicate that political outcomes will be limited in their impact rather than affecting the totality of an individual's social relations. When the vulnerabilities of participants are contained, so are the risks of political engagement. Limiting risks also makes it easier for participants to talk, listen, negotiate, compromise, generate new ideas, and seek common interests. Put negatively, cognitive reasoning in political situations will be difficult if participants are faced simultaneously with multiple threats, the limiting case of which is war. But if trust is pervasive in a *differentiated* society, it is likely that trust in those areas of life that are, for the moment, shared and unproblematic can serve to contain the corrosive forces of the distrust characteristic of politics.

But it is easier to see how trust and deliberative decision-making might be complementary than it is to see how political deliberation *itself* might generate trust, given the conflicts that define and pervade politics. Clearly, one role of deliberation is to enable challenge, which may (and should) *diminish* trust by exposing conflicts of interest and identity that participants mistakenly had thought to be common. Disillusioning *unwarranted* trust, however, is an essential moment in building warranted trust. The question is whether deliberative processes can generate *warranted* trust. Although there is no definitive theoretical answer to this question (there may be empirical answers if we know what to look for), we ought to investigate several theoretical possibilities.

First, political deliberation is a distinctive way of making public judgments, the characteristics of which can combat the subjective cognitive biases toward the past. Deliberation enlarges the perspectives of individuals by introducing them to new perspectives, voices, experiences, and knowledge (Arendt 1982; Habermas 1996; Warren 1992). When one is forced by argumentation to consider and respond to alternative perspectives, then one gains the resources to break with the limits of one's past and to embrace new possibilities. Enlarging one's perspective may help participants find shared interests, discover new interests, or reprioritize their own in ways more consistent with others. Clearly, the incentives for these transformational processes stem from the pressures for collective action within institutions that mitigate nondiscursive influences such as coercion and money. Under these circumstances, deliberation may help transform and align interests, a precondition of warranted trust.[25]

---

[25] For qualifications, see Warren (1992).

Second, narratives of distrust, conspiracy, betrayal, and fear thrive in discursive vacuums in large part because narrative is one way of focusing and containing perceived risks and threats. In political situations, these tendencies are magnified: Because politics combines social groundlessness with risk, it is especially conducive to narratives that demonize opponents (Warren 1996b). Deliberation can challenge such narratives by providing alternative narratives. These may have the effect of containing and focusing areas of disagreement and conflicting interests, in this way containing the perceptions of threat that are corrosive of trust. As Earle and Cvetkovich (1995) have noted, deliberative arenas provide opportunities for narrative self-presentation that can provide assurances. Deliberative arenas – unlike, say, those of the mass media – provide opportunities to explain oneself, one's group, one's problems. Because mutual respect and tact are more likely in face-to-face relations, narratives are more likely to focus upon self-characterization and to do so in ways that function as assurances, focusing not simply on differences, but also on shared commonalities and predicaments.[26] These in turn may check the imagined vulnerabilities (if, in fact, they are only imagined!) that political situations inevitably magnify. To be sure, any such effects would be tendencies, and their desirability is relative to the effects of nondiscursive forms of politics.

Third, deliberative decision-making should tend to mitigate perceptions of betrayal by providing reasons that justify compromised interests and identities. There are two different possibilities at work here. The first has to do with the *open* and *public* character of deliberative decision-making. While it is hard to imagine a fully transparent politics, deliberative politics tends toward open displays of reasons, justifications, and motivations. In examining the case of the Keating Five, Dennis Thompson (1993) argues convincingly that we should think of corruption in a democracy as decision-making that responds to influences other than public reasoning. In this case, the corrupting influence was money: corrupting because money produced a *non*public, semisecret mode of decision-making about matters of *public* concern (cf. Gutmann and Thompson 1996). Clearly, where politics is conducted in this way – where decisions are made privately in response to money – constituents will rightly suspect betrayals not only of their own interests, but also of the public trust placed in representatives. The second force at work here is the display of *public*

---

[26] Thus, to consider an unlikely example, it has often been reported that in the trench warfare of World War I, soldiers from opposing sides talked across the frontier, thus presenting themselves as more alike than different. These opportunities of self-presentation, limited though they were by circumstances, nonetheless contradicted official propaganda and very likely dampened the willingness of soldiers to kill one another.

reasons and reasoning. An apparently puzzling fact about American politics is that significant numbers of people seem to rank the "sincerity" of politicians ahead of policy preferences, suggesting that they can tolerate principled disagreements but not betrayals of trust. What this may suggest is that even when political representatives must compromise interests and identities, *if* they can put their reasons on display, then they have not *betrayed* their constituents but rather pressed for their cause within a context that requires compromise, departures from campaign promises, and new solutions (Johnson 1993: 11). It may be that displays of reasons can help to break vicious cycles of trust, betrayal, and cynicism in favor of a more benign and progressive principled opposition of arguments.

Fourth, a politics that works within the medium of speech will, owing to the internal logic of language use, generate trust as a condition of communication. Deliberative situations place a premium upon successful argumentation – that is, persuasion. Successful communication requires understanding the cognitive content of the statements of others. Even if one disagrees with the statement, even if it is merely the beginning of an argument, in responding to the cognitive content of a claim, one recognizes the other person as a speaker. In an important way, this recognition is an initial extension of trust that a speaker will say things that he/she considers true, sincere, or normatively right (Habermas 1984, 1987). Such trust may be and often is disappointed: The fact that individuals talk does not automatically generate trust between them. But where there is a basis for trust in shared interests, the initial extension of trust implied in discourse may be the first step toward generating more trust (cf. Mansbridge, this volume, chapter 10). Even in the limiting case of war, this dynamic is one reason why diplomats place such importance on getting the belligerents to talk.

Finally, trust is necessary for promising, unless one holds to the Hobbesian view that promises are good only if enforced by the sword. Successful resolutions of political conflicts imply promises: promises for future performances or promises to forgo future tactics. The one who accepts a promise is also extending a trust in the goodwill of the one who promises, thus creating relationships of obligation that mitigate, in Hannah Arendt's (1958) terms, some of the uncertainty that is inherent in future-oriented, intersubjective actions. As Arendt emphasized, deliberative forms of politics are likely to be more robust in creating promises and the trust they imply, simply because a promise is, initially, a discursive bond rooted in shared understandings communicated in speech (cf. Harré, this volume, chapter 8).

My argument, then, is that there are homologies and complementarities between politics and trust that deliberative forms of democracy are best suited to develop and that could cultivate the future-oriented and trans-formative potentials of politics. But because the risks of politics make trust problematic, the relationship between democracy and trust remains one of tension. The tensions, however, can be eased if we pay special attention to the structure of protections and assurances within political relations necessary for the fragile powers of discourse to do their work. If institutions can be designed in ways that mitigate these tensions, then we shall have taken an important step toward meeting the challenges of the late-modern/postmodern era. Ultimately, democracy and trust do not need to refer to anything outside of the potentials already embedded in con-tingent social relations; they do not need metaphysics, nor do they need to rely on unquestioned tradition. Yet they together name and evoke the normative potentials already existing within social relationships for a good society of reflective, self-governing individuals.

REFERENCES

Arendt, Hannah, 1958. *The Human Condition*, Chicago: University of Chicago Press
    1982 *Lectures on Kant's Political Philosophy*, Ronald Beiner (ed. and trans.), Chicago: University of Chicago Press
Ayres, Ian and Braithwaite, John, 1992. *Responsive Regulation: Transcending the Deregulation Debate*, New York: Oxford University Press
Baier, Annette, 1986. Trust and antitrust. *Ethics* 96, 231–260
Barber, Bernard, 1983. *The Logic and Limits of Trust*, New Brunswick, NJ: Rutgers University Press
Bianco, William T., 1994. *Trust: Representatives and Constituents*, Ann Arbor: University of Michigan Press
Braithwaite, Valerie, 1998. Institutionalizing distrust, enculturating trust, in Valerie Braithwaite and Margaret Levi (eds.), *Trust and Governance*, New York: Russell Sage
Cohen, Jean L. and Arato, Andrew, 1992. *Civil Society and Political Theory*, Cambridge, Mass.: MIT Press
Cohen, Joshua and Rogers, Joel, 1995. Secondary associations and democratic governance, in Eric Olin Wright, *Associations and Democracy*, New York: Routledge, 7–98
Coleman, James S., 1990. *Foundations of Social Theory*, Cambridge, Mass.: Harvard University Press
Earle, Timothy C. and Cvetkovich, George T., 1995. *Social Trust: Toward a Cosmopolitan Society*, Westport, CT: Praeger
Eisenstadt, S. N. and Roniger, L., 1984. *Patrons, Clients, and Friends: Interpersonal Relations and the Structure of Trust in Society*, Cambridge: Cambridge University Press
Fukuyama, Francis, 1995. *Trust: The Social Virtues and the Creation of Prosperity*, New York: Free Press

Gambetta, Diego, 1988. Mafia: The price of distrust, in Diego Gambetta (ed.), *Trust: Making and Breaking Cooperative Relations*, Oxford: Basil Blackwell, 158–175

Giddens, Anthony, 1990. *The Consequences of Modernity*, Stanford: Stanford University Press

Green, Donald P. and Shapiro, Ian, 1994. *Pathologies of Rational Choice Theory: A Critique of Applications in Political Science*, New Haven: Yale University Press

Gutmann, Amy and Thompson, Dennis, 1996. *Democracy and Disagreement*, Cambridge, Mass.: Harvard University Press

Habermas, Jürgen, 1984. *The Theory of Communicative Action*, vol. I, Thomas McCarthy (trans.), Boston: Beacon Press

1987. *The Theory of Communicative Action*, vol. II, Thomas McCarthy (trans.), Boston: Beacon Press

1990. *Moral Consciousness and Communicative Action*, Christian Lenhardt and Shierry Weber Nicholsen (trans.), Cambridge, Mass.: MIT Press

1996. *Between Facts and Norms: Contributions to a Discourse Theory of Law and Democracy*, William Rehg (trans.), Cambridge, Mass.: MIT Press

Hardin, Russell, 1991. Trusting persons, trusting institutions, in Richard J. Zeckhauser (ed.), *Strategy and Choice*, Cambridge, Mass.: MIT Press, 185–209

1993. The street-level epistemology of trust. *Politics and Society* 21, 505–529

1995. Trust in government. Paper presented at the Pacific Division meeting of the American Philosophical Association, San Francisco, April

Johnson, Peter, 1993. *Frames of Deceit: A Study of the Loss and Recovery of Public and Private Trust*, Cambridge: Cambridge University Press

Keohane, Robert O., Haas, Peter M., and Levy, Marc A., 1993. The effectiveness of international environmental institutions, in Peter M. Haas, Robert O. Keohane, and Marc A. Levy (eds.), *Institutions for the Earth: Sources of Effective International Environmental Protection*, Cambridge, Mass.: MIT Press, 3–24

Lefort, Claude, 1986. *The Political Forms of Modern Society: Bureaucracy, Democracy, Totalitarianism*, Cambridge: Polity Press

Luhmann, Niklas, 1979. Trust: A mechanism for the reduction of social complexity, in *Trust and Power: Two Works by Niklas Luhmann*, Chichester: John Wiley and Sons

1988. Familiarity, confidence, trust: problems and alternatives, in Diego Gambetta (ed.), *Trust: Making and Breaking Cooperative Relations*, Oxford: Basil Blackwell, 94–107

McAllister, Daniel J., 1995. Affect- and cognition-based trust as foundations for interpersonal cooperation in organizations. *Academy of Management Journal* 38, 24–59

Misztal, Barbara A., 1996. *Trust in Modern Societies: The Search for the Bases of Social Order*, Cambridge, Mass.: Blackwell Publishers

Morin, Richard and Balz, Dan, 1996. Americans losing trust in each other and institutions. *The Washington Post*, Sunday, January 28

The Pew Research Center for the People and the Press, 1997. *Trust and Citizen Engagement in Metropolitan Philadelphia: A Case Study*, Washington, DC: The Pew Research Center

Preuss, Ulrich, 1995. *Constitutional Revolution: The Link Between Constitutionalism and Progress*, Deborah Lucas Schneider (trans.), Atlantic Highlands, NJ: Humanities Press

Seligman, Adam B., 1992. Trust and the meaning of civil society. *International Journal of Politics, Culture and Society* 6, 5–21

1997. *The Problem of Trust*, Princeton: Princeton University Press

Silver, Allan, 1997. "Two different sorts of commerce" – friendship and strangership in civil society, in Jeff Weintraub and Krishan Kumar (eds.), *Public and Private in Thought and Practice*, Chicago: University of Chicago Press, 43–74

Teubner, Günther, 1983. Substantive and reflexive elements in modern law. *Law and Society Review* 17, 239–285

Thompson, Dennis F., 1993. Mediated corruption: The case of the Keating Five. *American Political Science Review* 87, 369–381

Walzer, Michael, 1983. *Spheres of Justice: A Defense of Pluralism and Equality*, New York: Basic Books

Warren, Mark E., 1990. Ideology and the self. *Theory and Society* 19, 599–634

1992. Democratic theory and self-transformation. *American Political Science Review* 86, 8–23

1996a. Deliberative democracy and authority. *American Political Science Review* 90, 46–60

1996b. What should we expect from more democracy? Radically democratic responses to politics. *Political Theory* 24, 241–270

1999. What is Political? *Journal of Theoretical Politics* 11, 207–231

Weber, Max, 1946. The Protestant sects and the spirit of capitalism, in H. H. Gerth and C. Wright Mills (eds.), *From Max Weber: Essays in Sociology*, Oxford: Oxford University Press, 302–322

Williams, Bernard, 1988. Formal structures and social reality, in Diego Gambetta (ed.), *Trust: Making and Breaking Cooperative Relations*, Oxford: Basil Blackwell, 3–13

Zucker, Lynne G., 1986. Production of trust: Institutional sources of economic structure, 1840–1920. *Research in Organizational Behavior* 8, 53–111

12   Conclusion

Mark E. Warren

The problem of establishing a good form of collective rule, Rousseau explained in *The Social Contract*, "is to find a form of association which will defend and protect with the whole common force the person and goods of each associate, and in which each, while uniting himself with all, may obey himself alone, and remain as free as before" (1913: Book I, chap. VI). In many ways Rousseau's problem in *The Social Contract* remains ours. But his solution – that individuals might develop and complete their human capacities through identifying with the General Will – has not worn as well as the problem. In designing political procedures that would evoke the General Will, Rousseau supposed a social homogeneity and structural simplicity rare even in his day, while implicitly seeking a unified form of community that is no longer possible, even were if it desirable. Yet Rousseau was not entirely misdirected: he designed the social contract for a society of egoists, one in which empathetic solidarity had little force. *The Social Contract* experimented with the question as to whether new forms of cooperation – the life-blood of society – might be induced by political design, but in ways that would enhance the flourishing of individuals by inducing transformations within society, culture, and identity.

But although this ideal cannot but remain with us, it can go wrong even without the fiction of the General Will. Politics – with the powers it evokes, the conflicts it occasions, and strategic maneuvering it incites – rarely provides a genial environment for such developmental effects. If we wish to keep before us the intriguing and paradoxical Rousseauian proposition that there are intrinsic relations between the late modernist/postmodernist ideals of freedom and human flourishing and democratic politics, we shall no doubt have look to the more gentle and indirect means of cultivating them.

Trust names one way of making a problem of the culture of democratic enablement, by indicating one means of engaging in extensive social cooperation that does not generate the experience that, in working with others, one is compromising one's freedom. To the contrary, when individuals can trust others, they can also develop and secure capacities of action, increase mobility and choice, and reduce existential anxieties. Trust indicates a generic and pervasive means through which the late modernist/ post-modernist ideals associated with democracy – freedom, reciprocity, recognition, and security – can be and often are achieved.

Yet to relate trust to politics – to see it as resolving Rousseau's paradox – entangles us in a new set of paradoxes. Insofar as politics is marked by conflicts of interests and identities against backgrounds of power, crucial conditions of trust are absent. Add to this problems of scale and complexity – that we may not know what we would need to know to trust or distrust large-scale institutions – and we may be forgiven for wondering whether trust has any place at all in politics, democratic or otherwise.

It has not been the aim of the essays in this volume to focus on trust proper. There already exists an extensive literature in sociology, social psychology, and economics that does so, a literature extensively invoked by these essays. Rather, the essays bring into focus the paradoxical quality of the relationship between trust and democratic politics, mostly by clarifying what is at issue. It turns out, however, that the focus on the paradoxical relationship between democracy and trust also sharpens our focus on problems of trust more generally – no doubt because the limiting cases that occur within politics help to clarify conceptual boundaries. I shall try to highlight some general conclusions, while noting the areas of significant disagreement that will be productive of future conversations. I hasten to add that the following assessments and reflections are mine and mine alone.

Declining trust in government

In the last few years, opinion leaders and media pundits have been quick to conclude that declining trust in government indicates a more general crisis of democracy. The essays in this volume are much more circumspect, and some quite skeptical of this claim. Most fundamentally, all distinguish between trust in government institutions, and the many other kinds of trust that democracy may require, while also questioning the meaning of "democracy." On balance, we do not have a clear enough conceptual picture of the relationship between trust and democracy to know whether declining trust in the governments of existing democracies should count as a problem for democracy. For example, several authors point out that declining trust in government is only bad for democracy if this is a decline in *warranted* forms of trust. Declining forms of trust in government could indicate that citizens are becoming more sophisticated about judging government officials, and often find them untrustworthy (see Inglehart, Patterson, Cohen, and Warren, this volume). If so, declining trust in government would be a gain for democratic accountability.

Alternatively, it may be that for most people, most of the time, government institutions are too distant for the basic condition of trust – knowledge of the interests of the trusted – to be met (Hardin, this volume). From this perspective, since the question of trust in government is misplaced, declining trust in government cannot be a problem let alone a crisis. Such a view does not rule out, however, that surrogates for trust, such as consistency and predictability, might be entirely appropriate expectations to place on governments.

What it means to "trust" an institution

Behind the question what it might mean to trust government is the even more generic question of what it means, if anything, to trust an institution. The answer is not obvious, not least because – as the authors of this volume agree – the *core* trust relation is interpersonal. Whatever it means to trust an institution is somehow scaled up from the domain of socially thick, face-to-face relations.

The essays in this volume take distinct positions on this theoretical issue. Russell Hardin argues that under contemporary circumstances the idea that one could trust or distrust a large-scale institution is meaningless, since one condition of trust – that the truster could know the interests and motivations of the trusted – cannot possibly be fulfilled, given the shear numbers of government officials and the distance between citizens and even the closest of governments. Hardin's assessment builds on his view of trust as "encapsulated interest": the truster must have sufficient knowledge of the trusted for the truster to know that the trusted has his interests in view and is motivated to act on behalf of them.

Other essays take positions that differ in ways that are quite significant for the question of whether and how trust can be extended to institutions. Importantly, the other authors do not question the core of Hardin's view of trust as encapsulated interest – at least insofar as he insists on the importance of individuals being able somehow to judge the interests and motivations of the trusted. Rather, the differences have to do with how knowledge is achieved, how it is extended beyond face-to-face relations, and how the motivations of the trusted are affected by being the subject of trusting expectations (cf. Offe, Mansbridge). Harré, for example, sees trust in institutions as a special case of trust in persons. Thus, for example, I do not *know* the officials of the bank with which I deal. But, all other things being equal, it is reasonable for me to trust them. In doing so, I am operating on the presumption that they have internalized the ethical and other normative expectations of their offices – or, in any case, they are motivated to act in accordance with them owing to external rewards or sanctions. This *shared* knowledge of institutional rules gives the information I need to extend trust. Because the rules of an institution can be known and generalized to a very large number of strangers, the truster can extrapolate these rules to individuals about whom he has little direct knowledge.

Likewise, Patterson notes that what he calls "indirect personal trust" can be achieved through intermediaries that vouch for the integrity of the trusted, so that an individual's powers of judgment can extended through social networks to reach a far larger number of persons than could be known individually. Offe notes that such extensions of judgments need not depend on extended social networks; they can be formalized through institutions because the constitutive rules of institutions always have a normative content. They include expectations for the performance of persons that inhabit the roles established by the rules. So, "trusting an institution" is a way of saying that one knows the normative *idea* of the institution, which one extends to the individuals who populate it on the assumption that they are motivated to abide by its normative expectations. Under these circumstances, judgments to trust depend more upon judgments of the robustness of institutional norms than upon judgments of individuals within institutional roles.

Patterson extends this idea of "trusting an institution" into another dimension as well. Drawing on Coleman (1990) he develops the category of "indirect impersonal" trust, or "delegated trust," where the idea is that third parties guarantee transactions (as do banks, trust companies, etc.), and in this way create the effects of trust through third party enforcement. This point can be extended to the workings of law, as suggested in the essays by Offe, Cohen, and myself. One reason that we can trust (or *ought* to be able to trust) many large-scale institutions is that their functions are specified by law. But what this means is that (a) we know the *normative* idea of the law and thus the normative expectations it places on officials; and (b) the law creates incentives over and beyond the normative incentive for officials to act in accordance with the shared expectations of law, thus reducing the risks of trust (cf. Habermas 1996). Thus, to "trust an institution" means that the truster knows the normative idea of the institution, and has some confidence in the sanctions that provide additional motivation for officials to behave according to this idea. Expectations can be disappointed, of course. But, assuming shared normative expectations that are enforced at their limits, it can make sense to trust an institution.

What it means to "trust an institution" depends, on this account, on shared knowledge and legitimacy of the (legal) rules that establish institutions. This is what cannot be taken for granted, and why Offe, Cohen, and I emphasize the important role of democratic discourse in mediating institutions by constantly testing, revising, invigorating, and communicating norms. In this sense, the relationship between democracy and legitimacy goes to the heart of whether it can ever make sense to "trust an institution".

The difference between these kinds of positions and Hardin's, then, is not on the issue of whether trust involves an "encapsulated interest." Hardin's important contribution, it seems to me, is that he establishes precisely what is at risk in trust relations, and has identified the conditions that must be met for trust to be warranted. There is, I think, a broad consensus among these essays on this point. The differences have to do with (a) how the truster can know the interests and motivations of the trusted, and (b) whether the identity of the trusted, and thereby his motivations, are structured by the shared normative ideas embedded in the constitutive rules of institutions, and (c) whether structures of reward and sanction serve to align motivations when normative incentives are weak. These issues in turn depend upon different conceptions of the subject and subjective judgment, one instrumentally rational, and the other, for want of a better term, "social-psychological" in orientation. Not surprisingly, this is the issue that ultimately divides rational choice accounts of social life from most others.

What does it mean that "trust in government" is declining?

Nonetheless, these considerations do allow us to further specify what declining trust in government might mean. There are several possibilities. (a) Officials may be becoming more untrustworthy measured by divergences from institutional norms. (b) Citizens are becoming more sophisticated and leveling higher expectations on officials. (c) Citizens are becoming more cynical because their expectations have increased without a corresponding increase in the trustworthiness of officials. (d) Institutional norms are increasingly opaque, conflicted, or otherwise fail to provide a normative framework of expectations that citizens can read onto officials. (e) Information about officials' interests and performance is increasingly complex, scarce, or otherwise inaccessible, so that sophisticated citizens will, in the absence of information, simply withhold trust. These possibilities are difficult to assess in any general way, given the current deficits in both theory and evidence. Nonetheless, it is unlikely, as Inglehart notes, that government officials are less trustworthy than in the past – at least in the established democracies – so that declining trust in government probably stems from combinations of the other four circumstances.

Moreover, "trust in government" will mean different things depending upon whether "government" indicates administrative performance, or whether it indicates institutionalized political processes. The case of administrative performance is especially interesting because administration has become politicized to the point that administrative rule-making is now widely viewed as part of the political process. As a result, in the area of administrative performance the normative and informational deficits ((d) and (e) above) are now quite pronounced. At the same time, some of the more interesting innovations in deliberative and other direct forms of democracy can be found in administrative law-making and enforcement, directed precisely at the normative and informational conditions of trust (cf. Freeman, 1997; Pritzker and Dalton, 1995). The history of the (US) Environmental Protection Agency's (EPA) handling of the Superfund program (for cleaning up sites contaminated by toxic wastes) is a case in point.[1] In the aftermath of the stewardship of Ann Burford, a Reagan appointee who sought to undermine the EPA's function and mission, Congress was faced with the problem of restoring public trust in the Superfund program. The 1986 Superfund Amendment and Reauthorization Act implemented a number of measures aimed at developing conditions of trust in a what had become a highly politicized environment. Citizens gained the standing to sue, and citizens' groups could now apply for Technical Assistance Grants to hire independent technical experts. In addition, EPA regional offices were required to keep, compile, and make available all information used to select Superfund clean-up sites. While these strategies can appear to further politicize an already overpoliticized agency, I think they are better seen as aimed at providing the informational and normative conditions of warranted trust, which would ideally replace the more deferential forms of trust shattered by Ann Burford's leadership.

More generally, I think the notion of "trust in government" makes sense if it means trust in established government agencies, especially those with relatively settled normative purposes, and which are monitored by interested publics for adherence to these purposes (cf. Warren 1996). These would be necessary conditions to assure citizens that their interests converge with those of government officials.

---

[1] I am grateful to Wesley Joe for providing this example.

It is quite a different matter, however, if "trust in government" refers to the arenas of institutionalized politics, and to the elected officials who populate these arenas. What it means for something to be "political" is, in part, that the normative ideas that define institutions are contested, and not yet codified into law. In contrast, most administrative agencies benefit from the fact that their enabling legislation was based on some degree of consensus about their purpose – at least in those cases in which the purposes were clear, or have been clarified over time. In the case of the EPA, for example, the broad normative issues are now relatively settled, with the broad public support for environmental protection finding an institutional locus within the agency. Moreover, notwithstanding the Burford years, the EPA tends to hire people who share in this normative consensus. The fact that there is an institutional location of a (nonetheless always evolving) normative consensus means that one condition of trust – normative indicators of converging interests – already exists. Beyond this, building trust is a matter of enabling discursive arenas to handle emerging normative conflicts, while ensuring that there exist the means to relate information to the normative consensus.

But within arenas lacking the same level of normative consensus – arenas that are more "political" – is it less easy for citizens to learn what kinds of motivations and interests elected officials have. The case of elected officials in the US Congress, for example, is especially problematic. Even assuming a system cleansed of money, each elective representative faces the task of representing multiple and conflicting interests and identities. Lacking the information and certainties that come with institutional trust, and encouraged by campaigns that focus on the qualities of persons rather than issues or party platforms, it is tempting for individuals to revert to the expectations of face-to-face trust. But here the conditions of interpersonal trust could not possibly obtain. So in these cases, Hardin is no doubt right that it makes little sense either to trust or distrust since the conditions of trust do not exist.

Yet I think it remains worth asking, *pace* Offe, Cohen, and myself, whether attending to the discursive dimensions of institutions might introduce conditions of trust, especially by designing institutions so that the force of argument cannot be bypassed by the powers of money and coercion. If declining "trust in government" indicates declining trust in elected representatives, this probably indicates that something is wrong – not relative to a better past, but relative to changing expectations, and thus to the developing potentials for democracy that fail to find institutional expression (cf. Inglehart, this volume, chapter 4). It may also be the case, as suggested by Offe, Cohen, and myself (cf. Beck 1992), that the threshold of legitimacy could be changed by pushing issues into new political venues where the conditions of trust might be more easily satisfied. This being said, in any *political* arena, precisely because normative expectations *are* unsettled, the mechanisms that extend trust to institutions are likely to be weak at best – a point that is congruent with Inglehart's observation that transitions to democracy correlate with low levels of trust. Again, democracy requires a delicate balance of trust where matters are settled, and monitoring of decision-makers where they are not.

Where "democracy" is located: state, civil society, economy

If different meanings of "trust" are in play in these essays, there are also differing meanings of "democracy." Clearly, differing conceptions of democracy will affect how, and in what ways, one judges trust to be good for democracy.

The most straightforward approaches are represented by Hardin, Inglehart, and Uslaner, where "democracy" refers to "democratic government" – the arenas of formal, state-centered institutions that meet certain requirements, including a representative structure based on a broad franchise, political rights including freedom of speech and rights to associate, protections for minorities and other related conditions. Inglehart and Uslaner rely on this broad and widely accepted conception of democracy in part because their work is located within the tradition of empirical survey research. In Inglehart's case in particular, this conception of democracy fits with the available comparative survey data, and any conception that is either more stringent in what counts as "democracy" or broader in its domains of application would make comparisons difficult. Likewise, the surveys typically include only a few highly general questions about trust that focus on just two kinds of trust relations: trust in government (and other institutions), and interpersonal trust. Thus, the problem of "democracy and trust" is narrowed by the available data to the problem of "liberal-democratic government and trust".

Working within the terms of this problem, Inglehart and Uslaner both note that democratic governments do just fine with either high or low degrees of trust *in government*. What both note, however, is that stable democracies seem to depend more upon higher degrees of *interpersonal* trust as well as what Inglehart refers to as a "culture of trust" than do authoritarian governments. But interpersonal trust is enhanced only at the margins by democratic government. There is, Inglehart argues, no evidence that democracy contributes to trust. Rather, interpersonal trust is, Inglehart argues, an effect of economic development, cultural, and other historical factors.

These findings may support Hardin's theoretical claim that judgments of trust and distrust are simply misplaced when applied to government. Alternatively, they may support the notion that democratic government depends upon the vigilance of the governed more than it does on their trust – one of the interpretations offered by Inglehart. But such findings also raise by implication the question (which cannot be adequately answered based on existing survey data) as to whether a more expansive conception of democracy would lead us to focus on different kinds of relations between democracy and trust. The issue is raised implicitly by Inglehart's and Uslaner's discussions: in addition to the contributions of economic well-being and cultures of trust, both find support for Putnam's Tocquevillian conclusion that stable democracies are associated with a robust associational life.

But Tocqueville's idea was that democratic government depends in part on a broader democratic culture, itself partly an effect of non-governmental democratic arrangements. Tocqueville relied on a quite generic conception of democracy. Wherever people bypass hierarchical intermediaries to address problems requiring collective action, this is democracy. These associational experiences, Tocqueville held, help to generate a democratic culture. Tocqueville thus invoked a broad conception of political organization, and this in turn enabled him to extend the concept of democracy to any venue of collective decision and action.

Tocqueville's use of the term "democracy" was, of course, so broad, diffuse, and often abstract that one might question its analytic usefulness. Nonetheless, his usage does retain the essential normative connection between democracy and self-government, which he then uses analyze numerous kinds of collective action. The point is that because Tocqueville's use of the term "democracy" is less stipulative than formal, state-centered conceptions, it allows us to ask whether there might be direct and significant relations between democracy and trust, particularly within non-governmental venues – in civil society and even within some sectors of the economy. These spaces of association may be more likely to meet the conditions of trust because they provide opportunities for arguing, demonstrating, deliberating, and empathizing – that is, democratic experiences that are remote and scarce in the formally-organized, state-centered domains of politics. Likewise, it may be that the meaning "democracy" should extend to the deliberations of public spheres, where the power of deciding is weak at best, but the forces of opinions are nonetheless forged and then become effective in governmental or other venues. Such experiences provide "sociological" content to democracy, and this in turn alters how we cast the problem of democracy and trust.

So the conclusion that democracy does not depend upon trust in government, but does depend on interpersonal trust is, at best, a provisional formulation that leads to another set of questions about the relation between democracy and trust. But these questions depend on broader conceptions of "democracy." This is what we find, implicitly or explicitly, in other essays in this volume. Implicitly, "social capital" arguments already suggest the inadequacy of state-centered conceptions of democracy. This is in part because such arguments presume capacities for collective action and decision within civil society and economy, capacities that make democracies work by enabling groups to call governments to account, to take on problems best resolved by non-governmental means, and to serve as the schools of democratic dispositions. To understand these possibilities, however, would require a close analysis of varying kinds of political venues within civil society and economy to discover where democratic structures might exist, what dimensions of democracy they include, and how they interface with other institutions, power structures, and systems, questions that Cohen raises in the conclusion to her essay. Within democratic theory this kind of work is still in its infancy.

The analyses of Harré, Scott, Offe, Cohen, Mansbridge, and myself all presuppose expansive conceptions of democracy – albeit sometimes differing conceptions – and thus raise questions that are somewhat different than those of Inglehart, Uslaner, and Hardin. Harré and Scott emphasize the limits of state-centered institutions and rule-based (law-based) means of coordinating collective actions. The conceptual weight of their conceptions of democracy is centered on the self-organizing capacities of society. What Harré refers to as "thick democracy" resides in social capacities to do things, capacities that can be protected and indirectly facilitated by state-guaranteed liberties, but which cannot be engineered. One ought, on this account, build a conception of democratic process out of the essential good of the self-organization of society. Clearly, if one places the conceptual weight of "democracy" here, then trust will turn out to be an essential and generic means of the self-organization of society.

A similar point is made by Mansbridge. Where the essays by Harré and Scott are, in many ways, defensive – that is, focused on how to preserve "thick" street-level social organization – Mansbridge examines the more specific question of how to generate these capacities within contexts of distrust. In this way, she relates a similar appreciation for the "democratic" potentials of the spontaneous self-organization of society to "political" situations in which trust is missing or damaged. To risk extending trust can be, Mansbridge argues, a moral virtue. But it can only be judged a moral virtue from the perspective of generating social cooperation, that is, from an "altruistic" perspective. In contrast to Hardin, not only is a different conception of trust is at work here, but also a different conception of the subject (self), as well as a different conception of democracy – one that places the weight of democracy on the self-organization of society.

The essays by Offe, Cohen, and myself take a similar approach to the meaning of democracy, but focus as well on the indirect and enabling functions of the state with respect to the self-organization of society. The conceptual differences here have less to do with where democracy is centered than on how the means available to the state – primarily the deployment of legitimate (legal) coercion – might be used to protect and generate the self-organizing capacities of society. In contrast to the essays by Harré and Scott, the emphasis here is on how democratic processes, suitably structured, might generate trust, building on those interpersonal forms of trust that are warranted, while recognizing the corrosive effects of power, conflict, and high-level systems effects. As I emphasize at the end of my essay, because of the shifting venues of democracy, and because of the unique difficulties posed by politicized contexts, the business of identifying the "productive" side of democracy with respect to trust is still quite undeveloped.

Good and bad trust: the political psychology of trust

Although the term "democracy" remains contested in this volume, there is broad agreement that not all forms or kinds of trust are good for democracy. Depending upon the conception and dimension of democracy, democratic theorists hold that individuals ought to display civic virtues, critically examine their interests, possess a sense of political efficacy (or agency), tolerate principled differences, and be able to know, represent, and argue for their interests. Some of these dispositions may be undermined by some kinds of trust.

The problem can be clarified by noting that there exist different psychologies of trust. Within the category of interpersonal trust, for example, Uslaner distinguishes generalized and particularized trust. Generalized trust indicates a willingness to extend trust to strangers, while particularized trust indicates group bonds that are exclusive of others, as in ethnic and some kinds of religious and clan-based identities. Particularized trust undermines democratic dispositions because the psychological investment that creates the bond depends on opposition to those who do not possess the characteristic in question, such as the proper ethnicity, relation to God, or skin color. To extend empathy, tolerance, or recognition to the Other thus immediately threatens the bond of trust. Moreover, because such bonds depend on investments in some similar trait, they also serve to suppress conflicts of interest within the group – such as class differences. Indeed, the culture of deliberation, challenge, and self-investigation is incompatible with particularized trust, since questions and challenges addressed to the group are *ipso facto* expressions of disloyalty.

Patterson's typology likewise identifies particularized trust, which he views as a species of "direct impersonal trust" in which the "stranger" in our midst serves the function of defining who is one of "us" and who is one of "them." This was, according to Patterson's analysis, the social psychological basis of the white, *herrenvolk* democracy of the American South. What is interesting about Patterson's analysis of this category, however, is that he sees the "particularizing" effect as only one possibility; the "stranger" within our midst may also be a person upon whom we rely, and with whom we have everyday interactions, as with the Chinese grocer in Jamaica. There is often a social basis here for generalizing trust, at least insofar as practical dealings over time build confidence, often in spite of the particularizing effects that exist at the same time.

We find a similarly interesting psychological proposition in Harré's suggestion that confidence and trust – often distinguished in the literature on the basis of whether risks are known or unknown – are really quite similar forms of judgment. From the perspective of generalizing trust to political situations, this is a promising point, because it suggests a psychological continuum from predictability to confidence to trust. If so, then out of predictability might come trust. This possibility is important from a political perspective, since much "social repair" work begins with predictability in the form of explicit laws, treaties, contracts, and (in diplomacy especially) "confidence building" measures. If Harré's psychological observations are correct, trust cannot be engineered but its locations may be protected and its soil cultivated so as to encourage its growth.

But these are merely suggestions within this volume. Although these essays perform the crucial task of distinguishing among alternative psychologies of trust, a key question they do not address has to do with what might be called the "convertibility" of trust relations – from forms of trust that are bad for democracy to those that are good. There are at least two kinds of issues here. The first has to do with how close these alternative kinds of trust are within personality structures. If an individual's identity includes particularized trust, is this so constitutive of the personality that democratic forms of trust would be all but impossible to achieve? Second, if there is, indeed, some convertibility, then are there forms of association, or even kinds of democratic venues, that might evoke such conversions? As far as I am aware, these questions move us into uncharted territory.

Egalitarian pluralism: should democracy involve an epistemic division of labor?

We are left with at least one more troubling issue. If we were to accept, despite Hardin's skepticism, that democracy and trust are mutually supportive, we would also have to accept that democracies must build upon epistemic divisions of labor? That is, if I am willing to trust an advocacy group, a government agency, or an official, I am also assuming that there are at least some others who are monitoring the organization or official in question. I may trust their judgments to avoid the trouble of participation. Or, I may do so because I want to focus the epistemic resources that *distrust* requires into those (politicized) arenas where I judge trust is not warranted. If I take the latter route, and most other people do likewise, then we can speak of trust enabling an epistemic division of labor, which could in turn underwrite egalitarian patterns of participation in complex, large-scale societies. In doing so, however, I would not be taking on responsibility for participating in *every* decision within the polity – which is impossible in any case. Rather, my participation would be focused, although it would shift arenas and issues as problems change, my participatory resources change (say, because of life-cycle), or my interests change. If most people do as I do, then trust would enable highly pluralized but relatively egalitarian patterns of participation. The pattern would be pluralized because at any point in time individuals selectively focus their participatory resources. The pluralism would be egalitarian if every individual possessed participatory resources (time, knowledge, security, rights of voting, association, and speech, etc.) that provide them with roughly equal chances to influence political outcomes, should they choose to do so.

While such a possibility is implied by many of the essays in this volume, it is perhaps only Hardin's skepticism about the democratic functions of trust that reminds us of the significant change in the ethos of democratic theory it would entail. Most democrats accept the *fact* that there is a political division of labor, but only owing to the necessities of conducting politics within large-scale, complex societies. Democrats do not, for the most part, accept the *principle*: the very the idea of divided labor seems out of place in democratic politics. Unlike the division of labor for the sake of collective action, democrats do not think the epistemic labors of citizenship – their responsibility to decide – should be divided or in any way differentially distributed. Democratic politics is unique in this respect: it is the *only* sphere in which everyone is entitled to speak and vote, regardless of merit, knowledge, rank, power, or wealth.

We now maintain the fiction of equal citizenship – that we all attend equally to all matters of public concern – while recognizing that the ideal cannot be realized in societies like ours, even in principle. We democrats are perpetually disappointed. Our disappointment may not be cost free, however, if it distracts us from the less global possibility of an alternative conception of citizen capacities and obligations that would focus on maximizing the quality as well as the quantity of participation. Our disappointment sometimes allows us to avoid responsibility for asking what kinds of divisions of political attentiveness would be warranted, how would they be enabled, and how would they direct the resources of citizenship to the arenas in which they are most needed.

By implication, many of the essays in this volume take a step in the direction of such a revision of democratic theory, if only by recognizing the many roles that trust may play in enabling democracy, not least through providing an epistemic division of democratic judgment. The very concept of trust in such a context thus suggests an altered ethos of democratic theory – away from strictly egalitarian conceptions of the responsibilities of citizenship, and toward a pluralized egalitarianism. The concept of trust raises the question as to the means and mechanisms through which such a pluralized conception might become operative. It suggests that there may be better and worse pluralisms, and that epistemic divisions of labor may be better or worse, warranted or unwarranted, hierarchical or egalitarian. These essays also help to clarify the difficulties of such a shift in focus, not the least of which is that the conditions of trust are particularly problematic in politics, for it is precisely here that we should not take convergent interests for granted.

But this volume only steps onto the threshold of this issue. To take on this issue implies a new frontier in the ethos of democratic theory – the challenge of crafting an egalitarian pluralism appropriate for late modern/ postmodern societies. I do not saddle the other authors with this assessment, although many undoubtedly find it congenial.

REFERENCES

Beck, Ulrich, 1992. *Risk Society: Toward a New Modernity*, trans. Mark Ritter. London: Sage Publications
Coleman, James S., 1990. *Foundations of Social Theory*, Cambridge, Mass.: Harvard University Press
Freeman, Jody, 1997. Collaborative governance in the administrative state, in Ian Ayres and John Braithwaite (eds.), *Responsive Regulation: Transcending the Deregulation Debate*, New York: Oxford University Press

Habermas, Jürgen, 1996. *Between Facts and Norms: Contributions to a Discourse Theory of Law and Democracy*, William Rehg (trans.), Cambridge, Mass.: MIT Press

Pritzker, David M. and Dalton, Deborah S, 1995. *Negotiated Rulemaking Sourcebook*, Washington, DC: Office of the Chairman, Administrative Conference of the United States

Rousseau, Jean-Jacques. 1913. *The Social Contract and Discourses*, G. D. H. Cole (trans.), London : Dent

Warren, Mark E. 1996. Deliberative democracy and authority. *American Political Science Review* 90, 46–60

Index

affective trust, 330–1
affirmative action, 19, 177, 203, 235n
African-Americans: campaign ads and, 193–4; distrust and, 11, 168, 172, 282; interests of, 176; media news and, 194; otherness and, 157; religion and, 202; slavery and, 163–4; trust in government and, 18; voting and, 199, 203. *See also* racism, segregation, slavery
Algeria, 99
Almond, Gabriel, 97, 99, 101, 105, 113, 131n, 210
altruistic trust, 17–18, 25, 290–307
American Association of Retired People, 224
American colonies, 10–11; development of democracy in, 161–3; trust within, 334n
American National Election Study, 126
Anderson, Perry, 213
Andrews, Charles M., 108, 118, 162
anonymity, 55, 57, 60–1, 67, 70–1, 73, 83
Anti-Federalists, 22
anti-Semitism, 276
Arato, Andrew, 12, 209, 211, 215, 228, 229n, 326, 337
Arendt, Hannah, 312–13, 340, 342, Argentina, 101
associations, 123, 208; modernization and, 210; civil society and, 212–19; family as core of, 232–8; global, 244; membership in, 131; neocommunitarians and, 228–39; neoconservatives and, 13, 19; non-traditional, 14; non-virtuous, 125; rights and, 326; risk and, 334; social capital and, 217–21; sports and 145–6; television and, 137
Atlanta, 201
Austen, Jane, 304, 306

Austin, J. L., 265
Austria, 99
authoritarianism, 104, 123, 141–2, 144; collapse of, 97, 99, 100; economics and, 99; high-modernism and, 284; overcoming, 58; social orders and, 273; Soviet, 284; subjective well-being and, 111
authority, 154, 261, 276; collective knowledge and, 37; delegation of, 36; democracy and, 56, 261; democratic, 42; governmental, 85; knowledge and, 38; law and, 81; respect for, 8, 268; rights and, 325; as superior to power, 67
Axelrod, Robert M., 89

Baier, Annette, 1, 298n, 303n, 324, 328, 339
Baker, Kendall L., 104, 251
Banfield, Edward, 48, 89, 101, 123
bargaining, 62–3, 83, 339
Baston, C. Daniel, 291n
Bates, Robert H., 123
Bayesian individual, 335
Beck, Ulrich, 228, 230
Belarus, 108–9
Bendor, Jonathan, 124, 132
betrayal, 51, 167, 265, 316, 339; as a cultural practice, 306; deliberative democracy and, 341
Bill of Rights, 270
Black, Earl and Black, Merle, 166, 168
block-watch associations, 277
Bobbio, Noberto, 209
Bollen, Kenneth A., 99–100
Bolsheviks, 284–5
Bosnians, 144
bowling, 145, 147, 169
Boynton, G. R., 104
Bradford, E. M., 167
Bradley, Bill, 211

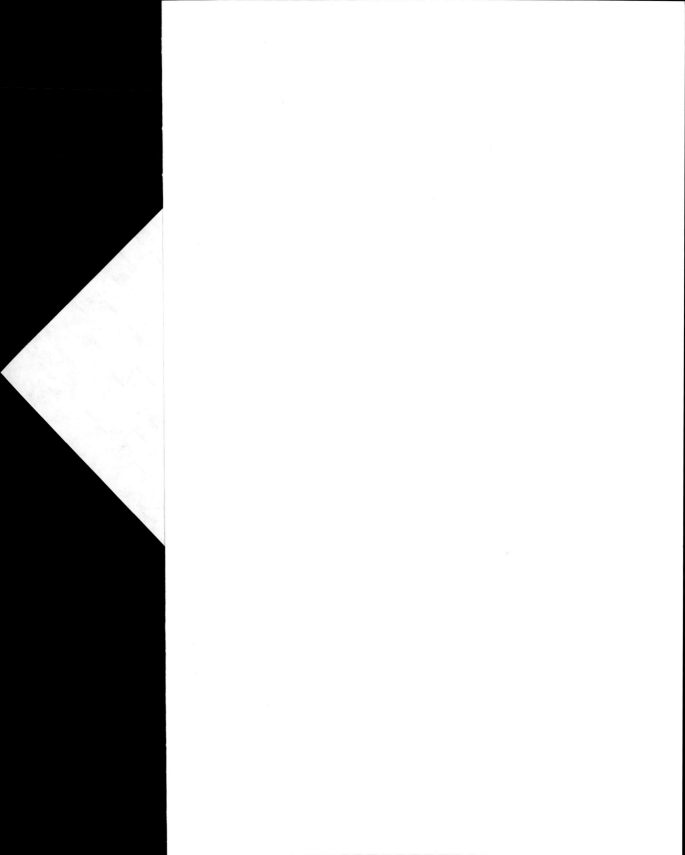

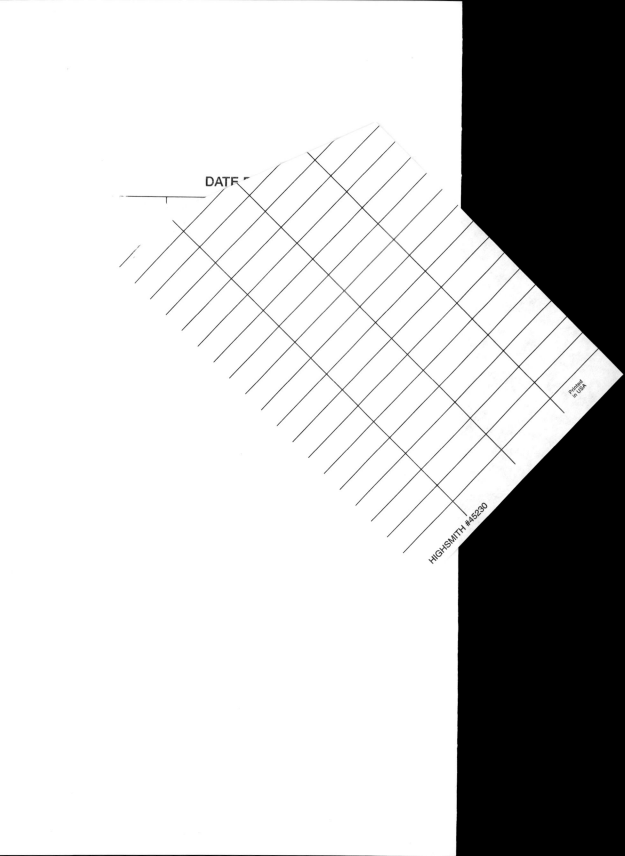

DATE

HIGHSMITH #45230

Printed
in USA